Family Instructions for the Yan Clan
and Other Works by Yan Zhitui (531–590s)

Library of
Chinese Humanities

Family Instructions for the Yan Clan and Other Works by Yan Zhitui (531–590s)

Translated, with introduction and notes, by Xiaofei Tian

Volume edited by Paul W. Kroll

De Gruyter

This book was prepared with the support of the Andrew W. Mellon Foundation.

ISBN 978-1-5015-1140-0
e-ISBN (PDF) 978-1-5015-0319-1
e-ISBN (EPUB) 978-1-5015-0313-9
ISSN 2199-966X
DOI https://doi.org/10.1515/9781501503191

Library of Congress Control Number: 2020943599

Bibliografische Information published by the Deutsche Nationalbibliothek
The Deutsche Nationalbibliothek lists this publication in the Deutsche Nationalbiblio-
grafie; detailed bibliographic data are available in the Internet at http://dnb.dnb.de.

© 2021 Xiaofei Tian, published by Walter de Gruyter Inc., Boston/Berlin
The book is published with open access at www.degruyter.com.

Typesetting: Meta Systems Publishing & Printservices GmbH, Wustermark
Printing and binding: CPI books GmbH, Leck

www.degruyter.com

Table of Contents

In memory of my mother,
許建華 (1938–2020)

La bella donna che cotanto amavi
Subitamente s'è da noi partita …

Acknowledgments

Translating Yan Zhitui's works was part of a larger research project on early medieval Chinese court culture and literature. Several years ago I had translated Yan Zhitui's autobiographical rhapsody, "Viewing My Life," for the benefit of my students in a graduate seminar. However, the lion's share of work on this volume was carried out during a year-long sabbatical leave that was made possible by a research fellowship from the American Council of Learned Societies: In 2019–2020, I was awarded the ACLS Donald J. Munro Centennial Fellowship in Chinese Arts and Letters, which enabled me to finish the translation. I am grateful to the ACLS and Harvard University, my home institution, for their sponsorship.

I thank Kang-i Sun Chang and Paul W. Kroll for their friendship and support. I am deeply indebted to Paul Kroll for editing the manuscript through those stressful first weeks of the pandemic lockdown.

I also thank the wonderful administrators at my department, Alison Howe, Gustavo Espada, and Susan Kashiwa, as well as the outstanding editorial staff at De Gruyter, Andre Borges, Stefan Diezmann, Birgit Sievert, and Katrin Stein, for their indispensible help in producing the volume.

When I am engaged in research and writing, I become completely absorbed, obsessively spending numerous hours that turn into long days and nights, weeks, and months. I cannot possibly have done this without the steadfast support of Stephen Owen, my beloved husband of more than twenty years, who, despite his own busy schedule, has always done everything he could to help ease all the grinds of daily life for me. I appreciate the maturity of my son, George, the sweetest, the most independent, empathetic, and humorous young boy I have known. Thank you, Steve and George, for all the laughs and all the encouragement. I am profoundly grateful to my family. I would have accomplished nothing without them.

Little did I know, when I started working on this book, that a global pandemic would break out and, like so many others, I was unable to travel for months, that my dear mother would pass away, suddenly and unexpectedly, during this time, and that our visit to my parents in December 2019 would be the last I ever saw of her in this life. Her abrupt departure overwhelmed me with grief and regret, and left a void in my heart that would never be filled. Born in the war-torn China in 1938, my mother almost lost all members of her immediate family when she was still an enfant; she grew up deprived of parental guidance and love, and so she did her best to compensate, in all the ways she knew, by giving me all her affection, love, and "family instructions" in the Yan Zhitui sense, when I was growing up. Without her I would have never become the person and the scholar I am today. I dedicate this book to my mother's memory.

Mid-autumn Festival, 2020   X. F. T.

Introduction

Today Yan Zhitui (531–590s) is primarily remembered for his *Family Instructions for the Yan Clan*, a book of twenty chapters, written in lucid, unpretentious, but gracious prose, on an assortment of topics ranging from household management and remarriage to religious belief, cultural pursuits, and codes of behavior in everyday life. Addressing his sons, the book's intended readers, as "you boys" throughout, he begins with a statement of his purpose for writing such a book, and ends with his last will and testament. Across fifteen centuries, we can still vividly hear the voice of a father and a man who lived through one of the most chaotic periods in Chinese history, and who was intent on the preservation of his family in terms of physical survival, spiritual well-being, and social status. We also learn much information about sixth-century Chinese society, culture, and customs from the perspective of a mode of writing that evokes a private monologue overheard. This is the earliest extant book-length "family instructions"; it is also one of the few books from early medieval China that is still regularly translated into modern vernacular Chinese intended for the general audience and published in large print runs over and again.

The success of Yan Zhitui's *Family Instructions* sometimes obscures his other remarkable achievements, chief among which was a long auto-biographical rhapsody, "Viewing My Life," interspersed with the author's self-annotations in prose. Self-exegesis would become a prevalent feature in Chinese poetry from the late eighth century onward; Yan Zhitui's self-annotations in his rhapsody mark an important milestone.

This volume includes an annotated translation of Yan Zhitui's *Family Instructions*, his extant poems and rhapsodies, and his biography in the dynastic histories. In the following pages, I will sketch Yan Zhitui's life and the complicated times in which he lived, offer an account of his beliefs and values, discuss his literary accomplishments, and conclude with some notes on the text and editions and on translation.

Life and Times

Yan Zhitui lived most of his life during an age of division. The history of this period, referred to as "early medieval China" or, in Chinese terms, the Northern and Southern Dynasties, is notoriously difficult and complicated. It was a period of migrations and separations, brutality and violence, but also one of cultural innovations and artistic brilliance. Yan Zhitui's life embodies all the multifarious facets of his age.

After the collapse of the Han empire and the ensuing Three Kingdoms period, China was briefly unified in 280 under the rule of the Jin dynasty. In the early fourth century, non-Han nomadic peoples invaded from the north, and the Jin capital Luoyang fell. The ruling elite were forced to cross the Yangzi River to the south, where they reestablished the Jin regime, with Jiankang 建康 (modern Nanjing) as the new capital. With the Yangzi River as a natural barrier, and with the support of the great families, the Jin monarchy lasted another one hundred years, until it was toppled by a powerful general, who founded the Song 宋 dynasty (420–479), also known as the "Liu Song" 劉宋 to be distinguished from the later dynasty of the same name. The Liu Song was succeeded by a series of short-lived, sophisticated dynasties: Qi 齊 (479–502), Liang 梁 (502–557), and Chen 陳 (557–589). The Liang in particular enjoyed nearly half a century of material prosperity and literary vitality under the energetic and steady Emperor Wu 武帝 (r. 502–549), one of the longest-ruling monarchs in Chinese history. Yan Zhitui was born eleven years into Emperor Wu's reign, and grew up at a time when the Liang was at the height of its power.

Yan Zhitui's ancestors hailed from Linyi of Langye 琅邪臨沂 (in modern Shandong). His ninth-generation ancestor, Yan Han 顏含 (ca. 260s– ca. 350s), had served on the staff of the Prince of Langye, who became the founding emperor of the Eastern Jin (r. 317–323), and so was among the first who crossed the Yangzi River to settle in the south. In the stringent hierarchical society of the Southern Dynasties, the Yan clan of Langye, though not of the top echelon, was high up as an old northern noble family, and their early migration to the south was further considered a political advantage.[1] Although he did not seem to have any distinguished achievements, Yan Han was nevertheless enfeoffed as a marquis.[2] Perhaps an important factor in Yan Han's prestige

---

[1] Northern gentry who crossed the Yangzi River to the south late were treated as inferior to those who immigrated earlier, and there was a strong prejudice against them in official recruitment. See *Song shu* 65.1720–721.

[2] *Jin shu* 88.2285.

was his direct kinship connection with Wang Dao 王導 (276–339), also from Langye, the powerful minister who played a crucial role in the founding of the Eastern Jin.[3]

Yan Zhitui descended from Yan Han's eldest son. He had a culturally illustrious forebear, Yan Yanzhi 顏延之 (384–456), who was in the direct line of descent from Yan Han's youngest son.[4] One of the literary giants of the early fifth century, Yan Yanzhi had a reputation not only for broad learning and brilliant literary writing, but also for drinking, unrestrained behavior, and a volatile temper.[5] Some of Yan Yanzhi's traits – erudition and propensity for writing, defiance of authority, hot-blooded stubbornness – seem to have run in the Yan family: Yan Zhitui's grandfather committed suicide as a political protest; his elder brother, Yan Zhiyi 顏之儀 (523–591), several times almost lost his life for defying emperors in the north;[6] an eighth-century descendant, Yan Zhenqing 顏真卿 (709–785), died defying a rebel governor.[7] Yan Zhitui himself was known for his indulgence in alcohol and unconventional behavior in his youth, and once even lost an official appointment because of drinking.[8] Perhaps most importantly, Yan Yanzhi wrote "Instructions from the Courtyard" (*Ting gao* 庭誥) for his sons, the gist of which is preserved in his dynastic history biography.[9] This may well have served as an inspiration for Yan Zhitui's *Family Instructions*.

Yan Zhitui's grandfather, Yan Jianyuan 顏見遠 (d. 502), was married to a daughter of the Xie clan of Chen commandery 陳郡謝氏 (in mod-

---

3 The epitaph for Yan Han, written shortly after his death by a relative, Li Chan 李闡, records a conversation in which Yan Han referred to Wang Dao by his baby name Ah Long 阿龍 and positioned himself as a *zhangren*, Elder, to Wang Dao. Yan Kejun, *Quan Jin wen* 133.2225. Here *zhangren*, rather than father-in-law, refers to a senior relative on either paternal or maternal side (see *Family Instructions*, VI.24). Albert Dien does not mention this connection, but notes Yan Han's kinship ties with Wang Shu 王舒 (d. 333), Wang Dao's cousin, and Huan Wen 桓溫 (312–373), the powerful general (Dien 2–3).

4 Yan Zhitui mentions a Yan Yanzhi who was a disgraced general (XIV.1b). This must be Yan Yan, a general killed in battle, not to be confused with the writer Yan Yanzhi.

5 See Yanzhi's biography in *Song shu* 73.1891–904.

6 *Zhou shu* 40.720–21.

7 *Jiu Tang shu* 128.3595–596.

8 See *BQS* 2 in Appendix.

9 *Song shu* 73.1893–902.

ern He'nan), which was one of the two top clans in the south, the other being Wang Dao's clan.[10] Yan Jianyuan, who had served the last Qi emperor, was "a square man and did not fit in with the crowd."[11] He was primarily known for starving himself to death upon Liang's replacement of Qi, an unusual act at the time and a topic to which we will return below.[12] For this reason, Yan Zhitui's father, Yan Xie 顏協 (498–539), declined the summons of the court and chose to serve only on a princely staff.[13] His patron was Emperor Wu's seventh son, Xiao Yi 蕭繹 (507–555). Yan Xie was a well-read man with an interest in the esoteric and a renowned calligrapher whose calligraphy once graced many steles in Jingzhou;[14] but he was not trained in the courtly style of writing and was not a member of the contemporary literary community.

Yan Zhitui was likely born in Jiangling 江陵 (in modern Hubei), the provincial capital of Jingzhou where Xiao Yi was governor in 531. A child bears the influence of the parents in various ways, sometimes straightforwardly, sometimes negatively. In *Family Instructions*, Yan Zhitui exhorts his sons to be good with calligraphy, but not too good, because he does not want them to be enslaved by requests for their writing from the rich and powerful; he may very well be thinking of his own father (XIX.1–2). Since Yan Xie authored biographies of Jin immortals, Yan Zhitui concedes that "the talk of deities and immortals may not be entirely nonsense" (and even has an extant poem on the topic of immortals), but advises his sons not to get involved in pursuing immortality by taking drugs (XV.1). He was once fascinated by the art of divination, perhaps as a result of his father's interest in omens, but eventually gave it up, discouraging his sons from engaging in it as well (XIX.12).

When Yan Zhitui was eight years old, his father died. He was subsequently brought up by his two elder brothers (mentioned in *Family*

10 We know this because after Yan Jianyuan died in 502, his son Yan Xie was raised by his maternal uncle, Xie Jian 謝暕 of Chen commandery. *Liang shu* 50.727.

11 This comment was made by Yan Zhenqing. *Quan Tang wen* 339.3341.

12 *Liang shu* 50.727.

13 Ibid.

14 He authored *Biographies of Jin Immortals* 晉仙傳 and *Diagrams of the Disasters Presaged by the Sun and Moon* 日月災異圖. *Liang shu* 50.727; *Nan shi* 72.1785.

Instructions, I.3 and I.4).[15] At eleven years, Yan Zhitui listened to the prince Xiao Yi's lectures on *Laozi* and *Zhuangzi* along with other students, although he claims he was not interested in the metaphysical discourse (VIII.22), and his biography describes him as devoted to the pursuit of his "family specialty" in the *Zuo Tradition* and the *Rites of Zhou*.[16] Throughout *Family Instructions* Yan Zhitui mentions Xiao Yi many times. It is clear that, although capable of being cruel toward his own flesh and blood, the prince had treated the Yan brothers, and their late father, with kindness and generosity.[17] Consequently, in his "Rhapsody on Viewing My Life," Yan Zhitui gives as euphemistic an account of Xiao Yi as possible regarding the prince's behavior in the Hou Jing Rebellion. This forms a glaring contrast with the scathing criticism of Xiao Yi made by the preeminent writer of the age, Yu Xin 庾信 (513–581), in his autobiographical rhapsody, "Lament for the South" ("Ai Jiangnan fu" 哀江南賦).

Though orphaned at a tender age, had the Liang not collapsed, Yan Zhitui probably would have enjoyed a fine career on the prince's staff and a predictably smooth life; he might even have been summoned to court like his father and had a stint in the splendid capital city. But when Yan Zhitui was seventeen years old, the Hou Jing Rebellion broke out.

In the fifth century, north China was ruled and unified by the Northern Wei 魏 dynasty. In 534, the Wei succumbed to civil war, and split

---

15 Because only the name of one elder brother is known, some scholars speculate that one of the elder brothers must have been a cousin. This is doubtful, for Yan Zhitui is so punctilious about the correct terms of kinship. Yan Xie's biography in the dynastic histories states that he had two sons, "Zhiyi and Zhitui, who both became well-known at a young age" (*Liang shu* 50.727; *Nan shi* 72.1785). The phrasing may imply that there were other brothers even though these two were the best-known among them. Indeed, two centuries later, a famous descendant of the Yan clan, Yan Zhenqing, mentions another brother, Yan Zhishan 顏之善, although Yan Zhishan is recorded as a younger brother to Yan Zhitui. *Quan Tang wen* 340.3449. However, Yan Zhiyi is also recorded as Yan Zhitui's younger brother in the *Bei shi* biography (83.2796), all of which shows there is much fluidity in textual records and memories.

16 *BQS* 1 in Appendix.

17 Yan Zhiyi, for instance, received a personal note from Xiao Yi commending him for his "Ode on Jingzhou" 荆州頌 (or "Ode to the Divine Prefecture" 神州頌). *Bei shi* 83.2796; *Zhou shu* 40.719.

into two states: the Western Wei, with its capital in Chang'an (modern Xi'an); and the Eastern Wei, with its capital in Ye (in modern Hebei). Hou Jing 侯景 (503–552), a treacherous Eastern Wei general, first defected to the Western Wei and then asked to surrender to the Liang. Emperor Wu accepted Hou Jing's capitulation against the counsel of many of his ministers. Hou Jing then rebelled against the Liang in 548 and with shocking speed advanced to the capital, which fell after a bloody siege of five months. Emperor Wu died soon after, and the crown prince Xiao Gang 蕭綱 (503–551, r. 549–551) became emperor under Hou Jing's control. Instead of rushing to the rescue, Xiao Yi, who harbored imperial ambitions of his own, engaged in a bitter feud with his brothers and nephews. Xiao Yi only seriously turned his attention to Hou Jing after he eliminated what he perceived as competitors for the throne. Refraining from censuring Xiao Yi outright, Yan Zhitui nevertheless offers subtle reproach in ll. 83–84 of his "Rhapsody on Viewing My Life":

及荊王之定霸   Only after the King of Jing secured his hegemony
始雪恥而圖雪   did he begin to eradicate shame and take vengeance.

In 550, Yan Zhitui was assigned to the staff of Xiao Fangzhu 蕭方諸 (537–552), Xiao Yi's second son who was stationed at Ying prefecture. Xiao Fangzhu and his incompetent advisors were easily defeated by Hou Jing's generals, and Yan Zhitui was captured and taken back to Jiankang as a prisoner. He did not get back to Jiangling until Hou Jing was defeated in 552. His experience during this time – including the harrowing episode of almost being executed by Hou Jing's men, and the traumatic sight of a ruined Jiankang – is narrated in detail in his "Rhapsody on Viewing My Life."

Upon Hou Jing's death, Xiao Yi took the throne near the end of 552, and against the advice of many of his courtiers, stayed in Jiangling instead of going to the capital Jiankang. Yan Zhitui spent the next two years in Jiangling participating in the collation of the emperor's book collection, which was much expanded by books transported from the Liang imperial library in Jiankang. In 553, Xiao Yi enlisted the help of the Western Wei and defeated his younger brother Xiao Ji 蕭紀 (508–553), the governor of Yizhou in Shu (modern Sichuan), who had also proclaimed himself emperor. The strife between the brothers proved to be fatal for the Liang, for once the Western Wei army took control of the strategically important Shu region upstream of the Yangzi River, the Liang was doomed.

In the winter of 554, the Western Wei army attacked, and Jiangling fell. On the eve of the court's capture, Xiao Yi set fire to the imperial book collection, reportedly one hundred and forty thousand scrolls in total, which Yan Zhitui had worked on for the past two years. Xiao Yi was executed by suffocation in January 555. The Wei army took well over one hundred thousand Jiangling residents to Chang'an, with Yan Zhitui and Yan Zhiyi among them, and slaughtered the young and weak.[18] Only three hundred households were spared from captivity. Twenty to thirty percent of the captives died of cold and hardship on the way, and most of the surviving captives were made slaves and distributed amongst the Wei generals and soldiers.[19]

Yan Zhitui bore witness to many acts of violence and destruction through it all. One can only imagine how the traumatic experience changed him. In *Family Instructions* he records the death of three brothers at the hands of the Wei soldiers, as the two younger brothers clung to the elder brother and tried to shield him (III.7). In the *Account of Wronged Souls* (see below), he tells of a man surnamed Liu who had lost his entire family in the Hou Jing Rebellion except for a young son and, upon being taken captive, carried the little boy himself on the long journey to Chang'an. A Wei commander wrestled the boy away and abandoned him in snow, and whipped the father who begged for the child's life. The father, grief-stricken and suffering from his injuries, died soon after.[20] In his "Rhapsody on Viewing My Life," Yan Zhitui devotes as many as forty lines (ll. 171–210) to the devastation of Jiangling and the captives' journey north. He laments the destruction of the books that to him represented the essence of human civilization, and mourns the looting and annihilation of the precious objects and imperial paraphernalia that were symbolic of the power of the state.[21] He

---

18 *Liang shu* 5.135.
19 *Zizhi tongjian* 166.5123.
20 *Yuanhun zhi*, 88–89.
21 The looting of Liang treasures is narrated in the biography of the general Yu Jin 于謹 (493–568) in *Zhou shu* 15.248.

speaks of his shame as a survivor, and grieves over the miseries of his fellow captives. The intensity of feeling invested in these lines far surpasses his narration in the same rhapsody of the fall of the Northern Qi, a dynasty he served for a good part of his adult life.

Yan Zhitui was separated from his brother upon coming to the north. While Yan Zhiyi stayed in Chang'an, Yan Zhitui was dispatched to Hongnong (in modern He'nan) to serve on the staff of a Western Wei general. At the time, the Eastern Wei had been replaced by the Northern Qi 齊 established by Gao Yang 高洋 (525–559; r. 550–559). Learning that the Qi court was sending Liang detainees home, Yan Zhitui in early 556 made the drastic decision to flee to Qi in the hope that he, too, would be able to return to the south.[22] One evening, he took his family to board a pre-fitted boat and, riding on the flooded Yellow River, traveled seven hundred *li* in one night.

It was, however, not in Yan Zhitui's destiny that he would ever see the south again. After he arrived at the Qi capital, Ye 鄴 (in modern He'bei), word came that the general Chen Baxian 陳霸先 (503–559; r. 557–559) deposed Xiao Yi's ninth son, whom he had set on the throne earlier, and established the Chen dynasty. With the Liang now defunct, Yan Zhitui remained in Ye at the Qi court.

Ironically, it was under the Last Ruler of Qi, a notoriously foolish and frivolous emperor, that Yan Zhitui seems to have flourished, through his aptitude in literary learning and administrative competence. There is evidence that he was one of the main forces behind the establishment of the Grove of Letters Institute (Wenlin guan 文林館) in the spring of 573,[23] and was involved in several of the Institute's influential compilations.

Despite recognition from the emperor, life at the Qi court was perilous because of conflicts between Xianbei military officers and Han men of letters. Only by a stroke of luck did Yan escape death in a tragic incident in which six of his colleagues lost their lives for remonstrating

---

22 The Northern Qi had tried to put Xiao Yuanming 蕭淵明 (ca. 490s–556), Liang Emperor Wu's nephew, on the Liang throne, but eventually the Liang generals prevailed and established Xiao Yi's ninth son as emperor in the autumn of 555.

23 See *Bei Qi shu* 42.563, 45.603.

with the emperor. Referred to as "Han fellows in literary offices" ("Han'er wenguan" 漢兒文官), they were executed and their bodies were dumped in the Zhang River.[24]

The Northern Qi did not last long. Earlier, in 557, the Western Wei had been replaced by Zhou 周 (also known as the Northern Zhou). Now, in early 577, the Zhou army conquered Qi. Yan Zhitui once more made a bid to return to the south by trying to persuade the Last Ruler of Qi to flee to Chen, but he did not prevail.

After the Qi fell, Yan Zhitui was obliged to go to Chang'an with a group of seventeen other Qi courtiers, including some of the Qi's most prominent writers and poets such as Yang Xiuzhi 陽休之 (509–582) and Lu Sidao 盧思道 (535–586).[25] In Chang'an, Yan Zhitui was finally reunited with his brother Yan Zhiyi, who was by this point a prominent minister in the Zhou court and had become quite consumed by his life and career in the north. With the kind of foolhardy uprightness that ran in the Yan family, Yan Zhiyi almost lost his life defending the failing Zhou royal house against the powerful general Yang Jian 楊堅 (541–604; Sui Emperor Wen, r. 581–604), who deposed the child emperor of Zhou and established the Sui 隋 dynasty in 581.[26]

Yan Zhitui, in contrast, was merely lingering on. He laments in his rhapsody,

在揚都值侯景殺簡文而篡位, 於江陵逢孝元覆滅, 至此而三為亡國之人.

At Yangdu, Hou Jing assassinated Emperor Jianwen and usurped the throne. At Jiangling, Emperor Xiaoyuan met with destruction. By now I have three times become a man of a fallen state.

He compares himself to a bird whose home grove was burned and whose wings are clipped, or a fish out of water. With an acute sense of rootlessness, he writes, "Alas, so vast is the universe, / I am mortified

---

24 *Bei Qi shu* 39.513. See his rhapsody, ll. 265–70, and *BQS* 6 in Appendix.

25 See Lu Sidao's biography in *Bei shi* 30.1076 and Yuan Xinggong's 元行恭 (d. 590s) biography in 55.2006.

26 Yan Zhiyi was a tutor to the Crown Prince, who later became Emperor Xuan (559–580, r. 578–580), and was known at this time for his repeated blunt remonstrance with the emperor. *Zhou shu* 40.720.

there is no place to lodge this body of mine" (ll. 319–20). Unlike Lu
Sidao and Xue Daoheng 薛道衡 (540–609), who managed to go home,
however briefly, Yan Zhitui had no place to which to return.

He kept close company with the other Qi exiles. Yang Xiuzhi composed a poem on "Listening to the Singing Cicadas" ("Ting chan ming"
聽蟬鳴), to which Yan Zhitui and Lu Sidao wrote matching poems.[27]
Lu Sidao's piece "was highly valued by the contemporaries": Yu Xin,
the most revered literary master of the time, "read all the matching
poems and deeply admired [Lu Sidao's]."[28] One can perhaps see why:
Lu Sidao's piece is filled with nostalgia for the bygone dynasty and
home state, with which many could find emotional resonance;[29] Yan
Zhitui's, on the other hand, is marked by a clear-eyed observation of
the reality around him articulated with directness and irony:

關中滿季心	The land within the Pass is filled with the likes of Ji Xin;
關西饒孔子	to the west of the Pass, there is a rich store of Confuciuses.[30]
詎用虞公立國臣	Why bother using the Lord of Yu's state-defend-ing minister?
誰愛韓王游說士	Who'd be fond of the persuader in the court of the King of Han?[31]

That is, the Zhou had its own talented people and would not use the
services of the Qi courtiers. In many ways this was a prescient insight:
Sui Emperor Wen never trusted the former Qi courtiers as much as he
did the northwestern families, and the regional bias continued into the

27 Yang Xiuzhi's original piece is no longer extant. The title also reads "Ting ming
    chan" 聽鳴蟬.
28 *Sui shu* 57.1398.
29 Lu Qinli, 2637.
30 "Within the Pass" and "to the west of the Pass" refer to the northwest. Ji Xin
    (fl. third century BCE) was a chivalrous figure widely admired by people "within
    the Pass." Yang Zhen (d. 124 CE), a learned Eastern Han scholar, was referred
    to as "the Confucius to the west of the Pass."
31 Gong Zhiqi and Su Qin are figures for the Northern Qi courtiers (see notes to
    this poem in this volume).

early Tang.[32] Furthermore, the atmosphere in the Zhou and the early Sui court was quite different from the Qi: Qi was perhaps the most literarily-inclined of the northern dynasties; Zhou, on the other hand, was devoted to martial values,[33] and Sui Emperor Wen was well-known for his lack of cultural sophistication and open disdain for literary matters.[34]

Yan Zhitui continued to serve as a Senior Serviceman in the Censorate during the Zhou and the early years of the Sui. As he says in *Family Instructions,*

計吾兄弟，不當仕進；但以門衰，骨肉單弱，五服之內，傍無一人，
播越他鄉，無復資廕；使汝等沈淪廝役，以為先世之恥；故靦冒人
間，不敢墜失。兼以北方政教嚴切，全無隱退者故也。

As I see it, we brothers should not have entered public service. However, the fortune of our clan is in decline, and our blood and flesh do not enjoy much power and status in society. Indeed there is nobody among close and distant relatives on whom we can rely. Moreover, we have been displaced from our native land and migrated to another region, so there is no inherited title to be passed on to our offspring. Should you boys be debased to the status of servants, it would be a disgrace to our ancestors. For this reason we have brazenly taken official posts, not daring to let the family tradition fall away. Besides, governmental regulations in the north are so austere that no one is permitted to seek reclusion and retirement (XX.3).

Along with another former Qi courtier, Yan Zhitui was ordered by Emperor Wen to assist in the compilation of a new history of the Wei,

---

32 Tang Emperor Taizong (r. 626–649) once commented on the differences between those "from within the Pass" (northwesterners) and those "from east of the Taihang Mountains" (northeasterners), and a minister protested, saying that an emperor should regard all within the four seas as his home and not be confined by the boundary between east and west. The very incident reveals that regional bias was deeply rooted. *Jiu Tang shu* 104.4012.

33 See *Sui shu* 50.1316, 51.1329.

34 *Sui shu* 2.54. In 585, he issued an edict that memorials to the throne must be factual and plain, and he had a governor indicted because his memorial was ornate and flowery. *Sui shu*, 66.1545.

treating the Western Wei as the legitimate dynasty, as opposed to the
existing *History of the Wei*, since Sui followed from Zhou that in turn
received its mandate from the Western Wei.[35] In 582, a Chang'an resident accidentally excavated a scale dated to Qin times, and Yan Zhitui
was asked to work with a former Qi courtier to transcribe the writings
on the iron weight (XVII.23). In the same year, he memorialized the
emperor that the court's ritual music was still using non-Han melodies
and asked to "seek the ancient norms" by following the Liang example.
Emperor Wen dismissed this suggestion immediately: "The Liang music
is the 'sound of a fallen state' – why inflict it on Us?"[36] Ultimately,
however, the Sui officials could not work out a program of ritual music
of their own.[37] After the Chen was conquered in 589, one of the emper-
or's trusted advisors, as well as his own son, Yang Guang 楊廣 (later
Emperor Yang, r. 604–618), advocated the adoption of the southern
music, and the emperor finally acquiesced.

Perhaps shortly after 584, a debate broke out between the northwesterners and northeasterners about the new calendar. The debate was
referred to the Section of Legal Policies in the Censorate, where Yan
Zhitui was appointed, and he suggested that the matter fell outside
their jurisdiction and that they should not adjudicate it.[38] With some
glee, he recounts in *Family Instructions* how the one colleague who
refused to listen to him ended up in disgrace (XII.11).

In Chang'an Yan Zhitui also socialized with members of the southern
diaspora. Lu Fayan's 陸法言 preface to his phonological work, *Qie yun*
切韻, relates how, in the early years of the Kaihuang era (581–600), he and
a group of eight friends, including Yan Zhitui, discussed the southern and
northern sound systems together; Xiao Gai 蕭該 and Yan Zhitui were cred-

---

35 *Shi tong* "Gujin zhengshi" 古今正史, 751. This work of historiography is no
    longer extant.
36 *Sui shu* 14.345.
37 The emperor said angrily that, seven years after he founded the Sui, the court's
    ritual music was still praising the former dynasty. *Sui shu* 14.345.
38 Liu Xiaosun 劉孝孫 (d. ca. 594) and Liu Zhuo 劉焯 (542–608), both from
    Hebei ("to the east of the Taihang Mountains), criticized the new calendar
    presented to the throne in 584 by a northwestern Daoist Zhang Bin 張賓.
    Zhang Bin, who had ingratiated himself with Emperor Wen by predicting he
    would one day take the throne, prevailed. *Sui shu* 17.423.

ited as the main arbiters in these discussions.[39] Yan Zhitui himself devotes an entire chapter to phonology in *Family Instructions*; it testifies to the academic passion of a scholarly man and to the importance attached to correct pronunciation as a status symbol, a topic to which we will return below.

Perhaps most importantly, it was during the Sui that he finished his *Family Instructions*. Initially intended only for his sons, this book nevertheless ensured his lasting fame. Throughout the book he addresses his sons as "you boys" (*rucao* 汝曹 or *ercao* 爾曹). In Qi, Yan Zhitui had sired two sons: Silu 思魯 ("longing for Lu") and Minchu 愍楚 ("compassion for Chu"). In Sui he fathered another son, Youqin 遊秦 ("wandering in Qin").[40] Yan Zhitui mentions his wife's family a few times in *Family Instructions*, thus we know her surname was Yin 殷. Youqin, however, might have been born to a different mother than Silu and Minchu. In *Family Instructions*, Yan Zhitui gives an entire chapter to the topic of remarriage, in which he explains that sons by concubines are treated well in the south, but are despised and excluded from polite society in the north. He does not, however, appear to endorse remarriage, warning his sons that they must be careful about this matter and citing their maternal uncle's case to demonstrate the danger of remarriage. The prominence of such a topic in *Family Instructions* shows that it was a matter dear to Yan Zhitui's heart, and the story he ends the chapter with, about an Eastern Han man who was filial to his stepmother and generous to his younger brother's children, seems to mean more than he explicitly states.

During Yan Zhitui's last years, he received the recognition of Emperor Wen's eldest son, Yang Yong 楊勇 (ca. 560s–604), who was the Crown Prince until he was deposed in 600. Unlike his father, Yang Yong appreciated learning and literature; he made Yan Zhitui an Academician on his staff in the midst of the Kaihuang era and treated him with great respect.[41] Yan Zhitui did not live to see Yang Yong fall from grace. In 591, his elder brother, Yan Zhiyi, died at the age of sixty-eight, and Yan Zhitui passed away presumably not long afterward.

---

39 Yan Kejun, *Quan Sui wen* 27.4180. Lu Fayan's preface was written in 601. Xiao Gai was a grandson of Liang Emperor Wu's brother Xiao Hui 蕭恢 (476–526) and had expertise in phonology.

40 That Youqin was born in Sui is based on the assertion made in Yan Zhenqing's stele inscription. *Quan Tang wen* 339.3441.

41 See *BQS* 8 in Appendix.

Much of Yan Zhitui's *Family Instructions* is concerned with the importance of passing on the family legacy in learning. In this respect, his three sons did not disappoint him.[42] Yet, passing away in the newly unified empire at the apex of its power, Yan Zhitui could not anticipate that his sons would be caught in chaotic times again so soon. The Sui fell apart under the rule of Emperor Yang, with violent uprisings breaking out all over the country.[43] Minchu and his entire family were cannibalized by a hungry rebel army.[44] So intent on advising his sons about brotherly affection and household management, but having little to say about conjugal love and respect, Yan Zhitui might not have known or cared that his eldest son Silu had an unhappy relationship with his wife. It ultimately caused Silu's alienation from his own son, Yan Shigu 顏師古 (581–645), which apparently was public knowledge and became a stigma on Yan Shigu's reputation.[45]

Yan Shigu was, however, a classicist scholar far better known than both his father and grandfather.[46] His great-great-grandson Yan Zhenqing was a Tang loyalist who was martyred for his fierce outspokenness and righteousness, and, reminiscent of Zhitui's father, for his striking calligraphy, which is still avidly copied and studied today.

The Buddhist Faith

Yan Zhitui uses an entire chapter in *Family Instructions* exhorting his sons to adhere to the Buddhist faith. From the very beginning he makes it crystal-clear that Buddhism is the family religion:

---

42 Silu and Minchu were known for their learning. Youqin was appointed Governor of Lianzhou 廉州 (in modern Hebei) in the early years of Tang Gaozu's 高祖 reign (r. 618–626) and proved a good administrator; he was also the author of a philological work on the *Han History*. Though this work is lost, his nephew Yan Shigu (Silu's eldest son) reportedly adopted much of his work in writing his own commentary, still extant, on the *Han History. Jiu Tang shu* 73.2596.

43 *Sui shu* 4.83–93.

44 *Jiu Tang shu* 56.2275.

45 Silu married the daughter of Yin Yingtong 殷英童, a Northern Qi courtier who was the author of a collection of literary works (see *Jiu Tang shu* 47.2072). Yan Shigu tried to reconcile his parents and henceforth strained his relationship with his father. This was alluded to by the emperor in his critique of Yan Shigu. *Xin Tang shu* 198.5642.

46 See Yan Shigu's biography in *Jiu Tang shu* and *Xin Tang shu*.

三世之事，信而有徵，家世業此，勿輕慢也。其間妙旨，具諸經論，
不復於此，少能讚述；但懼汝曹猶未牢固，略重勸誘爾。

Our family has been devoted to Buddhism for generations; you
should not treat it lightly and casually. The marvelous doctrines
are fully expounded in the various sutras and abhidharmas, and I
will not be able to recapitulate them here. I only fear that you boys
are not quite confirmed in your faith yet, so I will briefly repeat
my encouragement (XVI.1).

And he is unequivocal about the superiority of Buddhism, not only to
the teachings of Laozi and Zhuangzi, but also to Confucianism. He
says of Buddhism:

明非堯、舜、周、孔所及也。

Clearly this is not what [the sage emperors] Yao and Shun, the
Duke of Zhou, and Confucius could ever match (XVI.2).

Ever being the pragmatic man, he concedes that certain things, such
as "hunts and battles, banquets and punishments [corporal punishment and punishment by death]," stem from human nature and so
cannot be eliminated all at once, but he believes that they must be
regulated so as not to become excessive, and stresses that this being
the case,

歸周、孔而背釋宗，何其迷也。

How deluded if one bows to the Duke of Zhou and Confucius but
turns one's back on Buddhism! (XVI.3)

Yet, despite Yan Zhitui's unambiguous declaration of his religious faith,
there has been a strong desire in the Chinese tradition to see Yan Zhitui
as a staunch Confucian, to the extent that some late imperial editions
of his *Family Instructions* even changed the text to fit this image. In the
final chapter, "Last Will," once again Yan Zhitui asks his sons not to
follow Confucian teachings in the matter of making sacrifices to deceased parents:

四時祭祀，周、孔所教，欲人勿死其親，不忘孝道也。求諸內典，則無益焉。

The four seasonal sacrifices are taught by the Duke of Zhou and Confucius with the hope that one shall not forget one's parents as soon as they die, but if you look into the Inner Scriptures [i.e., Buddhist scriptures], you will see that these sacrifices are completely useless (XX.5).

Instead, he asks them to offer his spirit a vegetarian meal from time to time, and to "do something at the Ullambana Festival on the fifteenth of the seventh month: that is all I expect from you" 及七月半盂蘭盆, 望於汝也. The Ullambana Festival, on which rituals are performed to relieve the sufferings of the dead, derives from the *Ullambana Sutra* in which Maudgalyāyana redeems his deceased mother from hell. Yet, in two late imperial editions, the citation above reads: "....and to practice to the best of your ability loyalty and trustworthiness, and to not bring shame to your parents: that is all I expect from you" 及盡忠信, 不辱其親, 所望於汝也.[47] None of the earlier editions contains this variant reading.

The reasons for the desire to label Yan Zhitui a Confucian are manifold. Buddhism, as a foreign religion, has always been regarded with skepticism and mistrust by many since its introduction into China, but the tendency was intensified in late imperial times, when neo-Confucianism became state orthodoxy and held powerful sway over the Chinese scholarly elite, and that has lasted well into the modern times, infused with a state-sponsored nationalistic agenda.

Such labeling, which implies an inflexible conviction about clear-cut boundaries between different systems of beliefs, may not have always made sense in the fifth and sixth century. Zhang Rong 張融 (444–497), a member of the southern elite and a prominent cultural figure, asked on his deathbed to be buried with "the *Classic of Filial Piety* and *Laozi* in my left hand and the *Lotus Sutra* in my right hand."[48] His attitude – an integration of values represented by a series of important texts – is revealing about the age in which he lived. There indeed were fierce

---

47 See XX.5 in Additional Notes.
48 *Nan Qi shu* 41.729. One wonders if Zhang Rong should be labeled as a "Buddho-Daoist-Confucian" if that would even mean anything.

debates about Confucian, Buddhist, and Daoist teachings at the time, but even if we wish to consider Yan Zhitui in those terms and impose "-ism" on his beliefs, it seems perverse not to follow a man's self-declaration of his faith and insist on imposing upon him a definition that he himself explicitly denies.

Upon close inspection, the Confucian label, even applied in a generalized and ahistorical manner, does not fit well with the values held by Yan Zhitui, either. Yan Zhitui has been regarded as a Confucian primarily on the grounds that he cared deeply about family tradition, and that he never entered the religious order himself or encouraged his sons to become monks.[49] And yet, in the *Vimalakīrti-nirdeśa Sutra*, one of the most popular Buddhist scriptures in early medieval China, Vimalakīrti was a lay Buddhist with a family and a luxuriant secular lifestyle who nevertheless was deeply enlightened and approved by the Buddha as a role model. In the *Ullambana Sutra* mentioned above, Maudgalyāyana goes through extraordinary trials and tribulations to redeem the suffering soul of his deceased mother from hell, performing a supreme act of filial piety in fulfillment of his religious destiny. Filial piety is not a virtue monopolized by Confucianism, nor should Confucianism, which has gone through many transformations throughout history, be equated only with the love of one's family.

The changes that have taken place in the Confucian tradition itself can be seen most clearly in the notion of loyalty, a topic of utmost importance to a neo-Confucian of late imperial China. Teng Ssu-yü claims, "Loyalty is highly desired by Yen Chih-t'ui."[50] But his claim is based on a misunderstanding of Yan Zhitui's own words, not to mention that his citation in support of the claim omits an important part of the passage in question.[51] This is the passage in its entirety:

---

49 For instance, see Teng Ssu-yü, "Introduction," xxix–xxxii.
50 Teng, "Introduction," xxix.
51 On p. xxix, Teng's citation reads: "Not bend the knee before two imperial families was the integrity of Po I and Shu Ch'i; to refuse to serve an illegitimate ruler was the principle of I-yung and Ch'i-tzu. But if you cannot help it, and suddenly have to bend your knees in serving another ruler, you should not change your thought about the former chief, whether he still exists or not." Cf. the translation in Teng, p. 92.

不屈二姓，夷、齊之節也；何事非君，伊、箕之義也。自春秋已來，
家有奔亡，國有吞滅，君臣固無常分矣；然而君子之交絕無惡聲，一
旦屈膝而事人，豈以存亡而改慮？陳孔璋居袁裁書，則呼操為豺狼；
在魏製檄，則目紹為蛇虺。在時君所命，不得自專，然亦文人之巨患
也，當務從容消息之。

Not submitting to two royal houses – this is the integrity shown
by Bo Yi and Shu Qi. "Any lord one serves is one's ruler" – this is
the principle upheld by Yi Yin and Jizi. Ever since the Spring and
Autumn period, many clans have fled into exile, and many states
have been conquered: the relationship between a prince and a minister cannot remain unchanged. Yet, when a gentleman severs his
relationship with another, he will not speak ill of his former friend.
Once a man bends his knee to serve another, how can he change
his thoughts about his former lord? When Chen Kongzhang was
writing a letter on behalf of Yuan Shao, he called Cao Cao a jackal
and a wolf; when he composed a proclamation on behalf of the
Wei, he described Yuan Shao as a poisonous snake. He did what
his current lord ordered and had no control over his action. But
this is a great problem for a man of letters. You must consider this
most carefully if you ever find yourself in such a situation. (IX.6)

In the opening statement, Yan Zhitui cites two opposite cases: in the
case of Bo Yi and Shu Qi, they starved themselves to death rather than
serve a different dynasty than the one they were born into; in the case
of Yi Yin and Jizi, they were flexible about which ruler to serve because,
according to Yi Yin, "To serve a lord who is not the right lord: now
what harm lies in that?....The important thing here is to manage the
world on behalf of Heaven and hopefully be able to practice the Way"
事非其君者, 何傷也……要欲為天理物, 冀得行道而已矣.[52] In the *Family
Instructions* context, clearly the Yi Yin–Jizi model is the one Yan Zhitui
approves, as he plainly tells his sons that "the relationship between a
prince and a minister cannot remain unchanged."[53] His advice to them

---

52 *Mengzi zhushu* 3A.56a.
53 Remarkably, the phrase, "Any lord one serves is one's ruler," again has a textual
    variant in a late imperial edition, which makes no sense (see Additional Notes).

is not to adhere to one dynasty and one lord, but simply not to bad-mouth their former ruler, be he dead or alive.

Yan Zhitui's notion of loyalty would seem woefully inadequate to the late imperial scholarly elite. Yet, while in later times Bo Yi and Shu Qi received unanimous acclaim for their loyalty to the Shang, their reception in early medieval times was mixed, and they were censured for their foolhardy adherence to a dynasty that had lost Heaven's mandate.[54] Similarly, when Yan Zhitui's grandfather, Yan Jianyuan, starved himself to death upon Liang's replacement of Qi in 502, his behavior stood out as being highly singular: it was not the norm of the age, and it was not necessarily considered commendable either. Liang Emperor Wu's comment is telling:

我自應天從人, 何預天下士大夫事, 而顏見遠乃至於此也.[55]

I have responded to the call of Heaven and followed the will of men [in establishing the Liang]. Does this have anything to do with the gentry of the world?! That Yan Jianyuan should have done a thing like this!

At any rate, Yan Zhitui himself served four dynasties – Liang, the Northern Qi, Zhou, and Sui; and he clearly did not want his sons to emulate his grandfather. He might have regarded loyalty as an impor-tant quality, but his definition of loyalty requires a nuanced historical

---

54 There were many writings from the third and fourth century that testify to the mixed reception of Bo Yi and Shu Qi. Wang Can's 王粲 (d. 217) "Lament for Yi and Qi" 弔夷齊文 states: "Keeping themselves pure, they indulged in their aims, / they went against the great principle of sagely and wise men" 絜己躬以騁志, 怨聖哲之大倫. Yan Kejun, *Quan hou Han wen*, 106.966. Mi Yuan's 麋元 (fl. 3rd century) piece on the same topic goes even further: "You recited sagely writings, listened to sagely music, lived in a sagely time, and yet deviated from the sagely mind" 誦聖之文, 聽聖之音, 居聖之世, 而異聖之心. *Quan sanguo wen* 38.1267. The great writer Ruan Ji 阮籍 (210–263) questions how they pursued reputation at the expense of their life: "They acted rashly regarding lifespans and were not at ease, contesting for good name as their measure" 肆壽夭而弗豫兮, 競毀譽以為度. Yan Kejun, *Quan sanguo wen* 44.1304; translation Stephen Owen's, in Ruan Ji 173.

55 *Liang shu* 50.727.

understanding that takes us far beyond the entrenched neo-Confucian ideology of late imperial and modern China.

To Yan Zhitui, the core concepts of Confucianism are "benevolence, integrity, decorum, wisdom, and trustworthiness," of which he finds perfect counterparts in Buddhist prohibitions against killing, stealing, impropriety, licentiousness, and dissembling (XVI.3). But there is also a set of values and convictions he imparts to his sons more implicitly, and no less self-consciously.

Values and Beliefs

When Yan Zhitui was taken to Jiankang as a captive by Hou Jing's forces, he witnessed a city in ruins. More devastating was the termination of the great families:

> 中原冠帶隨晉渡江者百家，故江東有百譜，至是在都者覆滅略盡。

> Of the "caps and sashes" of the Central Plain, those who had crossed the River with the Jin house amounted to a hundred clans.[56] Hence there were a hundred clan genealogies to the east of the Yangzi River [i.e., the south]. By now, however, those in the capital were almost completely destroyed.

The Southern Dynasties was very much an aristocratic society with a stringent social hierarchy and an absolute division between gentry and commoners, but the destruction brought about by the Hou Jing Rebellion, and the disorder and dislocation that ensued, finally broke down the entrenched social structure. It was a world full of menaces and opportunities.

Faced with this new reality, those who could not adjust were simply washed away. At a time of quick rise and fall of fortunes, the fluidity of social status, and the dissolution of social distinction between gentry and commoners, Yan Zhitui is concerned, not only about the family's physical survival, but also about preserving the elite identity of the family.

---

56 "Caps and sashes" refers to the gentry.

自荒亂已來，諸見俘虜，雖百世小人，知讀論語、孝經者，尚為人師；
雖千載冠冕，不曉書記者，莫不耕田養馬。

In the recent times of chaos, of those who have become captives,
if one knows how to read the *Analects* and the *Classic of Filial Piety*,
be he from a family that has been lowly for a hundred generations,
he can still be a teacher to someone else; but if a man does not
know how to write, be he from a family that has been patrician
for a thousand years, he will still have to plow the field and tend
horses (VIII.5).

He observed, with alarm and pity, the scions of aristocratic families
falling from grace:

及離亂之後，朝市遷革，銓衡選舉，非復曩者之親；當路秉權，不見
昔時之黨....兀若枯木，泊若窮流，鹿獨戎馬之間，轉死溝壑之際。

After the disorder and dispersion, court and marketplace were
changed. Those in charge of government recruitment are now no
longer their relatives; the powers that be are no longer the members
of their clique....Stupefied like a withered tree, shallow like an
exhausted stream, they wander aimlessly in the midst of military
horses and eventually die off in a ditch (VIII.4b).

For the old elite, family lineage is no longer everything. One must
possess "learning and skills" (*xueyi* 學藝). The desire to maintain family
social status is a driving motivation behind his exhortation of his sons
to study, to master philological and literary skills, and to continue the
family legacy in *suye* 素業, "pure profession," a term that in this period
referred specifically to an engagement in cultural learning and classical
scholarship as opposed to martial skills. The chapters on the importance
of study, literary writings, evidential learning, and phonology take up
the lion's share of the book.

Yet, education and learning are far from being "the only distinction
between nobles and commoners."[57] This is most obvious in Chapter
VI, "Manners and Etiquette," one of the longest chapters in the book.

---

57 Teng, xxvi.

In it, Yan Zhitui sets out in great detail the rules of conduct that govern a gentry member's everyday life, such as how to handle taboo names (i.e., names of deceased ancestors), the correct forms of addressing a relative, weeping at parting and during mourning, the observation of mourning rituals, and the celebration of birthdays. What may appear superficial and trivial to a modern reader proved to be of crucial importance to a member of the elite like Yan Zhitui, because it is in such details of speech and action that one sees the distinguishing traits of a well-born genteel man. It must also be noted that none of these codes of conduct has anything to do with morality. Although their ages and circumstances were far apart, Yan Zhitui is reminiscent of Baldesar Castiglione (1478–1529), the Renaissance Italian author of *The Book of the Courtier*, known as "a handbook for gentlemen." There is a remarkably similar preoccupation with social distinction and outward appearances.

At the opening of this chapter, Yan Zhitui makes a pointed comment on the profound difference of life between south/past and north/present:

> 學達君子，自為節度，相承行之，故世號士大夫風操。而家門頗有不同，所見互稱長短，然其阡陌亦自可知。昔在江南，目能視而見之，耳能聽而聞之；蓬生麻中，不勞翰墨。汝曹生於戎馬之間，視聽之所不曉，故聊記以傳示子孫。

....learned and wise gentlemen took it upon themselves to lay down rules, which have subsequently spread to others. The world refers to such rules as the manners and etiquette of the gentry. Even though each family has its own style, and some may regard certain rules as either superior or inferior to others, we can still discern the basic ways of carrying oneself. In the old days, back in the south, one witnessed proper conduct with one's own eyes and heard it with one's own ears. "Pigweed grows in the midst of hemp" – one did not need to bother using brush and ink [to write down the rules].[58] You boys, however, were born and raised among war hors-

---

58 The full saying is "Pigweed in the midst of hemp naturally grows up straight." It appears in the philosophical *Xunzi* and refers to the influence of one's environment. Yan Zhitui implies that the south in the old days had been much more conducive for a child's proper education in manners and etiquette.

es, and have not had a chance to see or hear about those proprieties. Thus I have to record them so as to pass them on to my sons and grandsons.

Yan Zhitui's sons were all born and raised in the north. But Yan Zhitui's family was one of the oldest elite émigré clans in the south and had enjoyed superiority even to the native families of the south. It is this deeply rooted sense of elite family identity that proved to be the most important thing to Yan Zhitui.

It is this sense of identity that is carried over in the chapter on phonology. He is emphatic about teaching his children the correct pronunciations from their early childhood:

吾家子女，雖在孩稚，便漸督正之；一言訛替，以為己罪矣。

The sons and daughters of my family, even during their early childhood, are drilled and corrected little by little. If they ever pronounce one thing wrong, I consider it my fault.

Like manners and etiquette, pronunciation and accent are an outward sign of the inner identity.

According to Yan Zhitui, the only places where pronunciation can serve as a standard are the former Southern Dynasties capital, Jiankang, and the former Eastern Han/Western Jin capital, Luoyang (XVIII.2). As Chen Yinke long ago pointed out, Yan Zhitui is certainly not referring to the contemporary Luoyang speech, but rather to the Luoyang speech preserved by the northern elite clans – like his own – that migrated to the south after the fall of the Western Jin.[59] By Jiankang Yan Zhitui does not mean the Wu dialect (*Wu yu*) spoken by the native southern families either, but again to the speech of the old elite émigrés.

To many scholars of the history of this period, the numerous comparisons between south and north, made throughout *Family Instructions*, are of great interest. Albert Dien correctly notes that, "The period that he had spent in the South was an extremely important one to him, for those were his formative years. In his *Instructions* the southern cus-

---

59 Chen Yinke, 1–18.

toms and attitudes loom large."[60] But it is worthwhile to bear in mind
that he had also spent more than two decades of his adult life in the
Northern Qi, and anecdotes and reminiscences about Qi abound. For
this reason, we should add an important provision about his north-
south comparisons: his notion of the north is perhaps not the generalized "north China," but rather the northeast.

One of the most striking points of difference between south and
north is woman's lifestyle and sphere of influence, an issue on which
Yan Zhitui shows his most southern, and conservative, attitude. He
admits that daughters are "truly a burden" from a financial point of
view, since parents must provide a daughter with a dowry; but from a
humanitarian perspective opposes infanticide, practiced by many of his
contemporaries (V.15): this is as far as his "liberalism" goes. He stresses
women should be only allowed to take care of material provisions for
a family, and must not be allowed to intervene in state or family affairs;
he also writes with approval that (elite) women in the south had very
little social intercourse even with their relatives.

It is noteworthy, however, that he paints a very different picture of
women's activities in the northeast:

鄴下風俗，專以婦持門戶，爭訟曲直，造請逢迎，車乘填街衢，綺羅
盈府寺，代子求官，為夫訴屈。

The customs of Ye are, however, quite different: they let the wife
take charge of the family. The womenfolk are involved in disputes
and lawsuits; they pay visits and receive guests; their carriages
crowd the streets, and official quarters swarm with their silk dresses.
They seek office for their sons or make pleas to authority on behalf
of their husbands (V.12).

Whether or not this was really a legacy of the Northern Wei of Xianbei
origin as Yan Zhitui suggests, this was the culture that saw the emergence of powerful women in the northern dynasties' politics. During
Yan Zhitui's lifetime, Sui Emperor Wen's wife, Empress Dugu 獨孤
(544–602), of a mixed Xianbei and Han ethnicity, was well known for

---

60 Dien, 9–10.

being the emperor's equal partner in state governance.[61] This was also the very culture that would eventually give rise to Wu Zetian (624–705), the only woman emperor who established her own dynasty and one of the most competent rulers in Chinese history.

Literary Accomplishments

Yan Zhitui's *Family Instructions* is written in clear and fluent prose, but his contemporaries would without a doubt look to poetry (*shi*) and rhapsodies (*fu*) as the most privileged forms of literary expression. Yan Zhitui only has five poems (one of dubious attribution) and one rhapsody that are extant in their entirety. In both of these genres, Yan Zhitui cannot be said to represent the mood of the age.

In *Family Instructions*, Yan Zhitui states that not a single piece of his father's literary writings was selected into *A Record of the New Writings of the Western Headquarters*, an anthology commissioned by the prince Xiao Yi; the "western headquarters" refers to Xiao Yi's headquarters. He puts a good face on the exclusion as much as possible by saying that this was because his late father's writings "had an orthodox elegance and did not follow the contemporary fashion" (IX.12). He also mentions that his father's writings were destroyed in a house fire and thus not transmitted. Conflagration was indeed one of the primary culprits for textual losses in the age of manuscript culture; nevertheless, it also shows that Yan Xie's writings were not circulating far and wide during his lifetime, so no one had a second copy of them.

In the south, one of Yan Zhitui's ancestors, Yan Yanzhi, had been the foremost court poet in the Liu Song dynasty. In the last decades of the fifth century, Yan Yanzhi's densely allusive style yielded to the so-called Yongming 永明 Style, whose leading representatives promoted verbal limpidity and self-conscious euphony, wearing their learning very lightly. The Yongming Style evolved further in the sixth century into the Palace Style (*Gongti* 宮體), named after the Eastern Palace (Donggong 東宮) that was the official residence of the Crown Prince. The Palace Style was exemplified by the poetry of Xiao Gang, Xiao Yi, and members of their intimate circles, including the aforementioned Yu Xin

---

61 *Sui shu* 22.622, 38.1109.

and his father Yu Jianwu 庾肩吾 (480s–ca. 552). Their poetry continued to manifest the limpidity advocated by the Yongming poets; but it possesses an unprecedented degree of intricacy and delicacy and a sophisticated subtlety of expression. It is also a poetry informed by the Buddhist consciousness of the ephemerality of the world of physical phenomena and the beauty resulting from such ephemerality.

In terms of being free of linguistic opaqueness, Yan Zhitui's poetic writings may indeed be considered "limpid." Yet, whether it is due to his family tradition, personal predilection, his upbringing in the provinces and lack of exposure to the Jiankang court society, or all of the above, his poetic compositions are characterized by a straightforward plain-spokenness that does not fit the criteria of southern courtly poetics. Nevertheless, it is important to note that Yan Zhitui is not part of the conscious reaction against the southern style that occurred during Sui Emperor Wen's reign. In his chapter on literary writings, Yan explicitly gives praise to the modern style:

今世音律諧靡，章句偶對，諱避精詳，賢於往昔多矣。

Today's writings, in terms of harmonious metrical pattern, refined parallelism, and meticulous avoidance of taboos, are much superior to former times (IX.11).

While he disapproves of ornateness on principle, as everyone else does, he states:

時俗如此，安能獨違？但務去泰去甚耳。

This, however, is the contemporary trend; how can you alone fight it? Just try to avoid extremes and excesses (IX.10).

The fact that he values literary writings is not only seen in devoting an entire chapter, one of the longest in *Family Instructions*, to the topic of literary writings, but also in his opening statement of that chapter:

朝廷憲章，軍旅誓誥，敷顯仁義，發明功德，牧民建國，不可暫無。

In creating court statutes, issuing military oaths and announcements, manifesting benevolence and integrity, and demonstrating achievements and virtue, governing the people as well as establishing the state, we cannot do without literary writings even for one moment (IX.1).

Interestingly, for *buke zanwu* 不可暫無 ("we cannot do without literary writings even for one moment"), the "Song edition" notes that it also reads *shiyong duotu* 施用多途 ("[literary writings] have many practical applications"). This variant reading is adopted in nearly all later editions. Such a variant, certainly not a copyist error resulting from graphic or phonological similarity, seems to be among those of an ideological origin, reflecting the well-known bias against literature on the part of neo-Confucian thinkers from the Song (960–1279) onward.

Yan Zhitui also launches into an extensive and vehement critique of the Western Han writer Yang Xiong (53 BCE–18 CE) for his dismissal of belletristic writings, echoing the declaration of Xiao Gang, Liang Emperor Jianwen:

不為壯夫, 楊雄實小言破道; 非謂君子, 曹植亦小辯破言。論之科刑,
罪在不赦。

"A grown man does not practice it" – Yang Xiong truly marred the Way with his petty discourse. "Writing rhapsodies is not fitting employment for a gentleman" – Cao Zhi also damaged Discourse with his trivial rhetoric. Should we discuss legal punishment for their offenses, their crime must be classified as unpardonable.[62]

Yan Zhitui's advice to his sons about writing is characteristically pragmatic: he counsels them to get plenty of feedback from family and friends before making their works public (IX.5). He shows a remarkable awareness of the existence of an inborn aptitude in the making of a great writer: "As long as you become a learned man, you can establish yourself in the world; but if you have no genius, don't force yourself to take up the writing brush" (IX.4). Many of Yan Zhitui's specific comments on literary writings focus on *shi* poetry. He brings up revealing differences in northeastern and southern views of poetry, and his sympathies clearly lie with his southern peers (IX.32 and IX.33).

---

62 Yan Kejun, *Quan Liang wen* 11.3010.

One particularly notable feature about Yan Zhitui's own writings is the self-annotations of his "Rhapsody on Viewing My Life." Prior to it, only two rhapsodies are known to have self-exegesis: the great southern poet Xie Lingyun's 謝靈運 (385–433) "Rhapsody on Dwelling in the Mountains" ("Shanju fu" 山居賦), and the northern astronomer Zhang Yuan's 張淵 (fl. 383–429) "Rhapsody on Viewing Celestial Phenomena" ("Guan xiang fu" 觀象賦). The former includes a prose commentary that explains among other things the local topography as well as flora and fauna represented in the rhapsody, and the latter, a commentary explaining the constellations and astronomical lore. Unlike either of these writers, Yan Zhitui's exegetical notes inserted in his rhapsodic poem strictly consist of an explanation of larger historical events and his own life story. They furnish information that is essential in a standard biography from a dynastic history, and sometimes provide data that we do not get in any other historical source from this period, such as in the case where he lists all the people collating books in Xiao Yi's Jiangling library and their offices. The duet of the two distinct voices of the same author, in the rhapsodic poem and in the prose notes, paints a full picture of a specific historical individual against the general backdrop of a chaotic age, and it is a fleshed-out historical record that no third-person historical writing can accomplish on its own.

Yan Zhitui compiled two collections of stories: one is entitled *A Collection of Records of Spirits* (*Jiling ji* 集靈記), now lost except for a few fragments;[63] the other, *An Account of Wronged Souls* (*Yuanhun zhi* 冤魂志), has been reconstituted from encyclopedia and compendium sources; its current version includes sixty brief stories recounting wrongful death and retribution manifesting Yan Zhitui's Buddhist faith. The stories from recent times in particular, such as the aforementioned one about the father and son captives who died on their way to Chang'an, might bring a sense of comfort to those who, like Yan Zhitui, witnessed and heard about violent, traumatic events.[64]

---

63 The longest item appears in *Taiping yulan* 718.3315. For others, see Zhang Aitang 436–37.

64 This work was translated and annotated by Alvin Cohen as *Tales of Vengeful Souls* (Taipei: Ricci Institute, 1982). It is not included in the present volume, per the Chinese convention of not including story compilations in a writer's "collection of literary works" (*wenji* 文集). *Yanshi jiaxun*, on the other hand,

Yan Zhitui was the author of several philological works. Unfortunately they are all lost except for small fragments. Several chapters in his *Family Instructions* are acclaimed for being a trove of philological and phonological knowledge. Even though some of his observations have been questioned by later scholars, they are valuable in allowing us a glimpse into early medieval scholarship. We also learn a great deal about the fluid, messy world of textual circulation in the age of manuscript culture, as versions of classics and histories differed from south to north.

Perhaps most notably, Yan Zhitui comes across as someone with a strong sense of curiosity about the world he lived in, from a relative's pet bird to a plant found in southern courtyards. His knowledge is not only grounded in book learning but also in his extensive travels from south to north. We see this curiosity in his "Rhapsody on Questioning the Sages" ("Jisheng fu" 稽聖賦), which is extant in fragments. It seemed to consist of a series of questions about cosmological and natural phenomena, probably not unlike those he poses in his chapter on Buddhism in *Family Instructions*.

Notes on Text and Editions

Yan Zhitui's *Family Instructions* was a popular text. Apart from independent circulation, it was also selectively included in Buddhist works such as *Guang Hongming ji* 廣弘明集 (*Expanded Collection on the Propagation of the Light*) compiled by the monk Daoxuan 道宣 (596–667) and *Fayuan zhulin* 法苑珠林 (*A Forest of Pearls in the Garden of Dharma*) compiled by another monk Daoshi 道世 (d. 683); it was also partially copied in what are sometimes referred to by scholars as "Dunhuang encyclopedias," such as *Qin dushu chao* 勤讀書鈔. It was printed more than once in the Song. In a colophon written by Shen Kui 沈揆 (1160 *jinshi*) in 1180, Shen Kui mentions that he collated a Min (Fujian) print edition in his family collection against an edition printed in Shu (Sichuan). The Min edition, he says, is full of errors, whereas the Shu

---

belongs to the genre of "instructions to my sons" (*jiezi* 誡子) that indeed gets included in a literary collection, even though in Yan Zhitui's case his "family instructions" is of an unusal length and from early on has circulated independently from his collected works (see *BQS* 8 in Appendix).

edition has been collated and corrected in red ink by Xie Jingsi 謝景思, who referenced He Ning's 和凝 (898–955) edition and other books. It is unclear whether "He Ning's edition" refers to a printed edition collated by He Ning or a manuscript copy from He Ning's collection. The edition with Shen Kui's colophon is referred to as the "Song [dynasty] edition" (*Song ben* 宋本). *Family Instructions* was subsequently reprinted throughout the Yuan, Ming, and Qing dynasties.

There are two major systems of editions, marked not by any substantial differences in terms of content, but by the division of fascicles (*juan*). One is based on the "Song edition" and divided into seven fascicles; the other is based on Ming printed editions and divided into two fascicles. However, it is important to note that no copy of the original 1180 print is available now. As in the case of many legendary "Song editions," what one gets to see are its later (i.e., Yuan, Ming, and Qing) incarnations, which all eagerly tout themselves as having descended from a "Song edition," either as a "revised reprint" (*buxiu chongke ben* 補修重刻本) or as a "shadow copy" (*ying chao* 影鈔, i.e., an exact copy) or based on a "shadow copy."

The great Qing book collector Bao Tingbo's 鮑廷博 (1728–1814) printed edition, which is part of his Zhibuzu zhai 知不足齋 book series, is exactly such an edition. He describes this edition as "a reprint of the shadow copy of the Song edition in the collection of Shugu tang 述古堂," which was the studio name of the bibliophile and book collector, Qian Zeng 錢曾 (1629–1701). Bearing the printer's seal of the "Tian Family of Liantai" 廉臺田家, this edition is considered, rightly or wrongly, by many as a Yuan 元 dynasty (1271–1368) revised reprint of the "Song edition."[65]

The most popular edition claiming to be based on the Song edition is the one annotated by Zhao Ximing 趙曦明 (1705–1787, courtesy name Jingfu 敬夫) and Lu Wenchao 盧文弨 (1717–1796), the so-called Baojing tang 抱經堂 edition. It was first printed in 1789, and then a

---

65 Wang Liqi 12, based on the speculation of Qian Daxin 錢大昕 (1728–1804), who believes *liantai* to be a reference to Lianfangsi 廉訪司 (Provincial Surveillance Commission) established in the Yuan (cited in Wang 610–11). This is, however, highly doubtful, as Liantai is very likely used here as a place name rather than the abbreviation of an office name.

revised and collated edition, with a list of correction notes by Lu
Wenchao, was printed in 1792. Subsequently, many Qing and modern
editions took the Lu Wenchao annotated edition as their base edition,
including 1) the Yan Shihui 嚴式誨 (1890–1976) edition, first printed
in Chengdu in 1929, later reprinted with Yan Shihui's collation notes
dated 1931; 2) the *Congshu jicheng* 叢書集成 edition (first series printed
in 1935–1937), Vol 33; 3) Zhou Fagao's 周法高 (1915–1994) collated
edition; and 4) Wang Liqi's 王利器 (1912–1998) collated edition, which
is the most commonly used scholarly edition today. It is, however, important to note that Zhou Fagao and Wang Liqi both have consulted
other editions and in many cases chose not to follow the Lu Wenchao
edition.

The "Song edition" system divides the twenty chapters into seven
fascicles, with Chapters 1–5 as *juan* 1, Chapters 6–7 as *juan* 2, Chapter
8 as *juan* 3, Chapters 9–11 as *juan* 4, Chapters 12–16 as *juan* 5, Chapter 17 as *juan* 6, and Chapters 18–20 as *juan* 7. The other edition
system simply divides the twenty chapters into two fascicles, with ten
chapters each. This latter system is seen only in a number of Ming
dynasty editions, including: 1) the Cheng Rong 程榮 (fl. late 16th c.)
edition in the *Han Wei congshu* 漢魏叢書 series (1592), with a preface
by Yan Zhibang 顏志邦 in 1578 and an earlier preface by Yan Rugui
顏如環 in 1518, who claims to have collated this edition with an incomplete copy in his family collection, a handwritten copy of the Song
printed edition, and a copy of *Xu Jiaxun* 續家訓 (*Sequel to Family Instructions*) by Dong Zhenggong 董正功/工 (fl. 11th c.?); 2) the Fu Yue
傅鑰 (Fu Taiping 傅太平) (1482–1540) edition with Zhang Bi's 張璧
1524 preface; and 3) the Yan Sishen 顏嗣慎 edition printed in 1575
and the Luo Chun 羅春 edition from the Chenghua 成化 era (1465–
1487), referenced in Wang Liqi and Zhou Fagao.

These Ming editions tend to contain the kind of ideological variants
discussed earlier. It is with some amusement that I note scholars such
as Lu Wenchao and Zhou Fagao often refer to the same editions differently, either as "Ming edition(s)" or as "vulgar editions" (*suben* 俗本 /
sujian ben 俗閒本), largely depending on whether a variant from those
editions meets their approval.

The Chinese text in this volume is based on the Bao Tingbo edition
and the Lu Wenchao edition, collated with the aforementioned edi-

tions. All meaningful textual variants that, if adopted, involve a change in connotation are noted in Additional Notes.

Yan Zhitui's literary collection in thirty fascicles was long lost and was not even recorded in the "Bibliography" of Sui and Tang dynastic histories. A few of his poems are extant through Tang and Song encyclopedia and compendium sources. His "Rhapsody on Viewing My Life" is preserved in entirety through its inclusion in his biography in the *Northern Qi History*, which is its earliest source. Although the original *Northern Qi History* was incomplete and over three-fifths was supplemented by later hands, the part that contains Yan Zhitui's biography is considered to belong to the original version. His "Rhapsody on Questioning the Sages," circulating independently in the Tang and Song, was lost after the Song, and the fragments have been reconstituted by Wang Liqi from various Tang and Song sources. I have offered some corrective observations on his annotations of a few entries and added two more entries to his list.

Notes on Translation

In working on this volume I am indebted to the pioneering work of Teng Ssu-yü and Albert Dien, who translated most of Yan Zhitui's writings in the 1960s and 1970s. My translations have departed significantly from theirs, in no small part owing to the transformations in the field of early medieval Chinese studies since then. In general, I have leaned toward a literal translation without compromising the readability of the English. I did not always succeed, and only take comfort in the hope that I have erred on the side of awkwardness rather than of distortion.

The paragraphs in *Family Instructions* are given breaks and numbered for the sake of ease of reading and looking things up in the Additional Notes. These breaks are my own; in Chinese editions many passages run much longer.

I use *pinyin* Romanization throughout the volume. For Middle Period Chinese pronunciations I consulted Paul W. Kroll's *A Student's Dictionary of Classical and Medieval Chinese* (rev. ed., Brill 2017).

In the traditional Chinese system of reckoning age, people are born at the age of one, and one year is added to their age on each Chinese

New Year's Day, rather than on one's birthday. Thus, when Yan Zhitui says nine *sui*, it means, roughly speaking, eight years old.

This volume, as a work of translation, does not have a standard bibliography; but the books and articles mentioned in this volume are given in the list of Abbreviations. Following the conventions of the Library of Chinese Humanities, footnotes are reserved for explanatory material deemed essential for understanding the translation, including historical information about persons and events. I reserve more scholarly matters, such as textual sources and variants, for Additional Notes. Yan Zhitui's writing is eminently lucid. Modern readers, particularly native speakers of Chinese, may be lured to take lucidity for transparency. Yet, there are cases in which he uses a word or phrase in a peculiar way, characterized by period usage, and not to be taken for granted. Occasionally, I explain my reason for choosing a certain translation in an endnote.

顏氏家訓
Family Instructions for the Yan Clan

序致第一

I.1

夫聖賢之書，教人誠孝，慎言檢迹，立身揚名，亦已備矣。魏晉已來所著諸子，理重事複，遞相模斆，猶屋下架屋，牀上施牀耳。吾今所以復為此者，非敢軌物範世也，業以整齊門內，提撕子孫。

I.2

夫同言而信，信其所親；同命而行，行其所服。禁童子之暴謔，則師友之誠不如傅婢之指揮；止凡人之鬭鬩，則堯舜之道不如寡妻之誨諭。吾望此書為汝曹之所信，猶賢於傅婢寡妻耳。

I. An Account of Intent

I.1

There are abundant books by sages and worthies that teach a man to be sincere and filial,[1] to exercise care in speech and caution in conduct, and to establish oneself and propagate one's name far and wide. Since the Wei and Jin dynasties [220–420 CE], various masters' works have been repetitive in stating principles and citing facts, emulating one another like constructing another roof underneath a roof or putting another bed above a bed. Now I apply myself to yet another such work not because I dare to presume I can determine a course for events and set up a model for the world. Rather, I hope to regulate my household with it and get the ears of my sons and grandsons.

I.2

When a man hears the same advice from different people, he trusts it when it comes from those dear to him; when he receives the same order from different people, he acts on it whe it comes from those he respects. Thus, to put a stop to a child's mischiefs, a teacher's or a peer's council is not as effective as the instructions from a maidservant; to break up a fight between two ordinary fellows, the way of Yao and Shun is not as powerful as the persuasion from the principal wife.[2] I nonetheless hope that this book of mine will do better with you boys than the words of a maidservant or of a wife.[3]

---

1 As Wang Liqi notes (1–2), the intended phrase here may have been "*loyal* and filial" (*zhong xiao* 忠孝), but *zhong*, loyal, being the personal name of Sui Emperor Wen's father was a taboo character in the Sui (581–618), and thus many contemporary sources used "sincere" (*cheng*) to replace "loyal" (*zhong*).
2 Yao and Shun are legendary sage emperors in antiquity.
3 "You boys" refers to Yan Zhitui's sons (see Introduction).

I.3

吾家風教，素為整密。昔在齠齔，便蒙誨
誘；每從兩兄，曉夕溫凊。規行矩步，安
辭定色，鏘鏘翼翼，若朝嚴君焉。賜以優
言，問所好尚，勵短引長，莫不懇篤。

I.4

年始九歲，便丁荼蓼，家塗離散，百口索
然。慈兄鞠養，苦辛備至；有仁無威，導
示不切。雖讀禮傳，微愛屬文，頗為凡人
之所陶染，肆欲輕言，不備邊幅。

I.5

年十八九，少知砥礪，習若自然，卒難洗
盪。三十已後，大過稀焉；每常心共口
敵，性與情競，夜覺曉非，今悔昨
失，自憐無教，以至於斯。

---

1 For the two elder brothers, see Introduction.
2 Literally, "we suffered from the acrimonious taste of sowthistle and knotweed."
3 It is possible to understand *li zhuan* more generally as "the books of rites" here. I take them to refer specifically to the *Rites of Zhou* (*Zhou li* 周禮, aka *Zhou Offices*) and the *Zuo Tradition*, in light of Yan Zhitui's family specialty in the study of these two works, and also given the fact that his official biography clearly

I.3

Our family's customs and teachings have always been regular and strict. When I was a young boy, I received instructions from my parents. I always followed my two elder brothers in paying respect to our parents in the morning and at evening.[1] We would walk with measured, steady steps, and speak calmly and with a composed countenance. We moved about in such an orderly, respectful manner as if we were visiting an awe-inspiring prince. Our parents would bestow on us encouraging words, and asked about our particularly interests. They were ever earnest in urging us to overcome our shortcomings and develop our strengths.

I.4

As soon as I turned nine *sui*, we suffered the painful loss of our parents.[2] Our family fortune declined, and all of our family members were scattered. In the course of bringing me up, my loving brothers encountered all manner of hardships. Being kind, they did not inspire any fear in me, and they were not strict in their teaching and guidance. Although I studied the *Rites* and *Tradition*, and was somewhat fond of literary composition, I fell under the influence of ordinary fellows;[3] indulging in my desires, I spoke rashly, and was inattentive to my personal appearance.[4]

I.5

At the age of eighteen or nineteen *sui*, I began to learn about self-cultivation. But habits had become my second nature, and it was hard to get rid of them in a flash. After I reached thirty *sui*, I managed to make fewer grave mistakes. Still, my mouth and my mind remained mutual enemies; my nature and my passions contended with each other. Each night I would recognize my errors committed in the morning; each day I regretted my misdeeds from the day before. I lament that I did not have a proper upbringing, and was brought to such a state.

---

takes *li zhuan* as exact references, (see Yan Zhitui's *Bei Qi shu* biography in Appendix, *BQS* 1–2).

4 This forms an interesting contrast with his father, Yan Xie 顏協 (d. 539), who is described in his biography as a man who "cared about his appearance" 修飾邊幅 (*Nan shi* 72.1785).

I.6

追思平昔之指，銘肌鏤骨，非徒古書之
誡，經目過耳。故留此二十篇，以為汝曹
後車耳。

I.6

As I recall my past, it is carved into my flesh and engraved on my bones. Those are not just things I learned from ancient books, but what I have seen with my own eyes or heard with my own ears. Therefore I leave these twenty chapters for you boys, so that my experience will be like an overturned cart that serves as a warning to those coming after.

教子第二

II.1

上智不教而成，下愚雖教無益，中庸之
人，不教不知也。

II.2

古者，聖王有胎教之法：懷子三月，出居
別宮，目不邪視，耳不妄聽，音聲滋味，
以禮節之。書之玉版，藏諸金匱。子生咳
嘷，師保固明仁孝禮義，導習之矣。凡庶
縱不能爾，當及嬰稚，識人顏色，知人喜
怒，便加教誨，使為則為，使止則止。比
及數歲，可省笞罰。父母威嚴而有慈，則
子女畏慎而生孝矣。

II. Educating Children

II.1

Those who are of highest intelligence become accomplished without teaching, but it is useless to teach those who are of extreme stupidity. As for those in the middle, they do not learn anything unless taught.

II.2

In the ancient times, sage kings had the method of pre-natal teaching: namely, women who were pregnant for three months must stay in a separate residence; they were not to look at inappropriate things or listen to inappropriate sounds, and they would regulate speech with proper etiquette. These rules were written on a jade tablet kept in a metal case. When a son is still in early childhood, his teacher and tutor well-versed in [the principles of] filial piety, benevolence, ritual propriety, and righteousness should already begin to guide and instruct him in those principles. Even though ordinary people are unable to do this, they should nevertheless teach a child as soon as the child becomes conscious of the parents' facial expressions and understands their pleasure and displeasure. The child should do what the parents ask him to do and stop when the parents ask him to stop. Thus trained in a few years, the child will manage to avoid corporal punishment altogether. If the parents are strict yet kind, then their son or daughter will naturally hold them in awe and act with caution, and a sense of filial piety will be born.

II.3

吾見世間，無教而有愛，每不能然；飲食運為，恣其所慾，宜誡翻獎，應訶反笑。至有識知，謂法當爾。驕慢已習，方復制之，捶撻至死而無威，忿怒日隆而增怨，逮于成長，終為敗德。孔子云"少成若天性，習慣如自然"是也。俗諺曰："教婦初來，教兒嬰孩。"誠哉斯語！

II.4

凡人不能教子女者，亦非欲陷其罪惡；但重於訶怒傷其顏色，不忍楚撻慘其肌膚耳。當以疾病為諭，安得不用湯藥鍼艾救之哉？又宜思勤督訓者，可願苛虐於骨肉乎？誠不得已也。

II.5

王大司馬母魏夫人，性甚嚴正；王在湓城時，為三千人將，年踰四十，少不如意，猶捶撻之，故能成其勳業。

II.3

I have seen many parents acting otherwise, as they love their children but do not teach them proper behavior. Instead, they indulge their children and let them eat, drink, and act as they please, praising them when they should be admonished, and smiling at them when they should be reprimanded. When their children are older, they believe this is how things should be. If parents only try to control a child after the habits of arrogance and insouciance have already been formed, then by that time they will have no authority [over the child] even if they beat the child to death; their rage may grow every day, and it will only increase the child's resentment. Such a child will ultimately come to no good when he grows up. As Confucius said, "What one learns in childhood is like one's inborn temperament; the habits one forms become second nature." A popular saying goes, "Educate your wife when she is still a new bride; educate your son when he is still an infant." How true these words are!

II.4

If parents are unable to educate their son or daughter, it is not that they want to lead their children into bad behavior or misdeeds; it is simply that they cannot bear to upset their children with angry rebukes or bring pain to their body through corporal punishment. Such parents should think of the treatment of illness as a metaphor: how can one not save one's sick child with medicine and needles? They should also understand that those parents who diligently supervise and coach their children truly have no desire to abuse their own flesh and blood, but only do it because there is no other way.

II.5

Madame Wei, the mother of Grand Marshal Wang, was austere and strict by nature.[1] When Wang was in Pencheng, he was a commander of three thousand troops and over forty years old. Yet, if he did anything to incur her displeasure, she would still give him a beating. That was why he was able to accomplish his meritorious achievements.

---

1 This refers to Wang Sengbian 王僧辯 (d. 555), a famous Liang general who recovered the Liang capital Jiankang after the Hou Jing Rebellion.

II.6

梁元帝時,有一學士,聰敏有才,為父所
寵,失於教義:一言之是,徧於行路,終
年譽之;一行之非,揜藏文飾,冀其自
改。年登婚宦,暴慢日滋,竟以言語不
擇,為周逖抽腸釁鼓云。

II.7

父子之嚴,不可以狎;骨肉之愛,不可以
簡。簡則慈孝不接,狎則怠慢生焉。由命
士以上,父子異宮,此不狎之道也。仰搔
癢痛,懸衾篋枕,此不簡之教也。

II.6

At the time of Liang Emperor Yuan, there was a young scholar who was quick-witted and talented.[1] He was doted on by his father, who neglected to educate him properly. If he said one thing right, his father would tell the whole world about it, praising him all year long. If he did one thing wrong, his father would try to cover it up or make light of it, hoping that he would reform on his own. When he reached the age of getting married and entering public service, he had become increasingly insensitive and arrogant. Eventually, because he did not choose his words well, Zhou Ti disemboweled him and smeared the war drum with his blood as a sacrifice.[2]

II.7

The solemn relation between father and son should not be damaged by familiarity; the love of flesh and blood should not be sullied by casualness. When too casual, parental love and filial piety fail to meet each other; when too familiar, a sense of disrespect is born. For those with an official appointment, father and son should stay in different chambers: this is the way to avoid familiarity.[3] A child attends to the parents' discomfort such as itch or pain, hangs their coverlet and encases their pillows: this is the way to avoid casualness.[4]

---

1 Liang Emperor Yuan (r. 552–555) was Xiao Yi 蕭繹 (508–555); sometimes he is also referred to as Emperor Xiaoyuan by the author.

2 Zhou Ti may be Zhou Di 周迪 (d. 565), a military man who rose to prominence after the Hou Jing Rebellion. The scholar is unknown.

3 "For those with an official appointment, father and son should stay in different chambers": this is a nearly verbatim citation from *The Record of Rites*, one of the Confucian classics. The following sentence also represents the teachings from the same work.

4 The *Record of Rites* (*Li ji*) prescribes that a child tends to the parents' least discomfort and makes the parents' bed after they get up in the morning.

II.8

或問曰："陳亢喜聞君子之遠其子，何謂也?"對曰："有是也。蓋君子之不親教其子也。詩有諷刺之辭，禮有嫌疑之誡，書有悖亂之事，春秋有衰僻之譏，易有備物之象：皆非父子之可通言，故不親授耳。"

II.9a

齊武成帝子琅邪王，太子母弟也，生而聰慧，帝及后並篤愛之，衣服飲食，與東宮相準。帝每面稱之曰："此黠兒也，當有所成。"及太子即位，王居別宮，禮數優僭，不與諸王等，太后猶謂不足，常以為言。

II.8

Someone asked me, "Chen Kang was delighted to know about a gentleman's keeping distance from his son. Why was that?"[1] I replied, "It was indeed so. It means that a gentleman does not teach his son in person. *The Classic of Poetry* contains words of indirect criticism; *The Record of Rites* warns against jealousy and suspicion; *The Book of Documents* records rebellion and disorder; *The Spring and Autumn* makes sardonic comments about depraved deeds; *The Classic of Changes* shows the images of all things: none of these is a suitable topic of conversation between father and son. Hence a gentleman does not teach his son in person."

II.9a

The Prince of Langye was the son of Qi Emperor Wucheng and the younger brother of the Crown Prince by the same mother.[2] He was born bright; the emperor and empress loved him dearly. In food, drink, and clothing, he enjoyed the same treatment as the Crown Prince. The emperor would often praise him to his face, saying, "This is a smart boy. He will surely achieve great things." After the Crown Prince took the throne, the prince went to live in a separate palace. He enjoyed privileges that the other princes did not, and yet the Empress Dowager thought it was not enough, and often spoke of it [to the emperor].

---

1 Chen Kang was a disciple of Confucius. This statement is from an anecdote about Chen Kang and Kong Li (Confucius' son) recorded in the *Analects*.

2 Qi Emperor Wucheng was Gao Zhan 高湛 (538–569; r. 561–564). The Prince of Langye was Gao Yan 高儼 (558–571), son of Emperor Wucheng and Empress Hu. The Crown Prince Gao Wei 高緯 (556–577) was the last Qi emperor (r. 565–577).

II.9b

年十許歲，驕恣無節，器服玩好，必擬乘
輿；常朝南殿，見典御進新冰，鈎盾獻早
李，還索不得，遂大怒，曰：“至尊已
有，我何意無?”不知分齊，率皆如此。
識者多有叔段、州吁之譏。後嫌宰相，遂
矯詔斬之，又懼有救，乃勒麾下軍士，防
守殿門；既無反心，受勞而罷，後竟坐此
幽薨。

II.10

人之愛子，罕亦能均；自古及今，此弊多
矣。賢俊者自可賞愛，頑魯者亦當矜憐，
有偏寵者，雖欲以厚之，更所以禍之。共
叔之死，母實為之。趙王之戮，父實使
之。劉表之傾宗覆族，袁紹之地裂兵亡，
可為靈龜明鑒也。

---

1 Shu Duan (b. 754 BCE) was the younger son of Duke Wu of Zheng, favored by
his mother over his elder brother. Shu Duan plotted insurgence after his elder
brother succeeded to the dukedom and eventually died in exile. Zhouxu (d. 719
BCE) was the favorite son of Duke Zhuang of Wei; he murdered his elder half-
brother and became the duke himself, but was killed soon after.
2 He Shikai 和士開 (524–571), a powerful minister of the Northern Qi.

II.9b

When he was in his early teens, the prince was arrogant and unrestrained. He expected his attire and paraphernalia to be the same as the emperor's. Once he went to court in the Southern Palace, and saw the Chief Steward offering new ice and the Imperial Park Supervisor presenting early plums to the throne. After he returned to his residence, he demanded the same for himself; when he could not get what he wanted, he became furious and started cursing, saying, "His Majesty already has them; how come I still don't?" This was typical of his lack of any sense of propriety and proportion. Wise courtiers spoke ironically of his resemblance to Shu Duan and Zhouxu.[1] He disliked the Prime Minister, and had him executed by falsifying an imperial edict.[2] Worried there might be rescue [for the Prime Minister], he ordered soldiers to guard the palace gates. Since he did not intend to rebel, he desisted after being confronted by the emperor. He eventually died in imprisonment because of this.

II.10

Parental love is rarely distributed equally among all of one's children, and this has led to many disasters from the ancient times till today. One naturally admires and loves the worthy and talented sons, but should also have compassion for the senseless and stupid ones. If a parent is partial to one son, then the desire to favor him will turn out to harm him instead. The death of Gong Shu was really caused by his own mother; the murder of the Prince of Zhao was truly brought about by his own father.[3] Liu Biao's entire clan was destroyed, and Yuan Shao lost his troops and realm.[4] These cases can serve as omens and mirrors for us.

---

3 Gong Shu refers to Shu Duan (see note to II.9b); Gong was his fief. The Prince of Zhao was Liu Ruyi 劉如意 (d. 195/194 BCE), the young son of Liu Bang 劉邦, the founding emperor of Han known as Gaozu 高祖 (r. 202–195 BCE). Gaozu doted on Ruyi and wanted to make him his heir in place of the Crown Prince by his principal wife, Empress Lü. After Gaozu's death Empress Lü had Ruyi killed.

4 Liu Biao (142–208) and Yuan Shao (142–202) were warlords at the end of the Eastern Han dynasty. They had both favored a younger son over the older son and heir, which led to sibling conflict and weakened the family rule.

II.11

齊朝有一士大夫，嘗謂吾曰："我有一
兒，年已十七，頗曉書疏，教其鮮卑語及
彈琵琶，稍欲通解，以此伏事公卿，無不
寵愛，亦要事也。"吾時俛而不答。異
哉，此人之教子也！若由此業，自致卿
相，亦不願汝曹為之。

II.11

In the Qi court there was an official who once said to me: "I have a son who is seventeen *sui*. He knows quite a bit about writing letters. He has been taught the Xianbei language and how to play the *pipa* (i.e., Central Asian lute), and is becoming quite adept at both. He serves the ministers of the state with these skills, and everyone is terribly fond of him. This is really an important thing [we can do for our children]." I just lowered my head without replying. How strange is the way this man teaches his son! Now, even if you can achieve high office through such skills, I do not wish you to do it.

兄弟第三

III.1

夫有人民而後有夫婦，有夫婦而後有父子，有父子而後有兄弟：一家之親，盡此三而已矣。自茲以往，至於九族，皆本於三親焉，故於人倫為重者也，不可不篤。

III.2

兄弟者，分形連氣之人也，方其幼也，父母左提右挈，前襟後裾，食則同案，衣則傳服，學則連業，游則共方，雖有悖亂之行，不能不相愛也。及其壯也，各妻其妻，各子其子，雖有篤厚之行，不能不少衰也。娣姒之比兄弟，則疏薄矣；今使疏薄之人，而節量親厚之恩，猶方底而圓蓋，必不合矣，惟友悌深至不為旁人之所移者免夫。

III. Brothers

III.1

First there is the human species, and then there are husband and wife; once there are husband and wife, there are father and sons; there are father and sons, and then there are brothers. The closeness of a family comprises these three relationships. From this point on, all of the nine clans are based on these three kinships.[1] Hence they carry the most weight in all human relations, and you must not neglect to solidify them.

III.2

Brothers are connected by their vital energy despite having separate bodies. When they are little, their parents take one along on the left and another on the right, with one running in the front and another following behind. They share the same table when eating, and the elder brother passes down his clothes to the younger. They read the same books when studying, and stay together when traveling; even if they commit wicked acts, they cannot help feeling love for one another. When they grow up, each takes a wife, and each has one's own sons; even if they behave generously, they cannot help becoming slightly estranged. Sister-in-laws, compared to brothers, are much more distant from each other. If distant relatives are made to manage intimate and affectionate kin, it is like putting a round cover over a square base: it will certainly not fit. Only those brothers who are deeply bonded with each other can avoid being swayed by others.

---

1 The "nine clans" refers to one's own relatives plus the relatives of one's father, grandfather, great-grandfather, great-great-grandfather as well as of one's son, grandson, great-grandson, and great-great-grandson. Alternatively, it refers to the relatives on one's father's side, one's mother's side, and one's wife's side.

III.3

二親既歿，兄弟相顧，當如形之與影，聲
之與響；愛先人之遺體，惜己身之分氣，
非兄弟何念哉？兄弟之際，異於他人，望
深則易怨，地親則易弭。譬猶居室，一穴
則塞之，一隙則塗之，則無頹毀之慮；如
雀鼠之不恤，風雨之不防，壁陷楹淪，無
可救矣。僕妾之為雀鼠，妻子之為風雨，
甚哉。

III.4

兄弟不睦，則子姪不愛；子姪不愛，則羣
從疏薄；羣從疏薄，則僮僕為讎敵矣。如
此，則行路皆踏其面而蹈其心，誰救之
哉？人或交天下之士，皆有歡笑，而失敬
於兄者，何其能多而不能少也。人或將數
萬之師，得其死力，而失恩於弟者，何其
能疏而不能親也。

III.3

After their parents pass away, brothers should look upon each other as body and shadow, sound and echo. If a man love his body bequeathed by his late father, and cherishes the vital energy inherited from his parents, then who but his own brother should he think upon? The relation between brothers is different from other relations: when one has high expectations, one easily becomes resentful [when the expectation is not met], but since brothers are so close, it is also easy to patch things up. It is like living in a house: if you fill a hole as soon as you see it, and seal a crack as soon as you notice it, then you need never worry about the collapse of the house. However, if you do not care about [the damage caused by] sparrows and rats, and do not do anything to defend against wind and rain, then the walls will fall and the pillars will crumble, and there will be no hope for the house. Servants and concubines are like the sparrows and rats; wife and sons are like the wind and rain. How terrible!

III.4

If brothers do not get along, then sons and nephews will not love one another; if sons and nephews do not love one another, then cousins will become estranged from one another; if cousins are estranged from one another, then their servants will become enemies. If they carry on like this, then even strangers on the street will bully them, and who will ever come to their rescue? Some people can befriend men of the world and make them all happy, but fail to show respect for their elder brother. Why can they relate well with so many but not with one person? Some men can command tens of thousands of troops and gain their loyalty, but cannot care for their younger brother. Why can they deal with the distant ones so well, but not with their own kin?

III.5

娣姒者，多爭之地也，使骨肉居之，亦不
若各歸四海，感霜露而相思，佇日月之相
望也。況以行路之人，處多爭之地，能無
閒者鮮矣。所以然者，以其當公務而執私
情，處重責而懷薄義也；若能恕己而行，
換子而撫，則此患不生矣。

III.6

人之事兄，不可同於事父，何怨愛弟不及
愛子乎？是反照而不明也。沛國劉璡嘗與
兄瓛連棟隔壁，瓛呼之數聲不應，良久方
應；瓛怪問之，乃曰：“向來未著衣帽故
也。”以此事兄，可以免矣。

III.5

Sisters-in-law occupy a role that gives rise to many conflicts. Even when one's own flesh and blood occupies such a role, it is far better for them to each go off somewhere else within the four seas, for in that case they will miss each other when affected by frost and dew, and will stand in the sun or under the moon gazing toward each other with longing. When strangers become sisters-in-law to each other, it is even rarer for them [than for blood relations] to get along without grudges. This is because they hold onto their private interest in handling general family affairs and harbor little sense of justice in carrying out weighty family responsibilities. If only they can act with empathy and bring up each other's sons in exchange, then such trouble will not arise.

III.6

If a man is unwilling to treat his elder brother the way he treats his father, then why should he complain that his elder brother does not love him as much as he does his own son? That only shows how much he lacks in self-reflection and self-awareness. Liu Jin of Peiguo had lived in a room next to his elder brother Liu Huan.[1] Once Huan called out to Jin several times, but Jin did not answer for quite a while. Huan thought it was strange and asked him about it. Jin said, "It was because I was not dressed [when you called]." If a man treats his elder brother like that, then he will be without blame.

---

1 Peiguo is in modern Anhui. Liu Huan (434–489) was a prominent scholar of the Confucian classics. This story was well-known at the time, as it was recorded in the *History of the Southern Qi* compiled by Xiao Zixian 蕭子顯 (489–537).

III.7

江陵王玄紹，弟孝英、子敏，兄弟三人，
特相友愛，所得甘旨新異，非共聚食，必
不先嘗，孜孜色貌，相見如不足者。及西
臺陷沒，玄紹以形體魁梧，為兵所圍；二
弟爭共抱持，各求代死，終不得解，遂并
命爾。

III.7

Wang Xuanshao of Jiangling and his two younger brothers Xiaoying and Zimin were very loving to one another.[1] Whenever they got any delicacies or rare foods, none of them would taste it until they could share with the others. When they were together, they were happy and affectionate as if they could never get enough of one another. After the western capital fell, Xuanshao, who was tall and stalwart, was surrounded by soldiers.[2] His two younger brothers clung to him and each beseeched the soldiers to die in his place. They would not let go of him no matter what, and eventually died together.

---

1 Wang Xuanshao and his brothers are not attested elsewhere in historical records.
2 This refers to the fall of Jiangling to the army of the Western Wei in late 554 (see Introduction). Jiangling was to the west of Jiankang, the older capital of the Liang.

後娶第四

IV.1

吉甫，賢父也，伯奇，孝子也，以賢父御孝子，合得終於天性，而後妻閒之，伯奇遂放。曾參婦死，謂其子曰："吾不及吉甫，汝不及伯奇。"王駿喪妻，亦謂人曰："我不及曾參，子不如華、元。"並終身不娶，此等足以為誡。其後，假繼慘虐孤遺，離閒骨肉，傷心斷腸者，何可勝數。慎之哉，慎之哉。

IV.2

江左不諱庶孽，喪室之後，多以妾媵終家事。疥癬蚊虻，或不能免，限以大分，故稀鬭閱之恥。

IV. Remarriage

IV.1

Jifu was a wise father and Boqi was a filial son. When a wise father was matched with a filial son, they should have fulfilled their inborn nature; yet the father's second wife came between them and Boqi was exiled.[1] After his wife died, Zeng Shen said to his son: "I am not the equal of Jifu, nor are you the equal of Boqi."[2] When Wang Jun lost his wife, he likewise told people: "I am not the equal of Zeng Shen, nor are my sons the equal of Hua and Yuan."[3] Both Zeng Shen and Wang Jun never took a second wife. Such cases should serve as adequate warning. In later times, the stepmother would abuse the motherless children left behind by the first wife, causing alienation among those of the same flesh and blood and breaking their hearts. Such cases are numerous. Be careful! Be careful!

IV.2

To the left of the Yangzi River, people did not discriminate against sons by concubines.[4] Therefore, after the wife dies, many men rely on their concubine to manage the household. There may be small problems here and there, but the concubine is limited by her social position, and so the disgrace of domestic fights is rare.

---

1 Yin Jifu 尹吉甫 was a minister of King Xuan of Zhou (r. 828–783 BCE). After his wife died, he married again, and the second wife accused Boqi, the son left by the first wife, of making passes at her. Jifu exiled Boqi. Later he learned of the son's innocence and killed his second wife.

2 Zeng Shen (fl. fifth century BCE) was a disciple of Confucius. Hua and Yuan, referred to below, were his sons.

3 Wang Jun (d. 14 BCE) was an official of the Western Han.

4 "To the left of the Yangzi River" (or "to the east of the Yangzi River") refers to the south.

IV.3

河北鄙於側出，不預人流，是以必須重
娶，至於三四，母年有少於子者。後母之
弟，與前婦之兄，衣服飲食，爰及婚宦，
至於士庶貴賤之隔，俗以為常。身沒之
後，辭訟盈公門，謗辱彰道路，子誣母為
妾，弟黜兄為傭，播揚先人之辭迹，暴露
祖考之長短，以求直己者，往往而有。悲
夫！

IV.4

自古姦臣佞妾，以一言陷人者眾矣。況夫
婦之義，曉夕移之，婢僕求容，助相說
引，積年累月，安有孝子乎？此不可不
畏。

IV.3

To the north of the Yellow River, people despise sons by concubines and exclude them from polite society; therefore a man whose wife dies must remarry, even up to three or four times, and sometimes a mother is younger than her stepson. In all kinds of things, from food and clothing to marriage and government service, the treatment received by the younger brother from the second wife and the elder brother from the first wife can be so different as to evoke the distance separating the elite from the commoner or the nobility from the plebeian, but the society takes it for granted. In such cases, once the father passes away, accusations and lawsuits fill the courtroom, and insults and slanders are spread on the streets; a son may falsely call his stepmother a concubine, or a younger brother may relegate his elder brother to a servant; there are many who broadcast the private words and deeds of their deceased father and expose the shortcomings of their forebears in order to justify themselves. Alas, how sad!

IV.4

From ancient times there have been many wicked ministers and devious concubines who framed and ruined a man with a single word. How much more so when a wife talks to her husband morning and evening, with maids and servants seeking acceptance and aiding in her persuasion. If this goes on for months and years, how can there be a filial son left? One must remain apprehensive about such things.

IV.5

凡庸之性，後夫多寵前夫之孤，後妻必虐
前妻之子；非唯婦人懷嫉妒之情，丈夫有
沈惑之僻，亦事勢使之然也。前夫之孤，
不敢與我子爭家，提攜鞠養，積習生愛，
故寵之；前妻之子，每居己生之上，宦學
婚嫁，莫不為防焉，故虐之。異姓寵則父
母被怨，繼親虐則兄弟為讎，家有此者，
皆門戶之禍也。

IV.6

思魯等從舅殷外臣，博達之士也。有子
基、諶，皆已成立，而再娶王氏。基每拜
見後母，感慕嗚咽，不能自持，家人莫忍
仰視。王亦悽愴，不知所容，旬月求退，
便以禮遣，此亦悔事也。

IV.5

Among people of mediocre caliber, the second husband tends to favor the son left by the previous husband, but the second wife always abuses the previous wife's son. It is not just because women are jealous by nature or men tend to be infatuated, but also because the circumstances make it so. The son of the previous husband does not dare to fight over family property with the son of the second husband, who cares for him, brings him up, and gradually grows to love him. In contrast, the son of the previous wife is placed above the son of the second wife, who feels obliged to guard against him in matters such as studies, public service, and marriage, and hence mistreats him. If a son with a different surname is favored, then the parents are resented [by their own sons]; if the stepmother mistreats her stepson, then the half-brothers become enemies. When this happens in a family, it never bodes well for the household.

IV.6

Yin Waichen, you boys' maternal uncle, was a learned and wise man. His two sons, Ji and Chen, had both grown up. He then married a second wife neé Wang. Every time Ji visited his stepmother, he was overcome by longing for his birth mother and could not help sobbing, and the members of the family could not bear to look at him. Even Madame Wang herself was saddened, and did not know what to do. In about a month's time she asked to leave, and so she was sent away with proper rites. This was a regrettable affair.

IV.7

後漢書曰：安帝時，汝南薛包孟嘗，好學
篤行，喪母，以至孝聞，及父娶後妻而憎
包，分出之。包日夜號泣，不能去，至被
毆杖。不得已，廬於舍外，旦入而洒掃。
父怒，又逐之，乃廬於里門，昏晨不廢。
積歲餘，父母慚而還之。後行六年服，喪
過乎哀。既而弟子求分財異居，包不能
止，乃中分其財：奴婢取其老者，曰："與
我共事久，若不能使也。"田廬取其
荒頓者，曰："吾少時所理，意所戀
也。"器物取其朽敗者，曰："我素所服
食，身口所安也。"弟子數破其產，還復
賑給。建光中，公車特徵，至拜侍中。包
性恬虛，稱疾不起，以死自乞。有詔賜告
歸也。

IV.7

The *History of the Later Han* records the life of a man named Xue Bao of Ru'nan, whose courtesy name was Mengchang, during the reign of Emperor An.[1] He was a good man who loved study, and was known for extreme filial piety at the time of his mother's death. His father remarried and grew to loathe Bao, so he sent Bao away. Weeping day and night, Bao could not tear himself away until beaten with a cane. He then built a hut outside his family home, and would come in every morning to sweep the courtyard for his parents. His father was furious and drove him away again. This time he built a hut in the neighborhood, and came to pay respects to his parents every morning and evening. After a year so, his parents felt ashamed of what they had done and took him back. Later, [after his parents passed away,] Bao observed mourning rites for six years, much longer than the required period [of three years]. His younger brother's sons wanted to divide the family property and live separately. Bao could not stop them, so he split the property equally among them. He himself took the old servants and maids, saying, "They have served me for a long time; you won't be able to use them." He took the barren fields and derelict cottages, saying, "I have cared for them since my youth; I am attached to them." He took the broken and dilapidated household utensils, saying, "I am accustomed to them and feel comfortable with them." His nephews went bankrupt several times, and he would always help them out. In the Jianguang era [121–122 CE] he was summoned to court. When he arrived, he was appointed to the post of Court Attendant. Modest by nature, Bao claimed illness and would rather die than serve. The emperor finally issued an edict to let him go.

---

1 The *History of the Later Han* was compiled by Fan Ye 范曄 (398–445). Ru'nan is in modern He'nan. Emperor An ruled from 106 to 125 CE.

治家第五

V.1

夫風化者，自上而行於下者也，自先而施
於後者也。是以父不慈則子不孝，兄不友
則弟不恭，夫不義則婦不順矣。父慈而子
逆，兄友而弟傲，夫義而婦陵，則天之兇
民，乃刑戮之所攝，非訓導之所移也。

V.2

笞怒廢於家，則豎子之過立見；刑罰不
中，則民無所措手足。治家之寬猛，亦猶
國焉。

V.3

孔子曰：“奢則不孫，儉則固；與其不孫
也，寧固。”又云：“如有周公之才之
美，使驕且吝，其餘不足觀也已。”然則
可儉而不可吝也。儉者，省約為禮之謂
也；吝者，窮急不恤之謂也。今有施則
奢，儉則吝；如能施而不奢，儉而不吝，
可矣。

V. Managing the Household

V.1

The civilizing influence is applied from above to below, from the earlier generation to the later generation. Therefore, if the father is not benevolent, then the son is not filial; if an elder brother is not affectionate, then the younger brother is not respectful; if a husband is not just, then the wife is not obedient. If a father is benevolent but the son is rebellious, or an elder brother is affectionate but the younger brother is arrogant, or a husband is just but the wife is defiant, then they are truly the wicked people of the world. They can only be brought into submission by punishment, but will not be moved by teaching and guidance.

V.2

If there is no disciplinary flagellation in a household, the faults of servants will immediately appear; if punishment is not properly meted out, the people will not know how to behave. The leniency and severity in managing a household are the same as in managing the state.

V.3

Confucius said, "Extravagance leads to immodesty; frugality leads to coarseness. It is better to be coarse than to be immodest." He also said, "If a man possesses the Duke of Zhou's talent, but is arrogant and parsimonious, his abilities will not be worth much."[1] Thus, one can be frugal but must not be parsimonious. Frugality means being economical in social life; but being parsimonious means showing no compassion for those in dire need. Nowadays, those who give alms are extravagant, and those who are frugal tend to be parsimonious. If one can be generous without being extravagant, frugal without being parsimonious, that will be ideal.

---

1 Both citations are from the *Analects*.

V.4

生民之本，要當稼穡而食，桑麻以衣。蔬
果之畜，園場之所產；雞豚之善，塒圈之
所生。爰及棟宇器械，樵蘇脂燭，莫非種
殖之物也。至能守其業者，閉門而為生之
具以足，但家無鹽井耳。今北土風俗，率
能躬儉節用，以贍衣食；江南奢侈，多不
逮焉。

V.5

梁孝元世，有中書舍人，治家失度，而過
嚴刻，妻妾遂共貨刺客，伺醉而殺之。

V.6

世間名士但務寬仁，至於飲食餉饋，僮僕
減損，施惠然諾，妻子節量，狎侮賓客，
侵耗鄉黨：此亦為家之巨蠹矣。

V.4

The essence of nourishing the folk is to farm for food and to plant mulberries and hemp for clothing. The stock of vegetables and fruit is produced in gardens; delicacies such as chickens and pigs are to be found in chicken coops and pig pens. From those things down to rafters, tools, firewood, and candle oil, all come from sowing and growing. Those who can hold on to their property have everything they need for their livelihood behind closed gates, and the only thing missing would be the salt-well. Nowadays, it is customary in the north to provide clothes and food by living economically and moderating expenditures. By contrast, life in the south is profligate, and in this regard it largely remains inferior to the north.

V.5

At the time of Liang Emperor Xiaoyuan, there was a Secretarial Drafter who mismanaged his household by being too harsh.[1] As a result, his wife and concubine conspired to hire an assassin, who murdered him when he was intoxicated.

V.6

But [it is equally harmful when] the eminent gentlemen of the world are only bent on leniency. When they offer food and drink to people, their servants secretly reduce the amount; when they make a promise to give alms, their wife and children control the quantity. The servants and family members thus insult the guests and raid the neighbors, proving to be the vermin in a household.

---

1 Emperor Xiaoyuan refers to Emperor Yuan.

V.7

齊吏部侍郎房文烈，未嘗嗔怒，經霖雨絕
糧，遣婢糴米，因爾逃竄，三四許日，方
復擒之。房徐曰："舉家無食，汝何處
來？"竟無捶撻之意。嘗寄人宅，奴婢徹
屋為薪略盡，聞之顰蹙，卒無一言。

V.8

裴子野有疏親故屬飢寒不能自濟者，皆收
養之；家素清貧，時逢水旱，二石米為薄
粥，僅得徧焉，躬自同之，常無厭色。

V.9

鄴下有一領軍，貪積已甚，家童八百，誓
滿千人。朝夕肴膳以十五錢為率，遇有客
旅，便無以兼。後坐事伏法，籍其家產，
麻鞋一屋，弊衣數庫，其餘財寶，不可勝
言。

V.7

Fang Wenlie, the Attendant Gentleman in the Ministry of Personnel in the Northern Qi, was never angry.[1] Once, it had been raining for days, and there was no grain left in his house. He sent a maidservant out to buy rice, but the maid availed herself of the opportunity and ran away. They did not capture her until three or four days later. Fang said amicably, "The whole family has had nothing to eat. Where have you been?" He had no intention to flog her for her offence. On another occasion, he lent his house to someone else as temporary lodging, whose servants almost tore the house down for firewood. When he heard of it, he merely frowned, but never spoke a word.

V.8

Pei Ziye gave shelter to all of his distant relatives and former subordinates who could not support themselves.[2] His own family was not well-to-do; when there was drought or flood, they would make thin gruel with two bushels of rice, which was barely enough to feed everyone. Pei Ziye himself shared the gruel with his family and never showed any discontent.

V.9

At Ye there was a General of the Palace Guard who was a greedy hoarder.[3] He had eight hundred servants, but vowed he would acquire one thousand. He allowed fifteen cash for his daily meals, and would not increase the budget even when there were guests. Later he was executed for some offense and his property was confiscated. They found hemp shoes that filled one entire room, several storehouses of worn-out clothes, and numerous treasures in addition.

---

1 Fang Wenlie (fl. mid-6th century) was from a prominent family in the north.

2 Pei Ziye (469–530) was a well-known scholar and writer in the Liang court.

3 This has been identified as the Northern Qi general Shedi Fulian 厙狄伏連 (d. 571).

V.10

南陽有人，為生奧博，性殊儉吝，冬至後
女婿謁之，乃設一銅甌酒，數臠獐肉；婿
恨其單率，一舉盡之。主人愕然，俛仰命
益，如此者再。退而責其女曰："某郎好
酒，故汝常貧。"及其死後，諸子爭財，
兄遂殺弟。

V.11

婦主中饋，惟事酒食衣服之禮耳，國不可
使預政，家不可使幹蠱；如有聰明才智，
識達古今，正當輔佐君子，助其不足，必
無牝雞晨鳴，以致禍也。

V.10

There was a man in Nanyang who amassed great wealth and was miserly by nature.[1] One year, his son-in-law visited him after the winter solstice, and was treated to one copper jug of ale and a few slices of venison. The son-in-law resented the modest fare, so he ate and drank everything in an instant. The shocked host ordered more to be brought out, and this was repeated several times. After the man retired, he rebuked his daughter, saying, "Your husband is too fond of drinking. That is why you will always be doomed to poverty." After he died, his sons fought over his wealth, and the elder brother killed the younger brother.

V.11

Women are in charge of family provisions and should only attend to the etiquette related to drink, food, and clothes. They should not intervene in state affairs, nor supervise family matters. If they have intelligence, talent, and a broad knowledge of the past and present, they should assist the man of the house and supplement his deficiencies. But a hen must never crow at dawn [like a rooster], for that would lead to disaster.[2]

---

1 Nanyang is in modern He'nan.
2 "A hen must not crow at dawn" is from the *Book of Documents*, one of the Confucian classics.

V.12

江東婦女，略無交遊，其婚姻之家，或十數年間未相識者，惟以信命贈遺致殷勤焉。鄴下風俗，專以婦持門戶，爭訟曲直，造請逢迎，車乘填街衢，綺羅盈府寺，代子求官，為夫訴屈。此乃恆、代之遺風乎。

V.13

南間貧素，皆事外飾，車乘衣服，必貴整齊；家人妻子，不免飢寒。河北人事，多由內政，綺羅金翠，不可廢闕，羸馬瘁奴，僅充而已；倡和之禮，或爾汝之。

V.14

河北婦人，織紝組紃之事，黼黻錦繡羅綺之工，大優於江東也。

V.12

Women to the east of the Yangzi River have little social intercourse.[1] Even women from families related by marriage may never meet one another for many years, and only convey good will to one another through messengers. The customs of Ye are, however, quite different: they let the wife take charge of the family. The womenfolk are involved in disputes and lawsuits; they pay visits and receive guests; their carriages crowd the streets, and official quarters swarm with their silk dresses. They seek office for their sons or make pleas to authority on behalf of their husbands. This, I am afraid, is the legacy of Heng and Dai.[2]

V.13

In the south even families with meager means are concerned about appearances. Wife, children, and servants may suffer from cold and hunger, but their carriages and clothes must be nice and neat when they go out.[3] In the north social life is managed by womenfolk, so fancy dresses and fine jewelry are indispensable, but scraggy horses and decrepit servants are considered adequate; often there is little etiquette between man and wife, as they address each other in disrespectfully intimate terms.

V.14

Nevertheless, in matters of weaving, braiding, and embroidering brocade and silk, women to the north of the Yellow River are much superior to their counterparts to the east of the Yangzi.

---

1 That is, women of the south.

2 The Northern Wei (386–534), a non-Han dynasty founded by the Tuoba or Tabgach clan, had its earlier capital at Pingcheng (in modern Shanxi), which belonged to the Dai commandery in Heng prefecture. "Heng and Dai" thus refers to the Northern Wei.

3 Interestingly, this recalls the description of Yan Zhitui's father, Yan Xie, in Yan Xie's biography in the *Southern History*: "Although Xie's family only had meager means, he cared about his appearance, and would not go out unless in a horse-drawn carriage" (*Nan shi* 72.1785).

V.15

太公曰："養女太多，一費也。"陳蕃曰："盜不過五女之門。"女之為累，亦以深矣。然天生蒸民，先人遺體，其如之何？世人多不舉女，賊行骨肉，豈當如此而望福於天乎？吾有疏親，家饒妓媵，誕育將及，便遣閽豎守之。體有不安，窺窗倚戶，若生女者，輒持將去；母隨號泣，使人不忍聞也。

V.16

婦人之性，率寵子婿而虐兒婦。寵婿，則兄弟之怨生焉；虐婦，則姊妹之讒行焉。然則女之行留，皆得罪於其家者，母實為之。至有諺云："落索阿姑餐。"此其相報也。家之常弊，可不誡哉。

V.15

Taigong said, "When one has too many daughters, it is a huge expense."[1] Chen Fan said, "A burglar does not visit a family of five daughters."[2] Daughters are truly a burden. However, heaven gives birth to the myriad people, and a daughter, too, receives her body from her forebears. What can one do about it? Many people refuse to raise daughters and would harm their own flesh and blood – how can one do this and yet expect to receive blessings from heaven? A distant relative of mine had many concubines and family entertainers. When any of them were getting close to the time of delivery, he would send a servant to keep watch. As the woman began to experience labor pains, the servant would peer into the window and lean by the door. If she gave birth to a girl, the baby would be immediately taken away. The mother would follow behind and wail; her cries were heart-wrenching to listen to.

V.16

A woman by nature dotes on her son-in-law but mistreats her daughter-in-law. When she dotes on her son-in-law, it creates resentment among the brothers-in-law; when she mistreats her daughter-in-law, it results in vilification among sisters-in-law. Thus a woman may cause offense no matter whether she lives at her native home or is married off, and that is all the mother's doing. Hence the proverb says, "Lonesome is the mother-in-law's meal." That is the payback for her behavior. This is a common problem in a family. How can you not be vigilant about it!

---

1 Taigong, also known as Taigong Wang and by several other names, was a legendary councilor of King Wen of Zhou (eleventh century BCE). The remark is from a military work attributed to Taigong.

2 Chen Fan (d. 168) was a famous Eastern Han minister. The remark was cited by Chen Fan as a contemporary proverb meaning the household with five daughters was so impoverished after marrying them off with required dowries that even a thief would pass up on stealing from it.

V.17

婚姻素對，靖侯成規。近世嫁娶，遂有賣
女納財，買婦輸絹，比量父祖，計較錙
銖，責多還少，市井無異。或猥婿在門，
或傲婦擅室，貪榮求利，反招羞恥，可不
慎歟。

V.18

借人典籍，皆須愛護，先有缺壞，就為補
治，此亦士大夫百行之一也。濟陽江祿，
讀書未竟，雖有急速，必待卷束整齊，然
後得起，故無損敗，人不厭其求假焉。或
有狼籍几案，分散部秩，多為童幼婢妾之
所點汙，風雨犬鼠之所毀傷，實為累德。
吾每讀聖人之書，未嘗不肅敬對之；其故
紙有五經詞義，及賢達姓名，不敢穢用
也。

V.17

That in forming marriage ties one should seek a decent family of moderate social status is a rule that was established by Marquis Jing.[1] In recent years there are those who sell their daughter for money or buy a daughter-in-law with silk. They compare the fathers' and grandfathers' positions, worry about the smallest things, ask for much but repay little, and behave no differently than men of the marketplace. In consequence, they either acquire a vulgar son-in-law in the family or witness an arrogant wife monopolizing the household. To covet prestige and pursue profit leads paradoxically to humiliation and shame. How can you not be careful about it!

V.18

When you borrow books from someone, you must cherish them. If a book comes in an imperfect condition, you should repair it. This is one of the one hundred fine actions that ought to be practiced by a genteel man. Even when he was in a hurry, Jiang Lu of Jiyang would always carefully roll up the scrolls before rising from his seat, so the books he read never suffered any damage, and people were never reluctant to lend him books.[2] Some people let books pile up on their desk or allow the scrolls to scatter all over the place; their young children, maids, or concubines often get the books dirty; wind, rain, dogs, and mice may spoil them. This is truly a blemish on their virtue. When I read the writings of the sages, I have always treated them with solemn respect. If an old piece of paper happens to contain phrases and principles of the Five Classics or the names of worthy men, I would not dare use it for irreverent purposes.

---

1 Marquis Jing was the posthumous title of Yan Han 顏含 (ca. 260s–ca. 350s), the ninth-generation ancestor of Yan Zhitui. He turned down marriage proposals made by two powerful families in the Eastern Jin (see Introduction).
2 The Jiang clan of Jiyang (in modern He'nan) was an eminent noble clan. Jiang Lu (fl. 530s) was granduncle of the famous poet Jiang Zong 江總 (519–594).

V.19

吾家巫覡禱請，絕於言議，符書章醮，亦
無祈焉，並汝曹所見也。勿妖妄之費。

V.19

In our family, as you boys have seen, we do not ever speak of praying and making pleas to gods through male or female spirit-mediums, nor do we ever resort to Daoist talismans and sacrifices. Do not waste your time on such ridiculous superstitions.

風操第六

VI.1

吾觀禮經，聖人之教，箕帚匕箸，咳唾唯諾，執燭沃盥，皆有節文，亦為至矣。但既殘缺，非復全書。其有所不載，及世事變改者，學達君子，自為節度，相承行之，故世號士大夫風操。而家門頗有不同，所見互稱長短，然其阡陌亦自可知。昔在江南，目能視而見之，耳能聽而聞之；蓬生麻中，不勞翰墨。汝曹生於戎馬之閒，視聽之所不曉，故聊記以傳示子孫。

VI. Manners and Etiquette

VI.1

I have observed, in the classic of rites, the teachings of the sage: in using dustpan, broom, spoon, and chopsticks, in coughing, spitting, and making replies, in holding candles and washing hands, there is always a set of protocols dictating the correct way of acting. The rules of conduct are indeed detailed and exhaustive.[1] However, the book has many lacunae and is no longer complete. For those things that are not mentioned in the ritual classic, and for those things that have changed with the times, learned and wise gentlemen took it upon themselves to lay down rules, which have subsequently spread to others. The world refers to such rules as the manners and etiquette of the gentry. Even though each family has its own style, and some may regard certain rules as either superior or inferior to others, we can still discern the basic ways of carrying oneself. In the old days, back in the south, one witnessed proper conduct with one's own eyes and heard it with one's own ears. "Pigweed grows in the midst of hemp" – one did not need to bother using brush and ink [to write down the rules].[2] You boys, however, were born and raised among war horses, and have not had a chance to see or hear about those proprieties. Thus I have to record them so as to pass them on to my sons and grandsons.

---

1 The classic of rites refers to the *Record of Rites*, one of the Confucian classics.
2 The full saying is "Pigweed in the midst of hemp naturally grows up straight." It appears in the philosophical *Xunzi* and refers to the influence of one's environment. Yan Zhitui implies that the south in the old days had been much more conducive for a child's proper education in manners and etiquette.

VI.2

禮曰："見似目瞿，聞名心瞿。"有所感觸，惻愴心眼。若在從容平常之地，幸須申其情耳。必不可避，亦當忍之；猶如伯叔兄弟，酷類先人，可得終身腸斷，與之絕耶？又："臨文不諱，廟中不諱，君所無私諱。"蓋知聞名須有消息，不必期於顛沛而走也。

VI.3

梁世謝舉甚有聲譽，聞諱必哭，為世所譏。又臧逢世，臧嚴之子也，篤學修行，不墜門風。孝元經牧江州，遣往建昌督事，郡縣民庶，競修箋書，朝夕輻輳，几案盈積，書有稱嚴寒者，必對之流涕，不省取記，多廢公事，物情怨駭，竟以不辦而還。此並過事也。

1 Xie Ju (d. 549) was a member of one of the most eminent clans, grandson of the famous writer Xie Zhuang 謝莊 (421–466) and son of Xie Yue 謝瀹 (454–498). He was known for his knowledge of Buddhism.

2 Zang Yan (d. 540s) was a scholar and writer, known for his expertise in the *Han History.* He had served on the staff of Xiao Yi (Emperor Xiaoyuan) for a long

VI.2

The *Record of Rites* says, "When a man sees someone who physically resembles [his late father], his eyes are startled; when he hears the name [of his late father], his heart is startled." It is because he is stirred by what he sees and hears, and his eyes and heart are deeply saddened. If this happens on an ordinary informal occasion, one may give expression to one's feelings. But if it is an unavoidable situation, a man should repress his feelings, for it would be as in the case of seeing his uncles or brothers: they look very much like his late father, but can he allow his heart to be so broken by seeing them that he severs relationship with them? The *Record of Rites* also states: "One should not avoid the name [of one's late father or grandfather] in one's writings and in the ancestral temple, nor should one avoid it in front of one's ruler." Thus we know that, when one hears the name [of one's late father or grandfather], one must carefully consider the circumstances; it is not necessary to become flustered and flee every time.

VI.3

Xie Ju of the Liang was a well-known man, but he would burst into tears whenever he heard his late father's name, and for this was ridiculed by his contemporaries.[1] Then again there was Zang Fengshi, son of Zang Yan.[2] He was diligent in study and virtuous in conduct, and kept up the fine reputation of his family. When Emperor Xiaoyuan served as governor of Jiangzhou, he sent Zang Fengshi to Jianchang as administrator. The people of the county vied to write to him. Letters arrived morning and evening, and his desk was piled with paperwork. But whenever an epistle mentioned *yanhan* ["severe cold"], his tears started flowing, and he could no longer deal with it.[3] Thus much official business was neglected, and people were all shocked and indignant. In the end he was dismissed from office because of incompetence. Both men had behaved excessively.

---

time. The incident related here took place when Xiao Yi was governor of Jiangzhou (in modern Jiangxi) from 540 to 547.

3 "Severe" (*yan*) was the personal name of Zang Fengshi's father and thus was a taboo character for him. Xiao Yi was appointed the governor of Jiangzhou (in modern Jiangxi) in 540. Jianchang was a commandery in Jiangzhou or Jiang prefecture, also in modern Jiangxi.

VI.4

近在揚都，有一士人諱審，而與沈氏交結
周厚，沈與其書，名而不姓，此非人情
也。

VI.5

凡避諱者，皆須得其同訓以代換之：桓公
名白，博有五皓之稱；厲王名長，琴有修
短之目。不聞謂布帛為布皓，呼腎腸為腎
修也。梁武小名阿練，子孫皆呼練為絹；
乃謂銷鍊物為銷絹物，恐乖其義。或有諱
雲者，呼紛紜為紛煙；有諱桐者，呼梧桐
樹為白鐵樹，便似戲笑耳。

---

1 Yangdu refers to Liang's old capital Jiankang (modern Nanjing).
2 The surname Shen is a different character from the character of the Yangdu
gentleman's personal name, although the two characters are pronounced alike.
3 Duke Huan refers to Duke Huan of Qi 齊 (d. 643 BCE), whose personal name
was Xiaobo 小白 (or Xiaobai in modern Mandarin). It is to be noted here that
the characters for the color "white" and the game Bo are different though pronounced alike.

VI.4

In recent years there was a gentleman in Yangdu whose personal name was Shen.[1] He was a very good friend with the Shen family. In his letters to this man, Mr. Shen would only write his own personal name without including his family name. This is not normal and natural behavior.[2]

VI.5

In avoiding someone's name we must replace the character with another character with similar meaning. Duke Huan was named Bo ["white"], and so in the game Bo, *wu bo* were called *wu hao* instead.[3] Prince Li was named Chang ["long"], and so a zither was described as either "tall" [*xiu*] or short.[4] Yet we have never heard anyone referring to "cotton and silk fabrics" (*bu bo*) as "cotton and *white*" (*bu hao*), or "kidney and intestines" (*shen chang*) as "kidney and tall" (*shen xiu*).[5] Liang Emperor Wu's baby name was Ah Lian, and his sons and grandsons would refer to *lian* ["white silk"] as *juan* ["raw silk"].[6] But they would go so far as to refer to *xiao lian wu* ["smelt metal things"] as *xian juan wu* [lit. "smelt raw silks"].[7] That, I am afraid, distorts the meaning of the phrase. For some people *yun* ["cloud"] is a taboo character, and so rather than saying *fen yun* ["copious" or "motley"], they say *fen yan* [lit. "profuse smoke"].[8] For some people *tong* is a taboo character, and so they call a *wutong* tree a *baitie* [lit. "white iron"] tree instead.[9] That is like a joke.

---

4 Prince Li refers to the Prince of Huainan named Liu Chang 劉長 (198–174 BCE), son of the founding Han emperor.

5 *Bo* in "cotton and silk fabrics" is a different character from *bo* (white) though pronounced alike.

6 Liang Emperor Wu ruled from 502 to 549 (see Introduction).

7 *Lian* in *xiao lian wu* is a different character from lian (white silk) though pronounced alike.

8 *Yun* (cloud) is a different characrer than *yun* in *fen yun* (copious) though pronounced alike.

9 *Tong* is homophonic with *tong* 銅 (copper), hence "white iron."

VI.6

周公名子曰禽，孔子名兒曰鯉，止在其
身，自可無禁。至若衛侯、魏公子、楚太
子，皆名蟣蝨；長卿名犬子，王修名狗
子，上有連及，理未為通，古之所行，今
之所笑也。北土多有名兒為驢駒、豚子
者，使其自稱及兄弟所名，亦何忍哉？

VI.7

前漢有尹翁歸，後漢有鄭翁歸，梁家亦有
孔翁歸，又有顧翁寵。晉代有許思妣、孟
少孤。如此名字，幸當避之。

VI.8

今人避諱，更急於古。凡名子者，當為孫
地。吾親識中有諱襄、諱周、諱清、諱
和、諱禹，交疏造次，一座百犯，聞者辛
苦，無憀賴焉。

---

1 Zhao Ximing believes that the prince of Wei is a mistake for the prince of Han
(Wang Liqi 67).
2 Zhangqing refers to Sima Xiangru 司馬相如 (ca. 179–117 BCE), famous Western Han writer. Wang Xiu (334–357), the eldest son of the nobleman Wang
Meng 王濛 (309–347), was known for his calligraphy like his father. In both
cases Quanzi and Gouzi were baby names.

VI.6

The Duke of Zhou named his son Qin ["fowl"] whereas Confucius named his Li ["carp"]. The name was limited to the person himself, so there was no need for prohibition. But the Marquis of Wei, the prince of Wei, and the heir apparent of Chu were all named Jishi ["flea's pupa"];[1] Zhangqing was named Quanzi ["son of a dog"], and Wang Xiu was named Gouzi ["pup"].[2] In these cases the name is related to the parent [in an unflattering manner], which is not a sensible thing to do. This practice of ancient times would be derided today. In the north many men named their son Lüju ["foal"] or Tunzi ["piglet"]. How unbearable it is to allow a man to refer to himself as such or be called such by his brothers!

VI.7

In the Former Han there was a Yin Wenggui [lit. father returns]; in the Later Han there was a Zheng Wenggui; the Liang likewise had a Kong Wenggui, and also a Gu Wengchong [lit. father's favorite].[3] In the Jin there were Xu Sibi [lit. longing for late mother] and Meng Shaogu [lit. orphaned when young].[4] I hope you will avoid using such personal names and courtesy names.

VI.8

People today avoid the names of their deceased ancestors even more strenuously than people in the olden days. So anyone in naming one's son must take his grandson into consideration. For some of my kin or acquaintances, [common characters such as] Xiang, Zhou, Qing, He, and Yu are all among tabooed characters. At a gathering, distant friends in a thoughtless manner might violate the taboos numerous times, causing those who hear it so much misery that it is hard to know what to do.

---

3 Yin Wenggui (d. 62 BCE) was a Former (Western) Han official. Kong Wenggui (fl. 530s) was a native of Kuaiji (in modern Zhejiang) and served on the staff of the Liang Prince of Nanping (476–533). Nothing is known about Zheng Wenggui of the Later (Eastern) Han (25–220) or Gu Wengchong of the Liang (502–557).

4 Xu Sibi was the courtesy name of Xu Yong 許永 (d. 329). Shaogu was the courtesy name of Meng Lou 孟陋 (fl. mid-4th century), well-known recluse and scholar of the Eastern Jin (317–420).

VI.9

昔司馬長卿慕藺相如，故名相如，顧元歎
慕蔡邕，故名雍。而後漢有朱張字孫卿，
許暹字顏回，梁世有庾晏嬰、祖孫登。連
古人姓為名字，亦鄙事也。

VI.10

昔劉文饒不忍罵奴為畜產，今世愚人遂以
相戲，或有指名為豚犢者。有識傍觀，猶
欲掩耳，況當之者乎？

VI.9

In the past, Sima Zhangqing admired Lin Xiangru, so he named himself Xiangru.[1] Gu Yuantan admired Cai Yong, so he named himself Yong.[2] In the Later Han, Zhu Zhang's courtesy name was Sunqing; Xu Xian's courtesy name was Yanhui.[3] In the Liang there were a Yu Yanying and a Zu Sundeng.[4] To take the surname of an ancient person as part of their personal name or courtesy name is a rather uncouth practice.

VI.10

In the past, Liu Wenrao could not bear having his slave called "an animal."[5] Yet in today's world fools use such words in jest, sometimes calling one another "pig" or "calf." Even a wise bystander would cover his ears, not to mention the one who is insulted.

---

1 For Sima Zhangqing, see note to VI.6. Lin Xiangru (fl. third century BCE) was a minister of the state of Zhao during the Warring States period.

2 Gu Yong (168–243), courtesy name Yuantan, was Wu's prime minister during the Three Kingdoms period. In his youth he had studied with Cai Yong (133–192), famous writer, scholar, and polymath.

3 Zhu Zhang (fl. 120s) was an Eastern Han minister whose name appears as Zhu Chang 朱偒 in the *History of the Later Han* and is emended accordingly by Wang Liqi (Wang 70). Sunqing is the philosopher Sun Qing or Xun Qing 荀卿 (fl. third century BCE), better known as Master Xun or Xunzi. Yan Hui was Confucius' favorite disciple who died young.

4 Yu Yanying was the son of a Liang minister Yu Yong 庾泳 (early sixth century). Yan Ying (d. 500 BCE) was a famous minister of the state of Qi. Zu Sundeng (fl. 570s) was a poet who served in minor office in the Chen dynasty (557–589). Sun Deng (fl. third century) was a well-known Daoist recluse.

5 Wenrao was the courtesy name of Liu Kuan (120–185), a prominent Eastern Han minister.

VI.11

近在議曹,共平章百官秩祿,有一顯貴,
當世名臣,意嫌所議過厚。齊朝有一兩士
族文學之人謂此貴曰:"今日天下大同,
須為百代典式,豈得尚作關中舊意?明公
定是陶朱公大兒耳。"彼此歡笑,不以為
嫌。

VI.11

Recently, at the Consultation Section, I participated in a discussion about the ranks and salaries of the officials. A certain nobleman, a famous minister of our times, thought that the salaries we set were too high. Several learned gentlemen of the Qi court said to this nobleman: "Today the world has become one. We must establish the standard and model for a hundred generations to come. How can we hold onto the old ideas from within the Pass?[1] Your sagacious highness must be the eldest son of Tao Zhugong!"[2] They all laughed merrily without any ill-feeling.[3]

---

1 The region "within the Pass" refers to the region to the west of the Hangu Pass (in modern Shaanxi), the territory ruled by the former Western Wei/Northern Zhou (see Introduction).

2 Tao Zhugong is Fan Li 范蠡 (fl. fifth century BCE), a man who had allegedly amassed immense wealth. His eldest son, who had experienced hardship in his youth, was tightfisted, and his miserliness cost the life of his younger brother as he begrudged the money his father gave him to use as bribery to get his younger brother out of jail.

3 Commentators disagree about the timing of this incident. Many believe the incident took place not only after the Northern Qi dynasty was conquered by the Northern Zhou in 577 but also after the Sui (replacing the Northern Zhou rule in 581) unified the empire in 589 (hence the comment "the world has become one").

VI.12

昔侯霸之子孫稱其祖父曰家公；陳思王稱
其父曰家父，母曰家母；潘尼稱其祖曰家
祖。古人之所行，今人之所笑也。及南北
風俗，言其祖及二親，無云家者，田里猥
人方有此言耳。凡與人言，言己世父，以
次第稱之，不云家者，以尊於父，不敢家
也。凡言姑姊妹女子子，已嫁，則以夫氏
稱之；在室，則以次第稱之。言禮成他
族，不得云家也。子孫不得稱家者，輕略
之也。蔡邕書集呼其姑姊為家姑家姊，班
固書集亦云家孫，今並不行也。

VI.13

凡與人言，稱彼祖父母、世父母、父母及
長姑，皆加尊字，自叔父母已下，則加賢
字，尊卑之差也。王羲之書，稱彼之母與
自稱己母同，不云尊字，今所非也。

---

1 Hou Ba (d. 37 CE) was a minister of the early Eastern Han.
2 Prince Si of Chen is Cao Zhi 曹植 (192–232), famous writer, son of the warlord Cao Cao 曹操 (155–220).
3 Pan Ni (fl. second to third century) was a Western Jin poet.

VI.12

In the past, Hou Ba's grandsons had referred to him as "my family's grandpa."[1] Prince Si of Chen referred to his father as "my family's father" and his mother as "my family's mother."[2] Pan Ni referred to his grandfather as "my family's grandfather."[3] These ancient practices are ridiculed nowadays. Whether in the south or north, when one speaks of one's grandfather or parents, no one uses the word "family" anymore; only the low-born country folk still do it. When a man mentions his father's elder brothers in conversation, he refers to them by the order of their births instead of saying "my family's uncles." This is because they are older than his father, and so he should not use the prefix "family" to debase them. When a man speaks of his father's sister and her daughters, if a woman is already married, then she should be referred to as Mrs. So-and-so; if she is unmarried, she should be referred to in the order of birth. This is because once married, a woman becomes a member of another family [her husband's family], and so one should not use the prefix "family" to refer to her anymore. As for one's own sons and grandsons, one does not use the prefix "family" to refer to them because one does not treat them seriously [as juniors]. Cai Yong's letters refer to his aunt and his elder sister as "my family's aunt" and "my family's elder sister." Ban Gu's letters refer to his grandson as "my family's grandson."[4] Nowadays both forms are obsolete.

VI.13

In conversations, when speaking of the conversation partner's grandparents, his father's elder brother and sister-in-law, his parents, or his father's elder sister, one should add a prefix saying, "your venerable X." When speaking of his father's younger brother and sister-in-law and members of the lower generation, one should use the prefix "worthy." This demonstrates the hierarchy between the older and younger generations. In his letters, Wang Xizhi had referred to the addressee's mother in the same way he referred to his own mother instead of saying "your venerable mother."[5] This is not considered proper today.

---

4 For Cai Yong, see note to VI.9. Ban Gu (32–92) was the main compiler of the *Han History.*

5 Wang Xizhi (303–361) was a member of a prominent aristocratic clan and a famous calligrapher, whose many family letters are preserved because of his calligraphy.

VI.14

南人冬至歲首，不詣喪家；若不修書，則
過節束帶以申慰。北人至歲之日，重行弔
禮。禮無明文，則吾不取。

VI.15

南人賓至不迎，相見捧手而不揖，送客下
席而已；北人迎送並至門，相見則揖，皆
古之道也，吾善其迎揖。

VI.16

昔者，王侯自稱孤、寡、不穀，自茲以
降，雖孔子聖師與門人言，皆稱名也。後
雖有臣僕之稱，行者蓋亦寡焉。

VI.17

江南輕重各有謂號，具諸書儀。北人多稱
名者，乃古之遺風，吾善其稱名焉。

VI.14

People in the south do not visit a bereaved family on the Winter Solstice Festival or the New Year's Day. If he did not write a letter, then after the festival he would pay a formal visit to express his condolences. In contrast, people in the north attach great value to performing the consolation ritual on these two festivals. Such a practice is not explicitly prescribed in the ritual texts, and so I do not recommend it.

VI.15

Southerners do not come to the door to greet their guest. Upon seeing each other they raise their clasped hands together but do not bow. To see off the departing guest, they merely get up from their seating mat, and that is all. Northerners, on the other hand, will come to the door to greet or bid farewell to their guest. Upon seeing each other, they always bow. All these are the ancient ways. I admire the greeting and the bowing.

VI.16

In the past, a king or a noble lord would refer to himself as "the Orphaned One," "the Solitary One," and "the Wretched One." As for those below, even Confucius the sage teacher would always call himself by name when speaking with his disciples. Later on, although a man might refer to himself as "Your Subject" or "Your Servant," these terms are rarely used.

VI.17

In the south there is a proper form of address for every person, whether high or low. These forms of address are listed in full in works on epistolary etiquette. Northerners simply address one another by personal name in most cases. This is the ancient way, which is what I prefer.

VI.18a

言及先人，理當感慕，古者之所易，今人
之所難。江南人事不獲已，須言閥閱，必
以文翰，罕有面論者。北人無何便爾話
說，及相訪問。如此之事，不可加於人
也。人加諸己，則當避之。名位未高，如
為勳貴所逼，隱忍方便，速報取了，勿使
煩重，感辱祖父。

VI.18b

若沒，言須及者，則斂容肅坐，稱大門
中，世父、叔父則稱從兄弟門中，兄弟則
稱亡者子某門中，各以其尊卑輕重為容色
之節，皆變於常。若與君言，雖變於色，
猶云亡祖亡伯亡叔也。吾見名士亦有呼其
亡兄弟為兄子弟子門中者，亦未為安貼
也。

VI.18a

When speaking of one's ancestors, one should be moved and filled with longing. This was easy for the ancients but is difficult for modern men. If people in the south must mention their clan history, they will invariably put it in writing; seldom do they discuss such matters in a face-to-face conversation. Northerners, however, speak of it or ask one another about it at the drop of a hat. You must not impose such a topic on others. If someone imposes it on you, you should do your best to evade it. Your reputation and position are not yet prominent; if you are pressed by a noble lord, you will have to put up with it, but act according to circumstances, and get over the subject as quickly as possible. Do not disgrace your grandfather and father by going into details.

VI.18b

If you have to mention your deceased forebears in a conversation, you should keep a somber face and sit up straight, and speak of "those who belong to the large clan." For your father's elder brother and younger brother, you should refer to them as "those of the family of my cousins"; and for your brothers, you should say "those of the family of the son of the deceased." You should adjust your countenance in accordance with their seniority and status, and under all conditions your face should assume a different expression than its normal appearance. But if you must speak of them in front of your ruler, then even if you change your demeanor, you may still refer to them simply as "my late grandfather," "my late senior uncle [father's elder brother]," and "my late junior uncle [father's younger brother]." I have observed that a certain eminent gentleman had once in his ruler's presence referred to his deceased elder and younger brothers as "the one of my elder brother's son's family" or "the one of my younger brother's son's family." That was not appropriate.

VI.19

北土風俗，都不行此。太山羊侃梁初入南，吾近至鄴，其兄子肅訪侃委曲，吾答之云："卿從門中在梁，如此如此。"肅曰："是我親第七亡叔，非從也。"祖孝徵在坐，先知江南風俗，乃謂之云："賢從弟門中，何故不解？"

VI.20

古人皆呼伯父叔父，而今世多單呼伯叔。從父兄弟姊妹已孤，而對其前呼其母為伯叔母，此不可避者也。兄弟之子已孤，與他人言，對孤者前，呼為兄子弟子，頗為不忍；北土人多呼為姪。案爾雅、喪服經、左傳，姪雖名通男女，並是對姑之立稱。晉世已來，始呼叔姪。今呼為姪，於理為勝也。

---

1 Yang Kan (496–549) was a famous general from the north. He defected to Liang in 529 and eventually died a hero defending the capital Jiankang during the Hou Jing Rebellion. The Yang clan of Taishan (in modern Shandong) was an eminent clan.

2 Xiaozheng was the courtesy name of Zu Ting 祖珽 (d. 570s), talented courtier of the Northern Qi.

VI.19

The northerners do not have such customs at all. Yang Kan of Taishan had gone to the south in the early years of the Liang.[1] After I arrived at Ye, his elder brother's son, Yang Su, inquired after him. I replied, "When the one from your cousin's family was in the Liang, he did such-and-such." Yang Su said, "He was my late seventh junior uncle, not my cousin." Zu Xiaozheng, who knew the southern customs well, was present.[2] He said to Yang Su, "He was from your worthy cousin's family. What is there not to understand?"

VI.20

The ancients would call their uncles "senior-uncle-father" [*bofu*, the father's elder brother] and "junior-uncle-father" [*shufu*, the father's younger brother], but in modern times people drop "father" [*fu*] from the address and simply call them "senior uncle" (*bo*) and "junior uncle" (*shu*). If the father of one's male and female cousins has passed away, it is unavoidable to refer to their mother as one's "senior-uncle's wife" (*bomu*) or "junior-uncle's wife" (*shumu*) in their presence; but if the son of one's elder brother or younger brother is orphaned, and in a conversation with others you refer to them in their presence as "my elder brother's son" or "my younger brother's son," you may find it unbearable.[3] Under such circumstances, northerners usually call them *zhi*, "nephew/niece." Now, according to the *Erya*, the *Classic of Mourning Dress*, and the *Zuo Tradition*, the term *zhi* can be used for both male and female, but in both cases it is defined in relation to one's paternal aunt; it was only since the Jin dynasty [265–420] that people began to use *zhi* in relation to one's paternal uncle.[4] The modern [northern] custom of referring to the son of one's paternal uncle as *zhi* makes better sense.

---

3 This is because it involves making a direct explicit reference to the deceased by saying "my elder brother" or "my younger brother."

4 The *Erya* is the oldest surviving Chinese dictionary, which has been dated to the third century BCE and earlier. The *Classic of Mourning Dress* is a chapter with the title "Mourning Dress" from the ritual classic, *Ceremonial Ritual* (*Yi li* 儀禮). The *Zuo Tradition*, a historical narrative of fourth century BCE, was regarded as an exegesis of the *Spring and Autumn Annals*.

VI.21

別易會難，古人所重。江南餞送，下泣言離。有王子侯，梁武帝弟，出為東郡，與武帝別，帝曰："我年已老，與汝分張，甚以惻愴。"數行淚下。侯遂密雲，赧然而出。坐此被責，飄颻舟渚，一百許日，卒不得去。北間風俗，不屑此事，歧路言離，歡笑分首。然人性自有少涕淚者，腸雖欲絕，目猶爛然；如此之人，不可強責。

VI.22

凡親屬名稱，皆須粉墨，不可濫也。無風教者，其父已孤，呼外祖父母與祖父母同，使人為其不喜聞也。雖質於面，皆當加外以別之。父母之世叔父，皆當加其次第以別之；父母之世叔母，皆當加其姓以別之；父母之群從世叔父母及從祖父母，皆當加其爵位若姓以別之。河北士人，皆呼外祖父母為家公家母；江南田里間亦言之。以家代外，非吾所識。

---

1 That is, he looked gloomy but shed no tears.

VI.21

Parting is easy, but reunion is difficult. The ancients took parting very seriously. In the south, when people see each other off, they weep at bidding farewell. A prince, who was the younger brother of Liang Emperor Wu, was leaving the capital to serve as governor at a prefecture to the east. Upon his departure the emperor said to him, "As I am getting on in years, I am very saddened by our separation." Thereupon he shed tears. But the prince only had "dark clouds,"[1] and blushed with embarrassment upon exit. He received a reprimand for his lapse. After lingering aboard boat on the way for over a hundred days, he was ultimately unable to go to his post.[2] Northerners, on the other hand, are contemptuous of such a practice, and take leave of one another with merry laughter at the fork of the road. Some people have few tears by nature; they may suffer from a broken heart, but their eyes remain dry. One should not be too demanding and critical of such people.

VI.22

We must take great care to distinguish the forms of addressing various relatives. Once his father passes way, a man without good upbringing might address his maternal grandparents in the same way he does his paternal grandparents, which is not pleasant to hear. Even when a man speaks to the maternal grandparents face to face, he should always add the prefix of "maternal" [*wai*, lit. external] to distinguish them from his paternal grandparents. His parents' elder and younger brothers should be distinguished by numbers indicating the order of their birth; his parents' elder brother's wife and younger brother's wife should be distinguished by their surnames; his parents' cousins, their uncles and aunts, and their granduncles and grandaunts must be distinguished by their official titles and ranks. The northern gentry all call their maternal grandparents "family grandfather" and "family grandmother," and the country folk in the south do the same. To use "family" (*jia*) in place of "maternal" (*wai*) is not something I recognize.

---

2 This prince may have been Xiao Dan 蕭憺 (478–522), the youngest brother of Emperor Wu. He was appointed the governor of Nan Yanzhou 南兗州 in the autumn of 509, but never went to the prefectural capital Guangling 廣陵 to the east of Jiankang, and was reappointed as the governor of Yizhou in the following spring.

VI.23

凡宗親世數，有從父，有從祖，有族祖。
江南風俗，自茲已往，高秩者，通呼為
尊，同昭穆者，雖百世猶稱兄弟；若對他
人稱之，皆云族人。河北士人，雖三二十
世，猶呼為從伯從叔。梁武帝嘗問一中土
人曰：「卿北人，何故不知有族？」答
云：「骨肉易疏，不忍言族耳。」當時雖
為敏對，於禮未通。

VI.24

吾嘗問周弘讓曰：「父母中外姊妹，何以
稱之？」周曰：「亦呼為丈人。」自古未
見丈人之稱施於婦人也。吾親表所行，若
父屬者，為某姓姑；母屬者，為某姓姨。
中外丈人之婦，猥俗呼為丈母，士大夫謂
之王母、謝母云。而陸機集有與長沙顧母
書，乃其從叔母也，今所不行。

VI.23

The relatives from one's paternal clan are divided by generation into paternal uncles, paternal granduncles, and paternal clan-grandfathers [i.e., paternal grandfather's male cousins]. To the south of the Yangzi River, with regard to a relative outside these relationships, if he occupies an eminent official position, one would address him as "venerable so-and-so." If two men share the same patrilineal ancestors, then even after a hundred generations they would still call each other "brother," and refer to each other as a "clansman" when speaking to others. To the north of the Yellow River, a gentry member would call such a relative a collateral senior uncle or a collateral junior uncle even after twenty or thirty generations. Liang Emperor Wu once put this question to a man from the Central Land: "You are a northerner; why is it that you don't know about 'clan'?" He replied, "Because blood relations become alienated all too easily, I cannot bear using the term 'clan.'"[1] Although contemporaries thought this was a clever answer, it was not ritually appropriate.

VI.24

I once asked Zhou Hongrang, "What do you call your parents' paternal and maternal female cousins?"[2] He said, "I call them 'Elder.'" From ancient times until today, I have never heard of the term "elder" (*zhangren*) applied to women. My relatives' practice is as follows: if the aunt is on the father's side, we call her "so-and-so [surname] paternal aunt [*gu*]." If she is on the mother's side, we call her "so-and-so [surname] maternal aunt [*yi*]." Among commoners, the wives of our elders on either paternal or maternal side are all called "elder-mother" (*zhangmu*), but members of the gentry call them "Mother Wang," "Mother Xie," and so on and so forth. Lu Ji's literary collection contains a "Letter to Mother Gu of Changsha."[3] The addressee of the letter was the wife of his father's younger cousin. This however is no longer in practice today.

---

1 This man is identified as Xiahou Dan 夏侯亶 (d. 529).

2 Zhou Hongrang (ca. 500s–560s) was a nephew of Zhou She 周捨 (469–524), one of the most prominent Liang courtiers, and was known for his broad learning and literary writings.

3 Lu Ji (261–303) was a descendant of a southern noble family and a famous writer.

VI.25

齊朝士子，皆呼祖僕射為祖公，全不嫌有
所涉也，乃有對面以相戲者。

VI.26

古者，名以正體，字以表德，名終則諱
之，字乃可以為孫氏。孔子弟子記事者，
皆稱仲尼；呂后微時，嘗字高祖為季；至
漢爰種，字其叔父曰絲；王丹與侯霸子
語，字霸為君房。江南至今不諱字也。河
北士人全不辨之，名亦呼為字，字固因呼
為字。尚書王元景兄弟，皆號名人，其父
名雲，字羅漢，一皆諱之，其餘不足怪
也。

VI.25

The elite members of the Qi court all called Lord Chamberlain Zu "Zu gong" without the least bit of distaste.[1] Some even jested about it to his face.

VI.26

In ancient times, one's given name was to articulate one's identity, while one's courtesy name was to give expression of his virtue; once a person passed away, his given name would become taboo [for his children], but his courtesy name could be used as a surname for his grandsons. When Confucius' disciples recorded his deeds, they all referred to him by his courtesy name, Zhongni. When Empress Lü was still lowly, she called Gaozu by his courtesy name, Ji.[2] In the Han dynasty, Yuan Zhong had called his junior uncle by his courtesy name Si; when Wang Dan was speaking with Hou Ba's son, he referred to Hou Ba by his courtesy name Junfang.[3] To the south of the Yangzi River, even today people do not treat a courtesy name as taboo. The gentry to the north of the Yellow River observe no such distinction: they treat a man's given name and courtesy name as the same. Wang Yuanjing, Minister [of Personnel], and his brothers are prominent men.[4] Their father was named Yun and his courtesy name was Luohan. The brothers treat both names as taboo. If even they behave like this, there is no wonder that the rest of the world would do the same.

---

1 Lord Chamberlain Zu is Zu Ting (see note to VI.19), who was made Lord Chamberlain in 572. "Zu gong" means "Lord Zu" but also means "grandfather."

2 Empress Lü was the principal wife of Han Emperor Gaozu (see note to II.10).

3 Si was the courtesy name of Yuan Ang (d. 148 BCE), a Western Han minister; Yuan Zhong was the son of his elder brother. Wang Dan lived in the first century CE. For Hou Ba, see note to VI.12.

4 Yuanjing was the courtesy of Wang Xin 王昕 (d. 550s) the eldest son of Wang Yun (d. 517). He and his eight brothers were all talented and known as "the nine dragons of the Wang family." The Minister of Personnel was Wang Xi's title granted posthumously in late 560s.

VI.27

禮閒傳云：“斬縗之哭，若往而不反；齊
縗之哭，若往而反；大功之哭，三曲而
偯；小功緦麻，哀容可也，此哀之發於聲
音也。”孝經云：“哭不偯。”皆論哭有
輕重質文之聲也。禮以哭有言者為號；然
則哭亦有辭也。江南喪哭，時有哀訴之言
耳；山東重喪，則唯呼蒼天，期功以下，
則唯呼痛深，便是號而不哭。

VI.28

江南凡遭重喪，若相知者，同在城邑，三
日不弔則絕之；除喪，雖相遇則避之，怨
其不己憫也。有故及道遙者，致書可也；
無書亦如之。北俗則不爾。

VI.27

According to the "Jian zhuan" chapter of the *Record of Rites*, "The weeping of those who wear the heaviest mourning clothes is of a sound that goes all the way and never diminishes; the weeping of those who wear the second-degree mourning clothes is of a sound that goes all the way but does diminish; the weeping of those who wear the third-degree mourning clothes is of a sound that twists and turns three times and remains sad; for those who wear the fourth- and fifth-degree mourning clothes, a sad expression suffices. This is how grief can be channeled through sound." The *Classic of Filial Piety* says, "[When weeping for a deceased parent,] the weeping goes all the way and does not taper off." These statements all demonstrate that the sounds of weeping vary: some light and some heavy, some plain and some polished. The *Record of Rites* considers speaking while weeping as "wailing" (*hao*). This shows that weeping may be accompanied with words. In the south, when people weep during mourning, they often talk to the dead at the same time. In the north, in cases of the heaviest mourning, the bereaved would only cry out "Gray Heavens!" In cases of second-degree mourning, people would cry out, "Alas! So deep is my pain!" This is wailing without weeping.

VI.28

In the south, when a family is in heavy mourning, if a friend living in the same city does not come to offer condolences within three days, the family would sever relationship with him. After the mourning period is over, when the bereaved family runs into this friend, they would avoid him, because they resent that he shows no compassion for them. If a friend is unable to come because of distance or other reasons, it is acceptable to send a letter of condolences instead; but if he sends no such letter, then he would be treated in the same way by the bereaved family [as the friend who does not come to offer condolences]. Northern customs are not like these.

VI.29

江南凡弔者，主人之外，不識者不執手；
識輕服而不識主人，則不於會所而弔，他
日修名詣其家。

VI.30

陰陽說云："辰為水墓，又為土墓，故不
得哭。"王充論衡云："辰日不哭，哭則
重喪。"今無教者，辰日有喪，不問輕
重，舉家清謐，不敢發聲，以辭弔客。道
書又曰："晦歌朔哭，皆當有罪，天奪其
算。"喪家朔望，哀感彌深，寧當惜壽，
又不哭也？亦不諭。

VI.29

In the south, when a man comes to offer condolences, except for the man of the house, he will not hold the hand of anyone he does not know. If he only knows a distant member of the bereaved family but not the man of the house, then he will not come to the funeral service, but will instead prepare a calling card and visit the bereaved family on another day.

VI.30

According to the *yin-yang* theory, "*Chen* is the tomb for the element of water and also for the element of earth; therefore one must not cry [on a *chen* day]."[1] Wang Chong states in his *Balanced Discourses*: "On a *chen* day one must not cry, for it will lead to double bereavement."[2] Today people who do not have a proper upbringing take this quite seriously: if a death occurs on a *chen* day, then no matter whether it is the death of a close or distant member of the family, the entire family remains silent and does not dare to make any weeping sound, declining all mourners. Then again a Daoist work says, "Anyone who sings on the last day of a month or cries on the first day of a month has committed a grave offense and will have his allotted years decreased by heaven." A bereaved family feels particularly grieved on the first and fifteenth day of a month. How can they begrudge their life and refuse to cry? I find it incomprehensible.

---

1 *The Great Principles of the Five Elements* 五行大義, a *yin-yang* work on the Five Elements (i.e., metal, wood, water, fire, earth) compiled by Xiao Ji 蕭吉 (d. 615), regards the life cycle of the five elements as being in harmony with the twelve earthly branches, which are used to calculate time (year, month, day, and hour). *Chen* is the fifth of the twelve earthly branches. The element of water is said to be buried in *chen*, and the element of wood is also supposed to be buried in *chen*. Thus *chen* indicates double burials for two of the Five Elements. Xiao Ji was a grandson of Liang Emperor Wu's elder brother Xiao Yi 蕭懿 (d. 500); his work was preserved in Japan (see citation in Wang Liqi 97).

2 Wang Chong (27–100) was an Eastern Han thinker whose main work is *Balanced Discourses* (*Lun heng*).

VI.31

偏傍之書，死有歸殺。子孫逃竄，莫肯在
家；畫瓦書符，作諸厭勝；喪出之日，門
前然火，戶外列灰，祓送家鬼，章斷注
連：凡如此比，不近有情，乃儒雅之罪
人，彈議所當加也。

VI.32

已孤，而履歲及長至之節，無父，拜母、
祖父母、世叔父母、姑、兄、姊，則皆
泣；無母，拜父、外祖父母、舅、姨、
兄、姊，亦如之：此人情也。

VI.33

江左朝臣，子孫初釋服，朝見二宮，皆當
泣涕；二宮為之改容。頗有膚色充澤，無
哀感者，梁武薄其為人，多被抑退。裴政
出服，問訊武帝，貶瘦枯槁，涕泗滂沱，
武帝目送之曰："裴之禮不死也。"

---

1 Pei Zhili (fl. 500s–530s) served under Emperor Wu; his son Pei Zheng (d. 590s) was a well-known courtier in Sui court.

VI.31

According to unorthodox books, the soul of a person will return home on a certain day after death. On such a day, the deceased person's children all flee from home and refuse to stay behind. They would paint on tiles and write a talisman to avert the soul's return. On the day when the coffin is carried out to the burial site, they light fires outside their house and spread ashes in front of the gate; they hold rituals to send away the family spirit, and send memorials to heaven to request immunity from disasters. Such behavior does not issue from natural human feelings. People who engage in such practice are offenders against the grace of the educated elite and should be publically censured.

VI.32

After the loss of a parent, on New Year's Day and on the day of winter solstice, if the lost parent was one's father, then one should bow to one's mother, grandparents, senior and junior uncle and their wives, aunts, elder brother, and elder sister, and all would weep. If the deceased parent was one's mother, then one should bow to the father, maternal grandparents, maternal uncle and aunt, elder brother, and elder sister, and they would all weep. This is in accordance with human feelings.

VI.33

To the left of the Yangzi River, when the sons and grandsons of the bereaved family first took off their mourning clothes and had an audience with the emperor and the crown prince, they were expected to weep, and the emperor and the crown prince would change their countenance for their sake. There were quite a few courtiers who looked radiant and full-fleshed on such occasions, showing no sign of grief. Liang Emperor Wu disdained their character and would either demote them or dismiss them from office. When Pei Zheng had completed his mourning period and paid respects to Emperor Wu, he was emaciated and gaunt, his tears flowing copiously. After he took leave, Emperor Wu gazed after him, saying, "Pei Zhili is not dead."[1]

VI.34

二親既沒，所居齋寢，子與婦弗忍入焉。
北朝頓丘李構，母劉氏夫人亡後，所住之
堂，終身鏁閉，弗忍開入也。夫人，宋廣
州刺史纂之孫女，故構猶染江南風教。其
父獎，為揚州刺史，鎮壽春，遇害。構嘗
與王松年、祖孝徵數人同集談讌。孝徵善
畫，遇有紙筆，圖寫為人。頃之，因割鹿
尾，戲截畫人以示構，而無他意。構愴然
動色，便起就馬而去。舉坐驚駭，莫測其
情。祖君尋悟，方深反側，當時罕有能感
此者。

VI.34

After the death of parents, their son and daughter-in-law cannot bear to enter their bedroom. In the north, after Madame Liu, mother of Li Gou of Dunqiu, passed away, her room was locked up.[1] Li Gou could not bring himself to set foot in it for the rest of his life. Madame Liu was the grand-daughter of Liu Zuan, the Governor of Guangzhou of the Song.[2] Therefore Li Gou was influenced by the manners and education of the south. His father, Liu Jiang, who had served as the governor of Yangzhou, was murdered at his headquarters, Shouchun. Li Gou once had been at a gathering with Wang Songnian and Zu Xiaozheng.[3] Xiaozheng was good at drawing. There happened to be a brush and some paper at hand, so he drew a human figure on a piece of paper. Later, when carving a deer's tail at meal, he playfully cut the painted figure in half to show Li Gou. He did not mean anything by it, but Gou's face changed and took on a very sad expression. He immediately rose from his seat and left on his horse. All the guests were shocked and could not fathom the reason for his departure.[4] Master Zu, however, soon realized his mistake and felt deeply uneasy. At the time there were few who understood.

---

1 Dunqiu is in modern He'nan. Li Jiang (d. 529) was a minister of the Northern Wei; Li Gou (fl. 540s–550s) was his eldest son who later served the Northern Qi.

2 The *History of the Song* (*Song shu* 宋書) completed in 488 records a Liu Zuan (d. 478) who was a member of the Song royal family. It is unknown if he had served as governor of Guangzhou.

3 Wang Songnian (fl. 550s–560s) was a Northern Qi courtier. For Zu Xiaozheng, see note to VI.19.

4 To cut the painted figure in half reminded Li Gou of the way in which his father was killed.

VI.35

吳郡陸襄，父閑被刑，襄終身布衣蔬飯，雖薑菜有切割，皆不忍食；居家惟以掐摘供廚。江陵姚子篤，母以燒死，終身不忍噉炙。豫章熊康父以醉而為奴所殺，終身不復嘗酒。然禮緣人情，恩由義斷，親以噎死，亦當不可絕食也。

VI.36

禮經：父之遺書，母之杯圈，感其手口之澤，不忍讀用。政為常所講習，讎校繕寫，及偏加服用，有跡可思者耳。若尋常墳典，為生什物，安可悉廢之乎？既不讀用，無容散逸，惟當緘保，以留後世耳。

VI.35

After Lu Xian, the father of Lu Xiang of the Wu commandery, was killed, Lu Xiang dressed in coarse cotton clothes and remained a vegetarian for the rest of his life.[1] He could not even bear eating vegetables that had been chopped or cut, and would only pinch off their leaves for cooking. The mother of Yao Zidu of Jiangling died in a fire, and Yao Zidu could not bring himself to eat roasted meat for the rest of his life. The father of Xiong Kang of Yuzhang, while drunk, was murdered by a slave, so Xiong Kang never drank alcohol for the rest of his life.[2] However, rites are developed from natural human feelings, and gratitude must be guided by principles. Suppose one's parent dies of choking, one should not stop eating because of that.

VI.36

According to the *Record of Rites*, with regard to the books handed down by one's father and the wooden cup left behind by one's mother, the son is moved by how they were touched by his father's hands and his mother's mouth and cannot bear to use them again. This is because the books are what the father had always studied, discussed, collated, and copied, the cup is what the mother had frequently handled, and the parents had left traces of use on them. If it is just ordinary books and utensils, how can one discard them all? The books one no longer reads and the utensils one no longer uses must not be allowed to scatter; they should be preserved and sealed in cases and passed down to posterity.

---

1 Wu commandery is in modern Jiangsu. Lu Xiang (480–549) was a Liang courtier. His father Lu Xian served on the staff of the Southern Qi prince Xiao Yaoguang 蕭遙光 (468–499) and was killed in Xiao's ill-fated rebellion.

2 Nothing is known about Yao Zidu or Xiong Kang.

VI.37

思魯等第四舅母，親吳郡張建女也，有第
五妹，三歲喪母。靈床上屏風，平生舊
物，屋漏沾溼，出曝曬之，女子一見，伏
床流涕。家人怪其不起，乃往抱持；薦席
淹漬，精神傷沮，不能飲食。將以問醫，
醫診脈云：「腸斷矣。」因爾便吐血，數
日而亡。中外憐之，莫不悲歎。

VI.38

禮云：「忌日不樂。」正以感慕罔極，惻
愴無聊，故不接外賓，不理眾務耳。必能
悲慘自居，何限於深藏也？世人或端坐奧
室，不妨言笑，盛營甘美，厚供齋食；迫
有急卒，密戚至交，盡無相見之理：蓋不
知禮意乎！

VI.37

You boys' fourth maternal uncle's wife was the daughter of Zhang Jian of the Wu commandery.[1] Her fifth younger sister had lost her mother at the age of three *sui*.[2] The screen behind her mother's spirit seat had been used by the mother all her life. It became wet because of a roof leak and was moved out to be sunned. As soon as the girl saw it, she lay down on her bed and wept. Family members were surprised that she did not get up [for a long time] and went to raise her to her feet. They found her mattress was soaked with her tears. She was sad and gloomy, unable to eat or drink. They took her to see the doctor, who upon examining her pulse said, "Her intestines are broken."[3] The girl vomited blood and died in a few days. People inside and outside her family all felt sorry for her and lamented her death.

VI.38

The *Record of Rites* says, "A son does not enjoy himself on the anniversary of a parent's death." Moved by the parent's immeasurable kindness and filled with longing,[4] the son is saddened and takes no pleasure in anything, which is why he does not receive outside visitors and does not deal with various affairs. If one feels genuine grief, why does he have to confine himself to a secluded room? Some people may sit upright in a hidden chamber, but that does not prevent one from talking and laughing, providing oneself with many delicacies and a rich array of vegetarian dishes; yet, should any urgent matter arise, even close relatives or best friends do not get to see him. Isn't this a misunderstanding of the real meaning of rites?

---

1 Like the Lu family of the Wu commandery, the Zhang family of the Wu commandery was an eminent southern clan in the Southern Dynasties.
2 Two years old by western reckoning.
3 "Broken intestines," like "a broken heart" in English, indicates extreme grief. Here it becomes literal.
4 Yan Zhitui alludes to a stanza from the poem "Lu'e" 蓼莪 in the *Classic of Poetry*: "Father gave birth to me, / mother nurtured me. / I want to repay their kindness, / which is as immeasurable as heaven."

VI.39

魏世王修母以社日亡。來歲有社，修感念
哀甚，鄰里聞之，為之罷社。今二親喪
亡，偶值伏臘分至之節，及月小晦後，忌
之外，所經此日，猶應感慕，異於餘辰，
不預飲讌、聞聲樂及行遊也。

VI.40

劉縚、緩、綏，兄弟並為名器，其父名
昭，一生不為照字，惟依爾雅火旁作召
耳。然凡文與正諱相犯，當自可避；其有
同音異字，不可悉然。劉字之下，即有昭
音。呂尚之兒，如不為上；趙壹之子，儻
不作一：便是下筆即妨，是書皆觸也。

---

1 Wang Xiu (fl. 190s–210s) was an official known for his integrity and had served
  the Cao Wei regime during the Three Kingdoms period.
2 That is, if a parent passes away on the last day of a Big Month (a month of 30
  days in the lunar calendar), then when the anniversary month comes around and
  falls on a Small Month (a month of 29 days in the lunar calendar), one should
  nevertheless mourn on the day after the last day of the Small Month.

VI.39

Wang Xiu of the Wei lost his mother on an Earth Sacrifice Day.[1] The following year, on the anniversary of her death, Wang Xiu was filled with sadness and longing for her. When his neighbors heard his cries, they called off the celebration of the Earth Sacrifice Day. In modern times, after the passing of one's parents, when encountering the Fu Sacrifice, the La Sacrifice, Summer Solstice, Winter Solstice, Spring Equinox, or Autumn Equinox, as well as the day right after the last day of a shorter month,[2] even if it falls outside the anniversary of the parent's death, one should nevertheless mark the day off as different from the other days of the year, and show longing and sadness by refusing to participate in banquets, listen to music, or go on outings.

VI.40

The Liu brothers – Tao, Huan, and Sui – were all talented men.[3] Their father's given name was Zhao 昭, so all their life they would not even write the homophonic character *zhao* 照; instead, they would write it as *zhao* 召 with a "fire" radical [that is, as *zhao* 炤], based on the *Erya*.[4] While one should indeed avoid the character used in his father's name, he should not shun all homophones. Otherwise, even the very character "Liu" contains a part that is pronounced *zhao*.[5] If homophones must be avoided, then Lü Shang's son could not write "above" (*shang*), nor would Zhao Yi's son be able to write "one" (*yi*), and they would have encountered taboo characters everywhere they turned.[6]

---

3 Liu Zhao (fl. early fifth century) was the brother-in-law of the famous poet Jiang Yan 江淹 (444–505) and known for his annotations of the *History of the Later Han*. Liu Tao (fl. 530s) was known for his expertise in the ritual classics. Liu Huan (d. ca. 540) was a well-known poet and served on the staff of Xiao Yi. Liu Sui is not recorded in the histories.

4 *Erya*: see note to VI.20.

5 The character Liu can be split into two parts: *jin* 金 and *zhao* 刂.

6 Lü Shang is also known as Taigong (see note to V.15); Zhao Yi (fl. 170s–180s) was an Eastern Han writer.

VI.41

嘗有甲設讌席，請乙為賓；而旦於公庭見
乙之子，問之曰："尊侯早晚顧宅？"乙
子稱其父已往。時以為笑。如此比例，觸
類慎之，不可陷於輕脫。

VI.42

江南風俗，兒生一期，為製新衣，盥浴裝
飾，男則用弓矢紙筆，女則刀尺鍼縷，並
加飲食之物，及珍寶服玩，置之兒前，觀
其發意所取，以驗貪廉愚智，名之為試
兒。親表聚集，致讌享焉。自茲已後，二
親若在，每至此日，嘗有酒食之事耳。無
教之徒，雖已孤露，其日皆為供頓，酣暢
聲樂，不知有所感傷。梁孝元帝年少之
時，每八月六日載誕之辰，常設齋講；自
阮修容薨歿之後，此事亦絕。

VI.41

Once, a Mr. X invited a Mr. Y to a banquet. When he saw Mr. Y's son at court in the morning, he asked him, "When will your venerable father grace my house with his presence today?" Mr. Y's son answered that his father was "already gone." It became a joke at the time.[1] You must be careful about similar things and do not commit the fault of flippancy.

VI.42

According to the custom of the south, on a child's first birthday, new clothes are made for the child, who is bathed and dressed up. In front of a boy they set out a bow, arrows, paper, and brush, and in front of a girl they set out scissors, a ruler, needles and thread, in addition to food, drink, clothing items, and other items of ornament, dress, or play. They will let the child pick something out to see if the child is moderate or greedy, smart or stupid. This custom is known as "testing the baby." Relatives on paternal and maternal sides all gather together for a banquet. From this point on, if one's parents are both alive, one will host a party on one's birthday. But those who lack good upbringing will still throw a birthday party even after they have lost a parent; they will prepare food and drink on that day and enjoy music and entertainment, knowing nothing about sentimentality for their deceased parent. When Liang Emperor Xiaoyuan was young, on his birthday, which was the sixth day of the eighth month, he would arrange for a Buddhist lecture and vegetarian banquet; but ever since Lady Ruan passed away, he stopped doing it.[2]

---

1 "Already gone" can mean "already dead." This is why the son's answer was laughed at by contemporaries.
2 Xiao Yi, Emperor Yuan, was born on September 16, 508. Lady Ruan was Ruan Lingying 阮令嬴 (477–543/540), Xiao Yi's mother.

VI.43

人有憂疾，則呼天地父母，自古而然。今
世諱避，觸途急切。而江東士庶，痛則稱
禰。禰是父之廟號，父在無容稱廟，父歿
何容輒呼？蒼頡篇有侑字，訓詁云："痛
而謼也，音羽罪反。"今北人痛則呼之。
聲類音于耒反，今南人痛或呼之。此二音
隨其鄉俗，並可行也。

VI.44

梁世被繫劾者，子孫弟姪，皆詣闕三日，
露跣陳謝；子孫有官，自陳解職。子則草
屩麤衣，蓬頭垢面，周章道路，要候執
事，叩頭流血，申訴冤枉。若配徒隸，諸
子並立草庵於所署門，不敢寧宅，動經旬
日，官司驅遣，然後始退。

1 Cang Jie is the name of the legendary creator of writing and historian of the Yellow Emperor. The *Cang Jie pian* is the name of a philological work attributed to Li Si 李斯 (d. 208 BCE). The character *xiao* is regarded by scholars as a graphic error for *you* 侑, pronounced as hjuwH in Middle Chinese (see Zhou Fagao 27a–b; Wang Liqi 118).

VI.43

Since ancient times, when people are anguished or sick, they would call out to heaven and earth, father and mother. Nowadays, people observe taboos strictly, so gentry and commoners to the east of the Yangzi River cry out "Ni" when they are in pain. Now, "Ni" is the father's posthumous title in the ancestral temple. If one's father is still alive, one cannot refer to him by his posthumous title; if the father is already gone, how can one call out to him so casually? The *Cang Jie pian* contains the character *xiao*;[1] the gloss states that it indicates the sound of crying out in pain, and should be pronounced as a combination of [the initial sound of] *yu* [MC hjuX] and [the final sound of] *zui* [MC dzwojH].[2] Today northerners make this sound when they are in pain. *Sound by Categories* gives its pronunciation as a combination of *yu* [MC hju] and *lei* [MC lwijX].[3] Today southerners make this sound when they are in pain. These two sounds respectively follow the regional customs and can be both used when necessary.

VI.44

During the Liang dynasty, when a man was impeached and imprisoned, his sons, grandsons, younger brothers, and nephews would go to the court and stay there for three days, wearing no cap or shoes, apologizing and asking for forgiveness. If his sons and grandsons occupied any office, they would hand in their resignations. His sons, wearing straw sandals and dressed in coarse clothes, with disheveled hair and unwashed face, would nervously wait on the road for the official in charge and, upon seeing him, would knock their head on the ground until it bled and state their case. If a man was sentenced to hard labor, his sons would all construct a straw hut outside the gate of the government office, not daring to stay comfortably in their house. They would carry on in that manner for a dozen days until being driven away.

---

2 Pronunciation began to be marked by giving the combination of the initial sound of a word and the final sound of another word in early medieval China.

3 *Sound by Categories* (*Sheng lei*) is a phonological work, now lost, authored by Li Deng 李登 (fl. third century).

VI.45

江南諸憲司彈人事，事雖不重，而以教義
見辱者，或被輕繫而身死獄戶者，皆為怨
讎，子孫三世不交通矣。到洽為御史中
丞，初欲彈劉孝綽，其兄溉先與劉善，苦
諫不得，乃詣劉涕泣告別而去。

VI.46

兵凶戰危，非安全之道。古者，天子喪服
以臨師，將軍鑿凶門而出。父祖伯叔，若
在軍陣，貶損自居，不宜奏樂讌會及婚冠
吉慶事也。若居圍城之中，憔悴容色，除
去飾玩，常為臨深履薄之狀焉。

VI.45

In the south, when censors impeached someone, even if it might not be a grave case, the accused could be disgraced according to the principles of moral teaching or jailed for a minor offence and die in prison. Should that happen, the family of the accused would become enemies of the family of the accuser, and their sons and grandsons would sever relationship for three generations. When Dao Qia was appointed Palace Aide to the Censor-in-Chief, he was going to impeach Liu Xiaochuo.[1] Qia's elder brother, Gai, was a good friend with Liu. He tried his best to talk Qia out of it but did not succeed. He subsequently paid a visit to Liu and bid farewell to him in tears.

VI.46

Weaponry is inauspicious and warfare is dangerous; they are not the way to safety. In ancient times, the Son of Heaven would supervise the troops in mourning clothes, and a general would go to war through a "baleful gate."[2] Should one's father, grandfather, senior paternal uncle, or junior paternal uncle serve in the army on the battlefield, one should live modestly and refrain from playing music, giving parties, or holding festive celebrations such as a wedding or capping ceremony.[3] If any [of those relatives] is in a besieged city, one should be haggard in appearance and get rid of all his ornaments and luxury items, looking anxious and vigilant as if he were standing on the edge of a deep precipice or walking on thin ice.

---

1 Dao Qia (477–527) was made Censor in 525 and had a reputation for strictness. He and his brother Dao Gai (477–548) were both known for their literary talent. Liu Xiaochuo (481–539) was a famous court writer in the Liang.

2 A "baleful gate" is the northern gate of a city through which funeral processions make their exit. A general leaves for battle through the "baleful gate" to show his determination to fight to the death.

3 The capping ceremony was held when a man reached twenty *sui* to mark his entering of adulthood.

VI.47

父母疾篤,醫雖賤雖少,則涕泣而拜之,
以求哀也。梁孝元在江州,嘗有不豫,世
子方等親拜中兵參軍李猷焉。

VI.48

四海之人,結為兄弟,亦何容易。必有志
均義敵,令終如始者,方可議之。一爾之
後,命子拜伏,呼為丈人,申父交之敬;
身事彼親,亦宜加禮。比見北人,甚輕此
節,行路相逢,便定昆季,望年觀貌,不
擇是非,至有結父為兄,託子為弟者。

VI.47

When one's parent is gravely ill, even if a physician is low-born or very young, one ought to prostrate before him in tears and beg for mercy. While serving as governor of Jiangzhou, Liang Emperor Xiaoyuan once fell sick.[1] His heir, Fangdeng, personally made obeisance to Liu You, who at the time was merely the Adjutant in the Inner Troops Section on the prince's staff.[2]

VI.48

How can it ever be easy for "men within the four seas" to form brother-hood?[3] Only those who share the same goals, cherish the same principles, and remain constant from beginning to end may talk about doing such a thing. Once brotherhood is formed, one should order one's sons to make obeisance to the sworn brother, call him "Elder," and extend to him the respect due the father's friends. One should also show special politeness to the sworn brother's parents. In recent years I have observed that northerners pay very little attention to such etiquette. They can form brotherhood even when meeting on the road for the first time, guessing ages by looking at each other's face without consideration of right or wrong. As a result, sometimes a member of one's father's generation may become an "elder brother," or a member of one's son's generation may become a "younger brother."

---

1 Xiao Yi served as governor of Jiangzhou from 540 to 547.
2 Xiao Fangdeng (528–549) was Xiao Yi's eldest son.
3 A reference to a saying in the *Analects*: "Men within the four seas are all brothers."

VI.49

昔者,周公一沐三握髮,一飯三吐餐,以接白屋之士,一日所見者七十餘人。晉文公以沐辭豎頭須,致有圖反之誚。門不停賓,古所貴也。失教之家,閽寺無禮,或以主君寢食嗔怒,拒客未通,江南深以為恥。黃門侍郎裴之禮,好待賓客,或有此輩,對賓杖之,僮僕引接,折旋俯仰,莫不肅敬,與主無別。

VI.49

In the past, the Duke of Zhou had held wet hair in his hand three times during one bath and spat out his food three times during one meal in order to rush out and greet gentlemen of a humble status. He would receive over seventy people each day. Duke Wen of Jin, on the other hand, refused to see a lowly retainer Touxu under the pretext of hair-washing, and was henceforth vilified for "aberrant thinking."[1] Not keeping guests waiting at the door was an important etiquette prized in ancient times. Ill-bred families have rude gate-keepers who turn away a visitor without announcing him, because the master is sleeping, eating, or in a bad mood. This is regarded as a matter of deep shame in the south. Pei Zhili, Attending Secretary at the Palace Gate, treated his guests well.[2] If one of his servants did something like this, he would have him caned in front of the guest. His retainers and servants, when receiving visitors, whether bending or bowing, maintained a serious and respectful demeanor and tone, and acted toward them no differently than they did their own master.

---

1 Duke Wen of Jin (d. 628 BCE) was a feudal lord in the Spring and Autumn period who led Jin to hegemony among the feudal domains. The duke had refused to see Touxu under the pretext of hair-washing; Touxu said that when one washed one's hair, one turned one's head upside down, and thus one's thinking would become aberrant.
2 For Pei Zhili, see note to VI.33.

慕賢第七

VII.1

古人云："千載一聖，猶旦暮也；五百年
一賢，猶比髆也。"言聖賢之難得，疏闊
如此。儻遭不世明達君子，安可不攀附景
仰之乎？吾生於亂世，長於戎馬，流離播
越，聞見已多；所值名賢，未嘗不神醉魂
迷向慕之也。

VII.2

人在年少，神情未定，所與款狎，熏漬陶
染，言笑舉對，無心於學，潛移暗化，自
然似之；何況操履藝能，較明易習者也？
是以與善人居，如入芝蘭之室，久而自芳
也；與惡人居，如入鮑魚之肆，久而自臭
也。墨子悲於染絲，是之謂矣。君子必慎
交遊焉。孔子曰："無友不如己者。"
顏、閔之徒，何可世得。但優於我，便足
貴之。

---

1 This saying has appeared in various forms in a number of early texts.
2 A reference to a remark attributed to Confucius in *Shuo yuan* 說苑 (*Garden of Persuasions*) compiled by Liu Xiang 劉向 (79–8 BCE).

VII. Admiring Worthies

VII.1

The ancients said, "If there is but one sage emerging every one thousand years, it is as fast as from morning to evening; if there is but one worthy man emerging every five hundred years, it feels as if they stood shoulder to shoulder."[1] This tells us how scarce sages and worthy men are, and how far apart they appear in history. That being the case, if one encounters an extraordinary and wise gentleman, how can one not attach oneself to him and look up to him? I was born in chaotic times and grew up among military horses. Dislocated, wandering from place to place, I have heard and seen a great deal. Whenever I came across a talented, well-known man, I would invariably become captivated and filled with admiration for him.

VII.2

When a man is young, his spirit and emotions are not yet settled. The friends with whom he closely associates are able to mold and color him, influence and shape him. He may not emulate them deliberately, but he can be moved and transformed unconsciously, and naturally becomes like them in talking, laughing, and carrying himself. How much more so in matters such as conduct and skills that are clearer to see and easier to mimic? Therefore, if one consorts with good people, it is like entering a chamber of basil and eupatorium, and after a while one becomes naturally sweet-scented; if one consorts with wicked people, it is like entering an abalone shop, and after a while one becomes naturally stinky.[2] That is why Mozi lamented the dyed silk.[3] A gentleman must be cautious in choosing friends. Confucius said, "Do not befriend those who are inferior to yourself."[4] Yet, how can one get to meet a Yan Hui or a Min Sun in every generation?[5] As long as a friend is superior to me in some way, he should be valued.

---

3 Mozi, Confucius's contemporary, commented on the white silk's susceptibility to dyes (in the same way a man is susceptible to external influences).

4 This is a remark in the *Analects*.

5 Yan Hui and Min Sun were two of the most outstanding disciples of Confucius.

VII.3

世人多蔽，貴耳賤目，重遙輕近。少長周旋，如有賢哲，每相狎侮，不加禮敬；他鄉異縣，微藉風聲，延頸企踵，甚於飢渴。校其長短，覈其精麤，或能彼不能此矣。所以魯人謂孔子為東家丘。昔虞國宮之奇，少長於君，君狎之，不納其諫，以至亡國，不可不留心也。

VII.4

用其言，棄其身，古人所恥。凡有一言一行，取於人者，皆顯稱之，不可竊人之美，以為己力；雖輕雖賤者，必歸功焉。竊人之財，刑辟之所處；竊人之美，鬼神之所責。

---

1 Alternatively, the sentence could be interpreted as: "When we compare the two men's strengths and weaknesses and examine their fine and coarse qualities, the one from afar may not compare favorably with the one nearby after all." See Additional Notes.

2 Qiu was the personal name of Confucius. This is from a story in *School Sayings of Confucius* (*Kongzi jiayu* 孔子家語), a collection of sayings of Confucius from the Han whose current version was compiled by the third-century scholar Wang Su 王肅 (see XIX.17).

VII.3

People in the world have many delusions: they cherish what they hear but scorn what they see; they value what is distant and overlook what is close. If the friend they grow up with is a wise and talented man, they treat him with familiarity and without respect. But if it is a man from another place, as soon as they hear the least rumor of his reputation, they crane their neck and stand on tiptoe with a longing for him that is more intense than hunger and thirst. When they compare the two men's strengths and weaknesses and examine their fine and coarse qualities, they may admire one but disparage the other.[1] This is why the people of Lu referred to Confucius as "that fellow Qiu from the eastern neighborhood."[2] Gong Zhiqi of the state of Yu was a friend of his ruler since their youth, and the ruler treated him with casual intimacy and so did not adopt his advice, which resulted in the fall of his domain.[3] You must exercise caution in this.

VII.4

To adopt a man's words but discard his person was considered shameful by the ancients.[4] If you ever adopt one remark from another man or emulate one act, you must state it explicitly. You must not steal another man's accomplishment and pretend that it is your own. No matter how insignificant or low-born that person is, you should give credit where credit is due. Stealing another's money is punishable by law; stealing another's accomplishment is condemned by gods and spirits.

---

3 In 658 BCE and 655 BCE, the state of Jin twice requested permission to go through the state of Yu in order to carry out an attack on the state of Guo. Gong Zhiqi advised the lord of Yu not to grant permission, but the lord of Yu refused to listen to him. Jin then conquered Yu after the conquest of Guo.

4 This refers to a story recorded in the *Zuo Tradition* that Sichuan 駟歂, a grandee of the state of Zheng, executed Deng Xi 鄧析 but adopted his ideas. This was censured as unjust.

VII.5a

梁孝元前在荊州，有丁覘者，洪亭民耳，
頗善屬文，殊工草隸；孝元書記，一皆使
典之。軍府輕賤，多未之重，恥令子弟以
為楷法，時云"丁君十紙，不敵王君一
字。"吾雅愛其手跡，常所寶持。

VII.5b

孝元嘗遣典籤惠編送文章示蕭祭酒，祭酒
問云："君王比賜書翰，及寫詩筆，殊為
佳手，姓名為誰？那得都無聲問？"編以
實答。子雲歎曰："此人後生無比，遂不
為世所稱，亦是奇事。"於是聞者稍復刮
目。稍仕至尚書儀曹郎，末為晉安王侍
讀，隨王東下。及西臺陷歿，簡牘湮散，
丁亦尋卒於揚州；前所輕者，後思一紙，
不可得矣。

---

1 Xiao Yi had served as governor of Jingzhou twice; this refers to his first tenure from 526 to 532. Hongting is in modern Hubei.
2 Xiao Yi was in charge of the military affairs of six prefectures including Jingzhou, so the princely establishment is also referred to as a "military headquarters."

VII.5a

When Liang Emperor Xiaoyuan was governor of Jingzhou, he employed Ding Chan, a commoner from Hongting.[1] Ding Chan was good at literary composition and skilled at calligraphy in draft script and clerical script. Emperor Yuan charged him with copying out all his correspondence and documents. The staff of the military headquarters looked down on his low birth and did not value his skill,[2] and people were too ashamed to allow their children to emulate him. At the time there was even a saying, "Ten sheets of paper by Mr. Ding cannot compare with a single character by Mr. Wang."[3] I loved Ding Chan's calligraphy and cherished his writings.

VII.5b

Emperor Xiaoyuan once sent Huibian, the Document Clerk, to take his literary compositions to Libationer Xiao.[4] Xiao asked, "The recent letters as well as the poems and prose pieces from the prince were all copied out with a beautiful hand. What is the scribe's name? How come he is not known at all?" Huibian told him the truth. Ziyun said with a sigh, "This man is without equal in the younger generation. How strange that he does not enjoy any reputation in the world!" When people heard of this, they began to have a somewhat higher opinion of him. He was made the Gentleman Attendant in the Section of Ceremonies in the Imperial Secretariat, and eventually became a tutor to the Prince of Jin'an and moved east with the prince.[5] After the western capital [Jiangling] fell, books and writings were destroyed and scattered, and Ding died in Yangzhou shortly after. People used to hold his calligraphy in contempt, but now they can no longer get hold of a single piece of it.

---

3 Mr. Wang refers to Wang Bao 王褒 (510–576), a member of the Langye Wang clan, which was one of the most prestigious aristocratic clans of the Southern Dynasties. He was a famous poet, writer, and calligrapher.

4 This refers to Xiao Ziyun 蕭子雲 (487–549), a member of the royal family of the Southern Qi (479–502) and an acclaimed calligrapher.

5 Prince of Jin'an was Xiao Yi's elder brother Xiao Gang 蕭綱 (503–551, Liang Emperor Jianwen 簡文, r. 549–551). He was made governor of Yangzhou in 530 and thus moved east to the capital region from his earlier post as governor of Yongzhou (in modern Hubei).

VII.6

侯景初入建業，臺門雖閉，公私草擾，各
不自全。太子左衛率羊侃坐東掖門，部分
經略，一宿皆辦，遂得百餘日抗拒兇逆。
於時城內四萬許人，王公朝士，不下一
百，便是恃侃一人安之，其相去如此。古
人云："巢父、許由，讓於天下；市道小
人，爭一錢之利。"亦已懸矣。

VII.7

齊文宣帝即位數年，便沈湎縱恣，略無綱
紀。尚能委政尚書令楊遵彥，內外清謐，
朝野晏如，各得其所，物無異議，終天保
之朝。遵彥後為孝昭所戮，刑政於是衰
矣。

---

1 Hou Jing (503–552), a northern general, capitulated to the Liang in 548 but
rebelled soon afterward. He besieged the capital and finally captured it in the
spring of 549 (see Introduction). The Hou Jing Rebellion dealt a fatal blow to
the Liang rule. Jianye was an old name of Jiankang, and the Palace City was the
inner city of Jiankang where the imperial palace complex was located.

2 For Yang Kan, see note to VI.19. The East Gate was a side gate to the right of
the South Gate of the Palace City.

VII.6

When Hou Jing first entered Jianye, although the gates of the Palace City were closed against him, officials and commoners were all in a panic, unable to protect themselves.[1] Yang Kan, Commandant of the Left Guards of the Crown Prince, sat at the East Gate and took charge of the situation.[2] He made defense plans and gave instructions, and everything was ready overnight. As a result, the capital was able to resist the fierce rebels for more than a hundred days. At the time, there were well over forty thousand people in the city, and no less than one hundred princes, nobles, and courtiers; but it was up to Yang Kan alone to keep them safe. How disparate were their abilities! The ancients said, "Chaofu and Xu You declined the rule of the world, whereas the petty men of the marketplace fight over a single coin."[3] The difference between men can be indeed as drastic as that.

VII.7

A few years after the Qi Emperor Wenxuan took the throne, he began to indulge in drinking and to act without restraint.[4] Nevertheless, he was able to entrust governance to Yang Zunyan, Director of the Imperial Secretariat, who managed to maintain order inside and outside the court.[5] Officials and commoners were all content, and everyone was in the right place. There was no discord throughout the Tianbao era [550–559]. As soon as Zunyan was killed by Emperor Xiaozhao, the government went downhill.

---

3 Chaofu and Xu You were legendary ancient recluses who declined the offer of the throne made by the sage-emperor Yao.

4 Qi Emperor Wenxuan was Gao Yang 高洋 (529–559, r. 550–559), the founder of the Northern Qi.

5 Zunyan was the courtesy name of Yang Yin 楊愔 (511–560), an able and loyal minister trusted by Emperor Wenxuan. After Emperor Wenxuan died, Yang Zunyan was killed by Emperor Wenxuan's younger brother Gao Yan 高演 (535–561, Emperor Xiaozhao, r. 559–561). Gao Yan subsequently deposed his nephew and became emperor himself.

VII.8

斛律明月，齊朝折衝之臣，無罪被誅，將
士解體，周人始有吞齊之志，關中至今譽
之。此人用兵，豈止萬夫之望而已哉！國
之存亡，係其生死。

VII.9

張延雋之為晉州行臺左丞，匡維主將，鎮
撫疆場，儲積器用，愛活黎民，隱若敵國
矣。眾小不得行志，同力遷之；既代之
後，公私擾亂，周師一舉，此鎮先平。齊
國之亡，啟於是矣。

VII.8

Hulü Mingyue was the kind of minister in the [Northern] Qi court who could "keep the enemy's chariots back."[1] After he was unjustly executed, the army fell apart, and the people of Zhou began to make plans against Qi. People within the Pass still praise him today. How could such a brilliant military strategist be only admired by ten thousand men? Truly the survival of the entire realm was tied to his life and death.

VII.9

When Zhang Yanjun was Assistant Director of the Left at the Branch Department of State Affairs at Jinzhou, he counseled and defended the commander-in-chief, pacified the border region, kept a good storage of weapons and supplies, and lovingly nurtured the common folk.[2] He truly played a crucial role in defending the realm.[3] [With him in charge,] the various evil-doers could not act as they pleased, so they conspired together to remove him. Once he was replaced, chaos broke out in public and private arenas. When the Zhou army invaded Qi, this region was the first to be conquered. That, I am afraid, was the beginning of the end for the Qi.

---

1 Mingyue was the courtesy name of Hulü Guang 斛律光 (515–572), the best general that the Northern Qi had. His death was celebrated by the Zhou emperor who later said he would never have been able to conquer Qi had Hulü Mingyue been alive.

2 Little else is known about Zhang Yanjun (ca. 570s).

3 Literally, "as formidable as a kingdom equal in power."

勉學第八

VIII.1

自古明王聖帝，猶須勤學，況凡庶乎！此事遍於經史，吾亦不能鄭重，聊舉近世切要，以啟寤汝耳。

VIII.2

士大夫子弟，數歲已上，莫不被教，多者或至禮、傳，少者不失詩、論。及至冠婚，體性稍定；因此天機，倍須訓誘。有志尚者，遂能磨礪，以就素業；無履立者，自茲墮慢，便為凡人。

VIII. Encouraging Study

VIII.1

From ancient times, even wise princes and sage emperors still have had to be diligent in study, let alone ordinary men! Examples abound in the classics and histories, and I do not wish to be repetitive. I will simply mention some of the essentials from modern times with the hope of enlightening you.

VIII.2

The sons of the gentry all begin to receive an education when they are a few years old. Those who study more are taught the ritual classics and the commentaries; even those who study less are taught the *Poems* and the *Analects*.[1] When they reach the age of capping and marriage, their body and mind are basically formed and stabilized; this is when they need more instructions and guidance to take advantage of their faculties. Those with noble aspirations can thus refine themselves and accomplish the pure enterprise; those without a strong character will become lazy and careless, and hence become ordinary men.

---

1 The commentaries refer to the three commentaries on the *Spring and Autumn Annals* (春秋三傳): the *Zuo Tradition* 左傳, the *Gongyang Tradition* 公羊傳, and the *Guliang Tradition* 穀梁傳. The *Poems* is the *Classic of Poetry.*

VIII.3a

人生在世，會當有業：農民則計量耕稼，商賈則討論貨賄，工巧則致精器用，伎藝則沈思法術，武夫則慣習弓馬，文士則講議經書。多見士大夫恥涉農商，羞務工伎，射則不能穿札，筆則纔記姓名，飽食醉酒，忽忽無事，以此銷日，以此終年。

VIII.3b

或因家世餘緒，得一階半級，便自為足，全忘修學。及有吉凶大事，議論得失，蒙然張口，如坐雲霧；公私宴集，談古賦詩，塞默低頭，欠伸而已。有識旁觀，代其入地。何惜數年勤學，長受一生愧辱哉。

VIII.3a

A man living in this world must have a profession: a farmer plans for plowing and planting; a merchant talks about goods and commodities; a craftsman invests his energy in tools and utensils; an artist contemplates methods and techniques;[1] a warrior practices archery and horsemanship; a man of letters discourses on classics. I have seen many members of the gentry who are ashamed of dealing with farming and trading and have no particular skills; in archery they cannot penetrate a coat of leather armor; in writing they can only manage their own names. Eating their fill and drunk on ale, they pass their time in a daze having nothing to do, thus whiling away days and ending their years.

VIII.3b

Some of them may receive a minor office through the legacy of their forebears, and they content themselves with it and forget all about studying. On those occasions when an auspicious or inauspicious affair requires discussion of right and wrong, their mouths hang open in a stupor and they look as if sitting in a fog.[2] Whether at a public banquet or a private gathering, when others are discussing history or composing poetry, they fall into silence and lower their head, and can only yawn and stretch [in boredom]. They make an insightful observer want to hide in the ground on their behalf. Why on earth would they begrudge a few years of diligent study and suffer humiliation for a lifetime like that?

---

1 By an "artist" Yan Zhitui refers to a man well-versed in a particular skill, such as divination or chess-playing. This is in contrast with "craftsmanship" such as that of a carpenter.
2 Auspicious affairs refer to the annual sacrifices, capping or marriage ceremonies; inauspicious affairs refer to death and obsequies. The use of the etiquette and ritual appropriate to each occasion was an important matter that was often publically discussed as a topic in court debate.

VIII.4a

梁朝全盛之時，貴遊子弟，多無學術，至
於諺云："上車不落則著作，體中何如則
祕書。"無不熏衣剃面，傅粉施朱，駕長
簷車，跟高齒屐，坐棋子方褥，憑斑絲隱
囊，列器玩於左右，從容出入，望若神
仙。明經求第，則顧人答策；三九公讌，
則假手賦詩。當爾之時，亦快士也。

VIII.4b

及離亂之後，朝市遷革，銓衡選舉，非復
曩者之親；當路秉權，不見昔時之黨。求
諸身而無所得，施之世而無所用。被褐而
喪珠，失皮而露質，兀若枯木，泊若窮
流，鹿獨戎馬之間，轉死溝壑之際。當爾
之時，誠駑材也。

VIII.4a

When the Liang dynasty was at the peak of its power, many of the noble scions had so little learning that there was a saying at the time: "If you don't fall off from a carriage, you can be an Editorial Director; if you can write 'How do you do?' you can be an Imperial Librarian." The young lords would all perfume their clothes, shave their face, and apply powder and rouge; they would drive around in a carriage with a long awning and wear high-teeth clogs, sit on square mats of chessboard pattern and recline against a bolster of variegated silk, with their fancy trinkets arrayed around them. Coming and going at a leisurely pace, they looked like gods from a distance. When seeking to pass the examination for the degree of "Understanding the Classics," they would hire someone to answer the essay questions; at public banquets with the Three Dukes and the Nine Ministers, they would rely on someone else to compose poems on their behalf. At that time, they were quite the dashing gentlemen!

VIII.4b

After the disorder and dispersion, court and marketplace were changed. Those in charge of government recruitment are now no longer their relatives; the powers that be are no longer the members of their clique. Looking upon themselves, they have absolutely nothing to offer; when being applied to the world, they have no use whatsoever. Wearing coarse clothes on the outside, they nevertheless do not possess any pearls within; having lost the tiger's pelt, they expose their true substance of a sheep. Stupefied like a withered tree, shallow like an exhausted stream, they wander aimlessly in the midst of military horses and eventually die off in a ditch. At a time like this, they turn out to be nothing but losers.

VIII.5

有學藝者，觸地而安。自荒亂已來，諸見俘虜，雖百世小人，知讀論語、孝經者，尚為人師；雖千載冠冕，不曉書記者，莫不耕田養馬。以此觀之，安可不自勉耶？若能常保數百卷書，千載終不為小人也。

VIII.6a

夫明六經之指，涉百家之書，縱不能增益德行，敦厲風俗，猶為一藝，得以自資。父兄不可常依，鄉國不可常保，一旦流離，無人庇廕，當自求諸身耳。諺曰："積財千萬，不如薄伎在身。"

VIII.5

A man who has learning and skills can find ease anywhere he goes. In the recent times of chaos, of those who have become captives, if one knows how to read the *Analects* and the *Classic of Filial Piety*, be he from a family that has been lowly for a hundred generations, he can still be a teacher to someone else; but if a man does not know how to write, be he from a family that has been patrician for a thousand years, he will still have to plow the field and tend horses. Seeing this, how can you not exert yourselves? If you can manage to hold onto several hundred scrolls of books, you will never sink to the lower depths of society.

VIII.6a

If one understands the meaning of the Six Classics and wades through the works of a hundred schools, even if it does not further enhance one's virtuous conduct or transform the people's customs, it is a useful skill that one can draw upon. One's father and elder brother cannot always be depended on; one's home state cannot always be held onto. If one day you are displaced, there will be no one to shade and protect you, and you will have to rely on yourself. A proverb says, "Accumulating tens of millions of cash is not as good as having one minor skill."

VIII.6b

伎之易習而可貴者，無過讀書也。世人不問愚智，皆欲識人之多，見事之廣，而不肯讀書，是猶求飽而嬾營饌，欲暖而惰裁衣也。夫讀書之人，自羲、農已來，宇宙之下，凡識幾人，凡見幾事，生民之成敗好惡，固不足論，天地所不能藏，鬼神所不能隱也。

VIII.7

有客難主人曰："吾見彊弩長戟，誅罪安民，以取公侯者有矣；文義習吏，匡時富國，以取卿相者有矣；學備古今，才兼文武，身無祿位，妻子飢寒者，不可勝數，安足貴學乎？"

VIII.6b

Among skills that are easy to master and yet much prized, nothing can compare with reading books. People in this world, be they stupid or smart, all desire to be able to discern the character of many men and to acquire a wide range of experiences, yet they do not want to read: that is just like seeking to be full but being too lazy to cook a meal, or seeking to be warm but being too indolent to make clothes. Those who read get to observe numerous people and witness numerous events [through books] from the times of emperors Fu Xi and Shennong and in the entire universe.[1] It goes without saying that they understand clearly the successes and failures as well as the likes and dislikes of mankind. Indeed nothing between heaven and earth could be hidden from them, not even by gods and spirits.

VIII.7

A visitor challenges his host, saying, "I have seen men who are enfeoffed as a duke or a marquis because they can punish evil and bring peace with a strong bow and a long halberd; I have seen men who are made a minister or a premier because, well-versed in cultural matters and skilled in administration, they can correct policies and enrich the state. But there are also numerous men who, erudite about the past and present, talented in both civil and martial affairs, do not have an official position and a salary, and their wife and children suffer from hunger and cold. Why should studying be prized at all?"

---

1 Fu Xi and Shennong are legendary sage emperors from high antiquity.

VIII.8a

主人對曰："夫命之窮達，猶金玉木石也；脩以學藝，猶磨瑩雕刻也。金玉之磨瑩，自美其礦璞；木石之段塊，自醜其雕刻。安可言木石之雕刻，乃勝金玉之礦璞哉？不得以有學之貧賤，比於無學之富貴也。

VIII.8b

"且負甲為兵，咋筆為吏，身死名滅者如牛毛，角立傑出者如芝草；握素披黃，吟道詠德，苦辛無益者如日蝕，逸樂名利者如秋荼，豈得同年而語矣。且又聞之：生而知之者上，學而知之者次。所以學者，欲其多知明達耳。必有天才，拔群出類，為將則闇與孫武、吳起同術，執政則懸得管仲、子產之教，雖未讀書，吾亦謂之學矣。今子既不能然，不師古之蹤跡，猶蒙被而臥耳。"

VIII.8a

The host replies, "The good or bad fortune in one's predestined fate is like gold and jade or wood and rock; to refine it with learning and skill is like polishing and carving. The polished gold and jade are naturally more beautiful than the unpolished gold and jade; the uncarved wood and rock are naturally more unsightly than the carved wood or rock. Yet, how can you say that the carved wood and rock are better than unpolished gold and jade? Similarly, we cannot compare the poverty of those who have learning with the riches of those who do not have learning.

VIII.8b

"Besides, soldiers wearing their armor and clerks chewing their brushes who die without leaving behind a name are as numerous as the hair of an ox, and those who stick out like a pair of horns and become prominent are as few as the numinous *zhi* plant. Nevertheless, if one can hold silk scrolls in hand and open up writings on yellowed paper, ponder morality and contemplate virtue, it would be as rare as a solar eclipse to work painstakingly to no avail, but as common as milk thistles in autumn to enjoy fame and fortune.[1] How can you then speak of them in one breath? In addition, I have heard that the best thing is to be born with innate knowledge and the second best thing is to study and gain knowledge. The reason for studying is to become knowledgeable and wise. Now, if one is a genius outshining his peers, who as a general deploys military strategies like a Sun Wu and a Wu Qi or as a governor embodies the teachings of Guan Zhong and Zichan, then even if he does not read a single book, I will still regard him as a learned man.[2] But since you are not like that, if you furthermore refuse to follow the tracks of the ancients, you will be as though lying down with bedcovers pulled over your head."[3]

---

1 Yellowed paper was paper that had been treated with a yellow dye, which acted as insecticide so that insects would not eat through the paper. Milk thistles grow profusely in autumn and so are a metaphor for something very common.
2 Sun Wu (fl. 510s–490s BCE) and Wu Qi (d. 381 BCE) were famous generals; Guan Zhong (d. 645 BCE) and Zichan (d. 522 BCE) were famous statesmen.
3 In other words, staying in the dark.

VIII.9a

人見鄰里親戚有佳快者，使子弟慕而學
之，不知使學古人，何其蔽也哉？世人但
見跨馬被甲，長矟彊弓，便云我能為將；
不知明乎天道，辯乎地利，比量逆順，鑒
達興亡之妙也。但知承上接下，積財聚
穀，便云我能為相；不知敬鬼事神，移風
易俗，調節陰陽，薦舉賢聖之至也。

VIII.9a

When people see an outstanding person in their neighborhood or among their relatives, they instruct their sons and younger brothers to respect and emulate him, but they do not know enough to have them learn from the ancients – how foolish they are! They only know that one can be a general if he is able to ride a horse, wear a coat of armor, wield a long halberd, and pull a strong bow; but they fail to understand the wonderful use of comprehending the ways of heaven, recognizing the advantages of the terrain, evaluating the pros and cons of a situation, and grasping the principles of rise and fall. They only know that one can be a minister if he is able to assist the ruler, manage subordinates, accumulate wealth, and store grain; but they fail to understand that the nuances of the position involve serving gods and spirits with respect, transforming the people's customs, harmonizing *yin* and *yang* forces, and recommending worthy men to offices.

VIII.9b

但知私財不入,公事夙辦,便云我能治
民;不知誠己刑物,執轡如組,反風滅
火,化鴟為鳳之術也。但知抱令守律,早
刑時捨,便云我能平獄;不知同轅觀罪,
分劍追財,假言而姦露,不問而情得之察
也。

VIII.9b

They only know that a man can govern the people if he is able to abstain from profiting his private pocket and deal with public affairs swiftly, but they fail to understand the methods of being sincere in one's ways to teach the people by example, holding the reins of state as easily as a set of woven ribbons, turning the direction of the wind around to extinguish a fire, and transforming an owl into a phoenix.[1] They only know that one can be a good judge if he adheres to the legal codes, metes out punishment quickly, and exercises leniency in a timely manner; they fail to understand the wise insight in the case of tying the offenders to the same shaft of a carriage to examine their crimes,[2] the case of taking away one's inheritance because of a contested sword,[3] the case of making up a lie to expose falsehood,[4] or the case of discovering the truth by using no interrogation.[5]

---

1 To hold the reins of state as easily as a set of woven ribbons is a line taken verbatim from a poem in the *Classic of Poetry*. Turning the direction of the wind to extinguish a fire refers to a story about Liu Kun 劉昆 (d. 57 CE), a virtuous magistrate in the Eastern Han who allegedly extinguished fires by kowtowing in front of the flames. The owl was considered an unfilial bird; the transformation of an owl into a phoenix refers to another Eastern Han virtuous magistrate, Qiu Lan 仇覽 (fl. second century), who moved an unfilial son to filial piety.

2 It is unclear what Yan Zhitui is alluding to.

3 A wealthy man died leaving all his wealth to his grown daughter and only a sword to his infant son, and said that the son should receive the sword when he reached fifteen *sui*. The daughter, however, refused to give the sword to the son when the son reached the age of fifteen, and the son sued the daughter. The magistrate was the wise official He Wu 何武 (d. 3 CE), who decided that the daughter was too covetous and it must have been the father's will to give the family property to the son.

4 This is supposedly a story about Li Chong 李崇 (d. 525), a judicious Northern Wei official. Two men had once fought over a kidnapped child and each claimed to be the father; Li Chong told them the child had died, and gave the child back to the man who cried sadly and punished the man who did not show any sign of grief.

5 Lu Yun 陸雲 (262–303), famous Western Jin writer and Lu Ji's brother (see note to VI.24), once had a woman arrested whose husband had died of murder. He released the woman after ten days without any inquiry, but had her followed with the instruction that both the woman and any man talking to her shortly after she left prison must be apprehended and taken back. The man turned out to be the woman's lover who had plotted with her to murder the husband.

VIII.9c

爰及農商工賈，廝役奴隸，釣魚屠肉，飯
牛牧羊，皆有先達，可為師表，博學求
之，無不利於事也。

VIII.10a

夫所以讀書學問，本欲開心明目，利於行
耳。未知養親者，欲其觀古人之先意承
顏，怡聲下氣，不憚劬勞，以致甘腝，惕
然憯懼，起而行之也。未知事君者，欲其
觀古人之守職無侵，見危授命，不忘誠
諫，以利社稷，惻然自念，思欲效之也。

VIII.9c

Down to farmers, merchants, craftsmen, servants, slaves, fisherman, butchers, cowherds, and shepherds, there are wise ones among them all who can be treated as one's teachers and role models. If you seek knowledge widely, you will always find ways of benefiting your life and career.

VIII.10a

The reason for reading and studying is to open one's mind and sharpen one's eyes in order to improve one's conduct. For those who do not know how to care for their parents, we want them to see how the ancients anticipated the parents' wishes and watched their facial expressions, spoke to their parents with an agreeable voice and a gentle air, and spared no effort to bring them delicious and soft foods; thus they may become disconcerted and feel ashamed of themselves, and begin to do the same things [as the ancients did]. For those who do not know how to serve their sovereign, we want them to see how the ancients adhered to their duty without transgression, gave up their lives in a crisis, and never forgot to offer the ruler advice and admonition in order to benefit the state; thus they may reflect on themselves with sadness and wish to emulate the ancients.

VIII.10b

素驕奢者，欲其觀古人之恭儉節用，卑以
自牧，禮為教本，敬者身基，瞿然自失，
斂容抑志也。素鄙吝者，欲其觀古人之貴
義輕財，少私寡慾，忌盈惡滿，賙窮卹
匱，赧然悔恥，積而能散也。素暴悍者，
欲其觀古人之小心黜己，齒弊舌存，含垢
藏疾，尊賢容眾，苶然沮喪，若不勝衣
也。素怯懦者，欲其觀古人之達生委命，
彊毅正直，立言必信，求福不回，勃然奮
厲，不可恐懾也。

VIII.10c

歷茲以往，百行皆然。縱不能淳，去泰去
甚。學之所知，施無不達。

VIII.10b

For those who are supercilious and extravagant, we want them to see how the ancients were reverent and frugal, regarded humility as a guiding principle in self-cultivation, took decorum as the basis of education, and considered respectfulness as the foundation of one's self-identity; thus they may feel a sense of alarm and loss, assume a somber appearance, and restrain their desires. For those who are mean and stingy, we want them to see how the ancients valued integrity but scorned wealth, harbored no self-interest and few desires, had an aversion to things at their fullness, helped people in need and gave to the impoverished; thus they may with a blush feel regret and embarrassed, and be able to redistribute what they have accumulated. For those who are fierce and violent, we want them to see how the ancients, understanding that the tongue survives while the teeth decay, were cautious and self-effacing, tolerant and forgiving, respecting the worthy but putting up with the common men; thus they may become deflated and downcast, as if they could not bear the weight of their clothes. For those who are timid and cowardly, we want them to see how the ancients understood life and entrusted themselves to fate, remained upright and determined, kept their promises, and never deviated from the right path in seeking good fortune; thus they may rise stimulated and fired up, and henceforth refuse to be intimidated.

VIII.10c

From the above examples one may make a deduction about all one hundred conducts. Even if one cannot be perfect, one can at least get rid of excessiveness and extremity. The knowledge acquired from study can be applied to anything and everything in life.

VIII.11

今世人讀書者，但能言之，不能行之，忠
孝無聞，仁義不足；加以斷一條訟，不必
得其理；宰千戶縣，不必理其民；問其造
屋，不必知楣橫而梲豎也；問其為田，不
必知稷早而黍遲也；吟嘯談謔，諷詠辭
賦，事既優閑，材增迂誕，軍國經綸，略
無施用：故為武人俗吏所共嗤詆，良由是
乎。

VIII.12

夫學者所以求益耳。見人讀數十卷書，便
自高大，凌忽長者，輕慢同列；人疾之如
讎敵，惡之如鴟梟。如此以學自損，不如
無學也。

VIII.11

Nowadays those who read books can only talk but are unable to put knowledge into practice. Unknown for loyalty and filial piety, they are also found inadequate in benevolence and integrity. Furthermore, in judging a lawsuit they are unable to grasp the principle; put in charge of a small county of a thousand households, they are unable to govern the people properly. When asked about building a house, they do not know that lintel is horizontal and strut is vertical; when asked about plowing the field, they do not know that millet is planted early and glutinous rice is planted late. They chant and whistle, converse and jest, recite and intone poetic expositions. They are slow and laid-back in handling things, and their abilities are impractical. In martial matters and state affairs, they have no use whatsoever. They are despised and derided by soldiers and clerks truly for these very reasons.

VIII.12

The purpose of study is to benefit oneself. Yet I have seen people who, after reading several dozens of scrolls, become arrogant, slight their elders, and ridicule their peers. Others resent them like enemies and loathe them like owls. To thus bring harm to oneself through study, one might as well not study at all.

VIII.13

古之學者為己，以補不足也；今之學者為
人，但能說之也。古之學者為人，行道以
利世也；今之學者為己，脩身以求進也。
夫學者猶種樹也，春玩其華，秋登其實；
講論文章，春華也，脩身利行，秋實也。

VIII.14

人生小幼，精神專利，長成已後，思慮散
逸，固須早教，勿失機也。吾七歲時，誦
靈光殿賦，至於今日，十年一理，猶不遺
忘；二十之外，所誦經書，一月廢置，便
至荒蕪矣。

VIII.13

In ancient times, a man studied for the sake of himself, with a view of making up for what he lacked; in modern times, a man studies for the sake of others, with a view of showing off in conversation and nothing more. In ancient times, a man studied for the sake of others, carrying out the Way to profit the world; in modern times, a man studies for himself, embellishing himself to seek career advancement. Studying should be like planting a tree: one appreciates its flowers in spring and gathers its fruit in autumn. Discoursing and writing are the spring flowers; self-cultivation and self-improvement are the autumn fruit.

VIII.14

When a person is very young, his mind is focused and alert; when he grows up, his thoughts become scattered and distracted. Education must be carried out early so as not to lose the opportunity. When I was seven *sui*, I memorized the "Rhapsody on the Hall of Numinous Brilliance," and even today I can still recite it if I review it once every ten years.[1] As for the classics I read after turning twenty, I will forget them if I put them aside only for one month.

---

1 The rhapsody was composed by the Eastern Han writer Wang Yanshou 王延壽 (ca. 110s–130s). The full title is "Rhapsody (*Fu*) on the Hall of Numinous Brilliance in Lu" 魯靈光殿賦.

VIII.15a

然人有坎壈，失於盛年，猶當晚學，不可自棄。孔子云：“五十以學易，可以無大過矣。”魏武、袁遺，老而彌篤，此皆少學而至老不倦也。曾子七十乃學，名聞天下；荀卿五十，始來遊學，猶為碩儒；公孫弘四十餘，方讀春秋，以此遂登丞相；朱雲亦四十，始學易、論語，皇甫謐二十，始授孝經、論語，皆終成大儒，此並早迷而晚寤也。

VIII.15b

世人婚冠未學，便稱遲暮，因循面牆，亦為愚耳。幼而學者，如日出之光，老而學者，如秉燭夜行，猶賢乎瞑目而無見者也。

VIII.15a

However, a man may encounter difficult circumstances and miss his best years for study. If so, he should nevertheless apply himself to study later in life instead of giving up on himself. Confucius said, "If at fifty one studies the *Changes*, then one can be spared from major mistakes."[1] Wei Emperor Wu and Yuan Yi both studied even more intently as they advanced in years.[2] These are the examples of beginning study in youth and never growing tired of it even in old age. Master Zeng began study at seventy and became well-known throughout the realm; Master Xun began to travel for study at fifty, and still became an erudite scholar; Gongsun Hong began reading the *Spring and Autumn Annals* in his forties and finally became the prime minister through it; Zhu Yun was also forty when he began to study the *Changes* and the *Analects*; Huangfu Mi received instruction in the *Classic of Filial Piety* and the *Analects* after he turned twenty: they all became great Ru scholars in the end.[3] These are the examples of being lost in youth but awakening later in life.

VIII.15b

People in this world claim to be too late if they have not yet started studying at the age of capping and marriage, and subsequently continue being idle and "facing the wall": this is true ignorance.[4] To study at a tender age is like being illuminated by the light of the rising sun; to study in old age is like holding a candle while walking at night, which is nevertheless better than closing one's eyes and seeing nothing.

---

1 This remark is from the *Analects*.
2 Wei Emperor Wu is Cao Cao (see note to VI.12). Yuan Yi was an Eastern Han official, cousin of the warlord Yuan Shao 袁紹 (142–202).
3 Master Zeng is Zeng Shen (see IV.1). Xun Qing: see note to VI.9. Gongsun Hong (200–121 BCE) and Zhu Yun (fl. first century BCE) were both Western Han ministers. Huangfu Mi (215–282) was a Western Jin scholar and writer.
4 "Facing the wall" is a phrase in the *Book of Documents* and the *Analects* describing the benighted state of a person who does not study.

VIII.16

學之興廢，隨世輕重。漢時賢俊，皆以一
經弘聖人之道，上明天時，下該人事，用
此致卿相者多矣。末俗已來不復爾，空守
章句，但誦師言，施之世務，殆無一可。
故士大夫子弟，皆以博涉為貴，不肯專於
經業。

VIII.17

梁朝皇孫以下，總丱之年，必先入學，觀
其志尚，出身已後，便從文史，略無卒業
者。冠冕為此者，則有何胤、劉瓛、明山
賓、周捨、朱异、周弘正、賀琛、賀革、
蕭子政、劉縚等，兼通文史，不徒講說
也。洛陽亦聞崔浩、張偉、劉芳，鄴下又
見邢子才：此四儒者，雖好經術，亦以才
博擅名。如此諸賢，故為上品。

---

1 He Yin (446–531) was a scholar and writer who briefly served the Southern Qi.
Liu Huan: see note to III.6. Ming Shanbin (443–527) was a ritual specialist.
Zhou She: see note to VI.24. Zhu Yi (483–549) was Emperor Wu's favorite
courtier and an expert in ritual matters. Zhou Hongzheng (496–574), brother of
Zhou Hongrang (see note to VI.24), was a scholar and writer. He Chen (482–
550) and He Ge (479–540) were both renowned ritual specialists. Xiao Zizheng
(fl. early sixth century) had expertise in the *Classic of Changes*. Liu Tao: see note
to VI.40.

VIII.16

The flourishing and fading of study follow the times. In the Han dynasty, talented men all tried to expand the way of the sages through their expertise in one of the classics; understanding the heavenly order above and widely encompassing human affairs below, many became high ministers as a result. In a declining age this is no longer the case. Scholars keep to the chapter and verse commentaries and only repeat the words of their teachers, but nothing they know can be applied to practical matters. Hence the sons of the gentry families all prize reading widely but refuse to specialize in a single classic.

VIII.17

In the Liang dynasty, from the imperial grandsons down, a boy would be sent to school at the age of knotting up his hair for observation of his interests and aims; as soon as he entered public service, he would become a civil servant, and few would continue their study beyond that point. Those who could do so while serving in an official post included He Yin, Liu Huan, Ming Shanbin, Zhou She, Zhu Yi, Zhou Hongzheng, He Chen, He Ge, Xiao Zizheng, and Liu Tao; these gentlemen were also well-versed in literature and history, not just good at lecturing and discoursing [on the classics].[1] I have also heard of Cui Hao, Zhang Wei, and Liu Fang at Luoyang, and I have seen Xing Zicai at Ye: although these four scholars were fond of the classics, they were known for their broad learning as well.[2] Men such as them were of the highest order.

---

2 Luoyang was the Northern Wei capital from 494 to 534. Ye was the Northern Qi capital from 550 to 577. Cui Hao (381–450) was a Northern Wei minister and scholar. Zhang Wei (fl. mid-fifth century) was a well-known Northern Wei official and scholar of Confucian classics, as was Liu Fang (453–513), who was also a philologist. Xing Zicai was the courtesy name of Xing Shao 邢邵 (b. 496), famous writer who served the Northern Wei and Northern Qi.

VIII.18

以外率多田野閒人，音辭鄙陋，風操蚩拙，相與專固，無所堪能，問一言輒酬數百，責其指歸，或無要會。鄴下諺云：“博士買驢，書券三紙，未有驢字。”使汝以此為師，令人氣塞。孔子曰：“學也，祿在其中。”今勤無益之事，恐非業也。夫聖人之書，所以設教，但明練經文，粗通注義，常使言行有得，亦足為人；何必“仲尼居”即須兩紙疏義，燕寢講堂，亦復何在？爭此得勝，寧有益乎？光陰可惜，譬諸逝水。當博覽機要，以濟功業；必能兼美，吾無閒焉。

VIII.18

Apart from them, there are many rustic folks who are crude in accent and speech, ignorant and clumsy in manners, yet remain stubborn in their beliefs despite possessing few skills. If you ask them something in one sentence, they will answer you with several hundred words, but if you press them for the main point, they cannot give you a summary. As a Ye saying has it, "When an Erudite buys a donkey, he writes the contract in three sheets of paper, but you cannot even find the word 'donkey' in it." Should you take that as your model, I would be choked with indignation. Confucius said, "Study, and you will find emolument in it."[1] But if you diligently apply yourself to such useless study, I am afraid that will never make for a good occupation. Now, sages wrote books to teach people. As long as you understand the text of the classics and get the general meaning of the commentary, so that they can benefit your speech and action, it will be sufficient for establishing yourself. What is the point of writing a commentary in two sheets of paper on the phrase "Confucius' dwelling" and debating whether it was a sitting room or a lecture hall?[2] Even if you win such a debate, what is the use of it? Time is precious, and goes by like flowing water. You should read extensively and grasp the essentials in order to accomplish great things. Of course, if you can be good at both [practical knowledge and classical scholarship], then I will have no objection.

---

1 This remark is from the *Analects*.
2 The phrase appears at the opening of the *Classic of Filial Piety*.

VIII.19

俗間儒士，不涉群書，經緯之外，義疏而已。吾初入鄴，與博陵崔文彥交遊，嘗說王粲集中難鄭玄尚書事。崔轉為諸儒道之，始將發口，懸見排蹙，云：“文集只有詩賦銘誄，豈當論經書事乎？且先儒之中未聞有王粲也。”崔笑而退，竟不以粲集示之。

VIII.20

魏收之在議曹，與諸博士爭宗廟事，引據漢書，博士笑曰：“未聞漢書得證經術。”收便忿怒，都不復言，取韋玄成傳，擲之而起。博士一夜共披尋之，達明，乃來謝曰：“不謂玄成如此學也。”

VIII.19

The run-of-the-mill Ru scholars do not read widely. Apart from the classics and apocryphal prophetic texts, they only work on exegetical commentaries. When I first went to Ye, I became friends with Cui Wenyan of Boling.[1] With him I talked about Wang Can's criticism of Zheng Xuan's commentary on *The Book of Documents* in Wang Can's literary collection.[2] Cui conveyed our conversation to the Ru scholars. But almost as soon as he opened his mouth, there was much pushback. They said, "A literary collection only has poetry, rhapsodies, inscriptions, and eulogies. How can there be a discussion of the classics? Besides, we have never heard of a Wang Can among former Ru scholars." Cui withdrew with a chuckle, and did not even bother to show them Wang Can's collection.

VIII.20

When Wei Shou was in the Consultation Section, he argued with the Erudites about the ceremony in the ancestral temple, and cited from the *Han History* to support his point.[3] The Erudites all laughed, "We have never heard of finding supportive evidence for the classics in the *Han History*!" Wei Shou, enraged, said no more, but took out "Wei Xuancheng's Biography," threw it at them, and left.[4] The Erudites spent all evening checking it, and the next morning they came to apologize to him, saying, "We didn't realize Xuancheng was so learned."

---

1 The Cui clan of Boling (in modern Hebei) was an eminent northern clan. Cui Wenyan is unknown.
2 Wang Can (177–217) was a writer and poet well-versed in ritual matters. Zheng Xuan (127–200) was a late Eastern Han scholar and commentator.
3 Wei Shou (d. 572) was a famous northern writer and historian, the author of the *Wei History*. The *Han History* was compiled by Ban Gu (see note to VI.12).
4 Wei Xuancheng (d. 36 BCE) was a Western Han scholar official.

VIII.21a

夫老、莊之書，蓋全真養性，不肯以物累
己也。故藏名柱史，終蹈流沙；匿跡漆
園，卒辭楚相，此任縱之徒耳。何晏、王
弼，祖述玄宗，遞相誇尚，景附草靡，皆
以農、黃之化，在乎己身，周、孔之業，
棄之度外。而平叔以黨曹爽見誅，觸死權
之網也；輔嗣以多笑人被疾，陷好勝之窄
也；山巨源以蓄積取譏，背多藏厚亡之文
也；夏侯玄以才望被戮，無支離擁腫之鑒
也；

VIII.21a

As for the books of Laozi and Zhuangzi, they teach about preserving one's true self and nurturing one's nature without burdening oneself with external things. Therefore, Laozi concealed his name in being "a scribe by the pillar," and eventually went off to the desert wastes; Zhuangzi hid his tracks at Qiyuan and ultimately refused to be Chu's prime minister. These were wild fellows who followed their own heart. He Yan and Wang Bi emulated and expounded the Arcane Truth, admired and extravagantly praised each other.[1] Adhering [to Laozi and Zhuangzi] like shadow following the form or grass bending before the wind, they believed that the transformative powers of Shennong and the Yellow Emperor lay with themselves and gave no thought to the work of the Duke of Zhou and Confucius. Yet, Pingshu [He Yan] was executed for being a member of Cao Shuang's clique, and was caught in the snare of "dying for power."[2] Fusi [Wang Bi] was resented for mocking others, and fell into the trap of "loving to win." Shan Juyuan was criticized for amassing wealth, as he went against the teaching of "hoarding more, losing more."[3] Xiahou Xuan was put to death for his talent and repute, as he lacked the insight about the deformed Zhili and the unsightly tree.[4]

---

1 He Yan (d. 249), courtesy name Pingshu (see below), was well-versed in the "arcane learning" (*xuanxue*, also translated as "metaphysical learning") of *Laozi* and *Zhuangzi*. Wang Bi (226–249), courtesy name Fusi (see below), authored a commentary on *Laozi* and on the *Classic of Changes*.

2 Cao Shuang (d. 249) was a member of the Cao Wei royal family and lost his life in a power struggle with Sima Yi 司馬懿 (179–251).

3 Shan Juyuan was Shan Tao 山濤 (205–283), one of the "Seven Worthies of the Bamboo Grove." However, Shan Tao was not known as a hoarder. It is surmised that Shan Juyuan is an error for Wang Rong 王戎 (234–305), another of the "Seven Worthies."

4 Xiahou Xuan (209–254) was a cousin of Cao Shuang and also died by the hand of the Sima family. The deformed man Zhili and the unsightly tree are both from *Zhuangzi* parables about how malformed people and things get to live their natural lifespan due to their perceived uselessness.

VIII.21b

荀奉倩喪妻，神傷而卒，非鼓缶之情也；
王夷甫悼子，悲不自勝，異東門之達也；
嵇叔夜排俗取禍，豈和光同塵之流也；郭
子玄以傾動專勢，寧後身外己之風也；阮
嗣宗沈酒荒迷，乖畏途相誡之譬也；謝幼
輿賍賄黜削，違棄其餘魚之旨也。

VIII.21b

Xun Fengqian died of a broken heart after the passing of his wife – that was not Zhuangzi's feeling of "drumming on an earthenware pot."[1] Wang Yifu grieved over the loss of his son – that was not Dongmen Wu's philosophical attitude about death.[2] Ji Shuye's defiance of the mediocre people had led to disaster: was that "covering up one's light and sharing in the dust"?[3] Guo Zixuan exerted great influence due to his fame: was that "putting oneself last and giving up one's life"?[4] Ruan Sizong indulged in drinking and was lost in excess, thus discarding the warning about the "dangerous path."[5] Xie Youyu took bribery and was consequently demoted, thus defying the lesson of "discarding the leftover fish."[6]

---

1 Xun Fengqian was Xun Can 荀粲 (ca. third century), who was heart-broken after his wife's untimely death and himself died soon after at the young age of twenty-nine *sui*. After his wife died, Zhuangzi drummed on a pot and sang a song.

2 Wang Yifu was Wang Yan 王衍 (256–311), eminent minister of the Western Jin, known for his discourse on *Laozi* and *Zhuangzi*. Dongmen Wu was a man of Wei, who did not show grief when his son died; when asked, he said that he had had no son before his son was born and now he had no son again, so he was merely back to a previous state.

3 Ji Shuye was Ji Kang 嵇康 (224–263, also pronounced Xi Kang), famous poet and musician, one of the "Seven Worthies of the Bamboo Grove." He was married to a princess of the Cao Wei and was executed by the Sima family. The quotation is from *Laozi*.

4 Guo Zixuan was Guo Xiang 郭象 (d. 312), famous commentator on *Zhuangzi*. The quotation is from *Laozi*.

5 Ruan Sizong was Ruan Ji 阮籍 (210–263), famous poet and well-versed in Lao-Zhuang discourse, another member of the "Seven Worthies of the Bamboo Grove." The quotation is from *Zhuangzi*.

6 Xie Youyu was Xie Kun 謝鯤 (fl. early third century), a nobleman known for his love of *Laozi* and the *Classic of Changes* and his unconventional behavior. When Zhuangzi saw that his friend Huizi was followed by attendants riding in a hundred carriages but still felt dissatisfied, he discarded the extra fish in his meal as an admonishment to Huizi for his greed. The story is from the Western Han work *Huainanzi* 淮南子 (comp. second century BCE).

VIII.21c

彼諸人者，並其領袖，玄宗所歸。其餘桎
梏塵滓之中，顛仆名利之下者，豈可備言
乎。直取其清談雅論，辭鋒理窟，剖玄析
微，妙得入神，賓主往復，娛心悅耳，然
而濟世成俗，終非急務。

VIII.22

洎於梁世，茲風復闡，莊、老、周易，總
謂三玄。武皇、簡文，躬自講論。周弘正
奉贊大猷，化行都邑，學徒千餘，實為盛
美。元帝在江、荊間，復所愛習，故置學
生，親為教授，廢寢忘食，以夜繼朝，至
乃倦劇愁憤，輒以講自釋。吾時頗預末
筵，親承音旨，性既頑魯，亦所不好云。

VIII.21c

These gentlemen were leaders for the Lao-Zhuang admirers, who would turn to them for guidance. As for the rest of them, who are prisoners to the dusty mire of the mundane world, stumbling and falling over fame and gain, how can I possibly enumerate them all! Indeed, the only good things to be taken away from *Laozi* and *Zhuangzi* are the pure and elegant conversation, the sharpness of discoursing and the richness of principles, the examination of the arcane truths and the analysis of subtle principles, the marvelous achievement of the finest points, the exchange between the host and the guest that entertains the mind and pleases the ear; but when it comes to saving the world and forming good customs, these are not urgent necessities.

VIII.22

By the Liang times, this trend once again flourished. *Zhuangzi*, *Laozi*, and the *Classic of Changes* were together known as the Three Metaphysical Texts. Emperor Wu and Emperor Jianwen discussed and lectured on them in person. Zhou Hongzheng aided and assisted their great work, and their influence spread through the capital region. There were more than a thousand students, which was truly a magnificent sight. Emperor Yuan was likewise fond of the practice while he was governor in Jiangzhou and Jingzhou. He would gather students and teach them himself. Forgetting to sleep or eat, he did it day and night. Even when he was very fatigued, or worried and grieved, he would find comfort and release in lecturing on those texts. I, too, had participated in the lectures seated in the far back, and personally received the prince's instructions. But I was dull by nature, nor was I terribly interested.

VIII.23

齊孝昭帝侍婁太后疾，容色憔悴，服膳減
損。徐之才為灸兩穴，帝握拳代痛，爪入
掌心，血流滿手。后既痊愈，帝尋疾崩，
遺詔恨不見山陵之事。其天性至孝如彼，
不識忌諱如此，良由無學所為。若見古人
之譏欲母早死而悲哭之，則不發此言也。
孝為百行之首，猶須學以脩飾之，況餘事
乎。

VIII.24

梁元帝嘗為吾說："昔在會稽，年始十二，
便已好學。時又患疥，手不得拳，膝不得
屈。閑齋張葛幬避蠅獨坐，銀甌貯山陰甜
酒，時復進之，以自寬痛。率意自讀史
書，一日二十卷，既未師受，或不識一
字，或不解一語，要自重之，不知厭
倦。"帝子之尊，童稚之逸，尚能如此，
況其庶士，冀以自達者哉？

---

1 Empress Dowager Lou was named Lou Zhaojun 婁昭君 (501–562). A Xianbei
noblewoman, she was the mother to Emperor Wenxuan, Emperor Xiaozhao, and
Emperor Wucheng (see notes to VII.7 and II.9a).

VIII.23

Qi Emperor Xiaozhao waited upon Empress Dowager Lou when she was sick.[1] He became haggard in appearance and reduced his meals. Xu Zhicai administered moxibustion to two of her acupoints.[2] The emperor felt her pain so much that he clenched his fists, his fingernails cutting into his palms and blood covering his hands. Soon after the Empress Dowager recovered, the emperor himself fell ill and passed away. In his last edict he expressed regret that he could not live to supervise the burial of the Empress Dowager. He was so filial by nature, and yet so ignorant of what he should or should not say. This was very much due to the fact that he did not have any learning. Had he seen how the ancients mocked the man who wanted his mother to die early so that he could cry for her sadly, he would never have made a statement like that.[3] Filial piety is the foremost of one hundred virtuous actions, yet one still needs study to adorn it, not to mention other things!

VIII.24

Liang Emperor Yuan once told me this: "When I was at Kuaiji, I had just turned twelve *sui*, but was already fond of study.[4] At the time I was suffering from [sores caused by] scabies. I could not even close my hands or bend my knees. I would shut the doors of my studio and sit alone, hanging a hemp curtain to keep off the flies. I had a silver jug filled with the sweet wine of Shanyin, and drank it from time to time to alleviate the pain. I followed my whims and read history books on my own, finishing twenty scrolls each day. Since I did not learn them from a tutor, sometimes I might not know a character or understand a phrase, but in any case I loved it and never grew tired." If an exalted royal prince and a fun-loving child could do this, how much more so for an ordinary man who wishes to achieve prominence through study?

---

2 Xu Zhicai (d. 570s) was a legendary physician of his age. He was originally from a southern family and died at seventy-nine serving in the Northern Qi court.
3 This refers to a story in the Western Han work *Huainanzi*. In the story a young man wished his mother would die soon so that he could cry for her sadly.
4 Xiao Yi turned twelve *sui* or eleven years old in 519. His first administrative post was magistrate of Kuaiji.

VIII.25

古人勤學，有握錐投斧，照雪聚螢，鋤則
帶經，牧則編簡，亦云勤篤。梁世彭城劉
綺，交州刺史勃之孫，早孤家貧，常無
燈，折荻尺寸，然明讀書。孝元初出會
稽，精選寮寀，綺以才華，為國常侍兼記
室，殊蒙禮遇，終於金紫光祿。

VIII.26

義陽朱詹，世居江陵，後出揚都，好學，
家貧無資，累日不爨，乃時吞紙以實腹。
寒無氈被，抱犬而臥。犬亦飢虛，起行盜
食，呼之不至，哀聲動鄰，猶不廢業，卒
成大學，官至鎮南錄事參軍，為孝元所
禮。此乃不可為之事，亦是勤學之一人。

---

1 Su Qin 蘇秦 (fl. fourth century BCE) was an influential strategist in the Warring
  States period; he had allegedly pricked his thigh with an awl so he could stay
  awake and study. Wen Dang 文黨 was a native of Lujiang (in modern Anhui) in
  the Western Han. Once, when cutting wood in the mountains, he told his com-
  panions he wished to go away to pursue study. "I will throw my axe at a tall tree;
  if my axe is caught in the branches, I will go." The axe indeed was caught, and
  he subsequently went to the capital to study the classics. Sun Kang 孫康 (fl. fifth
  century), a Song official, had read at night by the light refracted from snow. Ju
  Yin 車胤 (d. 401), an Eastern Jin official, had gathered fireflies to use as light
  for reading at night because he was too poor to buy lamp oil.

VIII.25

Among the ancients who studied assiduously, there were those who held an awl, threw an axe, utilized the reflection of snow, or gathered fireflies.[1] Someone took the classics with him when plowing in the field; someone wove rushes together for writing when herding sheep.[2] They were truly diligent and devoted. During the Liang, there was Liu Qi of Pengcheng, who was the grandson of Liu Bo, the Governor of Jiaozhou.[3] He was orphaned at a young age and suffered from poverty. Having no lamp oil, he would break reeds into short pieces and light them to read at night. When Emperor Xiaoyuan was first appointed to Kuaiji, his staff members were all carefully selected.[4] Liu Qi was made Attendant-in-ordinary and Recorder on the prince's staff because of his remarkable talent, and was received with great respect by the prince. He ultimately passed away while in the post of Grand Master of the Palace with Golden Seal and Purple Ribbon.

VIII.26

Zhu Zhan of Yiyang, whose family had lived in Jiangling for generations, later went to Yangdu.[5] He was devoted to study. His family being poor, he could go several days with nothing to eat and sometimes swallowed paper to fill his stomach. He had no felt bedding in cold weather and would lie down in bed hugging his dog for warmth. His dog was also hungry and ran away to steal food elsewhere. He called out to the dog but it would not come back to him, and his pitiful cries moved his neighbors. Yet he never ceased studying, and eventually became a great scholar. He was appointed Administrative Supervisor to the Defender-of-the-south General, and was treated with esteem by Emperor Xiaoyuan. Such deeds are hard to achieve, but this is a fine example of someone bent on study.

---

2 These comments refer to two Western Han officials with a humble origin: the first is Ni Kuan 兒寬 (d. 103 BCE); the second is Lu Wenshu 路溫舒 (fl. first century BCE).

3 Pengcheng is in modern Jiangsu. The Liu clan of Pengcheng was a prominent clan in the Southern Dynasties. Liu Bo was made governor of Jiaozhou (modern Guangxi and northern Vietnam) in 468 and died on his way to the post. There is no record of Liu Qi in the histories. A Liu Qi is featured in several "linked verses" in the collection of the famous poet He Xun 何遜 (ca. 468–ca. 518).

4 See note to VIII.24.

5 Nothing else is known about Zhu Zhan. Yiyang was a county in Jingzhou or Jing prefecture (modern Hubei). Yangdu refers to the capital Jiankang.

VIII.27

東莞臧逢世，年二十餘，欲讀班固漢書，苦假借不久，乃就姊夫劉緩乞丐客刺書翰紙末，手寫一本，軍府服其志尚，卒以漢書聞。

VIII.28

齊有主書者內參田鵬鸞，本蠻人也。年十四五，初為閹寺，便知好學，懷袖握書，曉夕諷誦。所居卑末，使役苦辛，時伺閒隙，周章詢請。每至文林館，氣喘汗流，問書之外，不暇他語。及古人節義之事，未嘗不感激沈吟久之。吾甚憐愛，倍加開獎。後被賞遇，賜名敬宣，位至侍中開府。後主之奔青州，遣其西出，參伺動靜，為周軍所獲。問齊王何在，紿云："已去，計當出境。"疑其不信，歐捶服之，每折一支，辭色愈厲，竟斷四體而卒。蠻夷童丱，猶能以學著忠誠，齊之將相，比敬宣之奴不若也。

---

1 For Zang Fengshi, see note to VI.3. Dongguan is in modern Shandong.
2 For Liu Huan, see note to VI.40.
3 The Man people were a southern ethnic people treated as "barbarians."

VIII.27

Zang Fengshi of Dongguan, while in his twenties, wanted to read Ban Gu's *Han History*.[1] Since he could only keep the borrowed copy for a short time, he begged his elder sister's husband Liu Huan to give him the empty margins of visiting cards and letters, and used them to copy out the entire book for himself.[2] Everyone in the military headquarters admired his determination. In the end he became famous for his expertise in the *Han History*.

VIII.28

There was a palace attendant in the Qi whose name was Tian Pengluan. He was originally a Man barbarian.[3] He became a eunuch at the age of fourteen or fifteen and already had a desire for study. He would carry a book in his sleeve and read it aloud day and night. Because of his low status, he was engaged in toilsome service, but whenever he had a brief respite, he would go around making inquiries [about what he did not understand in his reading]. Every time he went to the Grove of Letters Institute, he would be panting and sweating from rushing and did not have time for anything beyond asking questions about the books he was reading.[4] Whenever he read about some heroic or upright deed of the ancients, he was always deeply moved and meditated upon it for a long time. I felt a strong affection for him, and would support and encourage him a great deal. Later he received recognition and favor from the emperor, who granted him the name Jingxuan and promoted him to the position of Palace Superintendent with his own office. When the Last Ruler fled to Qingzhou, he sent Jingxuan westward as a scout, and Jingxuan was captured by the Zhou army.[5] They asked him where the Qi ruler was. He deceived them, saying: "He is already gone. He is beyond the border by now." They suspected he was lying and tortured him. With every limb they broke, he only grew fiercer in his tone and demeanor. He finally died after all his four limbs were broken. Even a young barbarian lad could demonstrate such loyalty through study! The generals and ministers of Qi were not even fit to be Jingxuan's slaves.

---

4 The Grove of Letters Institute was an institute for scholars and writers that had been established in 573 by the Northern Qi emperor Gao Wei, known as the Last Ruler 後主 (see note to II.9a).

5 Qingzhou is in modern Shandong.

VIII.29

鄴平之後,見徙入關。思魯嘗謂吾曰:"朝無祿位,家無積財,當肆筋力,以申供養。每被課篤,勤勞經史,未知為子,可得安乎?"吾命之曰:"子當以養為心,父當以教為事。使汝棄學徇財,豐吾衣食,食之安得甘?衣之安得暖?若務先王之道,紹家世之業,藜羹縕褐,我自欲之。"

VIII.30

書曰:"好問則裕。"禮云:"獨學而無友,則孤陋而寡聞。"蓋須切磋相起明也。見有閉門讀書,師心自是,稠人廣坐,謬誤羞慙者多矣。

VIII.29

After Ye was conquered, we were obliged to moved inside the Pass.[1] Silu once said to me, "You have no salaried position in the court, and we have no wealth stored away. I should exert myself to provide for my parents. But you always urge me to work hard on the classics and histories instead. How can I, as a son, feel at ease?" I explained to him saying, "A son should indeed worry about providing for his parents, but a father should take the instruction of his son as his priority. If I make you give up study and pursue profit to enrich my food and clothes, how can the food taste good to me or the clothes feel warm to me? If, however, you can engage in the way of the former kings and continue our family's legacy, then pigweed stew and a coarse wadded robe are what I desire."

VIII.30

The *Book of Documents* says: "The one who likes to ask questions is enriched." The *Record of Rites* says, "The one who studies alone without friends remains superficial and benighted." One should seek inspiration and enlightenment by discussing with others. I have seen many a man who reads behind closed doors and takes no one's counsel but his own, believing himself to be correct, only to make a mistake and bring embarrassment upon himself in a large crowd.

---

1 Ye was conquered by Zhou in 577.

VIII.31

穀梁傳稱公子友與莒挐相搏，左右呼曰孟
勞。孟勞者，魯之寶刀名，亦見廣雅。近
在齊時，有姜仲岳謂："孟勞者，公子左
右，姓孟名勞，多力之人，為國所寶。"
與吾苦諍。時清河郡守邢峙，當世碩儒，
助吾證之，赧然而伏。

VIII.32

又三輔決錄云："靈帝殿柱題曰：'堂堂
乎張，京兆田郎。'"蓋引論語，偶以四
言，目京兆人田鳳也。有一才士乃
言："時張京兆及田郎二人皆堂堂耳。"聞
吾此說，初大驚駭，其後尋媿悔焉。

---

1 The *Guliang Tradition* (*Guliang zhuan*) is a Western Han work of exegesis of the *Spring and Autumn Annals*.

2 The *Expanded Ya* (*Guang Ya*) was a dictionary, now lost, compiled by Zhang Yi 張揖 (fl. early third century). It was based on, and expanded, the *Erya* (see note to VI.20), hence the name.

VIII.31

The *Guliang Tradition* says that, when Gongzi You was fighting with Ju Ru, his attendants cried out, "Menglao!"[1] Menglao was the name of a precious sword from the state of Lu. The name also appears in the *Expanded Ya.*[2] Recently, when I was serving in the Qi court, a man named Jiang Zhongyue said to me, "Meng Lao was one of Gongzi You's attendants. Meng was his surname and Lao was his given name. He was a man of great strength and was much prized by his state."[3] He argued with me most vigorously. Xing Zhi, the magistrate of Qinghe and a very erudite scholar of our age, sided with me and helped me prove my point.[4] Jiang finally submitted with a reddened face.

VIII.32

The *Conclusive Account of the Three Administrative Regions of Chang'an* states, "[Han] Emperor Ling wrote these words on the pillar of the palace hall: "'How imposing and majestic is Zhang!' So is Master Tian of the Metropolitan Area."[5] The emperor was pairing the *Analects* saying with a four-character phrase to evaluate Tian Feng, a native of the Metropolitan Area.[6] But a talented gentleman said, "At the time, Metropolitan Governor Zhang and Master Tian were both imposing and majestic." When he first heard my interpretation, he was terribly shocked at first, but was soon filled with shame and regret.

---

3 Jiang Zhongyue is otherwise unknown.

4 Xing Zhi (fl. 550s–560s) was a Northern Qi scholar. He was made magistrate of Qinghe (in modern Hebei) in 560.

5 *Sanfu juelu*, loosely translated here as *The Conclusive Account of the Three Administrative Regions of Chang'an*, was compiled by Zhao Qi 趙岐 (d. 201). Emperor Ling ruled from 168 to 189. Zhang is abbreviated from Zizhang 子張, the courtesy name of Zhuansun Shi 顓孫師, who was a disciple of Confucius known for his good looks. The quotation is from the *Analects*.

6 Tian Feng was a minister in Emperor Ling's court with an impressive demeanor. The emperor watched him depart from the court with admiration and wrote the above words.

VIII.33

江南有一權貴，讀誤本蜀都賦注，解"蹲
鴟，芋也"，乃為"羊"字。人饋羊肉，
答書云："損惠蹲鴟。"舉朝驚駭，不解
事義，久後尋跡，方知如此。

VIII.34

元氏之世，在洛京時，有一才學重臣，新
得史記音，而頗紕繆，誤反"頗項"字，
項當為許錄反，錯作許綠反，遂謂朝
士言："從來謬音'專旭'，當音'專
翾'耳。"此人先有高名，翕然信行；期
年之後，更有碩儒，苦相究討，方知誤
焉。

VIII.33

An important nobleman in the south once read a defective copy of the commentary on "The Rhapsody on the Shu Capital."[1] In the gloss "The 'squatting owl' refers to yam," "yam" (*yu*) is mistakenly copied as "lamb" (*yang*). Then someone gave the nobleman some lamb, and he wrote back saying, "Thank you for gracing me with the squatting owl." The entire court was shocked, having no idea what it meant. Only much later did people manage to trace the error and come to understand.

VIII.34

During the rule of the house of Yuan, in the capital Luoyang there was a great minister who was quite learned and talented.[2] He once acquired a copy of the *Phonological Glossary of the 'Historian's Record.'*[3] The glossary, however, contained many errors. For instance, in the name "Zhuanxu," *xu* should be glossed as a combination of *xu* and *lu*, but the glossary gives "a combination of *xu* and *yuan*" instead. The minister began to tell everyone, "We have been wrong all along to pronounce the name as Zhuanxu; it should be Zhuanxuan instead." Since this minister had always enjoyed a high reputation, people all believed and followed him. A year later, an erudite scholar devoted laborious research to the issue; only then did people realize the mistake.

---

1 The rhapsody was composed by the famous Western Jin writer Zuo Si 左思 (fl. 300). His contemporary Liu Kui 劉逵 authored a commentary.

2 The Northern Wei dynasty was ruled by the house of Tuoba (see note to V.12), but after Emperor Xiaowen (r. 471–499) moved the capital to Luoyang in 494, he had the royal surname changed to Yuan 元.

3 A book of this title, *Shi ji yin* 史記音, is recorded in the "Bibliography" of the *Sui History* (compiled in early seventh century); it is attributed to a minor Liang official, Zou Dansheng 鄒誕生 (fl. early sixth century). The *Historian's Record* (*Shi ji*) was authored by the Western Han historian Sima Qian 司馬遷 (ca. 145 BCE–ca. 86 BCE).

VIII.35

漢書王莽贊云："紫色鼃聲，餘分閏
位。"謂以偽亂真耳。昔吾嘗共人談書，
言及王莽形狀，有一俊士，自許史學，名
價甚高，乃云："王莽非直鴟目虎吻，亦
紫色蛙聲。"又禮樂志云："給太官挏馬
酒。"李奇注："以馬乳為酒也，挏挏乃
成。"二字並從手。挏挏，此謂撞擣挺挏
之，今為酪酒亦然。向學士又以為種桐
時，太官釀馬酒乃熟。其孤陋遂至於此。
太山羊肅，亦稱學問，讀潘岳賦"周文弱
枝之棗，"為杖策之杖，世本"容成造
歷，"以歷為碓磨之磨。

VIII.35

The *Han History* contains the following appraisal of Wang Mang: "He is like the color purple, the sound of a frog, or the surplus in a calendar occupying the intercalary position."[1] This means that the false is mixed up with the true. Once I was discussing books with friends and we talked about Wang Mang's appearance. A fine gentleman, a self-styled historian with an excellent repute, blurted out, "Wang Mang not only had an owl's eyes and a tiger's mouth; he was also purplish in his complexion and spoke with a croaky voice of a frog!" Then again "The Monograph of Rites and Music" in the *Han History* says, "The Imperial Provisioner was given the wine made of mare's milk." Li Qi's commentary states: "It is an alcoholic drink made from mare's milk by the *chong dong* method."[2] Both *chong* and *dong* have a "hand" radical; they mean to beat and churn. This is the same method employed in making kumiss today. The above-mentioned scholar, however, believed that the term means the Provisioner's wine-making is completed at the time when the *wutong* tree is planted. This, alas, shows the extent of his ignorance. Yang Su of Taishan was known as a learned man.[3] Yet, when he read in Pan Yue's rhapsody, "King Wen's date tree of delicate branches," he took *zhi* (branch) for *zhang* (hold [a staff]) as in *zhangce* (hold a staff).[4] When he read in the *Origins of Genealogies*, "Rongcheng invented the calendar," he took *li* (calendar) for millstone (*mo*) as in *duimo* (millstone).[5]

---

1 Wang Mang (45 BCE–23 CE) was the usurper of the Han throne and established the Xin 新 Dynasty (9–23).

2 Li Qi 李奇 (fl. second century) was a late Eastern Han scholar who authored a commentary on the *Han History*.

3 Yang Su was Yang Kan's nephew and an official of the Qi: see VI.19.

4 Pan Yue 潘岳 (d. 300) was a famous Western Jin writer. This line is from his "Rhapsody (*Fu*) on Dwelling in Leisure" 閑居賦.

5 *Li* 歷 and *li* 曆 are homophones and used interchangeably. The latter graph resembles the graph *mo*. *Origins of Genealogies* (*Shi ben*), extant only in fragments, is recorded in the *Han History*, a work giving account of surnames and genealogies in ancient times. Rongcheng was a minister of the mythical Yellow Emperor.

VIII.36

談說製文，援引古昔，必須眼學，勿信耳
受。江南閭里間，士大夫或不學問，羞為
鄙朴，道聽塗說，強事飾辭：呼徵質為周
鄭，謂霍亂為博陸，上荊州必稱陝西，下
揚都言去海郡，言食則餬口，道錢則孔
方，問移則楚丘，論婚則宴爾，及王則無
不仲宣，語劉則無不公幹。凡有一二百
件，傳相祖述，尋問莫知原由，施安時復
失所。

---

1 The Zhou court and the feudal domain of Zheng exchanged hostages in 720
  BCE; it was regarded as a violation of hierarchy between the Zhou king and a
  feudal lord as well as a loss of mutual trust. Bolu was the fief of Huo Guang
  霍光, a powerful Western Han minister. Perhaps because his surname was Huo,
  people referred to cholera, whose Chinese term is *huoluan* 霍亂, as Bolu.
2 Shaanxi was used to refer to the region to the west of Shaan (in modern He'nan)
  under the command of the Duke of Shao. Jingzhou was to the west of the capital
  city Jiankang and was one of the major prefectures in the Southern Dynasties;
  hence Jingzhou was referred to as "Shanxi."
3 This is perhaps because of a statement in the *Book of Documents*: "Between the
  Huai [River] and the sea there is the Yang prefecture." Jiankang was known as
  Yangdu (lit. Yang's capital), hence the "seaside commandery."
4 To "fill the mouth with gruel" is from the *Zuo Tradition*, in which it was used to
  refer to making a living by attaching oneself to a patron, thus it is not an appropriate term to indicate "eating."

VIII.36

In conversation or composition, when making a reference to an earlier text, you must do so through reading and not through hearsay. In the south, sometimes gentry members from a small town who did not have much learning were nonetheless ashamed of sounding uncouth, so they would strenuously add some rhetorical embellishments picked up from what they had heard on the street. They would call seeking collateral "Zhou and Zheng," and refer to cholera as "Bolu";[1] going to Jingzhou became "going to Shaanxi,"[2] and sailing downstream to Yangdu became "leaving for the seaside commandery";[3] speaking of eating, they would say "fill the mouth with gruel";[4] talking about money, they would say the "Square Hole";[5] inquiring about moving, they would say "Chuqiu";[6] discussing a wedding, they would say "yan'er";[7] referring to a man surnamed Wang, they would invariably call him Zhongxuan; every Mr. Liu was turned into a Gonggan.[8] There are no fewer than one or two hundred such examples, passed around from one person to another. If you asked them, no one knew the origin of the phrase; when they applied it to an occasion, it often turned out to be inappropriate.

---

5 "Square Hole" refers to a coin that is round in shape with a square hole in the middle. Lu Bao 魯褒, a late third century recluse, wrote a "Treatise on the Money God" ("Qian shen lun" 錢神論), in which he refers to money as "Brother Square Hole."

6 Chuqiu (in modern He'nan) was a place in the state of Wei. After Wei was invaded and the Duke of Wei went into exile, a new capital was built for Wei at Chuqiu in 658 BCE. It is not appropriate to use Chuqiu to speak of moving one's house.

7 "Yan'er" (at ease; cheerful) is from a line in the *Classic of Poetry*: "At ease in the new marriage" 宴爾新昏.

8 Zhongxuan was the courtesy name of the famous writer Wang Can (see note to VIII.19). Gonggan was the courtesy name of another famous writer from the same period, Liu Zhen 劉楨 (d. 217).

VIII.37

莊生有乘時鵲起之說，故謝朓詩曰：
"鵲起登吳臺。" 吾有一親表，作七夕詩
云："今夜吳臺鵲，亦共往填河。" 羅浮
山記云："望平地樹如薺。" 故戴暠詩
云："長安樹如薺。" 又鄴下有一人詠樹
詩云："遙望長安薺。" 又嘗見謂矜誕為
夸毗，呼高年為富有春秋，皆耳學之過
也。

---

1 Master Zhuang is the philosopher Zhuang Zhou. This remark appears in *Zhuangzi*.

2 Xie Tiao (464–499) was a Southern Qi courtier and famous poet. The line is from a poem entitled, "In Response to Fu, Magistrate of Wuchang, on Ascending the Old City-wall Built by Sun Quan" 和伏武昌登孫權故城. The poem is anthologized in the *Wen xuan* 文選, canonical sixth-century anthology compiled by Xiao Tong 蕭統 (501–531). The current version reads "Wu hills" ("Wu shan" 吳山) rather than "Wu terrace" ("Wu tai").

3 As the legend goes, the Weaver Woman and the Cowherd, lovers separated by the Heavenly River (the Milky Way), would annually reunite on the night of the seventh day of the seventh month, and magpies would build a bridge for them.

VIII.37

Master Zhuang has a phrase about taking the right opportunity to soar like a magpie.[1] Therefore Xie Tiao wrote a line of poetry saying, "[He] soared like a magpie and ascended the Wu terrace."[2] A relative of mine wrote a poem "On the Night of the Sevens," which contains the couplet: "Tonight, even the magpies on the Wu terrace / will all go to fill up the Heavenly River."[3] The *Record of Mount Luofu* says, "When you look down at the plain [from the mountain], the trees all seem like shepherd's-purse."[4] Hence Dai Gao wrote a line of poetry saying, "The trees in Chang'an are like shepherd's-purse."[5] Then a man at Ye wrote a poem about trees that contains the line, "I gaze afar at the shepherd's-purse of Chang'an." I have also encountered people who thought *jindan* (self-important and bragging) means *kuapi* (servile and fawning), or referred to old age as being "rich in springs and autumns."[6] These are all errors made by "learning by ear only."[7]

---

4 Mount Luofu is in Guangdong. A *Record of Mount Luofu*, extant in fragments, is attributed to Yuan Hong 袁宏 (fl. mid-fourth century). Shepherd's-purse is the name of a plant (*Capsella bursa-pastoris*).

5 Dai Gao was a Liang poet about whom little else is known. The line is from a *yuefu* poem, "Crossing the Guan Mountains" ("Du Guanshan" 度關山). The Guan Mountains referred to here are in modern Ningxia.

6 *Kuapi* contains the word *kua*, which by itself means boastful, hence the mistake. "Being rich in springs and autumns" means being rich in *future* years and refers to youth.

7 That is, learning from hearsay rather than from reading.

VIII.38

夫文字者，墳籍根本。世之學徒，多不曉
字：讀五經者，是徐邈而非許慎；習賦誦
者，信褚詮而笑呂忱；明史記者，專皮、
鄒而廢篆籀；學漢書者，悅應、蘇而略
蒼、雅。不知書音是其枝葉，小學乃其宗
系。至見服虔、張揖音義則貴之，得通
俗、廣雅而不屑。一手之中，向背如此，
況異代各人乎。

---

1 Xu Miao (345–398) was an Eastern Jin scholar who authored a phonological
  glossary of the five Confucian classics. He is often referred to as Xu Xianmin
  throughout Yan Zhitui's book. Xu Shen (d. ca. 149) was an Eastern Han scholar
  and the author of the *Shuowen jiezi* 說文解字 (*Explanation of Simple Graphs and
  Analysis of Composite Characters*, hereafter *Shuowen*).

2 Chu Quan may be Chu Quanzhi 褚詮之 (ca. fifth century), the author of the
  Bai fu yin 百賦音 (*Sounds of One Hundred Rhapsodies*). Lü Chen (ca. late third
  century) was a Western Jin author of the *Zi lin* 字林 (*Forest of Graphs*).

VIII.38

Language is the basis of books. Many students in this world do not
know anything about philology. When examining the five classics, they
agree with Xu Miao but disagree with Xu Shen;[1] when studying rhapsodies, they believe Chu Quan but scorn Lü Chen;[2] when exploring the
Historian's Record, they specialize in Pi and Zou but dismiss Zhuan and
Zhou scripts;[3] when studying the *Han History,* they take delight in Ying
and Su but ignore Cang and Ya.[4] They do not understand that phonology is the branches and leaves of learning but philology is the foundation, and even go so far as to prize the phonological glossaries by Fu
Qian and Zhang Yi, while scorning Fu Qian's *Common Writing* and
Zhang Yi's *Expanded Ya.*[5] Even in treating works by the same author
they show such great disparity, not to mention different authors from
different ages.

---

3 Zou is Zou Dansheng (see note to VIII.34). Pi is unknown, and is emended to
 Xu 徐 [Guang 廣] in Wang Liqi (Wang 221–22). Xu Guang was the younger
 brother of Xu Miao (see above) and authored a commentary of the *Shi ji.* Zhuan
 script is also known as the "lesser seal script" and Zhou script, the "greater seal
 script" or "the script of the historian Zhou."
4 Ying is Ying Shao 應劭 (fl. 170s–200s), and Su is Su Lin 蘇林 (fl. third century).
 Both have authored a commentary on the *Han History.* Cang refers to the "Three
 Cang Texts" (San Cang 三蒼), three philological works including the *Cang Jie
 pian* that circulated in the Western Han (see note to VI.43). Ya refers to the
 dictionary *Erya.*
5 Fu Qian 服虔 (d. ca. 180s) was a scholar of the classics who authored a commentary on the *Zuo Tradition* and also the *Common Writing* (*Tongsu wen* 通俗文).
 Zhang Yi's *Expanded Ya*: see note to VIII.31.

VIII.39

夫學者貴能博聞也。郡國山川，官位姓
族，衣服飲食，器皿制度，皆欲根尋，得
其原本；至於文字，忽不經懷，己身姓
名，或多乖舛，縱得不誤，亦未知所由。
近世有人為子制名：兄弟皆山傍立字，而
有名峙者；兄弟皆手邊立字，而有名機
者；兄弟皆水傍立字，而有名凝者。名儒
碩學，此例甚多。若有知吾鍾之不調，一
何可笑。

---

1 Yan Zhitui implies that 峙 is the correct form of 峙, which is the popular/
corrupted form. Thus, in naming a child with a character containing the mountain radical, the father was amiss in using 峙.
2 Yan implies that 機 is the correct form of 攕, which is the popular/corrupted
form. Thus, in naming a child with a character containing the hand radical, the
father was amiss in using 攕.

VIII.39

The reason for study is because we prize broad knowledge. For commanderies and princedoms, mountains and rivers, official titles and clan lineages, garments and victuals, utensils and customs, people usually desire to trace their roots and understand their origin. But when it comes to writing and words, they become casual and neglect to pay attention. Sometimes they even make mistakes about their own names; and even if they don't, they might not know how they come about. In recent years, when naming his son, someone chose characters with the "mountain" radical for all of them, but named one of the sons Zhi;[1] in choosing characters with the "hand" radical, another man nevertheless named one of his sons Ji;[2] in choosing characters with the "water" radical, yet another named one of his sons Ning.[3] Even famous Ruists and erudite scholars have erred like this. If there is a discerning person who knows the bells are not tuned, he will surely find this hilarious.[4]

3 Yan implies that 凝 is the correct form of 𣷯. Thus, in naming a child with a character containing the water radical, the father was amiss in using 𣷯.

4 Master Kuang, a legendary musician, once told Duke Ping of Jin that the bells were not tuned properly. The duke countered that all other musicians believed the bells to be well tuned. Master Kuang said, "If there is anyone who knows music at all, that person will surely know the bells are not tuned." This is a story from *Huainanzi*.

VIII.40

吾嘗從齊主幸并州,自井陘關入上艾縣,東數十里,有獵閭村。後百官受馬糧在晉陽東百餘里亢仇城側,並不識二所本是何地,博求古今,皆未能曉。及檢字林、韻集,乃知獵閭是舊礦餘聚,亢仇舊是縵欱亭,悉屬上艾。時太原王劭欲撰鄉邑記注,因此二名聞之,大喜。

VIII.41

吾初讀莊子"蝝二首",韓非子曰:"蟲有蝝者,一身兩口,爭食相齕,遂相殺也。"茫然不識此字何音,逢人輒問,了無解者。案爾雅諸書,蠶蛹名蝝,又非二首兩口貪害之物。後見古今字詁,此亦古之虺字,積年凝滯,豁然霧解。

---

1 Bingzhou is in modern Shanxi.
2 Jinyang is modern Taiyuan of Shanxi.
3 The *Forest of Graphs* was authored by Lü Chen (see note to VIII.38); the *Collection of Rhymes* (*Yun ji* 韻集) was a work by Lü Chen's brother Lü Jing 呂靜.

VIII.40

I once followed the Qi ruler to go to Bingzhou, entering Shang'ai county from the Jingxing Pass.[1] Several tens of leagues from the county there
was a village called Lielü. Later on, the courtiers all received fodder for
their horses at Kangchou City about a hundred leagues to the east of
Jinyang.[2] Nobody knew what these two places – Lielü and Kangchou –
had been in an earlier time. We sought widely in ancient and modern
books, but could not find their origins. Finally, I looked them up in
the *Forest of Graphs* and the *Collection of Rhymes*.[3] I subsequently
learned that Lielü was the remains of the old Lieyu Hamlet, and that
Kangchou had been Manqiuting in the olden days. Both places had
belonged to Shang'ai. At this time, Wang Shao of Taiyuan was planning
to compile a commentary on the *Record of Townships and Settlements*,
so I relayed the information to him.[4] He was overjoyed.

VIII.41

When I first read *Zhuangzi*, I encountered the statement that "*Kui* has
two heads." *Han Feizi* says, "There is a creature known as *kui*, which
has one body but two mouths. The two mouths fight for food and bite
each other, and eventually kill each other."[5] I had no idea how this
insect's name was pronounced. I would ask everyone I met, but nobody
knew. According to various lexical works such as the *Erya*, the silkworm's larva is called *kui*; but it does not have two heads and two
mouths, nor is it greedy and aggressive. Later, I saw in *A Glossary of
Archaic and Modern Characters* that this character was the same as *hui*
[a kind of venomous snake] in ancient times.[6] In an instant the doubt
of many years dissolved like a lifted fog.

---

4 Wang Shao (fl. 580s–610s) was the second son of Wang Songnian (see note to
   VI.34). He was known as a scholar of broad learning, but disparaged as a historian
   of the Qi and Sui.
5 *Han Feizi* (*Master Han Fei*) was authored by the Legalist philosopher Han Fei
   韓非 (d. 233 BCE).
6 This work was authored by the third-century philologist Zhang Yi (see note to
   VIII.31).

VIII.42

嘗遊趙州，見柏人城北有一小水，土人亦
不知名。後讀城南門徐整碑云："洦流東
指。"眾皆不識。吾案說文，此字古魄字
也，洦，淺水貌。此水漢來本無名矣，直
以淺貌目之，或當即以洦為名乎？

VIII.43

世中書翰，多稱匆匆，相承如此，不知所
由，或有妄言此忽忽之殘缺耳。案說
文："勿者，州里所建之旗也，象其柄及
三斿之形，所以趣民事。故忩遽者稱為匆
匆。"

VIII.42

Once, when I was in Zhaozhou, I saw a small river to the north of Boren City.[1] Even the locals did not know its name. Later I read in the stele inscription by Xu Zheng beside the south gate of the city that "The *bo* currents flow east."[2] None knew the character *bo*. I learned from *Shuowen* that the character was the ancient form of *po*, meaning shallow water. This river had had no name since the Han dynasty and was simply described as the shallows. Perhaps it should be named as Bo?

VIII.43

When people write letters, they often end with the expression *wuwu* ("in a rush") by habit, but no one knows how the expression came about. Some rashly speculate that it is the corrupted form of *huhu* ("in a hurry"). But according to the *Shuowen*, "*Wu* is a banner established in the country district. The graph imitates the form of a flagstaff with three streamers. The banner is to urge people to engage in farming [in a timely manner]. Therefore the phrase *wuwu* is used to refer to being in a rush."

---

1 Zhaozhou or Zhao prefecture is in modern Hebei. Yan Zhitui served in a post there in 564.
2 Xu Zheng (fl. third century) was a Wu official in the Three Kingdoms period.

VIII.44

吾在益州，與數人同坐，初晴日晃，見地上小光，問左右："此是何物？"有一蜀豎就視，答云："是豆逼耳。"相顧愕然，不知所謂。命將取來，乃小豆也。窮訪蜀士，呼粒為逼，時莫之解。吾云："三蒼、說文，此字白下為匕，皆訓粒，通俗文音方力反。"眾皆歡悟。

VIII.45

愍楚友婿竇如同從河州來，得一青鳥，馴養愛翫，舉俗呼之為鶡。吾曰："鶡出上黨，數曾見之，色並黃黑，無駁雜也。故陳思王鶡賦云：'揚玄黃之勁羽。'"試檢說文："鴆雀似鶡而青，出羌中。"韻集音分。此疑頓釋。

VIII.44

When I was in Yizhou, one day I was sitting around with several people.[1] The sky had just cleared up after rain, and the sun came out shining. I saw [something lit up by] a small light on the ground, and asked the attendants: "What is that?" A young servant from Shu went over to take a closer look and reported, "It is *dou bi*." We looked at one another in surprise, not understanding what he meant. We ordered him to bring it over, and it turned out to be an adzuki bean. I made inquiries all over the Shu region and found that the locals would say *bi* instead of *li* [lit. a grain (of sand or rice)]. At the time nobody understood [how the word *bi* came to be used as a measure word instead of *li*]. I said, "According to the Three Cang Texts and the *Shuowen*, this character is written as a *bai* plus a *bi* below [that is, as *bi* 皀, MC pik]. It is glossed as *li* [a grain of]. The *Common Writing* gives its pronunciation as a combination of *fang* [MC pjang] and *li* [MC lik]." Everyone was glad to be enlightened.

VIII.45

Dou Rutong, husband of Minchu's sister-in-law, came from Hezhou,[2] where he obtained a blue bird. He tamed the bird and kept it as a pet. Everyone in the family called it a pheasant. I said, "But the pheasant is from Shangdang.[3] I have seen it many times. Its color is yellow and black and has no other colors mixed in. Therefore the 'Rhapsody on the Pheasant' by Prince Si of Chen states, 'It raises its powerful pinions of dark and yellow.'"[4] Henceforth I looked it up in the *Shuowen* and found this definition of the *fen* quail: "The *fen* quail looks like a pheasant, but is of a blue color. It comes from Qiangzhong."[5] The *Collection of Rhymes* gives its pronunciation as *fen*. The doubt was resolved at once.

---

1 Yizhou was in Shu (modern Sichuan).
2 Minchu was Yan Zhitui's second son. His wife and Dou Rutong's wife were sisters. Nothing else is known about Mr. Dou. Hezhou is in modern Gansu.
3 Shangdang is in modern Shanxi.
4 Prince Si of Chen is Cao Zhi; see note to VI.12.
5 The *fen* quail is emended to the *jie* quail in the Lu Wenchao edition. See Additional Notes. Qiangzhong refers to the western lands (in modern Gansu, Qinghai, and Sichuan), from where Dou Rutong came.

VIII.46

梁世有蔡朗諱純，既不涉學，遂呼蓴為露
葵菜。面牆之徒，遞相倣效。承聖中，遣
一士大夫聘齊，齊主客郎李恕問梁使
曰：“江南有露葵否？”答曰：“露葵是
蓴，水鄉所出。卿今食者綠葵菜耳。”李
亦學問，但不測彼之深淺，乍聞無以覈
究。

VIII.47

思魯等姨夫彭城劉靈嘗與吾坐，諸子侍
焉。吾問儒行、敏行曰：“凡字與諮議名
同音者，其數多少，能盡識乎？”答
曰：“未之究也，請導示之。”吾曰：“凡
如此例，不預研檢，忽見不識，誤以問
人，反為無賴所欺，不容易也。”因為說
之，得五十許字。諸劉歎曰：“不意乃
爾！”若遂不知，亦為異事。

VIII.46

In the Liang there was a Cai Lang, who avoided *chun* as a taboo character. He was not an erudite man, and took to calling brasenia [*chun*] "dew mallow" [*kuicai*]. Those fellows "facing the wall" all mimicked him. During the Chengsheng era [552–554], a courtier was sent to the Qi as an envoy.[1] Li Shu, the Receptionist at the Qi court, asked the Liang envoy: "Is there dew mallow in the south?"[2] He replied, "Dew mallow is actually brasenia, a product of water areas. What you eat today is just the green mallow." Li was a learned man, but he did not know the depth of the envoy's knowledge, and could not investigate his claim on spot.

VIII.47

The husband of you boys' maternal aunt, Liu Ling of Pengcheng, once was sitting with me, and his sons were in attendance.[3] I asked [his sons] Ruxing and Minxing: "How many characters have the same sound as the Advisor's [Liu Ling] given name? Do you know them all?" They answered, "We have not looked into this. Please tell us." I said, "Well, if you don't study such characters ahead of time, should you encounter one of them and ask someone about it, you may be taken advantage of by a scoundrel. You should not be cavalier about it."[4] Thereupon I enumerated the characters, and there were over fifty of them. The Lius said with a sigh, "Who would have thought so!" It is remarkable that they actually had not known those characters.

---

1 Chengsheng was the name of Emperor Yuan's reign.
2 Late Qing scholar Li Ciming 李慈銘 (1830–1894) believes Li Shu 李恕 should be 李庶 (d. ca. 554) (see Wang Liqi 233).
3 The Liu clan of Pengcheng (in modern Jiangsu) was a prominent clan, although nothing else is known about Liu Ling or his sons.
4 That is, a scoundrel may make fun of them for not recognizing a taboo character.

VIII.48

校定書籍，亦何容易，自揚雄、劉向，方
稱此職耳。觀天下書未遍，不得妄下雌
黃。或彼以為非，此以為是；或本同末
異；或兩文皆欠，不可偏信一隅也。

VIII.48

Collating books is not an easy matter. Only those such as Yang Xiong and Liu Xiang were fit for the task.[1] If one has not read all the books in the world, one should not apply orpiment so lightly.[2] In some cases, what one version takes to be right is considered as wrong by another version; in some cases, the roots may be the same but the branches may differ; yet in other cases, both versions may be imperfect, and so one should not believe in either.

---

1 Yang Xiong (53 BCE–18 CE) was a prominent scholar and writer of the Western Han. For Liu Xiang, see note to VII.2.
2 That is, make corrections. In premodern times people used orpiment to mask mistakes like a correction fluid.

文章第九

IX.1

夫文章者，原出五經：詔命策檄，生於書
者也；序述論議，生於易者也；歌詠賦
頌，生於詩者也；祭祀哀誄，生於禮者
也；書奏箴銘，生於春秋者也。朝廷憲
章，軍旅誓誥，敷顯仁義，發明功德，牧
民建國，不可暫無。至於陶冶性靈，從容
諷諫，入其滋味，亦樂事也。行有餘力，
則可習之。

IX. Literary Writings

IX.1

Literary writings are derived from the Five Classics: imperial edicts, commands, decrees, and proclamations originate from *The Classic of Documents*; authorial prefaces, accounts, treatises, and disquisitions originate from the *Classic of Changes*; songs, chants, rhapsodies, and odes originate from the *Classic of Poetry*; sacrificial essays, ritual offering compositions, lamentations, and elegies originate from the *Record of Rites*; letters, memorials, admonitions, and inscriptions originate from the *Spring and Autumn Annals*. In creating court statutes, issuing military oaths and announcements, manifesting benevolence and integrity, and demonstrating achievements and virtue, governing the people as well as establishing the state, we cannot do without literary writings even for one moment. As for the way in which literary writings fire and smelt one's spiritual nature and help one phrase one's advice and admonition in graceful terms, if one can get into its tastes and flavors, then it is indeed a pleasure. If you still have surplus strength after doing other things, then you may try your hand at it.

IX.2a

然而自古文人，多陷輕薄：屈原露才揚
己，顯暴君過；宋玉體貌容冶，見遇俳
優；東方曼倩滑稽不雅；司馬長卿竊貲無
操；王褒過章童約；揚雄德敗美新；李陵
降辱夷虜；劉歆反覆莽世；傅毅黨附權
門；班固盜竊父史；趙元叔抗竦過度；馮
敬通浮華擯壓；馬季長佞媚獲誚；蔡伯喈
同惡受誅；

---

1 Qu Yuan (fl. fourth century BCE), supposedly an aristocrat of the state of Chu, was the putative author of *Li sao* 離騷 and several other poems in the *Lyrics of Chu* 楚辭. He lamented being misunderstood by his prince and committed suicide.

2 Song Yu was the putative author of a number of *sao*-style poems and is believed to be Qu Yuan's disciple, serving in the Chu court.

3 Dongfang Manqian is Dongfang Shuo 東方朔 (second century BCE), a writer in the court of Han Emperor Wu (r. 140–87 BCE), known for his wit and comic talent.

4 For Sima Zhangqing, see note to VI.6.

5 Wang Bao (first century BCE) was a famous Western Han writer. He wrote a comic piece of prose "Covenant for My Servant," in which he speaks of visiting a widow. Commentators believe this is the imperfection that Yan Zhitui alludes to.

6 For Yang Xiong, see note to VIII.48. The Xin dynasty was founded by Wang Mang, usurper of the Han throne (see note to VIII.35).

7 Li Ling (d. 74 BCE) was a Western Han general who was defeated by the Xiong-nu army and surrendered.

IX.2a

However, since ancient times men of letters often suffered from the flaw of frivolity and thoughtlessness. Qu Yuan displayed his talent and flaunted himself, and exposed the faults of his prince.[1] Song Yu sported a fancy appearance, and was treated like an entertainer.[2] Dongfang Manqian was comical and lacked dignity.[3] Sima Zhangqing stole from others and had no integrity.[4] Wang Bao's imperfection was revealed in his "Covenant for My Servant."[5] Yang Xiong's virtue was destroyed by his praise of the Xin dynasty.[6] Li Ling was brought to shame by surrendering to barbarians.[7] Liu Xin was inconsistent in his loyalty during Wang Mang's rule.[8] Fu Yi attached himself to a powerful clan.[9] Ban Gu plagiarized his father's historical writings.[10] Zhao Yuanshu was excessively proud.[11] Feng Jingtong was suppressed for being flowery and shallow.[12] Ma Jichang was derided for flattery.[13] Cai Bojie died for supporting an evil-doer.[14]

---

8 Liu Xin (d. 23 CE) was Liu Xiang's son (see note to VII.2) and an eminent scholar and bibliographer in his own right. He demonstrated his loyalty to Wang Mang first but later conspired against Wang Mang.

9 Fu Yi (fl. first century CE) was a distinguished Eastern Han writer. He was criticized for attaching himself to powerful imperial in-laws.

10 Ban Gu (see note to VI.12) had based the *Han History* on the work of his father Ban Biao 班彪 (3–54).

11 Zhao Yuanshu was the courtesy name of the Eastern Han writer Zhao Yi (see note to VI.40). He was known for his arrogance.

12 Feng Jingtong was Feng Yan 馮衍 (fl. 20s–ca. 60), Eastern Han writer who had had a checkered official career and tumultuous family life.

13 Ma Jichang was Ma Rong 馬融 (76–166), Eastern Han writer who was derided for flattering the powerful minister Liang Ji 梁冀 (d. 159).

14 Cai Bojie was Cai Yong (see note to VI.9), late Eastern Han polymath. He was imprisoned for expressing sympathy for the warlord Dong Zhuo 董卓 (d. 192) and died in prison.

IX.2b

吳質詆忤鄉里；曹植悖慢犯法；杜篤乞假
無厭；路粹隘狹已甚；陳琳實號麤疎；繁
欽性無檢格；劉楨屈強輸作；王粲率躁見
嫌；孔融、禰衡，誕傲致殞；楊修、丁
廙，扇動取斃；阮籍無禮敗俗；嵇康凌物
凶終；傅玄忿鬥免官；孫楚矜誇凌上；陸
機犯順履險；潘岳乾沒取危；顏延年負氣
摧黜；謝靈運空疏疎亂紀；王元長凶賊自
詒；謝玄暉侮慢見及。

---

1 Wu Zhi (177–230) was a writer and courtier favored by Cao Pi 曹丕 (187–226;
   Wei Emperor Wen, r. 220–226), Cao Cao's son and heir (for Cao Cao, see note
   to VI.12).
2 Cao Zhi, talented writer and Cao Cao's favorite son, was involved in fierce rivalry
   with his elder brother Cao Pi (see note above), and eventually lost his father's
   favor after he violated the law by riding his chariot down the speedway of the
   imperial palace.
3 Du Du (d. 78) made frequent requests and appeals to a friend who was a magistrate and became resentful when his demands were not met.
4 Lu Cui (d. 214) served on Cao Cao's staff. He was known for intolerance.
5 Chen Lin (d. 217) served on Cao Cao's staff and composed letters and proclamations on his behalf.
6 Po Qin (d. 218) served on Cao Cao's staff. The comments on his character and
   on Chen Lin's character above were made by their contemporary, Wei Dan 韋誕
   (179–253).
7 Liu Zhen (see note to VIII.36) was punished for showing disrespect for Cao Pi's
   wife.
8 For Wang Can, see note to VIII.19.
9 Kong Rong (153–208) and Mi Heng (173–198) were both renowned writers
   of the day, known also for their arrogance and outspokenness. Both died by
   execution.

IX.2b

Wu Zhi offended his fellow countrymen.[1] Cao Zhi was insolent and broke the law.[2] Du Du knew no end in making appeals and demands.[3] Lu Cui was extremely parochial.[4] Chen Lin was called truly careless.[5] Po Qin had no self-restraint.[6] Liu Zhen was condemned to hard labor because of his pig-headedness.[7] Wang Can gave offense because of his impetuousness in seeking advancement.[8] Kong Rong and Mi Heng were killed for their wild arrogance.[9] Yang Xiu and Ding Yi incurred death by political instigation.[10] Ruan Ji had no sense of decorum and damaged the customs.[11] Ji Kang met a violent end through condescension.[12] Fu Xuan was dismissed from office for his angry bout with a colleague.[13] Sun Chu was conceited and humiliated his superior.[14] Lu Ji deviated from the right path and trod in danger.[15] Pan Yue courted trouble because of his greed.[16] Yan Yannian was exiled on account of his temper.[17] Xie Lingyun breached regulations with his slackness.[18] Wang Yuanchang brought disaster upon himself by his fierceness and violence.[19] Xie Xuanhui was ruined by his impertinence.[20]

---

10 Yang Xiu (175–219) and Ding Yi (d. 220) were supporters of Cao Zhi in his rivalry with his elder brother Cao Pi for designation as heir to their father.

11 For Ruan Ji, see note to VIII.21b.

12 For Ji Kang, see note to VIII.21b.

13 Fu Xuan (217–278) was a prolific poet and writer.

14 Sun Chu (d. 293) was a Western Jin writer.

15 Lu Ji (see note to VI.24) was slandered and killed by the prince he served.

16 For Pan Yue, see note to VIII.35. He was implicated in a rebellion plot and executed.

17 Yan Yannian is Yan Yanzhi 顏延之 (384–456), a court poet who offended people with his hot temper and outspokenness. He was one of Yan Zhitui's forebears (see Introductoon).

18 Xie Lingyun (385–433) was a famous poet and writer best known for his landscape poetry. He was exiled for reckless behavior and eventually executed for plotting rebellion.

19 Wang Yuanchang is Wang Rong 王融 (467–493), a famous poet, who lost his life by supporting the wrong prince for the throne.

20 Xie Xuanhui is Xie Tiao: see note to VIII.37. He was slandered by someone he had scorned and wrongly executed.

IX.2c

凡此諸人，皆其翹秀者，不能悉記，大較
如此。至於帝王，亦或未免。自昔天子而
有才華者，唯漢武、魏太祖、文帝、明
帝、宋孝武帝，皆負世議，非懿德之君
也。自子游、子夏、荀況、孟軻、枚乘、
賈誼、蘇武、張衡、左思之儔，有盛名而
免過患者，時復聞之，但其損敗居多耳。

IX.3

每嘗思之，原其所積，文章之體，標舉興
會，發引性靈，使人矜伐，故忽於持操，
果於進取。今世文士，此患彌切，一事愜
當，一句清巧，神厲九霄，志凌千載，自
吟自賞，不覺更有傍人。加以砂礫所傷，
慘於矛戟，諷刺之禍，速乎風塵，深宜防
慮，以保元吉。

---

1 Han Emperor Wu was Liu Che 劉徹 (156–87 BCE, r. 140–87 BCE). The three
Wei emperors refer to Cao Cao (posthumously made Emperor Wu 武帝, also
known as Taizu), Cao Pi (see note to IX.2b), and Cao Rui 曹叡 (205–239,
r. 226–239), Cao Pi's son. Song Emperor Xiaowu was Liu Jun 劉駿 (430–464),
who left a sizable literary collection.

IX.2c

The above-mentioned men were the most outstanding among writers. I cannot make a note of all, but this list can give you a rough idea. Indeed even emperors and kings are not free from fault. From ancient times, only Han Emperor Wu, Wei Emperor Taizu, Wei Emperor Wen, Wei Emperor Ming, and Song Emperor Xiaowu were rulers with literary talent.[1] They were all subjected to criticism, and none is considered a prince of splendid virtue. As for men such as Ziyou, Zixia, Xun Kuang, Meng Ke, Mei Sheng, Jia Yi, Su Wu, Zhang Heng, and Zuo Si,[2] who enjoyed a great reputation but were unburdened by mistake or mishap, I have heard of such from time to time; but on the whole those who brought ruin to themselves constitute the majority.

IX.3

I often ponder this phenomenon and try to trace the hidden reasons. As I see it, the essence of literary writings is such that they reveal one's emotional stirrings and responses, give expression to one's spiritual nature, and cause one to draw upon and show off one's talent; so an author neglects the cultivation of integrity but is decisive in advancing himself. This problem is even more pronounced in today's men of letters: if they use a single appropriate textual reference and craft a single ingenious line, their soul soars to the ninth heaven and their aspiration transcends a thousand years; chanting and admiring their own composition, they become completely oblivious to people around them. In addition, a grain of sand and a pebble can wound more deeply than spears and halberds; the calamity caused by satire and mockery can happen more quickly than a thunderstorm. You should be deeply circumspect and cautious about this so as to safeguard the great blessings in your life.

---

2 Ziyou and Zixia were Confucius' disciples. Xun Kuang was Xunzi (Master Xun) or Xun Qing (see note to VI.9). Meng Ke was the philosopher Mencius (fl. fourth century BCE). Mei Sheng (d. 140 BCE) and Jia Yi (200–168 BCE) were Western Han writers. Su Wu (d. 60 BCE) was a Han courtier who refused to surrender to the Xiongnu through many years of hardship and detainment; many poems are (spuriously) attributed to him. Zhang Heng (78–139) was a famous Eastern Han writer and scientist. For Zuo Si, see note to VIII.33.

IX.4

學問有利鈍，文章有巧拙。鈍學累功，不妨精熟；拙文研思，終歸蚩鄙。但成學士，自足為人。必乏天才，勿強操筆也。吾見世人，至無才思，自謂清華，流布醜拙，亦以眾矣，江南號為詅癡符。近在并州，有一士族，好為可笑詩賦，誂撆邢、魏諸公，眾共嘲弄，虛相讚說，便擊牛釃酒，招延聲譽。其妻，明鑒婦人也，泣而諫之。此人歎曰："才華不為妻子所容，何況行路！"至死不覺。自見之謂明，此誠難也。

IX.5

學為文章，先謀親友，得其評裁，知可施行，然後出手；慎勿師心自任，取笑旁人也。自古執筆為文者，何可勝言。然至於宏麗精華，不過數十篇耳。但使不失體裁，辭意可觀，便稱才士；要動俗蓋世，亦俟河之清乎。

IX.4

In scholarship some are sharp and some are dull; in literary composition some are skillful and some are clumsy. The dull scholar keeps up his efforts and may one day attain mastery; the clumsy writer will be crude and inferior no matter how hard he tries. As long as you become a learned man, you can establish yourself in the world; but if you have no genius, don't force yourself to take up the writing brush. I have seen quite a few people without the slightest talent, who nevertheless regard themselves as pure and magnificent writers and allow their horrid and awkward compositions to spread through the world. In the south we used to call such men "sellers of their own folly." Recently, there was a gentry member in Bingzhou who wrote laughable poems and rhapsodies. Yet he would poke fun at eminent gentlemen such as Xing and Wei.[1] People mocked him by heaping on him false praise, and he would happily butcher oxen and strain ale to feast them in order to enhance his reputation. His wife, a wise woman, remonstrated with him with tears in her eyes. The man said with a sigh: "Alas, my talent cannot even be tolerated by my own wife! How can I expect much from people on the street?" He remained deluded until death. "Self-knowledge is the true knowledge" – and that is difficult to achieve indeed.

IX.5

When one is learning to write, one should consult one's relatives and friends and get their assessment and feedback first. After one is assured that the piece is acceptable, then one may let it out of hand. You must by no means follow your own heart and trust your own judgment, for you may well be a laughingstock to others. Since ancient times, numerous men have taken up a brush to write, and yet, when it comes to magnificent and superb writings, there have been no more than a few dozen. As long as one's writing has a clear structure and presentable expressions, one may be considered talented. If one seeks to stun the public and surpass the entire world, he might as well wait for the Yellow River to clear up first.

---

1 Bingzhou is in modern Shanxi. Xing and Wei refer to Xing Shao (see note to VIII.17) and Wei Shou (see note to VIII.20).

IX.6

不屈二姓，夷、齊之節也；何事非君，
伊、箕之義也。自春秋已來，家有奔亡，
國有吞滅，君臣固無常分矣；然而君子之
交絕無惡聲，一旦屈膝而事人，豈以存亡
而改慮？陳孔璋居袁裁書，則呼操為豺
狼；在魏製檄，則目紹為蛇虺。在時君所
命，不得自專，然亦文人之巨患也，當務
從容消息之。

IX.6

Not submitting to two royal houses – this is the integrity shown by Bo Yi and Shu Qi.[1] "Any lord one serves is one's ruler" – this is the principle upheld by Yi Yin and Jizi.[2] Ever since the Spring and Autumn period, many clans have fled into exile, and many states have been conquered: the relationship between a prince and a minister cannot remain unchanged. Yet, when a gentleman severs his relationship with another, he will not speak ill of his former friend. Once a man bends his knee to serve another, how can he change his thoughts about his former lord? When Chen Kongzhang was writing a letter on behalf of Yuan Shao, he called Cao Cao a jackal and a wolf; when he composed a proclamation on behalf of the Wei, he described Yuan Shao as a poisonous snake.[3] He did what his current lord ordered and had no control over his action. But this is a great problem for a man of letters. You must consider this most carefully if you ever find yourself in such a situation.

---

1 Bo Yi 伯夷 and Shu Qi 叔齊 (fl. eleventh century BCE) were brothers who protested against King Wu of Zhou's conquest of Shang and starved to death in the mountains.

2 Yi Yin 伊尹 was a minister of Shang in high antiquity. Jizi 箕子 was the uncle of the last Shang king, Zhou 紂; he remonstrated with King Zhou and was imprisoned, and after King Wu of Zhou conquered Shang, Jizi offered counsel to King Wu. The comparison between Bo Yi and Yi Yin is made by Mencius, who comments that the two men "did not share the same way": Bo Yi "would not serve any lord except for his lord [the lord of his choice]" 非其君不事, whereas for Yi Yin, "any lord he served was his lord" 何事非君. The commentary states that Yi Yin once said, "To serve a lord who is not the right lord: now what harm lies in that?....The important thing here is to manage the world on behalf of Heaven and practice the Way." *Mengzi zhushu* 3A.55b–56a.

3 Chen Kongzhang was Chen Lin (see note to IX.2b). He first served the warlord Yuan Shao (see note to II.10) and later served Cao Cao.

IX.7

或問揚雄曰：“吾子少而好賦？”雄曰：
“然。童子雕蟲篆刻，壯士不為也。”余
竊非之曰：“虞舜歌南風之詩，周公作鴟
鴞之詠，吉甫、史克雅、頌之美者，未聞
皆在幼年累德也。孔子曰：‘不學詩，無
以言。’‘自衛返魯，樂正，雅、頌各得
其所。’大明孝道，引詩證之。揚雄安敢
忽之也？若論‘詩人之賦麗以則，辭人之
賦麗以淫’，但知變之而已，又未知雄自
為壯夫何如也？著劇秦美新，妄投於閣，
周章怖慴，不達天命，童子之為耳。袁亮
以勝老子，葛洪以方仲尼，使人歎息。此
人直以曉算術，解陰陽，故著太玄經，為
數子所惑耳；其遺言餘行，孫卿、屈原之
不及，安敢望大聖之清塵？且太玄今竟何
用乎？不啻覆醬瓿而已。”

---

1 This dialogue is taken from Yang Xiong's work, *Model Sayings* (*Fa yan* 法言).
2 Yu Shun was a sage emperor in antiquity.
3 The "Owl" piece is a poem from the *Classic of Poetry*, attributed to the Duke of Zhou.
4 Yin Jifu was a minister in the court of King Xuan of Zhou (827–782 BCE). Shi Ke or Historian Ke was a historian in the state of Lu in the seventh century BCE.
5 Both remarks by Confucius are from the *Analects*.
6 This is from the *Model Sayings*.
7 Yang Xiong's essay was to praise the Xin dynasty established by the usurper Wang Mang (see note to VIII.35). He threw himself off a tower to escape arrest for

IX.7

Someone asked Yang Xiong, "Were you, sire, not fond of rhapsodies when you were young?" He replied, "Yes, I was. It is like a boy's carving of the insect script and the tally script. A grown man does not do it."[1] I humbly beg to differ. Yu Shun chanted the poem of "South Wind";[2] the Duke of Zhou composed the "Owl" piece;[3] Jifu's and Shi Ke's verses are among the most beautiful of the *Odes* and the *Hymns*.[4] I have never heard that their virtue was hurt by poetry-writing in their youth. Confucius said, "If one does not study the Poems, one will not know how to speak," and "I rectified music upon returning to Lu from Wei, and the *Odes* and the *Hymns* each found its proper place."[5] When expounding the way of filial piety, he also cited the *Poems* to prove his point. How could Yang Xiong dare to ignore poetic writings? As for his statement, that "the rhapsodies of a Poet are beautiful and proper while those of a rhetorician are beautiful but excessive,"[6] he only knows how to distinguish the two kinds, but how about his own behavior when he became a grown man? He wrote the essay on "Criticizing the Qin and Praising the Xin," and threw himself off the tower for nothing;[7] panicked and terrified, he had no comprehension of the Heavenly Mandate – this was all a boy's doing. It is lamentable that Yuan Liang should have regarded him as superior to Laozi and that Ge Hong should have compared him to Confucius.[8] They were both deceived by this fellow simply because he knew something about mathematics and the *yin* and *yang* principles and was thus able to write the *Classic of Great Mystery*. His words and conduct cannot even match those of Sun Qing and Qu Yuan;[9] how could he possibly look up to the pure dust of those great sages? Besides, what is the use of the *Great Mystery* today? It is only good for covering sauce jars.[10]

---

being associated with Liu Xin's son, who was to be executed by Wang Mang (see note to IX.2a).

8 Yuan Liang (fl. 250s) was a Wei minister known for his integrity and learning; he had written a treatise, now lost, criticizing He Yan 何晏 (d. 249), who admired Laozi and Zhuangzi, and Deng Yang 鄧颺 (d. 249). It is unknown if he made any comment on Yang Xiong. In all other editions "Yuan Liang" is emended to Huan Tan 桓譚 (23 BCE–56 CE), who praised Yang Xiong as superior to the "masters" including Laozi (see Additional Notes). Ge Hong (283–343) was an Eastern Jin Daoist thinker.

9 For Sun Qing, see note to VI.9. For Qu Yuan, see note to IX.2a.

10 This is what Liu Xin said to Yang Xiong about the *Great Mystery*.

IX.8

齊世有席毗者，清幹之士，官至行臺尚
書，嗤鄙文學，嘲劉逖云："君輩辭藻，
譬若朝菌，須臾之翫，非宏才也；豈比吾
徒千丈松樹，常有風霜，不可凋悴矣。"
劉應之曰："既有寒木，又發春華，何如
也？"席笑曰："可哉。"

IX.9

凡為文章，猶乘騏驥，雖有逸氣，當以銜
勒制之，勿使流亂軌躅，放意填坑岸也。

IX.10

文章當以理致為心腎，氣調為筋骨，事義
為皮膚，華麗為冠冕。今世相承，趨本棄
末，率多浮豔。辭與理競，辭勝而理伏；
事與才爭，事繁而才損。放逸者流宕而忘
歸，穿鑿者補綴而不足。時俗如此，安能
獨違？但務去泰去甚耳。必有盛才重譽，
改革體裁者，實吾所希。

IX.8

During the Qi there was a gentleman named Xi Pi, who was an efficient man of integrity and reached the position of Minister of the Branch Department of State Affairs. He despised literary learning. Once he taunted Liu Ti, saying, "The fine words of your ilk may be likened to the morning hibiscus: it provides a momentary pleasure, but is no great timber. How can you compare with people like us, who are pine trees of a thousand fathoms tall and never wither despite frequent wind and frost?"[1] Liu replied, "How about being a cold-resisting tree *and* sprouting spring flowers?" Xi laughed, "That would be all right, I guess."

IX.9

Writing is like riding a fine steed: even if it has a noble air, you must control it with the bit and reins. Don't let it go off the tracks, gallop to its heart's content, and fall into a ditch somewhere.

IX.10

Literary writings should take ideas and feelings as the heart and kidney; tone as the sinews and bones; textual references as the skin; beautiful flourishes as the cap on the head. Nowadays writers all follow one another in abandoning the roots and pursuing the branches, and most of them are ornate and superficial. Rhetoric and ideas compete with each other; rhetoric wins out and ideas are compromised. Textual allusions contend with the author's talent; talent is injured by too many allusions. A writer who is wild and unrestrained wanders off and forgets to return to the topic at hand; a writer who strains to make things work puts together various pieces and is still found wanting. This, however, is the contemporary trend; how can you alone fight it? Just try to avoid extremes and excesses. Suppose you have great talent and enjoy a high reputation and can reform the literary style, that is truly what I hope to see.

---

1 Liu Ti (525–573) was a Northern Qi courtier who was good at composing poetry.

IX.11

古人之文，宏材逸氣，體度風格，去今實
遠；但緝綴疎朴，未為密緻耳。今世音律
諧靡，章句偶對，諱避精詳，賢於往昔多
矣。宜以古之製裁為本，今之辭調為末，
並須兩存，不可偏棄也。

IX.12

吾家世文章，甚為典正，不從流俗。梁孝
元在蕃邸時，撰西府新文紀，無一篇見錄
者，亦以不偶於世，無鄭衛之音故也。有
詩賦銘誄書表啟疏二十卷，吾兄弟始在草
土，並未得編次，便遭火盪盡，竟不傳於
世，銜酷茹恨，徹於心髓。操行見於梁史
文士傳及孝元懷舊志。

IX.11

The ancients' writings demonstrate magnificent talent and noble air. Their structure and style are very different from today; it is just that their organizing and phrasing are rough and simple, not meticulous and subtle. Today's writings, in terms of harmonious metrical pattern, refined parallelism, and meticulous avoidance of taboos, are much superior to former times. You should take the ancients' tailoring and structuring as basis and today's diction and sound as the branches: both must be preserved; do not discard either.

IX.12

The literary writings of my late father had an orthodox elegance and did not follow the contemporary fashion.[1] When Liang Emperor Xiaoyuan was still a prince, he compiled *A Record of the New Writings of the Western Headquarters*, which did not include a single piece by my late father, because his writings stood apart from the world and contained no sounds of Zheng and Wei.[2] He had twenty scrolls of poems, rhapsodies, inscriptions, elegies, letters, memorials to the throne, and other official communications. When my brother and I were still in the mourning period, they were destroyed by fire before we could compile them, and so they were never transmitted to the world. The sorrow and bitter regret we felt penetrated the inner core of our heart. His moral standing and conduct can be found in the "Biographies of Literary Men" in the *Liang History* as well as in Emperor Xiaoyuan's *Recollections of Old Friends*.[3]

---

1 Yan Zhitui's father, Yan Xie, served on the staff of Xiao Yi when Xiao Yi was first made governor of Jingzhou in 526 (see Introduction).

2 This anthology is no longer extant. It was commissioned by Xiao Yi and compiled by Xiao Shu 蕭淑. Western Headquarters refers to Xiao Yi's headquarters at Jingzhou, which was to the west of the capital Jiankang. The "sounds of Zheng and Wei" describe frivolous and excessive music, which is considered the opposite of the restrained, elegant music of an orderly state.

3 As has been pointed out by Liu Pansui 劉盼遂 (1896–1966), this refers to the *Liang shi* 梁史 compiled by Xu Heng 許亨 (517–570), not the *Liang shu* 梁書 we see today that was completed by Yao Silian 姚思廉 (557–637).

IX.13

沈隱侯曰：“文章當從三易：易見事，一也；易識字，二也；易讀誦，三也。”邢子才常曰：“沈侯文章，用事不使人覺，若胸臆語。”深以此服之。祖孝徵亦嘗謂吾曰：“沈詩云‘崖傾護石髓’。此豈似用事邪?”

IX.14

邢子才、魏收俱有重名，時俗準的，以為師匠。邢賞服沈約而輕任昉，魏愛慕任昉而毀沈約，每於談讌，辭色以之。鄴下紛紜，各為朋黨。祖孝徵嘗謂吾曰：“任、沈之是非，乃邢、魏之優劣也。”

IX.13

The Reticent Marquis Shen said, "Writing should follow three kinds of easiness: the first is easiness of understanding the allusions; the second is easiness of recognizing the words; the third is easiness of reading aloud."[1] Xing Zicai often said, "Marquis Shen uses allusions in such a way that the reader is unaware of them being allusions. Rather, they sound as though coming directly from his heart."[2] He admired Shen deeply for that. Zu Xiaozheng once also said to me, "Shen's poem reads, 'The cliffs slant, protecting rocks' marrow.' That certainly doesn't sound like an allusion at all."[3]

IX.14

Xing Zicai and Wei Shou both enjoyed great fame. Contemporaries looked up to their writings as the standard and regarded them as great masters. Xing admired Shen Yue and scorned Ren Fang; Wei loved Ren Fang and criticized Shen Yue.[4] Every time they fell to talking about it at parties and banquets, their argument became quite heated. People at Ye were all abuzz about it and took different sides, so that each man had his own clique and circle of supporters. Zu Xiaozheng once said to me: "Ren's and Shen's pros and cons exactly reflect Xing's and Wei's strengths and weaknesses."

---

1 The Reticent Marquis was Shen Yue 沈約 (441–513), one of the most influential poets of the Southern Dynasties and compiler of the *History of the Song*.

2 Zicai was the courtesy name of Xing Shao (see note to VIII.17).

3 This line may contain an allusion to a story about Ji Kang (see note to VIII.21b), who was given melted "rock's marrow" or stalactite to drink.

4 Ren Fang (460–508) was a prominent southern writer. His contemporaries considered him as a master of prose whereas Shen Yue was regarded a master of poetry.

IX.15

吳均集有破鏡賦。昔者，邑號朝歌，顏淵
不舍；里名勝母，曾子斂襟：蓋忌夫惡名
之傷實也。破鏡乃凶逆之獸，事見漢書，
為文幸避此名也。

IX.16

比世往往見有和人詩者，題云敬同，孝經
云：「資於事父以事君而敬同。」不可輕
言也。梁世費旭詩云：「不知是耶非。」
殷澐詩云：「飄颻雲母舟。」簡文曰：「旭
既不識其父，澐又飄颻其母。」此雖悉古
事，不可用也。

IX.15

Wu Jun's collection has a "Rhapsody on A Broken Mirror" ["Pojing fu"].[1] In the old days, when a town was called Zhaoge ["singing in the morning"], Yan Yuan would not spend the night there; when a hamlet was named Shengmu ["defeating the mother"], Master Zeng pulled his clothes together.[2] It was because they disliked how a bad name could hurt the reality. Pojing ["broken mirror"] is an evil unfilial beast, which is mentioned in the *Han History*. One should strive to avoid referring to such names in one's writings.

IX.16

In recent years I have often seen people write a poem in response to another; they would entitle the poem, "Respectfully Responding [to So-and-so]" ("*Jing tong*"). The *Classic of Filial Piety* states, "In serving one's lord one takes one's cue from how one serves one's father: the reverence is the same (*jing tong*)." The phrase *jing tong* should not be used lightly. In the Liang, Fei Xu's poem contains the line, "I do not know if it is her or it is not her."[3] Yin Yun's poem contains the line, "Tossed on the waves, the boat decorated with mica."[4] Emperor Jianwen said, "Xu does not know his father while Yun tosses his mother."[5] Although both are allusions to earlier texts, they should not be used.

---

1 Wu Jun (469–520) was a famous southern poet whose distinctive style was dubbed "Wu Jun Style." This rhapsody is no longer extant.

2 Yan Yuan was Yan Hui, Confucius' favorite disciple (see VII.2). Zeng Shen was another disciple, well-known for his filial piety (see IV.1). Zeng Shen allegedly refused to enter Shengmu because he abhorred its name.

3 Fei Xu 費旭 is believed to be the same as Fei Chang 費昶 (fl. early sixth century), a Liang poet. In this line, *ye* 耶, a modal word, also has the meaning of "Dad," hence Emperor Jianwen's derision below.

4 Yin Yun is unknown. Lu Wenchao suspects he is the same as Yin Yun 殷芸 (471–529) or a mistake for a Chu Yun 褚澐 who had served on the staff of Xiao Yi. In this line, *yunmu* (mica) can also mean "Yun's mother," which leads to mockery from Emperor Jianwen.

5 Emperor Jianwen was Xiao Gang (see note to VII.5b), Emperor Wu's third son who was designated as heir in 531.

IX.17

世人或有引詩"伐鼓淵淵"者，宋書已有"屢遊"之誚。如此流比，幸須避之。

IX.18

北面事親，別舅摛渭陽之詠；堂上養老，送兄賦桓山之悲，皆大失也。舉此一隅，觸塗宜慎。

IX.19

江南文制，欲人彈射，知有病累，隨即改之，陳王得之於丁廙也。山東風俗，不通擊難。吾初入鄴，遂嘗以忤人，至今為悔。汝曹必無輕議也。

---

1 Both have to do with the use of *fanyu* in early medieval China, a practice that inverts the initial sounds of a two- or three-character compound and produces a new compound. The taboo is to inadvertently use a phrase that turns out to have a negative meaning when the initials are inverted. In the first case, 伐鼓 ("beating the drums," MC bjot kuX) can be inverted as 骨腐 (MC kwot bjuX), which means "bones are rotten." The second case has not been identified in the *History of the Song* (*Song shu*), but there is speculation that "frequent outings" (*lü you* 屢遊) can be inverted to sound like the Song founding emperor's name, Liu Yu 劉裕 (see Zhou Fagao 61a).

IX.17

Some contemporaries cite this line from the *Classic of Poetry*, "Beating the drums with a vibrating sound." In the *History of the Song* there is already the derision of the phrase "frequent outings."[1] Such expressions should be avoided.

IX.18

While serving one's mother reverently, one quotes "the north shore of Wei" upon taking leave of one's maternal uncle; while caring for one's father at home, one expresses "the sorrow of Huanshan" upon sending off one's elder brother: both are grave mistakes.[2] I am only showing you one aspect of this issue; you should be careful everywhere you turn.

IX.19

In the south writers wanted others to point out the faults in their writings, so that they would, upon learning of any infelicities, immediately correct them. This is precisely what Prince of Chen had gained from Ding Yi.[3] But the northern customs do not endorse criticism. When I first came to Ye, I had offended someone because of this, and have regretted it ever since. You boys must never discuss other people's writings lightly.

---

2 In the first case, the poem "The North Shore of Wei" from the *Classic of Poetry* is attributed to Duke Kang of Qin who expressed longing for his deceased mother when he saw his maternal uncle. Thus it is inappropriate to cite this poem if one's mother is still alive and well. In the second case, the "sorrow at Huanshan" alludes to a story about family separation taking place after the father's death. Hence it is inappropriate to use this allusion if one's father is still alive and well.
3 Cao Zhi, Prince of Chen, related in a letter to Yang Xiu that his friend Ding Yi had asked him to polish and revise his writing, and that he admired Ding Yi's open-mindedness (for Yang Xiu's and Ding Yi's friendship with Cao Zhi, see note to IX.2b).

IX.20

凡代人為文，皆作彼語，理宜然矣。至於哀傷凶禍之辭，不可輒代。蔡邕為胡金盈作母靈表頌曰："悲母氏之不永，然委我而夙喪。"又為胡顥作其父銘曰："葬我考議郎君。"袁三公頌曰："狷獹我祖，出自有嬀。"王粲為潘文則思親詩云："躬此勞瘁，鞠予小人；庶我顯妣，克保遐年。"而並載乎邕、粲之集，此例甚眾。

IX.20

When writing on behalf of someone else, it is appropriate for the author to speak in that person's voice. But if it is about sorrow and mourning or some inauspicious and disastrous event, you should avoid doing it. Cai Yong's eulogy in the "spirit memorial" he wrote for Hu Jinying's mother states, "I am grieved that my mother did not live a long time; she forsook me and departed from the world too early."[1] He also wrote an inscription for Hu Hao's deceased father, saying, "I hereby bury my late father, Court Gentleman for Consultation."[2] His "Eulogy to the Three Dukes of the Yuan Clan" states: "O glorious were our forefathers, who descended from the Gui clan." Wang Can's poem, "Longing for My Mother," written on behalf of Pan Wenze, contains these lines: "You were wearied and fatigued / raising me by hand, your little child. / I wished that my dear mother / could enjoy a long life."[3] These compositions are nevertheless included in Cai Yong's and Wang Can's literary collection respectively. There are many such examples.

---

1 Cai Yong (see note to VI.9), being a prominent writer, composed many such commissioned pieces on behalf of his contemporaries. Hu Jinying was the daughter of the Eastern Han minister Hu Guang 胡廣 (91–172). This piece is still extant while the next two pieces mentioned here are lost.
2 Hu Hao was grandson of Hu Guang.
3 For Wang Can, see note to VIII.19. His poem written for Pan Wenze is still extant.

IX.21

古人之所行，今世以為諱也。陳思王武帝
誄，遂深永蟄之思；潘岳悼亡賦，乃愴手
澤之遺：是方父於蟲，譬婦為考也。蔡邕
楊秉碑云："統大麓之重。"潘尼贈盧景
宣詩云："九五思龍飛。"孫楚王驃騎誄
云："奄忽登遐。"陸機父誄云："億兆
宅心，敦敘百揆。"姊誄云："倪天之
和。"今為此言，則朝廷之罪人也。王
粲贈楊德祖詩云："我君餞之，其樂洩
洩。"不可妄施人子，況儲君乎？

---

1 Cao Zhi's elegy for his father, Cao Cao (posthumous title Emperor Wu), is still extant. Cao Zhi's word choice had already received criticism before Yan Zhitui, even though the dragon was considered as falling in the animal category of insects, albeit the most exalted specimen, and the *Classic of Changes* speaks of the "hibernation of dragons and snakes."

2 Pan Yue's rhapsody is extant but the line criticized here is missing from the current version. "Traces left by hands" is a phrase referring to the deceased father in the *Record of Rites*.

3 Yang Bing (92–165) was a prominent Eastern Han minister. Cai Yong's stele inscription is extant but the line criticized here is missing from the current version. To occupy the "weighty position of the Great Commander" is used to describe Emperor Shun in the *Book of Documents*. Dalu is alternatively interpreted as "the great mountain forest," but also applies to Shun.

4 For Pan Ni, see note to VI.12. A poem to Lu Jingxuan by Pan Ni is extant, but the criticized line is missing from the current version. "Nine in the fifth place" and "dragon soaring" are from the *Classic of Changes* and normally describe ascending the throne.

IX.21

Many practices of the ancients have become taboos in today's world. Prince Si of Chen composed an elegy for Emperor Wu, in which he expresses sorrow over his father's "eternal hibernation."[1] Pan Yue, in his rhapsody lamenting his wife, describes his sadness upon seeing the traces of use on everyday objects left by her hands.[2] The former likened his father to an insect; the latter compared his wife to a deceased father. Cai Yong's stele inscription for Yang Bing describes him as "occupying the weighty position of the Great Commander."[3] Pan Ni's poem to Lu Jingxuan says, "Nine in the fifth place evokes the soaring of the dragon."[4] Sun Chu's elegy for Cavalry General Wang states: "Suddenly he ascended to the distant heaven."[5] Lu Ji's elegy for his father says: "A myriad people willingly submitted to you, who governed and harmonized a hundred officials." His elegy for his elder sister says: "You were like the little sister of the Heavenly God."[6] If an author writes like this nowadays, he would be considered an offender by the court. Wang Can's poem, "Presented to Yang Dezu," contains this couplet: "Our lord held a farewell banquet for you, / at which there were joy and harmony." This allusion cannot be casually applied to any son, even less to the heir apparent.[7]

---

5 For Sun Chu, see note to IX.2b. This piece is no longer extant. The particular phrase, *dengxia* (ascending the distant heaven), had a universal application but came to specifically designate the death of an emperor.

6 Lu Ji's father was Lu Kang 陸抗 (226–274), famous Wu general in the Three Kingdoms period. This piece is extant but the lines criticized here are missing from the current version. The line evokes an emperor or king rather than a minister. Lu Ji's elegy for his sister is no longer extant. The line is quoted verbatim from a poem in the *Classic of Poetry*, which praises the wife of King Wen of Zhou. The last character of the line should be *mei* 妹 rather than *he* 和 (see Additional Notes).

7 Yang Dezu was Yang Xiu (see note to IX.2b). This poem is no longer extant. The second line was a quotation from Lady Jiang 姜 upon her reunion and reconciliation with her son, Duke Zhuang of Zheng 鄭莊公 (757–701 BCE). Thus Yan Zhitui considers it inappropriate to apply it to just any son, not to mention the heir apparent (i.e., Cao Pi).

IX.22

挽歌辭者，或云古者虞殯之歌，或云出自
田橫之客，皆為生者悼往告哀之意。陸平
原多為死人自歎之言，詩格既無此例，又
乖製作大意。

IX.23

凡詩人之作，刺箴美頌，各有源流，未嘗
混雜善惡同篇也。陸機為齊謳篇，前敍山
川物產風教之盛，後章忽鄙山川之情，疎
失厥體。其為吳趨行，何不陳子光、夫差
乎？京洛行，何不述赧王、靈帝乎？

---

1 Tian Heng (d. 202) had been a member of the royal house of Qi who proclaimed
   himself King of Qi at the end of the Qin dynasty. After the Han founder Liu
   Bang unified the empire, he summoned Tian Heng to court. Tian Heng committed suicide on the way rather than become a Han subject. His retainers sang a
   dirge for him lamenting his death.

2 Lu Pingyuan is Lu Ji, who had served as Magistrate of Pingyuan. He wrote a
   dirge, still extant, that assumes the first-person voice of the deceased.

3 This poem is still extant. The last couplet criticizes Duke Jing of Qi's 齊景公
   (d. 490 BCE) sigh at the Ox Hill (where he wishes he could live forever to enjoy
   the beautiful landscape and his pleasure outings). Yan Zhitui feels that there is a
   disconnection between the main body of the poem and the ending.

IX.22

Regarding the genre of dirge, some say that it originated with the funeral song "Yubin" in ancient times; some say that it came from Tian Heng's retainers.[1] In any case, it is a poem in which the living mourn the dead and express their grief. Most of the dirges composed by Lu Pingyuan are, however, the deceased person's self-lamentation.[2] There is no such precedent in the established poetic tradition, and it also goes against the general intent of such compositions.

IX.23

With regard to the works of poets, be it satire, admonition, praise, or eulogy, each has its own source and tradition, and does not mix commendation and criticism in the same piece. Lu Ji's "Song of Qi" depicts the beauty of the mountains and rivers and the richness of the products and customs of the Qi region in the first part, but suddenly turns to the poet's disdain for sentimentality about mountains and rivers in the last part: this deviates from the normative style.[3] [Should this be acceptable,] in his "Ditty of Wu," why does he not mention Ziguang and Fuchai?[4] Similarly, in his "Ballad of the Capital Luoyang," why does he not refer to King Nan and Emperor Ling?[5]

---

4 The "Ditty of Wu" is still extant, which praises Wu, Lu Ji's homeland. Ziguang is Gongzi Guang (Prince Guang 公子光), better known as King Helü of Wu (r. 514–496 BCE), who died from injuries sustained in his invasion of the neighboring state Yue. Fuchai, son of Helü, ruled Wu from 496 BCE to 473 BCE. He was bent on taking revenge for his father when he first became king, but after defeating Yue he became self-satisfied, and Wu was eventually conquered by Yue.

5 This poem is no longer extant. Luoyang was the capital of the Eastern Zhou and Eastern Han. King Nan (r. 314–256 BCE) was the last king of the Eastern Zhou; Emperor Ling (168–189) was the last emperor of the Eastern Han who held actual power.

IX.24

自古宏才博學，用事誤者有矣；百家雜
說，或有不同，書儻湮滅，後人不見，故
未敢輕議之。今指知決紕繆者，略舉一兩
端以為誡云。

IX.25

詩云："有鷕雉鳴。"又曰："雉鳴求其
牡。"毛傳亦曰："鷕，雌雉聲。"又
云："雉之朝雊，尚求其雌。"鄭玄注月
令亦云："雊，雄雉鳴。"潘岳賦曰：
"雉鷕鷕以朝雊。"是則混雜其雄雌矣。

IX.24

From ancient times, even a talented and erudite writer might occasionally make a mistake in using textual allusions. The miscellaneous discourses of a hundred schools sometime contain variant versions, and if one of the books to which a writer alludes is lost, the source of the allusion will become inaccessible to the later-born. For this reason we should not criticize lightly. I will only cite a few examples of what we know for sure are erroneous to serve as warnings.

IX.25

A poem from the *Classic of Poetry* has a line that reads: "*Yao yao* a pheasant cries." Another line reads: "A pheasant cries, seeking her mate." The "Mao Commentary" notes: "*Yao yao* is the sound made by a female pheasant."[1] A couplet from another poem reads, "A pheasant cries [*gou*] at dawn, / it seeks a female." Zheng Xuan's gloss on the "Monthly Ordinances" says: "*Gou* is the cry of a male pheasant."[2] Pan Yue's rhapsody says, "A pheasant goes *yaoyao*, it cries [*gou*] at dawn."[3] Here Pan Yue confuses the male and female pheasants.[4]

---

1 The "Mao Commentary" is a Western Han commentary on the *Classic of Poetry*, reputedly compiled by Mao Heng 毛亨 (fl. 129 BCE) and his successor Mao Chang 毛萇.
2 The "Monthly Ordinances" is a chapter from the *Record of Rites*. For Zheng Xuan, see note to VIII.19.
3 Pan Yue's rhapsody, still extant, is "Rhapsody on Shooting Pheasants" ("Shezhi fu" 射雉賦). It is anthologized in the sixth-century anthology *Wen xuan*.
4 It was pointed out by an early commentator, Xu Yuan 徐爰 (394–475), that this line actually describes the cries of both male and female pheasants (see Wang Liqi 288).

IX.26

詩云：“孔懷兄弟。”孔，甚也；懷，思
也，言甚可思也。陸機與長沙顧母書，述
從祖弟士璜死，乃言：“痛心拔惱，有如
孔懷。”心既痛矣，即為甚思，何故方言
有如也？觀其此意，當謂親兄弟為孔懷。
詩云：“父母孔邇。”而呼二親為孔邇，
於義通乎？

IX.27

異物志云：“擁劍狀如蟹，但一螯偏大
爾。”何遜詩云：“躍魚如擁劍。”是不
分魚蟹也。

IX.28

漢書：“御史府中列柏樹，常有野鳥數
千，棲宿其上，晨去暮來，號朝夕鳥。”
而文士往往誤作烏鳶用之。

---

1 This letter is mentioned in VI.24.
2 Presumably this was the *Yiwu zhi* authored by Yang Fu 楊孚 (fl. 77). A "sword-holder" is a kind of crab.

IX.26

A poem from the *Classic of Poetry* contains the line, "I greatly miss my brothers" ("Kong huai xiongdi"). *Kong* means "greatly" and *huai* means "miss," so this line is saying one cherishes a passionate longing for one's brothers. When Lu Ji, in his "Letter to Mother Gu of Changsha," talks about the death of Shihuang, his younger cousin descending from the same great-grandfather, he says, "My heart and mind are pierced with grief, as if I had lost the one 'greatly missed.'"[1] Now, if one's heart is pained by someone's death, it shows that he is indeed greatly missing the deceased person; why say "as if"? In this case, I believe that by "the one 'greatly missed'" he is referring to brothers born of the same parents [as opposed to cousins]. But then, there is a line from a poem in the *Classic of Poetry* that reads, "My father and mother are very close." If one should henceforth refer to one's parents as "[those who are] very close," would that make any sense?

IX.27

The *Account of Exotica* says, "A 'sword-holder' looks like the common crab but one of its claws is much bigger than the other."[2] He Xun's poem says: "A leaping fish is like a sword-holder."[3] He is confusing fish with crab.

IX.28

The *Han History* says, "On the rows of cypresses in the courtyard of the Censorate, there were always several thousands of wild birds nesting. They would fly away in the morning and come back to roost at night, and were known as the 'Morning and Night Birds.'" Literary men often mistakenly referred to the birds as crows.[4]

---

3 He Xun 何遜 (ca. 468–ca.518) is a famous Liang poet. This line is from a poem entitled "Crossing Lianqi" 渡連圻. A variant reads: 魚游若擁劍.

4 As commentators point out, "crow" rather than "bird" has been the mainstream reading (Wang Liqi 290).

IX.29

抱朴子說項曼都詐稱得仙，自云：“仙人以流霞一杯與我飲之，輒不飢渴。”而簡文詩云：“霞流抱朴椀。”亦猶郭象以惠施之辨為莊周言也。

IX.30

後漢書：“囚司徒崔烈以銀鐺鎖。”銀鐺，大鎖也；世間多誤作金銀字。武烈太子亦是數千卷學士，嘗作詩云：“銀鎖三公腳，刀撞僕射頭。” 為俗所誤。

IX.29

The *Master of Embracing Simplicity* mentions that Xiang Mandu falsely claimed to be an immortal;[1] he would tell people that the gods had given him a cup of cloud vapor to drink and that subsequently he no longer suffered from hunger and thirst. Liang Emperor Jianwen's poem says, "Rosy cloud vapor flows into Baopu's goblet." This is like Guo Xiang taking Hui Shi's argument to be Zhuang Zhou's.[2]

IX.30

The *History of the Later Han* says: "The Minister of Education Cui Lie was shackled with the *lang dang* chains."[3] *Lang dang* refers to a big and heavy chain, but many people mistakenly write *lang* with a "metal" radical as *yin*, meaning silver. Crown Prince Wulie, himself a fine scholar who had read several thousand scrolls of books, once wrote a poem that says, "Silver chains bind the feet of the Three Dukes, / a sword knocks the head of the Lord Chamberlain."[4] He, too, was misled by the crowd.

---

1 The *Master of Embracing Simplicity* (*Baopuzi*) was a work authored by the Eastern Jin Daoist thinker Ge Hong (see note to IX.7).

2 Guo Xiang was a commentator on *Zhuangzi* (see note to VIII.21b). Hui Shi (fourth century BCE), a late Warring States thinker and so-called "terminologist" (*mingjia*) or casuist, is featured as a friend and conversation partner of Zhuang Zhou in the *Zhuangzi*.

3 Cui Lie (d. 192) was a late Eastern Jin official who was imprisoned by the warlord Dong Zhuo (see note to IX.2a).

4 Crown Prince Wulie was Xiao Yi's eldest son, Xiao Fangdeng (528–549; see VI.47). After he died in battle during the Hou Jing Rebellion, he was given the posthumous title Crown Prince Zhongzhuang 忠壯; the title was changed to Crown Prince Wulie after Xiao Yi took the throne in 552.

IX.31

文章地理，必須愜當。梁簡文雁門太守行
乃云："驚軍攻日逐，燕騎蕩康居，大宛
歸善馬，小月送降書。"蕭子暉隴頭水
云："天寒隴水急，散漫俱分瀉，北注徂
黃龍，東流會白馬。"此亦明珠之纇，美
玉之瑕，宜慎之。

IX.32

王籍入若耶溪詩云："蟬噪林逾靜，鳥鳴山
更幽。"江南以為文外斷絕，物無異議。簡
文吟詠，不能忘之，孝元諷味，以為不可復
得，至懷舊志載於籍傳。范陽盧詢祖，鄴下
才俊，乃言："此不成語，何事於能？"魏收
亦然其論。詩云："蕭蕭馬鳴，悠悠旆旌。"
毛傳曰："言不諠譁也。"吾每歎此解有情
致，籍詩生於此耳。

---

1 "Ballad of the Yanmen Magistrate" is an old ballad title. This poem is extant, but
   attributed to Chu Xiang 褚翔 (505–548), a Liang courtier. Yanmen in the title
   of the ballad is in modern Shanxi. The four lines here contain five proper names:
   Rizhu was the title of a Xiongnu chieftain; Yan is in modern Hebei; Kangju and
   Dayuan were kingdoms in Central Asia; Xiao Yue is Xiao Yuezhi 小月氏, a
   nomadic people living by the Qilian Mountains (in modern Gansu and Qinghai).
2 Xiao Zihui (fl. early sixth century) was brother of Xiao Ziyun (487–549; see note
   to VII.5b) and grandson of the Southern Qi founding emperor (r. 479–482). He
   was known for his literary writings. "Waters of Longtou" is a ballad title, to which
   many Liang poets had written poems. Xiao Zihui's piece is no longer extant.

IX.31

In literary writings geographical descriptions should be accurate. Liang Emperor Jianwen's "Ballad of the Yanmen Magistrate" says, "With the goose formation they mounted an attack on Rizhu; / the Yan cavalry swept Kangju clean. / Dayuan yielded their fine steeds; / Xiao Yue sent an epistle of surrender."[1] Xiao Zihui's poem "Waters of Longtou" says:[2] "In cold weather the Long River rushes forward; / scattered and dispersed, it flows in different directions. / To the north it hastens toward Yellow Dragon Fortress; / to the east it meets with White Horse Ford."[3] This is a flaw in a bright pearl and a blemish on beautiful jade. You should exercise caution in your own writings.

IX.32

Wang Ji's poem, "Entering Ruoye Creek," contains this couplet: "Cicadas noisily sing, the forest becomes quieter; / birds pipe up, the hills are even more serene."[4] People in the south regarded it as absolutely divine, and there was no disagreement. Emperor Jianwen chanted it over and over, unable to get it out of his mind. Emperor Xiaoyuan recited and savored it, and was of the opinion that we would never see anything like it ever again. He even mentioned it in Wang Ji's biographical note in his *Recollections of Old Friends*. However, Lu Xunzu of Fanyang, one of the Ye talents, had this to say: "It doesn't make any sense. What's so great about it?"[5] Wei Shou, too, echoed the sentiment. A couplet from the *Classic of Poetry* reads, "The horses whinny and neigh; / aflutter, the banners flow in the wind." The "Mao Commentary" says: "These lines describe the absence of clamoring [of the troops]." I have always admired the witty charm of this interpretation. Wang Ji's couplet derives from it.

---

3 The Long River originates from the Long Mountains (in modern Gansu). Yellow Dragon Fortress is in modern Liaoning and White Horse Ford is in modern He'nan.

4 Wang Ji (fl. 490s–ca. 547) was a Liang courtier and poet who had served on the staff of Xiao Yi.

5 Lu Xunzu (d. 566) was a Northern Qi courtier who was known for literary talent.

IX.33

蘭陵蕭愨，梁室上黃侯之子，工於篇什。嘗有秋詩云："芙蓉露下落，楊柳月中疏。"時人未之賞也。吾愛其蕭散，宛然在目。潁川荀仲舉、琅邪諸葛漢，亦以為爾。而盧思道之徒，雅所不愜。

IX.34

何遜詩實為清巧，多形似之言；揚都論者，恨其每病苦辛，饒貧寒氣，不及劉孝綽之雍容也。雖然，劉甚忌之，平生誦何詩，常云："'蘧居[車]響北闕，'懵懵不道車。"又撰詩苑，止取何兩篇，時人譏其不廣。

---

1 Xiao Que (fl. 550s–580s) was son of Xiao Ye 蕭曄 (Marquis of Shanghuang, d. ca. late 530s) and grandson of Xiao Dan 蕭憺 (478–522), Emperor Wu's younger brother. Lanling is in modern Shandong and was the ancestral home of the Xiao clan.

2 Xun Zhongju (fl. mid-sixth century) was a Liang official who was captured in 547 after a lost battle between the Liang and the Eastern Wei, and subsequently served the Northern Qi. Yingchuan, in modern He'nan, was the ancestral home of Xun Zhongju. Zhuge Han was a prolific writer also of southern origin (Langye, in modern Shandong, was his ancestral home); he had served in the Grove of Letters Institute along with Xiao Que and Yan Zhitui in 570s.

3 Lu Sidao (535–586) was a famous Northern Qi poet, and a clansman of Lu Xunzu (see IX.32).

IX.33

Xiao Que of Lanling was the son of the Marquis of Shanghuang of the Liang house.[1] He was skilled at writing poetry. He once wrote a poem about autumn, which contains this couplet: "The lotus drops its flowers under the dew; / willows grow sparse in the moonlight." People at the time did not appreciate it, but I am fond of the forlorn scene so vividly painted that I can see it right in front of my eyes. Xun Zhongju of Yingchuan and Zhuge Han of Langye share my opinion.[2] Lu Sidao and his like, however, are quite dismissive about it.[3]

IX.34

He Xun's poems are pure and well-crafted, with many vivid descriptions. But the critics at Yangdu [Jiankang] regretted his frequent complaint about hardships; they considered his poems as full of an air of cold destitution, not as genteel as Liu Xiaochuo's writings.[4] Liu Xiaochuo himself was nevertheless very jealous of He Xun. Whenever he talked about He Xun's poems, he would always say, "'Qu's carriage rumbles at the northern palace tower.' That must be a perverse and wicked carriage!"[5] When he compiled the *Garden of Poetry*, he only included two poems by He Xun, and was disparaged by his contemporaries for being so petty.[6]

---

4 Both were famous Liang poets (see note to VI.45 for Liu Xiaochuo and note to IX.27 for He Xun), although He Xun has fared much better than Liu Xiaochuo in literary history and proved more influential in later times.

5 This line is from He Xun's poem, still extant, entitled "What I Heard and Saw from My Carriage Going to Dawn Court" 早朝車中聽望. Qu refers to Qu Boyu 蘧伯玉 (fl. sixth century BCE), a Wei minister of high moral principles befriended and revered by Confucius. Once, late at night, Duke Ling of Wei 衛靈公 (r. 534–493 BCE) and his wife heard a carriage approach the palace with a rumbling sound but become quiet when it came to the palace tower, only to resume its louder passage afterward. The Duchess knew it must be Qu Boyu, because he was known to observe proper etiquette even with nobody around. Thus, He Xun's line is contrary to the traditional representation of Qu Boyu's character and becomes the target of Liu Xiaochuo's criticism.

6 The anthology is no longer extant.

IX.35

劉孝綽當時既有重名，無所與讓；唯服謝
朓，常以謝詩置几案間，動靜輒諷味。簡
文愛陶淵明文，亦復如此。

IX.36

江南語曰："梁有三何，子朗最多。"三
何者，遜及思澄、子朗也。子朗信饒清
巧。思澄遊廬山，每有佳篇，亦為冠絕。

IX.35

Liu Xiaochuo enjoyed a prominent reputation as a writer in his lifetime, and never deferred to anyone except Xie Tiao.[1] He kept Xie Tiao's poems on his desk, reading them and savoring them all the time. In the same way Liang Emperor Jianwen loved Tao Yuanming's writings.[2]

IX.36

In the south there was a saying, "The Liang has three He: Zilang is the best of them all."[3] The "three He" refers to Xun, Sicheng, and Zilang. Zilang's writings truly demonstrate an abundance of purity and artfulness. Whenever Sicheng visited Mount Lu, he would produce fine poems that indeed proved superior to his contemporaries as well.

---

1 For Xie Tiao, see note to VIII.37.
2 Tao Yuanming (365–427) is now considered one of the greatest Chinese poets. His poetry was very popular in his lifetime and during the Southern Dynasties. Apart from Xiao Gang's admiration mentioned here, Xiao Tong, Xiao Gang's elder brother, had compiled Tao Yuanming's collection and personally wrote a preface for it.
3 He Sicheng (ca. 480s–ca. 530s), He Zilang (fl. 510s), and He Xun were clansmen (Zilang was not son of Sicheng as Teng Ssu-yü claims; see Teng 107).

名實第十

X.1

名之與實，猶形之與影也。德藝周厚，則名必善焉；容色姝麗，則影必美焉。今不脩身而求令名於世者，猶貌甚惡而責妍影於鏡也。

X.2

上士忘名，中士立名，下士竊名。忘名者，體道合德，享鬼神之福祐，非所以求名也；立名者，脩身慎行，懼榮觀之不顯，非所以讓名也；竊名者，厚貌深姦，干浮華之虛稱，非所以得名也。

X. Name and Reality

X.1

Name and reality are like form and its reflection. With fine virtue and rich skills, one will certainly enjoy a good reputation, just as a lovely form will certainly have a beautiful reflection. If a man seeks a good reputation without cultivating himself, it will be as impossible as having a homely face but demanding to see a pretty reflection in the mirror.

X.2

A superior gentleman forgets about reputation; an average gentleman works to establish a reputation; an inferior gentleman steals reputation. The one who forgets about reputation embodies the Way, acts in accordance with virtue, and enjoys the blessings of spirits and gods; yet he does not seek reputation through this. The one who works to establish a reputation cultivates himself and is guarded in conduct, worrying that his fame and glory are not manifest for all to see; he will never yield a good name to anyone else. The one who steals reputation maintains a sincere appearance on the outside but harbors devious designs within, pursuing flowery but empty names: this is not the proper way to acquire reputation.

X.3

人足所履，不過數寸，然而咫尺之途，必
顛蹶於崖岸，拱把之梁，每沈溺於川谷
者，何哉？為其旁無餘地故也。君子之立
己，抑亦如之。至誠之言，人未能信，至
潔之行，物或致疑，皆由言行聲名，無餘
地也。吾每為人所毀，常以此自責。若能
開方軌之路，廣造舟之航，則仲由之言
信，重於登壇之盟，趙熹之降城，賢於折
衝之將矣。

---

1 Zhongyou was Zilu 子路 (542–480 BCE), a disciple of Confucius known for
his physical strength, valor, sense of justice, and rashness. This alludes to a story
in which someone claimed he did not need any oath as long as he could have a
verbal agreement from Zilu (from the *Zuo Tradition*, Duke Ai 14, 481 BCE).

X.3

A person's feet only stand on several inches of ground. But if he walks on a path that is one foot wide, he will stumble and fall off from the cliffs; if he walks on a narrow bridge that can be spanned with two hands, he would tumble over and drown in the river. Why is this? It is because there is no extra space around him. The same goes for a gentleman seeking to establish himself: the most sincere words may not be believed; the purest action may be doubted. This is due to the fact that he leaves no room in his speech, conduct, and reputation. Whenever I was slandered by others, I would blame myself thus. If one can open a wide path for carriages to proceed side by side, or widen the pontoon bridge by connecting many boats, then he will be like Zhongyou whose trustworthy words carried more weight than the oath sworn on an altar,[1] or Zhao Xi who with his good faith brought about the surrender of a city more readily than a general who could "keep the enemy's chariots back."[2]

---

2 Zhao Xi (3 BCE–80 CE) was known for his trustworthiness. During the post-Wang Mang civil war, a powerful local clan held a city refusing to surrender to the forces of the Gengshi 更始 emperor (r. 23–25 CE); they said they would yield only if the emperor could send Zhao Xi, a man of his word. As soon as Zhao was sent there, the clan surrendered. Zhao became a prominent official in the Eastern Han.

X.4

吾見世人，清名登而金貝入，信譽顯而然諾虧，不知後之矛戟，毀前之干櫓也。宓子賤云：“誠於此者形於彼。”人之虛實真偽在乎心，無不見乎跡，但察之未熟耳。一為察之所鑒，“巧偽不如拙誠”，承之以羞大矣。伯石讓卿，王莽辭政，當於爾時，自以巧密；後人書之，留傳萬代，可為骨寒毛豎也。

X.5

近有大貴，以孝著聲，前後居喪，哀毀踰制，亦足以高於人矣。而嘗於苫塊之中，以巴豆塗臉，遂使成瘡，表哭泣之過。左右童豎，不能掩之，益使外人謂其居處飲食，皆為不信。以一偽喪百誠者，乃貪名不已故也。

---

1 Fu Zijian's name was Fu Buqi 不齊, a disciple of Confucius famous for his capable governance as magistrate of Shanfu 單父 (in modern Shandong). The remark is also attributed to Confucius in early sources.

X.4

I have seen people who once having acquired a reputation for purity began to take cash, and who once having achieved credibility began to eat their words. They do not know that later spears and halberds can destroy earlier bucklers and shields. Fu Zijian once said, "Sincerity shown in one area will manifest in another."[1] A person's truth or falsity and candor or dishonesty are in his own mind, but are always revealed in outward traces. If you fail to see it, it is because you have not observed closely. Once it is detected through observation, then "clever deception is not as good as clumsy honesty," and the resulting shame will be great indeed. Boshi had refused the position of high minister; Wang Mang had declined ruling as regent.[2] At the time, they thought they were oh-so-clever-and-discreet; but their actions were recorded later and transmitted to posterity for ten thousand generations. Thinking of it gives one a chill in the bones and makes one's hair stand on end.

X.5

In recent years there was a great nobleman who was well-known for his filial piety. When he observed the mourning period for his parents, he demonstrated his grief well beyond ritual requirements. That was enough to show his superiority to others. Yet, he smeared his face with Ba beans to make sores, so as to create the appearance of excessive weeping. His servant-boys could not keep it secret. Once known, it made others believe that he was faking everything, from his living conditions to his food and drink during the mourning period. Thus he lost credit for a hundred acts of sincerity due to one act of hypocrisy, and it was all because he was too greedy for a good reputation and pursued it relentlessly.

---

2 Boshi (fl. 540s BCE) was an official in the state of Zheng. When the Duke of Zheng appointed him to be a high minister, he declined, but afterwards he asked for the appointment to be made again. He did this three times before he accepted. Wang Mang (see note to VIII.35) had repeatedly declined to act as regent when the young Han Emperor Ping took the throne in 1 BCE.

X.6

有一士族，讀書不過二三百卷，天才鈍拙，而家世殷厚，雅自矜持，多以酒犢珍玩交諸名士，甘其餌者，遞共吹噓，朝廷以為文華，亦常出境聘。東萊王韓晉明篤好文學，疑彼製作，多非機杼，遂設讌言，面相討試。竟日歡諧，辭人滿席，屬音賦韻，命筆為詩，彼造次即成，了非向韻。客各自沈吟，遂無覺者。韓退歎曰：“果如所量。”韓又嘗問曰：“玉珽杼上終葵首，當作何形？”乃答云：“珽頭曲圜，勢如葵葉耳。”韓既有學，忍笑為吾說之。

X.7

治點子弟文章，以為聲價，大弊事也。一則不可常繼，終露其情；二則學者有憑，益不精勵。

X.6

There was a dull-witted and inept gentry member who had merely read two or three hundred scrolls of books. But he came from a very wealthy family, and was conceited and self-important. He made friends with famous gentlemen by entertaining them with wine and food and offering them precious curiosities. Those who enjoyed the bait sang his praises, so that the court thought he was a fine literary man, and frequently sent him out of its borders as an envoy. Han Jinming, the Prince of Donglai, was fond of literature and cultural learning, and suspected that most of the man's writings were not his own creations.[1] So he decided to hold a party and test him in person. There were many men of letters among the invited guests, who enjoyed the gathering all day. They had writing brushes brought over and composed poems to designated rhymes. Our man in question dashed off a piece hastily, but it was not at all like the sort of poems he had supposedly written before. The guests were all deep in thought over their own poetry, and nobody noticed anything wrong. Han retired and said with a sigh, "This is exactly what I thought." On another occasion Han asked him, "'The jade scepter is pared down, so that its top resembles the head of a *zhongkui* [awl].' What shape should that be?"[2] He replied, "The scepter's head is curved and round, and looks just like a leaf of the mallow [*kui*] plant." Han was a learned man and told me the story with stifled laughter.

X.7

To polish the writings of one's children in order to promote them is a very bad practice. For one thing, it cannot be kept up, and truth will eventually come out. For another, a learner who has someone to rely on will even more not want to study hard.

---

2 The quotation is from the *Rites of Zhou* 周禮, one of the early ritual classics. The Eastern Han commentator Zheng Xuan (see VIII.19) glosses *zhongkui* as a *zhui* 椎 (awl); hence Han Jinming's derision of the gentry member, who took *kui* or *zhongkui* as the name of the Chinese mallow (*Malva verticillata L.*, not "sunflower" as Ssu-yü Teng says; see Teng 111). However, as scholars have pointed out, Zhongkui is indeed also the name of a plant with round-shaped leaves (*Basella rubra L.*), whose name and definition appear in the early dictionary *Erya* (cited in Wang Liqi 310). The gentry member might not have been entirely wrong as Han Jinming and Yan Zhitui believed.

X.8

鄴下有一少年，出為襄國令，頗自勉篤。
公事經懷，每加撫卹，以求聲譽。凡遣兵
役，握手送離，或齎梨棗餅餌，人人贈
別，云："上命相煩，情所不忍；道路飢
渴，以此見思。"民庶稱之，不容於口。
及遷為泗州別駕，此費日廣，不可常周。
一有偽情，觸塗難繼，功績遂損敗矣。

X.9

或問曰："夫神滅形消，遺聲餘價，亦猶
蟬殼蛇皮，獸迒鳥跡耳，何預於死者，而
聖人以為名教乎？"

X.8

There was a young man of Ye who was appointed the magistrate of Xiangguo.[1] He was quite conscientious and assiduous, and took public responsibilities very much to heart. He often showed solicitous care for people in order to build a fine reputation. Whenever men were conscripted, he would see them off by holding their hands. Sometimes he presented each one with fruit and cakes as farewell gifts, saying: "I am following orders from above, but I really feel bad about this. You may be hungry and thirsty on the road, and I hope to express my concern with these." The commoners sang his praises endlessly. Later, he was promoted to be Assistant Governor of Sizhou, where such expenses became increasingly cumbersome and he could no longer afford them.[2] Once a person has performed an act of hypocrisy, he cannot continue it in everything he does, and his achievements are thus spoiled.

X.9

Someone asked, "When the body ceases to exist and the spirit is gone, the reputation that is left behind and its value will be just like a cicada's shell or a snake's skin, the animal's tracks and the bird's traces. What do they have anything to do with the dead, and why should the sage establish the 'teaching of names'?"

---

1 Xiangguo is in modern Hebei.
2 Sizhou is in modern Jiangsu. The prefecture of Sizhou was known as Dongchuzhou 東楚州 in the Northern Qi and the name Sizhou was used in 580, at the very end of the Northern Zhou. Either the "young man of Ye" had served in Zhou after Zhou's conquest of the Northern Qi in 577 or this passage was written after 580 and Yan Zhitui uses the new name of the prefecture to refer back to Dongchuzhou.

X.10a

對曰:"勸也。勸其立名,則獲其實。且勸一伯夷,而千萬人立清風矣;勸一季札,而千萬人立仁風矣;勸一柳下惠,而千萬人立貞風矣;勸一史魚,而千萬人立直風矣。故聖人欲其魚鱗鳳翼,雜遝參差,不絕於世,豈不弘哉?四海悠悠,皆慕名者,蓋因其情而致其善耳。

X.10b

"抑又論之,祖考之嘉名美譽,亦子孫之冕服牆宇也,自古及今,獲其庇廕者亦眾矣。夫修善立名者,亦猶築室樹果,生則獲其利,死則遺其澤。世之汲汲者,不達此意,若其與魂爽俱昇,松柏偕茂者,惑矣哉。"

---

1 For Bo Yi, see note to IX.6. Bo Yi was the eldest son of the Lord of Guzhu 孤竹君, who wanted Shu Qi, his younger son, to be heir. After their father's death, Shu Qi deferred to Bo Yi to inherit their father's position, but Bo Yi refused and fled the state. Shuqi followed him.

X.10a

To him I replied, "It is all about encouragement. When you encourage a person to establish a name, you will obtain the reality. If you encourage them with one Bo Yi, then tens of thousands of people will become upright.[1] If you encourage them with one Ji Zha, then tens of thousands of people will become benevolent.[2] If you encourage them with one Liuxia Hui, then tens of thousands of people will become chaste.[3] If you encourage them with one Shi Yu, then tens of thousands of people will become honest.[4] The sage wants such people to become as numerous and varied as fish scales and phoenixes' wings, and to never cease appearing in the world. Isn't this a grand vision? Within the four seas there are countless people who admire a fine reputation, and the sage is simply taking advantage of such sentiments and helping fulfill the goodness in them.

X.10b

"Or let me put it another way: the fine reputation of one's ancestors is also the cap and clothes or walls and roof for their descendants. From past to present, there have been many people who obtained such protection from their forebears. Therefore, cultivating one's virtue and establish a fine reputation is like building a house or planting fruit trees: while alive, you profit from them; after death, you leave behind their benefits. People who rush about in the world do not understand this, as if their body would ascend to heaven along with their spirit or flourish together with the ever-green pines and cypresses – how mistaken they are!"

---

2 Ji Zha (fl. sixth century BCE) was the Wu king Shoumeng's 壽夢 (r. 585–561 BCE) youngest son, who was known for his worthiness. The king wanted to pass the throne to him, but Ji Zha refused and deferred to his elder brother.

3 Liuxia Hui (fl, seventh century BCE) was Zhan Huo 展獲 (also known as Zhan Ziqin 展子禽 or Zhan Qin 展禽), a minister of Lu (in modern Shandong) who was famous for his virtue. Liuxia (in modern Shandong) was his fief and his posthumous title was Hui.

4 Shi Yu (fl. 530 BCE) was Shi Qiu 史鰌, courtesy name Ziyu 子魚. He was a worthy official in the state of Wei.

涉務第十一

XI.1

士君子之處世，貴能有益於物耳，不徒高
談虛論，左琴右書，以費人君祿位也。

XI.2

國之用材，大較不過六事：一則朝廷之
臣，取其鑒達治體，經綸博雅；二則文史
之臣，取其著述憲章，不忘前古；三則軍
旅之臣，取其斷決有謀，強幹習事；四則
藩屏之臣，取其明練風俗，清白愛民；五
則使命之臣，取其識變從宜，不辱君命；
六則興造之臣，取其程功節費，開略有
術，此則皆勤學守行者所能辦也。人性有
長短，豈責具美於六塗哉？但當皆曉指
趣，能守一職，便無媿耳。

XI. Engaging in Affairs

XI.1

What is to be most prized about a gentleman in dealing with the world is his ability to bring benefit to people, not just dispensing great empty talk, with a zither on his left side and books on his right, wasting the emolument and position granted by his lord.

XI.2

There are, roughly speaking, no more than six ways for talented men to be deployed by the state: first, as officials in court, drawing upon their deep understanding of the principles of governance, and their broad learning and excellent morality in managing state affairs; second, as courtiers in cultural and historical learning, drawing upon their creating and transmitting the statutes and institutions, and keeping memories of the past alive; third, as military officers, drawing upon their decisiveness, resourcefulness, efficiency, and experience; fourth, as magistrates in the provinces, drawing upon their familiarity with the local customs, integrity, and love of the people; fifth, as diplomats and envoys, drawing upon their quick grasp of changing circumstances and sense of expediency, their ability to accomplish their mission with honor; sixth, as officials in charge of construction, drawing upon their capacity for gauging progress and saving expenses, their ingenuity in making and fashioning. Each of these positions can be achieved by someone who is assiduous in study and prudent in conduct. It is perfectly natural for a person to have strengths and weaknesses, so how can we expect anyone to be perfect in all six areas? As long as one knows their general import and can carry out his duty well in one of the areas, he may feel no shame about himself.

XI.3

吾見世中文學之士，品藻古今，若指諸掌，及有試用，多無所堪。居承平之世，不知有喪亂之禍；處廊廟之下，不知有戰陳之急；保俸祿之資，不知有耕稼之苦；肆吏民之上，不知有勞役之勤，故難可以應世經務也。

XI.4

晉朝南渡，優借士族；故江南冠帶，有才幹者，擢為令僕已下，尚書郎中書舍人已上，典掌機要。其餘文義之士，多迂誕浮華，不涉世務；纖微過失，又惜行捶楚，所以處於清高，蓋護其短也。至於臺閣令史，主書監帥，諸王籤省，並曉習吏用，濟辦時須，縱有小人之態，皆可鞭杖肅督，故多見委使，蓋用其長也。人每不自量，舉世怨梁武帝父子愛小人而疏士大夫，此亦眼不能見其睫耳。

XI.3

I have seen men of letters who evaluate and criticize the past and present as easily as if they were pointing to their own palm, but when being tested and employed themselves, they often fail at the task. Living in a peaceful age, they have not the faintest idea of the existence of disaster and chaos; lounging in the great halls of the ancestral temple and the court, they are unaware of the crisis of war; maintaining the sustenance from their salary, they know nothing about the toil of planting and plowing; lording over clerks and the common folk, they are unacquainted with the hardship of conscripted labor. For these reasons, they are hardly able to respond to the problems of the world and cope with practical affairs

XI.4

When the Jin royal house crossed the River to the south, they treated the gentry with great indulgence. Therefore, in the south a gentry member with any ability would be promoted to a position beneath the Director of Imperial Secretariat and Lord Chamberlain but above Secretarial Court Gentleman and Secretariat Drafter, entrusted with confidential matters of the state. The rest of the lot were men of literary learning who were mostly impractical and superficial, with no experience in handling worldly affairs. Being patrician, if they were ever found guilty of some minor offense, their superiors were reluctant to have them flogged; therefore they would be put in pure honorary positions as a way to protect them from their own shortcomings. As for the assistants working in the Imperial Secretariat, scribes, and military supervisors, or the Document Clerks and Departmental Clerks on the staffs of the princes, they were the ones familiar with all sorts of administrative duties and successfully answering to the needs of the times. Being low-born, if they ever acted in the manner of the low-born, they could be whipped and flogged, exhorted and disciplined; therefore they were often assigned to various offices and tasks as a way to make best use of their strengths. However, many gentry members had no self-awareness, and so throughout the country they resented Liang Emperor Wu and his sons for being fond of low-born men but keeping their distance from gentlemen. That was truly a case of "the eye being unable to see the eyelashes."

XI.5

梁世士大夫皆尚褒衣博帶，大冠高履，出則車輿，入則扶侍，郊郭之內，無乘馬者。周弘正為宣城王所愛，給一果下馬，常服御之，舉朝以為放達。至乃尚書郎乘馬，則糺劾之。及侯景之亂，膚脆骨柔，不堪行步，體羸氣弱，不耐寒暑，坐死倉猝者，往往而然。

XI.6

建康令王復性既儒雅，未嘗乘騎，見馬嘶歇陸梁，莫不震懾，乃謂人曰："正是虎，何故名為馬乎？"其風俗至此。

XI.5

The genteel courtiers of the Liang all favored loose robes, wide sashes, big hats, and high-teeth clogs. Going out they would ride in a carriage; coming inside they were supported by servants. Throughout the city and suburbs there was nobody on horseback. The Prince of Xuancheng was fond of Zhou Hongzheng and bestowed on him a "beneath-the-fruit-tree pony."[1] He rode it often, and the entire court thought him wild and unconstrained. They even went so far as to impeach any member of the imperial secretariat who would ride a horse. When the Hou Jing Rebellion broke out, they could not walk any distance with their delicate flesh and frail bones, nor could their fragile bodies and weak breath endure cold or heat. Thus many of them fell dead in the sudden crisis.

XI.6

Wang Fu, the mayor of Jiankang, was a refined and graceful man by nature and had never mounted a horse. Whenever he saw a horse whinny and snort and prance, he would be terrified. He said to people, "Verily, that beast is a tiger. Why should it be called a horse?" Such was the fashion of the day.

---

1 Zhou Hongzheng: see note to VIII.17. The Prince of Xuancheng was Xiao Daqi 蕭大器 (523–551), the eldest son of Xiao Gang, who was enfeoffed as Prince of Xuancheng in 531. The beneath-the-fruit-tree pony was a kind of miniature pony from southwestern Korea, which had been occasionally sent to China from the Eastern Han on through the Tang.

XI.7

古人欲知稼穡之艱難，斯貴穀務本之道
也。夫食為民天，民非食不生矣，三日不
粒，父子不能相存。耕種之，莜鉏之，刈
穫之，載積之，打拂之，簸揚之，凡幾涉
手，而入倉廩，安可輕農事而貴末業哉？
江南朝士，因晉中興，南渡江，卒為羈
旅，至今八九世，未有力田，悉資俸祿而
食耳。假令有者，皆信僮僕為之，未嘗目
觀起一塿土，耘一株苗；不知幾月當下，
幾月當收，安識世間餘務乎？故治官則不
了，營家則不辦，皆優閑之過也。

XI.7

The ancients wished to know the hardship of farming, which was the way of cherishing grain and heeding the foundation of life. "Food is people's heaven." People cannot survive without it. Without eating for three days, even father and son cannot properly greet each other. To plow and plant, to weed and hoe, to reap and harvest, to load and pile, to thresh and to sift: only after going through so many steps can the grain be stored in the granary. How can one disdain farming and prize the secondary professions instead? The courtiers of the south had crossed the Yangzi River for the sake of the Jin restoration and subsequently became lodgers in this land, where for eight or nine generations they never worked hard at farming but all lived on a salary instead. Even if there were a few who did farming, they would delegate it to their servants and retainers, and had never witnessed the breaking of one clod of earth or the weeding of one sprout. They had no idea in which month to seed and in which month to harvest. How then could they know other affairs of the world? Thus they were incompetent in state governance and sloppy in household management, and that was entirely due to leisure and idleness.

省事第十二

XII.1

銘金人云：“無多言，多言多敗；無多
事，多事多患。”至哉斯戒也。

XII.2

能走者奪其翼，善飛者減其指，有角者無
上齒，豐後者無前足，蓋天道不使物有兼
焉也。古人云：“多為少善，不如熟一；
鼫鼠五能，不成伎術。”近世有兩人，朗
悟士也，性多營綜，略無成名，經不足以
待問，史不足以討論，文章無可傳於集
錄，書跡未堪以留愛翫，卜筮射六得三，
醫藥治十差五，音樂在數十人下，弓矢在
千百人中，天文、畫繪、棊、博、鮮卑
語、胡書，煎胡桃油，鍊錫為銀，如此之
類，略得梗槩，皆不通熟。惜乎，以彼神
明，若省其異端，當精妙也。

XII. Saving Trouble

XII.1

The inscription on the bronze statue states: "Do not say many words: many words lead to many failures. Do not engage in many affairs: many affairs lead to many troubles."[1] How true is this warning!

XII.2

Those that can run are deprived of wings; those that are good at flying have their toes reduced; those with horns have no tusks; those with strong hind legs have no front ones. This is heaven's way of preventing creatures from having everything. The ancients said, "To do many things but excel at nothing is not as good as being skilled in one; a flying squirrel has five abilities but is consummate at none." In recent times there were two smart gentlemen who studied many things but did not make a name in any of them. Regarding the classics they did not know enough to answer queries; regarding histories they did not know enough to converse and debate; their literary writings were not good enough to be transmitted through anthologies; their calligraphy was not good enough to be appreciated and admired; in divination they got three out of six cases right; in medicine they cured five out of ten patients; their musical skills were below several dozens of people, and their archery was middling among several hundreds. As for astronomy, painting, *go* chess, the *liubo* game, Xianbei speech, the Hu script,[2] the extraction of walnut oil, and the refinement of tin into silver, they understood the basics of all of them but did not possess expertise in any. How regrettable! With their intelligence, had they curtailed their diverse interests, they would have been able to achieve mastery in one area.

---

1 There was a bronze statue with such an inscription on its back in Zhou's ancestral temple. This appears in several early sources, such as the *Shuo yuan* (*Garden of Persuasions*) of the first century BCE.
2 Wang Liqi believes that the Hu script here refers to the Xianbei script whereas the Xianbei speech refers to Xianbei spoken language (Wang 329). However, judging from contemporary sources, "Hu script" could also refer to Sanskrit.

XII.3

上書陳事，起自戰國，逮於兩漢，風流彌廣。原其體度：攻人主之長短，諫諍之徒也；訐群臣之得失，訟訴之類也；陳國家之利害，對策之伍也；帶私情之與奪，遊說之儔也。總此四塗，賈誠以求位，鬻言以干祿。或無絲毫之益，而有不省之困。幸而感悟人主，為時所納，初獲不貲之賞，終陷不測之誅，則嚴助、朱買臣、吾丘壽王、主父偃之類甚眾。良史所書，蓋取其狂狷一介，論政得失耳，非士君子守法度者所為也。

XII.3

The practice of presenting a memorial to the throne and discussing affairs began in the Warring States period. By the time of the Han dynasty, it became even more widespread. If we trace its various forms and styles, [we can divide them into four types:] those who criticize the faults of the ruler are remonstrators; those who expose the failings of a minister are litigators; those who argue about the pros and cons of the government are candidates answering examination questions; those who praise or condemn based on their personal feelings are in the category of traveling persuaders. All four types seek a position by hawking sincerity and pursue emolument by selling words. Often, instead of producing any benefit, they suffer the consequences of being misunderstood. If by any luck they move the ruler and their counsels are accepted for the time being, they may receive immeasurable rewards at first, but in the end execution will ensue without warning: this happened to Yan Zhu, Zhu Maichen, Yuqiu Shouwang, Zhufu Yan, and many others.[1] The good historian only recorded the ones among them who had aspirations and integrity and were able to discuss the successes and failures of governance; but it is not something that a gentleman who abides by law and order should do.

---

1 Yan Zhu (d. 122 BCE) was admired by Han Emperor Wu for his examination paper; Zhu Maichen (d. 115 BCE), Yuqiu Shouwang, and Zhufu Yan (d. 126 BCE) were appreciated and appointed by the same emperor for their memorials to the throne. They were all executed for one reason or another.

XII.4

今世所睹，懷瑾瑜而握蘭桂者，悉恥為之。守門詣闕，獻書言計，率多空薄，高自矜夸，無經略之大體，咸粃糠之微事，十條之中，一不足採，縱合時務，已漏先覺，非謂不知，但患知而不行耳。或被發姦私，面相酬證，事途迴穴，颭懼悠尤。人主外護聲教，脫加含養，此乃僥倖之徒，不足與比肩也。

XII.5

諫諍之徒，以正人君之失爾，必在得言之地，當盡匡贊之規，不容苟免偷安，垂頭塞耳；至於就養有方，思不出位，干非其任，斯則罪人。故表記云："事君，遠而諫，則諂也；近而不諫，則尸利也。"論語曰："未信而諫，人以為謗己也。"

XII.4

In today's world, as far as one can see, people who are talented and virtuous are all ashamed of acting on it. Those who wait at the palace gate to go to the court and submit a memorial to present their strategies are mostly empty and shallow, yet conceited and boastful; they know not the important fundamentals of government, and are full of trivial concerns. Of the ten proposals they make, not a single one is worth implementing. Even if something suits the needs of the time, it cannot lay any claim to far-sightedness, for it is not that people did not already know it, but rather the trouble is not being able to put it into practice. Sometimes they expose someone's treachery and are called upon to confront the accused; the process can be changeable and unpredictable, and they themselves may end up being charged with wrongdoing instead. The ruler, who wants to protect his repute and influence outside the court, might tolerate and excuse them. Such are fellows escaping harm by a stroke of luck, and are not worthy of your association.

XII.5

Men who remonstrate do so to correct the ruler's mistakes. If you are in a position where you are supposed to speak up, you ought to do your best to rectify and assist. You should not avoid trouble, try to have an easy time, lower your head, and cover your ears. But there is a proper way of serving one's lord, and one must not worry about things beyond the bounds of one's duty. If you overstep your responsibilities to intervene, you will have committed an act of transgression. Therefore the "Biaoji" chapter says, "In service, if a minister distant from the ruler remonstrates, he is trying to [be noticed and] curry favor; if a minister close to the ruler does not remonstrate, he is profiting from his position without doing anything to deserve it."[1] The *Analects* says, "If you remonstrate with a superior without gaining his trust first, he may think you are slandering him."

---

1 The chapter is from the *Record of Rites*.

XII.6

君子當守道崇德，蓄價待時，爵祿不登，信由天命。須求趨競，不顧羞慚，比較材能，斟量功伐，屬色揚聲，東怨西怒；或有劫持宰相瑕疵，而獲酬謝，或有誶聒時人視聽，求見發遣；以此得官，謂為才力，何異盜食致飽，竊衣取溫哉。

XII.7

世見躁競得官者，便為"弗索何獲"，不知時運之來，不然亦至也。見靜退未遇者，便為"弗為胡成"，不知風雲不與，徒求無益也。凡不求而自得，求而不得者，焉可勝算乎。

XII.6

A gentleman should follow the Way and enhance his virtue, cultivate his reputation and wait for the right moment. If he cannot rise to a high position with emolument, it is truly the will of heaven. Suppose he appeals and petitions, scuttles and contends, completely discards embarrassment and shame; suppose he compares his abilities with others, measures his achievements, and with a grim countenance and a raised voice, feels resentful about one and becomes irate with another; some blackmail the prime minister over some minor faults and thus receive a reward; some noisily call attention to themselves and request an assignment: should a man obtain a position by such methods and think this is due to his talent and abilities, how is that any different from stealing food to fill one's belly or pilfering clothes to keep warm?

XII.7

When people see those who are keen about getting ahead obtain an office, they say, "How could you gain anything if you don't seek it?" Yet they do not understand that when fortune smiles on you, opportunities will come without seeking. When they see those who are quiet and retiring have not yet been recognized, they say, "How could you achieve anything if you don't take action?" They do not understand that if wind and clouds do not oblige, you will be acting in vain. Look at those who find without seeking and those who seek but find nothing: how numerous are they!

XII.8

齊之季世，多以財貨託附外家，諠動女
謁。拜守宰者，印組光華，車騎輝赫，榮
兼九族，取貴一時。而為執政所患，隨而
伺察，既以利得，必以利治，微染風塵，
便乖蕭正，坑阱殊深，瘡痏未復，縱得免
死，莫不破家，然後噬臍，亦復何及。吾
自南及北，未嘗一言與時人論身分也，不
能通達，亦無尤焉。

XII.8

In the last years of the Qi, many men gave money and goods to their wife's or mother's family and sought advancement by way of women. Some managed to be appointed as governors, with burnished seals hanging on shiny ribbons and a splendid entourage. Their glory extended to all their close and distant relatives, and they enjoyed preeminence for the time being. Yet they were regarded as a headache by the authorities, who would have them monitored and investigated. Those who have risen through money will invariably fall from grace through money. If they were but a little stained by wind and dust, and deviated from the right path, the pit they fell into was deep, and the wounds could not heal easily. They might luckily escape death, but their family would be ruined without exception. They would then be regretful, but it would be as futile as trying to nibble one's own navel. From the south to the north, I myself have never discussed and flaunted my kinship connections. I was not able to make my way to the top through such means, but I have never erred and incurred punishment through such means, either.

XII.9

王子晉云："佐饔得嘗，佐鬥得傷。"此言為善則預，為惡則去，不欲黨人非義之事也。凡損於物，皆無與焉。然而窮鳥入懷，仁人所憫；況死士歸我，當棄之乎？伍員之託漁舟，季布之入廣柳，孔融之藏張儉，孫嵩之匿趙岐，前代之所貴，而吾之所行也，以此得罪，甘心瞑目。

XII.9

Prince Jin said, "Those who help with cooking get a bite; those who help with fighting get a wound."[1] This means one should have a hand in good deeds, but stay away from bad deeds, and never get involved in a clique for wicked purposes. If anything causes harm, then you should not be part of it. Still, even when a distressed bird flies into one's bosom, a kind man will feel pity for it; how can you reject a gentleman in desperation who turns to you for help? Wu Yun entrusted himself to a fishing-boat;[2] Ji Bu entered a funerary hearse;[3] Kong Rong concealed Zhang Jian;[4] Sun Song hid Zhao Qi.[5] These acts were esteemed in former times and are what I would choose to perform today. Even if I am punished by death for it, I would accept it most willingly.

---

1 Prince Jin was the Crown Prince of Zhou's King Ling (r. 571–545).

2 Wu Yun (d. 484 BCE) is better known as Wu Zixu, who escaped with his life after his father and elder brother were wrongfully executed by the king of Chu. A fisherman, knowing he was wanted by the king, nevertheless helped him cross the river to safety.

3 Han's founding emperor Liu Bang (r. 202–195 BCE) put up a handsome reward for Ji Bu, a Chu general who had fought against him, but a sympathizer hid Ji Bu in a large mortuary transport vehicle and moved him to a safe place.

4 Zhang Jian (115–198) offended a powerful eunuch and went to his friend's house to seek refuge from arrest. His friend was not home, but he was helped by his friend's younger brother, Kong Rong, who was only fifteen years old at the time (for Kong Rong, see note to IX.2b); later, Zhang Jian was pardoned, but Kong Rong's elder brother was executed.

5 Zhao Qi 趙岐 (d. 201), a famous scholar, made enemies with the powerful eunuchs at court and managed to survive after his entire family was executed. He was recognized by Sun Song, who offered to hide him in the layered walls of his house.

XII.10

至如郭解之代人報讎，灌夫之橫怒求地，游俠之徒，非君子之所為也。如有逆亂之行，得罪於君親者，亦不足恤焉。親友之迫危難也，家財己力，當無所吝；若橫生圖計，無理請謁，非吾教也。墨翟之徒，世謂熱腹，楊朱之侶，世謂冷腸；腸不可冷，腹不可熱，當以仁義為節文爾。

XII.10

However, as to Guo Jie who took revenge on behalf of others or Guan Fu who flew into a rage over land, those were strongmen and vigilantes;[1] a gentleman should not emulate them. A man who commits an act of evil and rebellion against his lord or his parents does not deserve any sympathy, either. If relatives and friends find themselves in danger and hardship, you must never begrudge money or efforts to help them out; but if they should produce a scheme out of the blue and come to you with an unreasonable request, that is not what I advise you to yield to. People like Mo Di are considered warm-hearted;[2] the likes of Yang Zhu are regarded as cold-blooded.[3] Blood should not be cold, nor should a heart get too warm. You should take kindness and a sense of right and wrong as your measure.

---

1 Guo Jie (d. 127 BCE) was a famous vigilante who loved to take revenge for others. Guan Fu (d. 131 BCE) was a tempestuous man who angrily rebuked the powerful minister Tian Fen 田蚡 (d. 130 BCE) for demanding land from his friend Dou Ying 竇嬰 (d. 131 BCE). He was eventually executed along with Dou Ying.
2 Mo Di is Mozi (fl. fifth century BCE), a thinker of the early Warring States period who espoused, among other things, the concept of "universal love."
3 Yang Zhu (fl. fourth century BCE) was another Warring States period philosopher often regarded as antithetical to Mozi in his emphasis on self-love.

XII.11a

前在修文令曹，有山東學士與關中太史競歷，凡十餘人，紛紜累歲，內史牒付議官平之。吾執論曰："大抵諸儒所爭，四分幷減分兩家爾。歷象之要，可以晷景測之；今驗其分至薄蝕，則四分疏而減分密。疏者則稱政令有寬猛，運行致盈縮，非算之失也；密者則云日月有遲速，以術求之，預知其度，無災祥也。用疏則藏姦而不信，用密則任數而違經。且議官所知，不能精於訟者，以淺裁深，安有肯服？既非格令所司，幸勿當也。"

XII.11a

Earlier, as I was serving in the section of legal policies [in the Censorate], scholars from east of the Taihang Mountains and the Grand Scribe from within the Pass had a disagreement about the calendar.[1] A dozen people discussed and argued for several years without any resolution. The Director of the Secretariat forwarded the discussion to the councilors [of my section] for judgment. I gave my opinion as follows: "The scholars can be roughly divided between two schools: the 'quarter-remainder calendar system' and the 'smaller decimal calendar system.' The essence of calendrical matters is measurement by the gnomon's shadow on a sundial. Now, if we examine the dates of the equinoxes, solstices, and eclipses, then the quarter-remainder calendar system is on a coarser scale while the smaller decimal calendar system is a finer scale. The supporters of the coarser scale claim that, just as government policies are sometimes relaxed and sometimes austere, the planetary movement can be slow or rapid, and so it is not the fault of calculation. Supporters of the finer scale hold that the sun and moon sometimes move faster and sometimes slower, and that if one bases the calculation on a certain method, then one can predict their progress and it is not a matter of good or bad omens. If we adopt the coarser scale, errors may be concealed, and people may not be convinced; but if we adopt the finer scale, then everything depends on calculation, and we may go against the teachings of the classics. Furthermore, the councilors' knowledge in this area cannot possibly be more profound than that of the disputants. If we arbitrate the connoisseurs with our own shallow expertise, how can we possibly persuade them? Since this matter does not fall under the jurisdiction of legal policies in any case, I humbly propose that we not adjudicate on this issue."

---

1 The incident described here took place in the early 580s under Sui Emperor Wen. The section of legal policies (*lingcao*) was part of the Censorate, where Yan Zhitui had served as a Senior Serviceman from 580 (toward the end of the Zhou; see *BQS* 8 in Appendix) into the early Sui. "East of the Taihang Mountains" refers to the northeastern region such as that of modern Hebei; "within the Pass" refers to the northwestern region such as that of modern Shaanxi (see Introduction).

XII.11b

舉曹貴賤，咸以為然。有一禮官，恥為此讓，苦欲留連，強加考覈。機杼既薄，無以測量，還復採訪訟人，窺望長短，朝夕聚議，寒暑煩勞，背春涉冬，竟無予奪，怨誚滋生，赧然而退，終為內史所迫：此好名之辱也。

XII.11b

All the councilors in the section, high or low, agreed with me. There was, however, one ritual officer who felt ashamed of the concession. He insisted on continuing the discussion and forced the opening of an investigation. Since his learning was limited, he could not gauge the depths of the problem. So he went back to interview the disputants and tried to look into the pros and cons of the two sides. He held meetings with them from morning to evening, and worked hard at it through seasons of cold and heat. Spring passed and winter came, and yet no conclusion was ever reached. He provoked much resentment and mockery, and had to withdraw in embarrassment, but not without being cornered and censored by the Director of the Secretariat in the end. This is an example of causing disgrace by the love of fame.

止足第十三

XIII.1

禮云:"欲不可縱,志不可滿。"宇宙可臻
其極,情性不知其窮,唯在少欲知足,為
立涯限爾。先祖靖侯戒子姪曰:"汝家書
生門戶,世無富貴;自今仕宦不可過二千
石,婚姻勿貪勢家。"吾終身服膺,以為
名言也。

XIII.2

天地鬼神之道,皆惡滿盈。謙虛沖損,可
以免害。人生衣趣以覆寒露,食趣以塞飢
乏耳。形骸之內,尚不得奢靡,己身之
外,而欲窮驕泰邪?周穆王、秦始皇、漢
武帝,富有四海,貴為天子,不知紀極,
猶自敗累,況士庶乎?

XIII. Being Content

XIII.1

The *Record of Rites* says, "Desire should not be indulged; aims should not be satisfied to the full." One can reach the end of the universe, but there are no known boundaries of human nature. We can only set a limit to it by reducing desires and learning to be content. Our ancestor, Marquis Jing, had left this warning to his sons and nephews: "Your family is one of scholars, and for generations there has never been someone rich and noble. Hereafter your official position should not exceed one with a salary of two thousand bushels, and in marriage do not covet alliance with a powerful clan."[1] All my life I have obeyed his words, regarding them as illustrious sayings.

XIII.2

Heaven and earth, spirits and gods all detest full measure. Only by remaining humble and moderate can one stay away from harm. In this life we dress to protect ourselves from cold and dew, and we eat to prevent hunger and deprivation. Even with regard to this body of ours, we cannot be extravagant and wasteful, not to mention being arrogant and lavish outside of our bodily needs. Zhou's King Mu, Qin's First Emperor, and Han Emperor Wu all enjoyed the possession of the four seas and the honor of being the Son of Heaven; yet, their desire knew no bounds, and they ended in failure and disaster.[2] How much more so for gentry and commoners?

---

1 Marquis Jing was Yan Zhitui's ninth-generation ancestor (see note to V.17).
2 King Mu (fl. tenth century BCE) was the fifth king of the Zhou dynasty; he had reputedly enjoyed touring his kingdom so much that he neglected governance. Qin's First Emperor (259–210 BCE) conquered the six rival states and unified the empire, but the Qin dynasty collapsed soon after he died. For Han Emperor Wu, see note to IX.2c.

XIII.3

常以二十口家，奴婢盛多，不可出二十
人，良田十頃，堂室纔蔽風雨，車馬僅代
杖策，蓄財數萬，以擬吉凶急速。不嗇此
者，皆以義散之；不至此者，勿非道求
之。

XIII.4

仕宦稱泰，不過處在中品，前望五十人，
後顧五十人，足以免恥辱，無傾危也。高
此者，便當罷謝，偃仰私庭。吾近為黃門
郎，已可收退；當時羈旅，懼罹謗讟，思
為此計，僅未暇爾。

XIII.3

I have always thought that, with a family of twenty members, even with a plethora of male and female slaves, there should not be more than twenty of them, as well as ten acres of good land, a house that is just adequate to provide shelter from wind and rain, a set of carriage and horses in place of a walking cane, and savings of several tens of thousands in preparation for auspicious and inauspicious events or some unforeseen crisis. If one's possessions exceed this, one should distribute the surplus with justness as one's guide; if one's fortune does not reach this, one should not seek to make up for the difference by wicked means.

XIII.4

To claim a decent public career you should aim at a middling rank, with fifty people ahead of you and fifty behind you. That will be sufficient for you to be free from embarrassment yet safe from danger and ruin. If you are ever promoted above that rank, you should decline the appointment and retreat to your private home. Recently, when I was made Gentleman of the Palace Gate, I should have taken retirement. But at that time, as a refugee and outsider, I was worried about incurring criticism and slander; so even though I had thought about this plan, I did not have a chance to do it.

XIII.5

自喪亂已來，見因託風雲，徼倖富貴，旦
執機權，夜填坑谷，朔歡卓、鄭，晦泣
顏、原者，非十人五人也。慎之哉。慎之
哉。

XIII.5

Since the breakout of chaos and war, I have seen many men who took advantage of the wind and clouds and seized riches and noble status by a stroke of luck. They held great power in the morning, but their bodies filled ditches and valleys in the evening; they might be as joyful as Zhuo and Zheng on the first day of the month, but ended up weeping over the fate of Yan and Yuan on the last.[1] Such men can be numbered in more than fives or tens. Be careful! Be careful!

---

1 Zhuo refers to the Zhuo family in Shu (modern Sichuan) that became wealthy from smelting iron in the third and second century BCE. Zheng refers to Cheng Zheng 程鄭, a man whose ancestors moved to Linqiong (in modern Sichuan) in the third century BCE; he also made a fortune through iron-smelting. Yan and Yuan refer to Yan Hui and Yuan Xian 原憲, disciples of Confucius living an impoverished life.

誡兵第十四

XIV.1a

顏氏之先，本乎鄒、魯，或分入齊，世以儒雅為業，徧在書記。仲尼門徒，升堂者七十有二，顏氏居八人焉。秦、漢、魏、晉，下逮齊、梁，未有用兵以取達者。春秋之世，顏高、顏鳴、顏息、顏羽之徒，皆一鬭夫耳。

XIV. Warning against Arms

XIV.1a

The ancestors of the Yan clan originated from Zou and Lu, with some branching out to go to Qi.[1] Through generations our family has engaged in cultural enterprises, which can be seen all over the written records. Confucius had seventy-two outstanding disciples, eight of whom belonged to the Yan clan.[2] Throughout the Qin, Han, Wei, and Jin dynasties, and as recently as the Qi and Liang dynasties, there has never been a single Yan who attained fame through the use of arms. In the Spring and Autumn period, Yan Gao, Yan Ming, Yan Xi, and Yan Yu were merely fighting men.[3]

---

1 Zou, Lu, and Qi are all in modern Shandong.
2 These are Yan Hui, Yan Hui's father Yan Wuyou 顏無繇, Yan Xing 顏辛, Yan Gao 顏高, Yan Zu 顏祖, Yan Zhipu 顏之僕, Yan Kuai 顏噲, and Yan He 顏何.
3 These four men were all from the domain of Lu, recorded in the *Zuo Tradition*.

XIV.1b

齊有顏涿聚,趙有顏冣,漢末有顏良,宋有顏延之,並處將軍之任,竟以顛覆。漢郎顏駟,自稱好武,更無事迹。顏忠以黨楚王受誅,顏俊以據武威見殺,得姓已來,無清操者,唯此二人,皆罹禍敗。頃世亂離,衣冠之士,雖無身手,或聚徒眾,違棄素業,徼倖戰功。吾既羸薄,仰惟前代,故寘心於此,子孫誌之。

XIV.1b

The domain of Qi had Yan Zhuoju; the domain of Zhao had Yan Ju; toward the end of the Han dynasty, there was Yan Liang; and in the Song there was Yan Yanzhi: they were all generals and fell from grace as such.[1] Yan Si, the Court Gentleman in the Han, professed a fondness of military arts, but he had no illustrious deeds.[2] Yan Zhong was executed for abetting the Prince of Chu;[3] Yan Jun was killed for occupying Wuwei.[4] Since our surname of Yan first appeared, these two men are the only ones who demonstrated no integrity, and both met with disaster and ruin. In recent times of disorder and dislocation, some gentry members, though devoid of physical prowess, nevertheless gathered a band of men, forsook their pure enterprises of old, and hoped against hope to achieve glory on the battlefield. Since I am frail and weak, I think back to our forebears and have decided to give up such ventures. I hope my offspring will keep this in mind.

---

1 Yan Zhuoju (also known as Yan Geng 顏庚) was a grandee who died in Qi's battle with Jin in 472 BCE. Yan Ju was a general of Zhao, under whose leadership the Zhao army was defeated by Qin; the king of Zhao and Yan Ju were both captured, and Zhao was conquered. Yan Liang (d. 200) was an Eastern Han general who was killed in battle. Yan Yanzhi is an error for Yan Yan (d. 398), an Eastern Jin general killed in battle.

2 Yan Si (second century BCE) was a minor official in the Western Han court who claimed he was not appreciated by Emperor Wen 文帝 (r. 179–157 BCE) because he was fond of military arts while Emperor Wen loved cultural learning.

3 Yan Zhong (d. 70) was accused of plotting rebellion with the Eastern Han prince Liu Ying 劉英 (d. 71) and was executed.

4 Yan Jun (d. 219) was a native of Wuwei (in modern Gansu) who proclaimed himself to be a general and rebelled against the Han. He was killed in local military strife.

XIV.2

孔子力翹門關，不以力聞，此聖證也。吾
見今世士大夫，纔有氣幹，便倚賴之，不
能被甲執兵，以衛社稷；但微行險服，逞
弄拳擊，大則陷危亡，小則貽恥辱，遂無
免者。

XIV.3

國之興亡，兵之勝敗，博學所至，幸討論
之。入帷幄之中，參廟堂之上，不能為主
畫規以謀社稷，君子所恥也。然而每見文
士，頗讀兵書，微有經略，若居承平之
世，睥睨宮闈，幸災樂禍，首為逆亂，詿
誤善良；如在兵革之時，構扇反覆，縱橫
說誘，不識存亡，強相扶戴：此皆陷身滅
族之本也。誡之哉。誡之哉。

XIV.2

Confucius was strong enough to raise a city-gate, but he was not well-known for his physical strength: this is evidence from a sage.[1] Yet, I have seen that some gentleman officials of today, so long as they have a little bit of corporeal rigor, immediately try to avail themselves of it. Unable to wear armor and bear arms to defend the country, they merely put on some sharp-looking clothes and go out in disguise, flexing and flaunting their muscles. In the worse cases it leads to danger and death, and in the best scenarios it causes them humiliation, truly without any exception.

XIV.3

Regarding the rise and fall of the country as well as the victory and failure of the army, if one's learning is broad enough to encompass these subjects, I indeed hope that you can deliberate and discuss them. If one enters the tent of a commander-in-chief or attends court in the palace hall, and yet is unable to draw up any plans for one's lord to benefit the state, it would be a cause of shame for a gentleman. However, I often see a man of letters who, having dipped into some military works and learned a little about strategies, if living in peaceful times, would spy on the palace, rejoice in misfortune, take the lead in plotting insurgence, and deceive and implicate good men; who, in times of war, would instigate and change sides, coax and persuade, establish and support a leader without recognizing who may survive. All these practices are the very root of personal ruin and family destruction. Take heed! Take heed!

---

1 It was Confucius' father, Shuliang He 叔梁紇, who had supposedly lifted a city-gate, but several early works attribute the feat to Confucius himself.

XIV.4

習五兵，便騎乘，正可稱武夫爾。今世士
大夫，但不讀書，即自稱武夫兒，乃飯囊
酒甕也。

XIV.4

If one is trained in using the five weapons and has mastered horseback riding, one may be called a warrior, no more and more less.[1] But the gentleman officials today proceed to call themselves "warriors" simply because they do not read books. They are, in fact, just rice sacks and wine pots.

---

1 The five weapons have various references. It is used as a general term for weapons.

養生第十五

XV.1

神仙之事，未可全誣；但性命在天，或難
鍾值。人生居世，觸途牽縶：幼少之日，
既有供養之勤；成立之年，便增妻孥之
累。衣食資須，公私驅役，而望遁跡山
林，超然塵滓，千萬不遇一爾。加以金玉
之費，鑪器所須，益非貧士所辦。學若牛
毛，成如麟角。華山之下，白骨如莽，何
有可遂之理？考之內教，縱使得仙，終當
有死，不能出世，不願汝曹專精於此。若
其愛養神明，調護氣息，慎節起臥，均適
寒暄，禁忌食飲，將餌藥物，遂其所稟，
不為夭折者，吾無間然。

1　Mount Hua, in modern Shaanxi, was reputedly the dwelling place of immortals
　and considered one of the Daoist holy mountains.

XV. Nurturing Life

XV.1

The talk of deities and immortals may not be entirely nonsense. It is just that one's lifespan depends on the will of heaven, and deities are perchance difficult to encounter. A man who lives in this world has entanglements everywhere: when he is a young boy, he toils serving his parents; when he reaches adulthood, he is burdened by wife and children; he is engaged in the pursuit of such necessities as food and clothes, and driven by public and private responsibilities and demands. He may aspire to hide his traces in mountains and groves and transcend the dusty world, yet we do not see a single such case among tens of thousands. In addition, the expense of gold and jade and other equipment needed for elixir-making is not something that an impoverished gentleman can manage. People who study the art of immortality may be as numerous as hairs on an ox, yet those who succeed are as rare as a unicorn's horn. At the foot of Mount Hua, bleached bones pile up like undergrowth.[1] Is there any possibility of achieving immortality? When one examines the Inner Teachings, one realizes that even if one becomes a god he will inevitably die and cannot leave the world behind.[2] Therefore, I do not want you boys to devote yourselves to this. However, should you lovingly nourish your spirit, regulate your breath, moderate periods of sleep and wakefulness, take measures to adapt to cold and heat, abstain from harmful food and drink and take preventive medicines so that you can suit your natural physical attributes and avoid premature death, then I certainly cannot find any fault with that.

---

2 The Inner Teachings refers to Buddhism.

XV.2

諸藥餌法，不廢世務也。庾肩吾常服槐
實，年七十餘，目看細字，鬢髮猶黑。鄴
中朝士，有單服杏仁、枸杞、黃精、朮煎
者，得益者甚多，不能一一說爾。

XV.3

吾嘗患齒，搖動欲落，飲食熱冷，皆苦疼
痛。見抱朴子牢齒之法，早朝建齒三百下
為良；行之數日，即便平愈，今恆持之。
此輩小術，無損於事，亦可脩也。

XV.4

諸欲餌藥，陶隱居太清方中總錄甚備，但
須精審，不可輕脫。近有王愛州在鄴學服
松脂，不得節度，腸塞而死，為藥所誤者
甚多。

---

1 Yu Jianwu (ca. 480–ca. 552) was a famous Liang court poet.

2 Boiling atractylodes is mentioned as a method of taking atractylodes 朮 by Tao
  Hongjing 陶弘景 (456–536), famous Daoist recluse and alchemist. A ninth-
  century poem by Pi Rixiu 皮日休 (ca. 834–ca. 883) uses the term boiled atractylodes 朮煎.

XV.2

The correct method of taking preventive medicines does not lead to the neglect of worldly affairs. Yu Jianwu often took locust seeds. Even in his seventies he was able to read tiny script, and his beard and hair were still black.[1] Many courtiers at Ye benefitted from taking apricot kernels, wolfberries, polygonatum, and boiled atractylodes individually.[2] I cannot enumerate them all.

XV.3

I once suffered from a loose tooth that was about to fall out; any cold or hot food or drink made it ache. I read about the method of preserving teeth in *Master of Embracing Simplicity*, that one should click one's teeth three hundred times every morning.[3] I did it for a number of days and my tooth was healed. Now I do it constantly. Such minor techniques are completely innocuous and you may very well try them.

XV.4

About the various medicines, Recluse Tao's *Grand Purity Prescriptions* gives a complete list of them.[4] But you must be careful and precise about it and cannot take them lightly. Recently at Ye, Governor Wang of Aizhou tried to take pine resin, but he did not get the dosage right and died of blockage in the intestines.[5] There have been many people who died of a misuse of drugs.

---

3 The work *Master of Embracing Simplicity* was authored by Ge Hong (see note to IX.7).

4 Recluse Tao refers to Tao Hongjing (see note to XV.2).

5 Aizhou, in modern Vietnam, was a prefecture established by the Liang in 523. Governor Wang of Aizhou presumably refers to a southerner surnamed Wang who was a former governor of Aizhou but later came to reside in Ye.

XV.5

夫養生者先須慮禍，全身保性，有此生然後養之，勿徒養其無生也。單豹養於內而喪外，張毅養於外而喪內，前賢所戒也。嵇康著養生之論，而以慠物受刑；石崇冀服餌之徵，而以貪溺取禍，往世之所迷也。

XV.6

夫生不可不惜，不可苟惜。涉險畏之途，干禍難之事，貪欲以傷生，讒慝而致死，此君子之所惜哉；行誠孝而見賊，履仁義而得罪，喪身以全家，泯軀而濟國，君子不咎也。

XV.5

Those who want to nurture their life must first worry about taking precautions against disaster and preserving body and spirit intact. Only when one has this life in hand can one then nurture it; when life is already lost, it will be futile to nurture it. Shan Bao nurtured his life from within but lost it on the outside; Zhang Yi nurtured his life on the outside but lost it from within: these are what former worthies warned us about.[1] Ji Kang wrote the treatise on "The Nourishment of Life," but was executed for his arrogance toward others; Shi Chong desired the effect of immortality drugs, but was ruined because of greed and infatuation: these are where past generations went astray.[2]

XV.6

Life should be treasured, but not at the expense of everything else. To go down a dangerous and fearful path, to intervene in misadventures, to harm life with avarice, and to suffer death through wickedness: these are what a gentleman should strive to avoid. But should one be slain for acting in a loyal or filial manner, punished for performing deeds of benevolence and integrity, lose one's life to protect one's family, or sacrifice oneself for the good of one's country: this is what a gentleman does not fault.

---

1 Shan Bao and Zhang Yi are figures in the *Zhuangzi*. The former lived in the mountains and never coveted fame and fortune; he looked like a young man at seventy, but was killed by a hungry tiger. The latter chased fame and fortune, and died at forty from "inner heat."

2 For Ji Kang, see note to VIII.21b. Shi Chong (249–300) was known for his wealth and extravagance; he loved a beautiful singing girl in his household and refused to give her up when a powerful minister demanded her. He was subsequently put to death. Shi Cong was said to be interested in immortality techniques.

XV.7

自亂離已來，吾見名臣賢士，臨難求生，
終為不救，徒取窘辱，令人憤懣。侯景之
亂，王公將相，多被戮辱，妃主姬妾，略
無全者。唯吳郡太守張嵊，建義不捷，為
賊所害，辭色不撓；及鄱陽王世子謝夫
人，登屋詬怒，見射而斃。夫人，謝遵女
也。何賢智操行若此之難？婢妾引決若此
之易？悲夫。

XV.7

Since the onset of disorder and dispersion, I have seen famous ministers and worthy men who begged for life in a predicament: in the end their entreaty was to no avail, and only brought humiliation and shame upon themselves. This fills me with vexation. During the Hou Jing Rebellion, numerous princes, dukes, generals, and ministers were disgraced and dispatched; almost none of the imperial consorts, princesses, ladies-in-waiting, and concubines escaped violation. There was only Zhang Sheng, the Magistrate of Wu commandery, who, having failed in his resistance efforts and facing death at the hands of the rebels, never yielded in words or demeanor.[1] There was also Lady Xie, wife of the Prince of Boyang's heir, who went up to the top of her house to angrily denounce the rebels, and was killed by arrows.[2] This lady was Xie Zun's daughter.[3] Alas, why is it so difficult for the worthy and wise to do what is right, yet so easy for maids and concubines to be so resolute in offering up their own life? How sad!

---

1 Zhang Sheng (d. 549), a southern nobleman, fought against Hou Jing's army and was defeated. He refused to submit and was executed along with a dozen family members.
2 The Prince of Boyang was Xiao Fan 蕭范 (499–550), Liang Emperor Wu's nephew. His heir was Xiao Si 蕭嗣 (d. 550), governor of Jinzhou 晉州 (in modern Anhui), who died fighting Hou Jing's army.
3 Xie Zun was presumably a member of the prominent Xie clan of Chen commandery.

歸心第十六

XVI.1

三世之事，信而有徵，家世業此，勿輕慢
也。其間妙旨，具諸經論，不復於此，少
能讚述；但懼汝曹猶未牢固，略重勸誘
爾。

XVI.2

原夫四塵五廕，剖析形有，六舟三駕，運
載眾生，萬行歸空，千門入善，辯才智
惠，豈徒七經、百氏之博哉？明非堯、
舜、周、孔所及也。

XVI. Turning to Buddhism

XVI.1

The transmigration of life in past, present, and future is true and has evidence. Our family has been devoted to Buddhism for generations; you should not treat it lightly and casually. The marvelous doctrines are fully expounded in the various sutras and abhidharmas, and I will not be able to recapitulate them here. I only fear that you boys are not quite confirmed in your faith yet, so I will briefly repeat my encouragement.

XVI.2

As we look into it, we see that the "four dusts" and "five aggregates" break down and account for all forms and phenomena, and the "six boats" and "three carriages" are vehicles to transport all living beings [to enlightenment].[1] Ten thousand actions will all return to emptiness, and a thousand gateways will all lead to good. As for eloquence and wisdom, how can they be confined to the breadth of the seven classics and the hundred schools?[2] Clearly this is not what [the sage emperors] Yao and Shun, the Duke of Zhou, and Confucius could ever match.

---

1 The "four dusts" refers to the [objects of the] four senses of sight, smell, taste, and touch; the "five aggregates" refers to the five components of a human being: form, perception, consciousness, active functions, cognition. The "six boats" are the six ways of achieving enlightenment: charity, the observation of precepts, patience, devotion, meditation, and wisdom. The "three carriages or vehicles" are three different kinds of teachings suited to people with different capacities: for voice-hearers, for cause-awakened ones, and for bodhisattvas.

2 The seven classics refer to the *Classic of Poetry*, the *Book of Documents*, the *Record of Rites*, the *Classic of Music*, the *Classic of Changes*, the *Spring and Autumn Annals*, and the *Analects*.

XVI.3

內外兩教，本為一體，漸極為異，深淺不
同。內典初門，設五種禁；外典仁義禮智
信，皆與之符。仁者，不殺之禁也；義
者，不盜之禁也；禮者，不邪之禁也；智
者，不淫之禁也；信者，不妄之禁也。至
如畋狩軍旅，燕享刑罰，固民之性，不可
卒除，就為之節，使不淫濫爾。歸周、孔
而背釋宗，何其迷也。

XVI.3

The Inner and Outer Teachings were originally one.[1] Their differences lie in the fact that one advocates enlightenment through gradual cultivation and progress while the other advocates absolute sagehood [that cannot be attained through study]; that one is profound while the other is shallow. For initiates, the Inner Scriptures establish five prohibitions; the principles of benevolence, integrity, decorum, wisdom, and trustworthiness prescribed in the Outer Scriptures tally with them perfectly. Benevolence corresponds to the prohibition against killing; integrity corresponds to the prohibition against stealing; decorum corresponds to the prohibition against impropriety; wisdom corresponds to the prohibition against licentiousness; trustworthiness corresponds to the prohibition against dissembling. As for hunts and battles, banquets and punishments,[2] they originate from human nature, and cannot be eliminated all at once; they are henceforth to be regulated so as not to become excessive. This being the case, how deluded if one bows to the Duke of Zhou and Confucius but turns one's back on Buddhism!

---

1 The Outer Teachings, as opposed to the Inner Teachings, are non-Buddhist teachings, here referring to Confucian teachings.
2 That is, corporal punishment and punishment by death.

XVI.4

俗之謗者，大抵有五：其一，以世界外事及神化無方為迂誕也，其二，以吉凶禍福或未報應為欺誑也，其三，以僧尼行業多不精純為姦慝也，其四，以糜費金寶減耗課役為損國也，其五，以縱有因緣如報善惡，安能辛苦今日之甲，利後世之乙乎？為異人也。今並釋之於下云。

XVI.5

釋一曰：夫遙大之物，寧可度量？今人所知，莫著天地。天為積氣，地為積塊，日為陽精，月為陰精，星為萬物之精，儒家所安也。星有墜落，乃為石矣；精若是石，不得有光，性又質重，何所繫屬？一星之徑，大者百里，一宿首尾，相去數萬；百里之物，數萬相連，闊狹從斜，常不盈縮。又星與日月，形色同爾，但以大小為其等差；然而日月又當石也？石既牢密，烏兔焉容？石在氣中，豈能獨運？

XVI.4

In general, there are five common objections to Buddhism: one, people regard things beyond this world and the boundless divine transformations as wild and absurd; two, people regard the sometimes slow occurrence of karmic retribution in the course of auspicious and inauspicious events or fortune and misfortune as lies; three, people regard Buddhist monks and nuns who are not pure and devoted as evil-doers; four, people regard the waste of gold and treasures and the reduction in taxation and corvée labor as harmful to the state; five, people wonder that, even though there may be karma and retribution, how can we make a person toil in this life to benefit another person in the next life, whom they regard as a different person altogether? Now I will respond to all these objections below.

XVI.5

My response to the first objection: How can distant and immense things ever be measured? Of all the things that people today know about, nothing stands out more than heaven and earth. Heaven is an accumulation of air, and earth is an accumulation of clods. The sun is the essence of *yang*, and the moon is the essence of *yin*, and the stars are the essence of the myriad things: these beliefs are what Ru scholars feel comfortable with. But sometimes a star falls to earth and turns out to be a rock.[1] If a star's essence is rock, then it should not have light. Besides, it has such a heavy substance; to what is it tied [as it hangs in mid-air]? The diameter of a star may be as great as a hundred leagues; the head and tail of a constellation are separated by as many as tens of thousands of leagues. A thing with a diameter of a hundred leagues is connected to another across tens of thousands of leagues; now how can their distance from each other and their layout remain constant and never vary? Furthermore, stars are just like the sun and moon in their light and color; only their sizes are different. Does that mean the sun and moon are rocks too? Since rocks are hard and dense, how can they contain within them the crow and the rabbit?[2] And how can a rock move around by itself in air?

---

1 This refers to a meteor.
2 It was believed that there was a three-legged crow on the sun and a rabbit on the moon.

XVI.6

日月星辰，若皆是氣，氣體輕浮，當與天
合，往來環轉，不得錯違，其間遲疾，理
宜一等；何故日月五星二十八宿，各有度
數，移動不均？寧當氣墜，忽變為石？地
既渾濁，法應沈厚，鑿土得泉，乃浮水
上；積水之下，復有何物？江河百谷，從
何處生？東流到海，何為不溢？歸塘尾
閭，漊何所到？沃焦之石，何氣所然？潮
汐去還，誰所節度？天漢懸指，那不散
落？水性就下，何故上騰？

XVI.6

Or, if the sun, moon, and stars are all made of air, since the substance of air is lightness and buoyancy, they should then all accord with heaven in their rotation; coming and going in orbit, they should not diverge from one another, and their speed, slow or fast, should be identical. Why then is it that the sun, moon, five planets and twenty-eight constellations each have their own measure and move at different paces?[1] And can it be possible that when something made of air falls to the earth, it will suddenly turn into a rock? Since the earth is turbid, it should in principle be solid and thick. But when people dig a hole in the ground, a spring comes out; does the earth then float on water? And what else is there underneath the water? Where do the large rivers and the hundreds of valley streams originate? They all flow east into the sea; but why does the sea never overflow? Where do the Gui Chasm and the Wei Abyss discharge the water?[2] What kind of gas ignites the stone of Scorched Waters?[3] Who regulates the ebb and flow of tides day and night? The Heavenly River hangs high above; how come it does not disperse and fall down?[4] Water by nature goes downward; why does it rise to the sky?

---

1 The five planets are Jupiter, Mars, Saturn, Venus, and Mercury. Traditional Chinese astronomers divided the celestial sphere into twenty-eight "lunar lodgings" comprising various constellations.

2 The Gui Chasm is mentioned in an early Daoist work *Liezi* as a bottomless ravine to the east of the Bohai Ocean, into which all waters flow. The Wei Abyss is another legendary place, mentioned in the *Zhuangzi*, through which rivers converge and are discharged.

3 Wojiao, "Scorched Waters," is a mythological hill to the south of the Eastern Sea. It is made of one massive rock of forty thousand square leagues that desiccates all the sea water that flows to it.

4 The Heavenly River is the Milky Way.

XVI.7

天地初開，便有星宿；九州未劃，列國未分，翦疆區野，若為躔次？封建已來，誰所制割？國有增減，星無進退，災祥禍福，就中不差；乾象之大，列星之夥，何為分野，止繫中國？昴為旄頭，匈奴之次；西胡東越，彫題交阯，獨棄之乎？以此而求，迄無了者，豈得以人事尋常，抑必宇宙外也？

XVI.7

When heaven and earth were first opened up, there were already stars and constellations. At that time, the nine provinces were not yet delineated, and the various states were not yet divided. Who created the boundaries and partitioned the lands, and how did the pattern of the stars above correspond to the sectioned territories below?[1] Since the establishment of feudal domains, who decided on the apportionment and separation? While the states on earth have appeared and vanished, stars have had no increase or decrease, and disastrous and fortunate events were reflected without missing a beat. But the heavenly bodies are vast and the stars are numerous; why should their division be tied to the Central Kingdom only? The Pleiades is the star cluster of the yak-tail banner that governs the Xiongnu region;[2] but how about the territories of the Western Hu, the Eastern Yue, and the southern barbarians of "tattooed foreheads and crossed toes"?[3] Should they be abandoned and forsaken then? If we explore such questions, there will be no end. Isn't it because human principles are mundane and we must seek the answers beyond the universe?

---

1 The *Book of Documents* divided "China" into nine provinces. It was believed that the prefectures below corresponded to the constellations in the celestial sphere above.

2 The Pleiades was also called "the star cluster of the yak-tail banner." The Xiongnu were nomadic peoples inhabiting the eastern Eurasian Steppe to the north of the Chinese empire.

3 The Western Hu refers to the ethnic peoples in the Western Regions, that is, Central Asia. The Eastern Yue refers to the peoples living in modern southeastern Zhejiang and northern Fujian. The "tattooed foreheads and crossed toes" were designations of ethnic peoples living in the far south. Unlike the case of the Xiongnu, no constellations were designated as corresponding to these various "barbarians."

XVI.8

凡人之信，唯耳與目；耳目之外，咸致疑焉。儒家說天，自有數義：或渾或蓋，乍宣乍安。斗極所周，管維所屬，若所親見，不容不同；若所測量，寧足依據？何故信凡人之臆說，迷大聖之妙旨，而欲必無恆沙世界、微塵數劫也？而鄒衍亦有九州之談。山中人不信有魚大如木，海上人不信有木大如魚；漢武不信弦膠，魏文不信火布；胡人見錦，不信有蟲食樹吐絲所成；昔在江南，不信有千人氈帳，及來河北，不信有二萬斛船：皆實驗也。

---

1 These were four major theories about heaven. The "celestial sphere" (*huntian* 渾天) theory considers heaven as being in the shape of an egg and earth as being like an egg yolk surrounded by the eggshell. The "hemispherical dome" (*gaitian* 蓋天) theory compares heaven to a covering and the earth to a plate. The "infinite empty space" (*xuanye* 宣夜) theory holds that the sun, moon, and stars float in air. The "heavens being at rest" (*antian* 安天) theory elaborates the "empty space" theory.

2 The Great Sage is the Buddha. "The sands of the Ganges River (in India)" is often used to describe something numerous. Kalpa is a Sanskrit word that means a relatively long period of time – such as millions of years – in Buddhist cosmology.

XVI.8

Average people only trust their ears and eyes; beyond the reaches of their hearing and sight, they become skeptical. Ru scholars have several theories in their discourses on heaven: some espouse the theory of the celestial sphere, and some the theory of a hemispherical dome; some advocate the theory of infinite empty space, and some the theory of the heavens being at rest.[1] As for the circumference of the revolution of the North Dipper, or the measurement of heaven's pivot and supports, if it is what one witnesses with one's own eyes, we will have to agree; but as it comes from speculation and conjecture, how can it be counted on? Why do people choose to believe the hypothetical ideas of ordinary people and disbelieve the marvelous teaching of the Great Sage, insisting that there cannot possibly be worlds as numerous as the sands of Ganges or kalpas as countless as dust motes?[2] Even Zou Yan had spoken of the "Nine Continents."[3] Yet, people living in the mountains do not believe there are fish as large as a tree, while people living by the sea do not believe there are trees as large as a fish; Han Emperor Wu did not believe there was bow-string glue;[4] Wei Emperor Wen did not believe there was fire-washed cloth;[5] when the Hu people saw brocade, they did not believe that it was produced from worms that eat tree leaves and spout silk; when I was in the south, I did not believe there was any felt tent that could shelter a thousand people; after I came to the north, people in the north did not believe there was any ship that could carry twenty-thousand piculs: these are all true occurrences.

---

3 Zou Yan (fl. third century BCE) was a Warring States thinker who espoused the theory that the world was divided into nine regions (also *jiuzhou* as in "nine provinces," see note to XVI.7) and the Chinese land known to the Ru scholars only comprised one of the eighty-one parts of the entire world.

4 Han Emperor Wu: see note to IX.2c.

5 Wei Emperor Wen: see note to IX.2b. He wrote in his work, *Authoritative Discourses* 典論, that there was no such a thing as the "fire-washed cloth" (i.e., asbestos). His son, Emperor Ming, had the work inscribed in stone, but later had to have this scraped off after the Wei court received the gift of asbestos from the Central Asia.

XVI.9

世有祝師及諸幻術，猶能履火蹈刃，種瓜
移井，倏忽之間，十變五化。人力所為，
尚能如此，何況神通感應，不可思量，千
里寶幢，百由旬座，化成淨土，踊出妙塔
乎？

XVI.10

釋二曰：夫信謗之徵，有如影響；耳聞目
見，其事已多，或乃精誠不深，業緣未
感，時儻差闌，終當獲報耳。善惡之行，
禍福所歸。九流百氏，皆同此論，豈獨釋
典為虛妄乎？項橐、顏回之短折，原憲、
伯夷之凍餒，盜跖、莊蹻之福壽，齊景、
桓魋之富強，若引之先業，冀以後生，更
為通耳。如以行善而偶鍾禍報，為惡而儻
值福徵，便生怨尤，即為欺詭；則亦堯、
舜之云虛，周、孔之不實也，又欲安所依
信而立身乎？

---

1 *Dhvaja* is a "victory banner" decorated with jewels at Buddhist temples. *Yojana* was a measure of distance used in ancient India; one yojana is about eight miles. The eleventh chapter "The Emergence of a Jeweled Stūpa" in the *Lotus Sutra* describes how a precious stūpa springs from the ground and floats in the air, from which a voice – that of the Buddha Prabhūtaratna – is heard praising the Śākyamuṇi Buddha and the *Lotus Sutra*.

2 Xiang Tuo was a child prodigy who had been a teacher to Confucius at seven *sui* and died young. Yan Hui was Confucius' favorite disciple.

XVI.9

There are in our times sorcerers with all sorts of illusionist arts. They can tread on fire and walk on knives, plant a melon [which grows and ripens in an instant] and move a well, producing various transformations in an instant. If even human abilities can conjure up such things, then how much more so for the divine powers to work unimaginable changes, revealing a bejeweled *dhvaja* as tall as a thousand leagues or a seat as wide as one hundred *yojanas*, turning a place into the Pure Land, and making a wondrous stūpa spring from the ground?[1]

XVI.10

My response to the second objection: the repayment for belief and disbelief follows a person like the shadow of a form or the echo of a sound; there are many such cases I myself have heard and witnessed in person. Sometimes, one's devotion is not yet deep and pure, and the causality of karma has not yet been fully manifested; but, even if the time may be slightly delayed, there will indeed be payback. Good and bad deeds respectively attract fortune and misfortune; this is a belief held by the nine schools and a hundred masters, so why should Buddhist scriptures alone be held as untrue? Xiang Tuo and Yan Hui died young;[2] Bo Yi and Yuan Xian suffered cold and hunger;[3] Robber Zhi and Zhuang Qiao enjoyed longevity and good fortune;[4] Duke Jing of Qi and Huan Tui were rich and powerful.[5] If we factor in their previous life and consider their next life, we will be able to explain it. But if one becomes resentful or feels deceived because good deeds accidentally lead to disaster or bad deeds inadvertently produce good fortune, then he may find that even [our beliefs about] Yao and Shun are false, and [our convictions about] the Duke of Zhou and Confucius are unreliable – what can such a man believe, and on what can he establish himself?

3 For Bo Yi, see note to IX.6. For Yuan Xian, see note to XIII.5.
4 Robber Zhi (fl. seventh century BCE) was a notorious bandit who killed many innocent people but died of natural causes. Zhuang Qiao (d. 256 BCE) was a general of Chu who had started off as a bandit; he later established himself as the king of Dian (modern Yunnan).
5 Duke Jing of Qi (d. 490 BCE) was an extravagant, self-indulgent ruler. Huan Tui (fl. 500–481 BCE) was a powerful but prodigal and corrupt minister of the domain of Song who once tried to have Confucius killed.

XVI.11

釋三曰：開闢已來，不善人多而善人少，何由悉責其精絜乎？見有名僧高行，棄而不說；若睹凡僧流俗，便生非毀。且學者之不勤，豈教者之為過？俗僧之學經律，何異世人之學詩、禮？以詩、禮之教，格朝廷之人，略無全行者；以經律之禁，格出家之輩，而獨責無犯哉？且闕行之臣，猶求祿位；毀禁之侶，何慚供養乎？其於戒行，自當有犯。一披法服，已墮僧數，歲中所計，齋講誦持，比諸白衣，猶不啻山海也。

XVI.11

My response to the third objection: since the creation of the world, bad people have been numerous and good people have been few. Why should we demand that everyone be pure? Moreover, when people see an eminent monk with noble conduct, they neglect mentioning him; but when they see a mediocre monk with crude behavior, they immediately begin criticizing him. But if a student is not diligent, is it his teacher's fault? How is an average monk's study of sutras and *vinaya* texts any different from a secular person's study of the *Poems* and *Rites*? If we use the teachings of *Poems* and *Rites* to measure the minister in court, few will be found perfect. If we use the prohibitions of the sutras and *vinaya* texts to measure those who have given up their families, how can they alone be blamed for their violations? Besides, a minister may be morally imperfect, yet he still seeks salary and position; why then should a monk or nun who violates the prohibitions feel ashamed of receiving provisions? They may have broken the precepts, but once they put on the dharma robes, they have become members of the Buddhist clergy, and if we enumerate how frequently they lecture at vegetarian assemblies, recite the scriptures, and observe their teachings all year, they still do so many more times than people in white clothes.[1]

---

1 Buddhist monks and nuns wear black clothes; people in white clothes refers to secular people.

XVI.12

釋四曰：內教多途，出家自是其一法耳。
若能誠孝在心，仁惠為本，須達、流水，
不必剃落鬚髮；豈令罄井田而起塔廟，窮
編戶以為僧尼也？皆由為政不能節之，遂
使非法之寺，妨民稼穡，無業之僧，失國
賦算，非大覺之本旨也。抑又論之：求道
者，身計也；惜費者，國謀也。身計國
謀，不可兩遂。誠臣徇主而棄親，孝子安
家而忘國，各有行也。儒有不屈王侯高尚
其事，隱有讓王辭相避世山林；安可計其
賦役，以為罪人？若能偕化黔首，悉入道
場，如妙樂之世，禳佉之國，則有自然稻
米，無盡寶藏，安求田蠶之利乎？

XVI.12

My response to the fourth objection: the Inner Teachings show many paths to enlightenment; leaving one's family for a monastery is only one of many. If a person has loyalty and filial piety in his heart, and takes kindness and charity as his basic principles, then like Sudatta and Jalavāhana it is not necessary to shave off one's beard and hair.[1] Who says that we must use all the lands to build pagodas and temples, and turn all tax-payers into monks and nuns? This only happens because of the incompetence of the authorities, so that illegal temples impede farmers from planting and plowing, and unemployed monks and nuns reduce the tax income of the state. This, however, is not the original intent of the Great Awakened One [the Buddha]. Let me consider it from another perspective: seeking the Way is to show concern for the individual self; saving expenses is to plan for the state. Individual concern and state planning cannot be both satisfied at the same time. A loyal minister abandons his family to die for his lord; a filial son secures his parents and forgets about the country: each follows an admirable course of action. Some Ru scholars do not bow to princes and nobles, but pursue high-minded reclusion; some hermits decline the offer of a throne or the position of prime minister to hide from the world in mountains and groves. How can we also demand from them taxation and corvée, and regard them as criminals? Indeed, if all the people are converted and enter monasteries, as in the age of marvelous joy in the Kingdom of Prince Saṅkha, then there will be naturally-grown glutinous rice and unlimited precious treasures.[2] Why would we need to seek the profit of farming and sericulture?

---

1 Sudatta was a wealthy merchant and a lay patron of Śākyamuṇi Buddha. Jalavāhana was another rich and charitable layman.
2 Prince Saṅkha (Ch. Rangqu) was the ideal ruler in ancient Indian mythology, a cakravartin or wheel-turning king who brought peace and prosperity to his people. Śākyamuṇi Buddha is said to have been a wheel-turning king in his previous incarnations. The age of marvelous joy is also understood by some commentators as the translated name of a kingdom in western India known as Saraushtra.

XVI.13

釋五曰：形體雖死，精神猶存。人生在
世，望於後身似不相屬；及其歿後，則與
前身似猶老少朝夕耳。世有魂神，示現夢
想，或降童妾，或感妻孥，求索飲食，徵
須福祐，亦為不少矣。今人貧賤疾苦，莫
不怨尤前世不修功業；以此而論，安可不
為之作地乎？夫有子孫，自是天地間一蒼
生耳，何預身事？而乃愛護，遺其基址，
況於己之神爽，頓欲棄之哉？凡夫蒙蔽，
不見未來，故言彼生與今非一體耳；若有
天眼，鑒其念念隨滅，生生不斷，豈可不
怖畏邪？

XVI.13

My response to the fifth objection: the physical body may die, but the spirit still lives. During this lifetime, a man may look to his future self as if it were a different person; but after he dies, the relation between his former self and himself will be like old age and youth, morning and evening. There have been many cases in which a spirit manifests itself in dreams and visions, sometimes appearing to maidservants, sometimes to wife and children, seeking food or requesting blessings. Nowadays, when a person is impoverished or suffers from illness, he invariably laments that he has not done virtuous deeds in a previous lifetime. When we consider this, how can we not make preparations for our future selves? Our son or grandson is just another human being in the universe; what do they have to do with our person? Yet we love and protect them, and bequeath to them our land and property; if so, then with regard to our own soul, why should we want to completely discard it? Ordinary men are blind and are unable to look into the future, so they believe that the self in this lifetime and the self in the next lifetime are not one; but if one has "heavenly eyes" and can see how birth and rebirth follow one another closely and life continues endlessly, how can one not be filled with fear and awe?[1]

---

1 The "heavenly eyes" are one of the "Five Kinds of Eyes" in Buddhist teachings. The "human or fleshly eyes" are our physical vision while the "heavenly eyes" can see into the future, obtainable through meditation.

XVI.14

又君子處世，貴能克己復禮，濟時益物。
治家者欲一家之慶，治國者欲一國之良，
僕妾臣民，與身竟何親也，而為勤苦修德
乎？亦是堯、舜、周、孔虛失愉樂耳。一
人修道，濟度幾許蒼生？免脫幾身罪累？
幸熟思之。汝曹若觀俗計，樹立門戶，不
棄妻子，未能出家，但當兼修戒行，留心
誦讀，以為來世津梁。人生難得，無虛過
也。

XVI.15

儒家君子尚離庖廚，見其生不忍其死，聞
其聲不食其肉。高柴、折像，未知內教，
皆能不殺，此乃仁者自然用心。含生之
徒，莫不愛命；去殺之事，必勉行之。好
殺之人，臨死報驗，子孫殃禍，其數甚
多，不能悉錄耳，且示數條於末。

XVI.14

Furthermore, a gentleman living in society values the ability to restrain himself and restore decorum, to help the world and benefit others.[1] He who manages the household desires the household to enjoy good fortune; he who manages the country desires the country to flourish. Otherwise, what kinship ties could possibly exist between oneself and one's subjects, that one should cultivate virtue and work tirelessly on their behalf? Wouldn't Yao, Shun, the Duke of Zhou, and Confucius have then sacrificed their own enjoyment for nothing? Then consider this most carefully: when a person pursues the Way, how many more people can he save, and how many more sinners can he redeem [than in managing a household or a country]? If you boys care about worldly matters and the interests of our clan, and cannot abandon your wife and children and leave your family behind, then you should at the very least refine your observation of the precepts and heed the recitation of sutras to provide salvation for your future lifetimes. The chance for this human life is hard to come by. Do not waste it!

XVI.15

Even a gentleman of the Ru school knows well to keep his distance from the kitchen, for having seen a living creature, he cannot bear to see it die, and having heard its cries, he cannot bring himself to eat its flesh.[2] Gao Chai and Zhe Xiang did not know anything about the Inner Teachings, yet they would not take a life, since that is the natural inclination of a kind person.[3] All living beings cherish their life; you must do your best to refrain from killing. Those who love to kill suffer retribution before death or cause their offspring misfortune. There are numerous such cases. I cannot record them all, but will just cite a few below.

---

1 To restrain oneself and restore decorum is a quotation from the *Analects*.

2 The sentence is taken from *Mencius*.

3 Gao Chai was a disciple of Confucius. Zhe Xiang was a man of the Eastern Han. Both were kind-hearted and refused to even snap new sprouts.

XVI.16

梁世有人，常以雞卵白和沐，云使髮光，
每沐輒破二三十枚。臨死，髮中但聞啾啾
數千雞雛聲。

XVI.17

江陵劉氏，以賣鱔羹為業。後生一兒頭俱
是鱔，自頸以下方為人耳。

XVI.18

王克為永嘉郡守，有人餉羊，集賓欲讌，
而羊繩解，來投一客，先跪兩拜，便入衣
中。此客竟不言之，固無救請。須臾，宰
羊為羹，先行至客。一臠入口，便下皮
內，周行徧體，痛楚號叫，方復說之。遂
作羊鳴而死。

XVI.16

In the Liang there was someone who always put egg whites in water for hair-washing, saying that it made hair shiny. Each time he washed his hair, he would break twenty or thirty eggs. When he was about to die, he heard nothing but the chirping of thousands of chicks coming from his hair.

XVI.17

A Liu family at Jiangling made a living by selling eel gumbo. Later on they had a son who was born with the head of an eel; only from his neck down did he have a human body.

XVI.18

When Wang Ke was magistrate of Yongjia, someone gave him a sheep, and he invited guests to a meal.[1] The rope tying the sheep was loosened, and the sheep went directly to one of the guests. It knelt down and bowed to him twice, and then it crept under his robe. The guest did not say anything about this, and certainly did not beg for its life. Soon afterward, the sheep was slaughtered to make a stew, and the platter was first presented to the said guest. As soon as he took one bite of the mutton, it somehow went under his skin and moved all over his body, making him call out in great pain. Only then did he tell the others what had happened. He subsequently died bleating like a sheep.

---

1 Wang Ke (fl. 540s–570s) was a member of the prominent Wang clan of Langye. He was captured after Jiangling fell to the Northern Zhou army and taken to Chang'an. He was allowed to return to the south in 556 and served the Chen dynasty. Yongjia is modern Wenzhou in Zhejiang.

XVI.19

梁孝元在江州時，有人為望蔡縣令，經劉敬躬亂，縣廨被焚，寄寺而住。民將牛酒作禮，縣令以牛繫剎柱，屏除形像，鋪設牀坐，於堂上接賓。未殺之頃，牛解，徑來至階而拜，縣令大笑，命左右宰之。飲噉醉飽，便臥簷下。投醒而覺體痒，爬搔隱疹，因爾成癩，十許年死。

XVI.20

楊思達為西陽郡守，值侯景亂，時復旱儉，飢民盜田中麥。思達遣一部曲守視，所得盜者，輒截手擊，凡戮十餘人。部曲後生一男，自然無手。

XVI.21

齊有一奉朝請，家甚豪侈，非手殺牛，噉之不美。年三十許，病篤，大見牛來，舉體如被刀刺，叫呼而終。

XVI.19

When Liang Emperor Xiaoyuan was governor of Jiangzhou, a man was made magistrate of Wangcai and took temporary lodging in a Buddhist temple, since the government building was burned down during Liu Jinggong's rebellion.[1] The locals presented him with an ox and ale. The magistrate had the ox tied to the pagoda's central pillar. He also removed the statues and set out seating mats to receive guests in the Buddha hall. Right before being slaughtered, the ox, freed from the ropes, went directly to the stairs and bowed. The magistrate laughed heartily and ordered his men to butcher it. After he ate and drank to his full, he lay down for a nap under the eaves. By the time he woke up, his body started to itch and he started scratching the hives on his skin, which eventually turned into leprosy. It took him over ten years to die.

XVI.20

When Yang Sida was magistrate of Xiyang, the Hou Jing Rebellion broke out.[2] That year there was a drought, and the harvest was bad. Hungry people stole wheat from the [government's] fields, so Yang Sida sent a soldier to watch the fields. Whenever he caught someone stealing, he would cut off the thief's hands, and a dozen people lost their hands. Later on the soldier had a son, who was born with no hands.

XVI.21

In the [Northern] Qi dynasty there was a Court Audience Attendant who was from a wealthy and extravagant family. Unless he slaughtered an ox by his own hand, he would not relish its taste. When he was in his thirties, he fell gravely ill, and saw many oxen coming to him. His entire body felt as if being stabbed by knives. He died crying and screaming.

---

1 Wangcai is in modern Jiangxi. Liu Jinggong's rebellion took place in 542 and was crushed by Xiao Yi, who was governor of Jiangzhou.

2 Xiyang is modern Hubei. Nothing else is known about Yang Sida.

XVI.22

江陵高偉，隨吾入齊，凡數年向幽州淀中
捕魚。後病，每見群魚齧之而死。

XVI.23

世有癡人，不識仁義，不知富貴並由天
命。為子娶婦，恨其生資不足，倚作舅姑
之大，蛇虺其性，惡口加誣，不識忌諱，
罵辱婦之父母，卻成教婦不孝己身，不顧
他恨，但憐己之子女，不愛其婦。如此之
人，陰紀其過，鬼奪其算，不得與為鄰，
何況交結乎？避之哉，避之哉。

XVI.22

Gao Wei of Jiangling followed me to go to Qi. For many years he would go fishing in the marshes of Youzhou.[1] Later, he contracted an illness, and died after always seeing a school of fish gnaw away at him.

XVI.23

There are ignorant people in this world who know nothing about benevolence and integrity and do not understand that wealth and nobility are heaven's will. When arranging a marriage for their son, they become resentful if the daughter-in-law does not bring enough of a dowry with her. Taking advantage of their senior status as parents-in-law, they behave like poisonous snakes and malign her with nasty tongues. Knowing no prohibitions, they even curse her father and mother. They only succeed in teaching their daughter-in-law to become unfilial to themselves. They do not care about her feelings, only showing affection for their own children but none for her. The Underworld will record the sins of such people, and the spirits will reduce their lifespan. You must not become neighbors with them, let alone socialize with them. Stay away from them, stay away from them!

---

1 Youzhou is modern Hebei.

書證第十七

XVII.1

詩云："參差荇菜。"爾雅云："荇,接
余也。"字或為莕。先儒解釋皆云:水
草,圓葉細莖,隨水淺深。今是水悉有
之,黃花似蓴,江南俗亦呼為豬蓴,或呼
為荇菜。劉芳具有注釋。而河北俗人多不
識之,博士皆以參差者是莧菜,呼人莧為
人荇,亦可笑之甚。

XVII. Evidential Learning

XVII.1

A line from the *Poems* says: "Now long, now short is floatingheart [*xing* plant]." The *Erya* glosses *xing* as *jieyu*. The character for *xing* has a variant form 荇. Earlier Ru scholars have described it as an aquatic plant with round leaves and a thin stalk, its length varying according to the depths of the water. Nowadays we see it wherever there is water. Its yellow flowers look like brasenia, and so in the south people also commonly call it "pig's brasenia," or just call it the *xing* plant. Liu Fang has a detailed explanation of it in his work.[1] However, ordinary men in the north mostly do not know it. All the Erudites regard the plant that is "now long, now short" as amaranth (*xian cai*), and even proceed to refer to *Acalypha australis* (*ren xian; Virginia copperleaf*) as *ren xing*. It is really too ridiculous.

---

1 For Liu Fang, see note to VIII.17.

XVII.2

詩云："誰謂荼苦?" 禮云："苦菜秀。" 爾雅、毛詩傳並以荼,苦菜也。案易統通卦驗玄圖曰："苦菜生於寒秋,更冬歷春,得夏乃成。" 今中原苦菜則如此也。一名游冬,葉似苦苣而細,摘斷有白汁,花黃似菊。江南別有苦菜,葉似酸漿,其花或紫或白,子大如珠,熟時或赤或黑,此菜可以釋勞。案郭璞注爾雅,此乃蘵,黃蒢也。今河北謂之龍葵。梁世講禮者,以此當苦菜;既無宿根,至春子方生耳,亦大誤也。又高誘注呂氏春秋曰:"榮而不實曰英。" 苦菜當言英,益知非龍葵也。

XVII.2

A line from the *Poems* says, "Who says the *tu* is bitter?" The *Record of Rites* says, "The sow thistle [lit. "bitter plant"] flowers." The *Erya* and the "Mao Commentary" both take *tu* to be sow thistle.[1] The *Diagrams Interpreting Hexagrams and Demonstrating the Mystery of the Summarized 'Changes'* says, "Sow thistle sprouts in chilly autumn months, continues growing through winter and spring, and ripens in summer."[2] The bitter plant of the Central Plains today is exactly like this. It is also known as "winter-roamer" (*youdong*). Its leaves resemble endive (*Cichorium endivia*) but are more slender, and exude a white juice when broken; its flowers are yellow like chrysanthemums. In the south there is another kind of "bitter plant," whose leaves resemble the sour-juice (*Physalis alkekengi* or bladder berry). It has purple or white flowers, and its seeds are like beads, turning red or black when ripe. This plant can relieve fatigue. According to Guo Pu's *Erya* annotations, this is cut-leaf ground berry (*Physalis angulata*).[3] Nowadays in the north people call it "dragon-mallow" (*longkui*). During the Liang, lecturers on the *Rites* took it to be sow thistle, but that was a gross mistake, since it has no perennial roots and only grows seeds in spring. Gao You's commentary to *Mr. Lü's Annals* states, "Flowering without bearing seeds is called *ying*."[4] The bitter plant of the north belongs to this category; hence it is all the more evident that it is not dragon-mallow [that does bear seeds].

---

1 The sow thistle is *Sonchus oleraceus*, in Chinese literally "bitter plant" or "bitter vegetable."

2 The author of this work, now lost, is unknown.

3 Guo Pu (276–324) was an Eastern Jin writer, scholar, and necromancer.

4 Gao You (fl. 205–212) was a late Eastern Han scholar. *Mr. Lü's Annals* (*Lüshi chunqiu*) was a philosophical work completed in 241 BCE by Lü Buwei 呂不韋, the prime minister of Qin, and his retainers.

XVII.3

詩云："有杕之杜。"江南本並木傍施
大,傳曰:"杕,獨皃也。"徐仙民音徒
計反。說文曰:"杕,樹皃也。"在木
部。韻集音次第之第,而河北本皆為夷狄
之狄,讀亦如字,此大誤也。

XVII.3

A line from the *Poems* says, "Solitary is the wild pear tree."[1] The character for "solitary" in all the southern editions is written as one with "big"
(*da*) beside a "wood" (*mu*) radical. The "Mao Commentary" glosses it
as "the look of being alone." Xu Xianmin's phonological gloss gives the
pronunciation as "ti" (a combination of "tu" and "ji").[2] *Shuowen* glosses
it as "descriptive of the look of a tree," and lists it under the "wood"
radical. In *Collection of Rhymes* it is pronounced as *di* like in the phrase
cidi (sequence). However, all the northern editions give the character
as *di*, as in the phrase *yidi* (barbarian), with the same pronunciation.
This is a gross mistake.

---

1 The wild pear here is the Callery pear.
2 Xianmin was the courtesy name of Xu Miao, fourth-century scholar (see note to
   VIII.38).

XVII.4

詩云："駉駉牡馬。"江南書皆作牝牡之
牡，河北本悉為放牧之牧。鄴下博士見難
云："駉頌既美僖公牧于坰野之事，何限
騲騭乎？"余答曰："案毛傳云：'駉
駉，良馬腹幹肥張也。'其下又云：'諸
侯六閑四種：有良馬，戎馬，田馬，駑
馬。'若作放牧之意，通於牝牡，則不容
限在良馬獨得駉駉之稱。良馬，天子以駕
玉輅，諸侯以充朝聘郊祀，必無騲也。周
禮圉人職：'良馬，四一人。駑馬，麗一
人。'圉人所養，亦非騲也；頌人舉其強
駿者言之，於義為得也。易曰：'良馬逐
逐。'左傳云：'以其良馬二。'亦精駿
之稱，非通語也。今以詩傳良馬，通於牧
騲，恐失毛生之意，且不見劉芳義證
乎？"

XVII.4

A line from the *Poems* says, "Large and strong are the steeds." In all southern editions, the character is written as *mu*, like in the term *pin mu* (mares and stallions), but in all northern editions it is written as *mu*, like in the phrase *fangmu* (to pasture). An Erudite at Ye challenged me, saying, "This ode praises Duke Xi for grazing horses in the suburbs. Why should it make a distinction between mares and stallions?" I replied, "According to the 'Mao Commentary,' '*Jiongjiong* describes a fine horse that has strong, powerful body and legs.' Later it also says, 'Feudal lords have six stables and four kinds of horses: fine horses, military horses, hunting horses, and inferior horses.' If you take *mu* to mean grazing that applies equally to both mares and stallions, then the term *jiongjiong* should not be limited to a fine horse [in the 'Mao Commentary']. Now, a 'fine horse' is used by the Son of Heaven to draw the imperial carriage and by the feudal lords for undertaking visits to the imperial court or holding sacrificial ceremonies at the suburban altar; it cannot be a mare by any means. The chapter "A Groom's Responsibilities" in the *Rites of Zhou* says, 'For a fine horse, a single groom may care for only one; for an inferior horse, a single groom may care for two.' The 'fine horse' cared for by the imperial groom here is no mare for sure. It is only proper that the poet uses strong fine horses [hence stallions] in praise of the duke. The *Changes* says, 'A fine horse gallops.' The *Zuo Tradition* says, 'He took two fine horses....' In both cases the phrase refers to a stallion, and is *not* a gender-inclusive term. If you take the 'fine horses' in the 'Mao Commentary' to include mares, I am afraid that you have missed the meaning of Master Mao. Besides, haven't you seen Liu Fang's commentary at all?"

XVII.5

月令云：“荔挺出。”鄭玄注云：“荔挺，馬薤也。”說文云：“荔，似蒲而小，根可為刷。”廣雅云：“馬薤，荔也。”通俗文亦云馬藺。易統通卦驗玄圖云：“荔挺不出，則國多火災。”蔡邕月令章句云：“荔似挺。”高誘注呂氏春秋云：“荔草挺出也。”然則月令注荔挺為草名，誤矣。河北平澤率生之。江東頗有此物，人或種於階庭，但呼為旱蒲，故不識馬薤。講禮者乃以為馬莧；馬莧堪食，亦名豚耳，俗名馬齒。江陵嘗有一僧，面形上廣下狹；劉緩幼子民譽，年始數歲，俊晤善體物，見此僧云：“面似馬莧。”其伯父縚因呼為荔挺法師。縚親講禮名儒，尚誤如此。

XVII.5

The "Monthly Ordinances" chapter [in the *Record of Rites*] says, "*Liting* appears." Zheng Xuan glosses *liting* as *Iris lactea* ("horse chives," *ma xie*).[1] *Shuowen* says, "*Li* looks like rushes but is smaller; its roots may be used to make brushes." The *Expanded Ya* says, "'Horse chives' (*ma xie*) is *li*." The *Common Writing* also calls it *ma lin*. The *Diagrams Interpreting Hexagrams and Demonstrating the Mystery of the Summarized 'Changes'* says, "If the *li* plant rises up (*ting*) but does not break the ground and appear, the country will suffer from many fires." Cai Yong's commentary to the "Monthly Ordinances" chapter states: "*Li* resembles *ting*."[2] Gao You's commentary to *Mr. Lü's Annals* says: "The *li* rises up [*ting*] tall." Then it seems that the "Monthly Ordinances" chapter is wrong to say the name of the plant is *liting*.[3] In the north this plant grows everywhere in the wetlands and marshes. In the south there is much of it as well, and sometimes people plant it in their courtyard and call it "drylands rushes." They do not recognize that it is *ma xie*. Scholars of the *Rites* thus thought it was actually purslane (*Portulaca oleracea*, or "horse amaranth" *ma xian*). Now purslane is edible; it is also known as "pig's ear," and colloquially called "horse-teeth." There was once a Buddhist monk in Jiangling whose face was broad in the upper part but narrow in the lower. Liu Huan's little son, Minyu, though still a young boy, had a quick wit and was good at describing things.[4] He blurted out upon seeing the monk, "His face looks like horse amaranth!" Henceforth his father's elder brother, Tao, would call the monk "Dharma Master Liting." Liu Tao himself was a well-known Ru scholar well-versed in the *Rites* and yet made such a mistake![5]

---

1 For Zheng Xuan, see note to VIII.19.
2 For Cai Yong, see note to VI.9. The meaning of this citation is unclear. Lu Wenchao suggests emending the text to "the *li* plant rises up and appears" 荔以挺出, based on a citation in *Bencao tujing* 本草圖經.
3 Yan Zhitui clearly takes *ting* as a verb, meaning "to emerge, to rise up." Some later scholars disagree with Yan's reading; see, for instance, Zhou Fagao 94a–b.
4 For Liu Huan and his brother Liu Tao, see note to VI.40.
5 Yan Zhitui implies that Liu Tao's mistakes are twofold: first, he mistook *Iris lactea*, "horse chives" (*ma xie*), for *Portulaca oleracea*, "horse-teeth amaranth" (*ma xian*); second, he thought the name of the plant was *liting*, rather than simply *li*.

XVII.6

詩云："將其來施施。"毛傳云："施
施,難進之意。"鄭箋云："施施,舒行
皃也。"韓詩亦重為施施。河北毛詩皆云
施施。江南舊本,悉單為施,俗遂是之,
恐為少誤。

XVII.7

詩云："有渰萋萋,興雲祁祁。"毛傳
云："渰,陰雲皃。萋萋,雲行皃。祁
祁,徐皃也。"箋云："古者,陰陽和,
風雨時,其來祁祁然,不暴疾也。"案:
渰已是陰雲,何勞復云"興雲祁祁"耶?
"雲"當為"雨",俗寫誤耳。班固靈臺
詩云："三光宣精,五行布序,習習祥
風,祁祁甘雨。"此其證也。

XVII.6

A line from the *Poems* says, "Perchance he will come leisurely (*shi shi*)." The "Mao Commentary" says, "*Shi shi* means advancing with difficulty." Zheng Xuan's commentary says, "*Shi shi* describes slow walking." The Han version of the *Poems* also gives *shi shi* as a duplicative phrase.[1] In the north all versions of the Mao *Poems* have *shi shi*. The older versions in the south, however, all give one *shi*, and people commonly accept it as correct. I am afraid it is a small mistake.

XVII.7

A couplet from the *Poems* says, "Pervasive are the moving clouds; / clouds rise slowly." The "Mao Commentary" says, "*Yan* describes the look of dark clouds; *qi qi* [in the first line] describes the movement of the clouds; *qi qi* [in the second line] describes slow motion." Zheng Xuan's commentary says, "In ancient times, when *yin* and *yang* were in harmony, wind and rain were timely, and their coming was slow rather than quick and violent." I note here that *yan* already describes dark clouds; why, then, should the poet bother to add "clouds rise slowly"? "Clouds" in this line should read "rain." It was an error made by common scribes. Ban Gu's poem "Numinous Terrace" says: "The three lights manifest their essence; / the Five Elements are arrayed in sequence. / Temperate is the good wind, / and slowly falls the sweet rain."[2] This furnishes a good piece of evidence.[3]

---

1 The Han version of the *Poems* was one of the three major "schools" or lineages that preserved, interpreted, and taught the *Classic of Poetry* in the Western Han.

2 The poem "Numinous Terrace" ("Lingtai") is part of Ban Gu's (32–92) "*Fu* on the Eastern Capital" ("Dongdu fu" 東都賦), preserved in the sixth-century anthology *Wen xuan*. The three lights refer to the sun, moon, and stars. The Five Elements refer to metal, wood, water, fire, and earth. Many later scholars disagree with Yan Zhitui's opinion here.

3 Many later scholars disagree with Yan's reading (see Wang Liqi 422–23).

XVII.8

禮云：“定猶豫，決嫌疑。” 離騷曰：“心猶豫而狐疑。” 先儒未有釋者。案：尸子曰：“五尺犬為猶。” 說文云：“隴西謂犬子為猶。” 吾以為人將犬行，犬好豫在人前，待人不得，又來迎候，如此返往，至於終日，斯乃豫之所以為未定也，故稱猶豫。或以爾雅曰：“猶如麂，善登木。” 猶，獸名也，既聞人聲，乃豫緣木，如此上下，故稱猶豫。狐之為獸，又多猜疑，故聽河冰無流水聲，然後敢渡。今俗云：“狐疑虎卜。” 則其義也。

XVII.8

The *Rites* says, "....to resolve hesitation (*youyu*) and settle doubts." *Li sao* says, "The heart is hesitating (*youyu*) and in doubts [like a fox] (*huyi*)."[1] No previous Ru scholar has explained the term *youyu*. I note that *Shizi* says, "A dog of five *chi* long is called *you*."[2] *Shuowen* says, "The people of Longxi call a puppy *you*." In my view, when a man walks with a dog, the dog loves to run in advance of (*yu*) the man, but when the man is slow in following, it will turn back to wait for him; it can run back and forth like that all day long. This is how *yu* takes on the meaning of indecisiveness, hence the compound *youyu*. Some people cite the *Erya*, "*You* looks like a muntjac and is good at climbing trees." *You* here is the name of a wild animal. When it hears the sound of people, it climbs up a tree in advance (*yu*); as a *you* climbs up and down like that, hence the term *youyu*. The fox is a suspicious animal, so it only crosses a frozen river when it listens to the ice and hears no sound of flowing water underneath. Nowadays a popular saying goes, "Fox is suspicious; tiger makes divination."[3] That is exactly what the saying refers to.

---

1 *Li sao* was a long poem attributed to Qu Yuan (see note to IX.2a).

2 *Shizi* was an early philosophical work attributed to Shi Jiao 尸佼, who had been a retainer of the Qin prime minister, Shang Yang 商鞅 (d. 338 BCE).

3 The tiger is observed to be fond of scratching the ground with its claws; it is believed to be making a divination before taking action.

XVII.9

左傳曰："齊侯痎，遂痁。"說文云："痎，二日一發之瘧。痁，有熱瘧也。"案：齊侯之病，本是間日一發，漸加重乎故，為諸侯憂也。今北方猶呼痎瘧，音皆。而世間傳本多以痎為疥，杜征南亦無解釋，徐仙民音介，俗儒就為通云："病疥，令人惡寒，變而成痁。"此臆說也。疥癬小疾，何足可論，寧有患疥轉作瘧乎？

XVII.10

尚書曰："惟景響。"周禮云："土圭測景，景朝景夕。"孟子曰："圖景失形。"莊子云："罔兩問景。"如此等字，皆當為光景之景。凡陰景者，因光而生，故即為景。淮南子呼為景柱，廣雅云："晷柱挂景。"並是也。至晉世葛洪字苑，傍始加彡，音於景反。而世間輒改治尚書、周禮、莊、孟從葛洪字，甚為失矣。

---

1 Du Yu 杜預 (222–284) was a Western Jin official who authored a commentary on the *Zuo Tradition*. After he died, he was granted the posthumous title "General-in-chief of the Southern Campaign" (Zhengnan dajiangjun 征南大將軍).

XVII.9

The *Zuo Tradition* says, "The Marquis of Qi contracted *jie*, which turned into *shan*." *Shuowen* says, "*Jie* is a malarial attack that occurs once every other day; *shan* is a malarial attack with a fever." I note here that the Marquis' illness had begun with an attack every other day and gradually worsened, hence causing the concern of the various feudal lords. Nowadays in the north people still call the disease *jie nüe*, with *jie* pronounced jie1 [MC keaj]. However, the widely-circulated versions often give jie4 [MC keajH, scabies] for jie1 [MC keaj, malarial attack every other day]. Even Southern Campaign General Du does not offer any explanation.[1] Xu Xianmin gives its pronunciation as jie4 [MC keajH]. The run-of-the-mill Ru scholars then offer this interpretation: "[The marquis] suffered from scabies, which caused him to have chills; later it turned into *shan* malaria." This is pure imagination. Scabies is a minor disease not worth mentioning. Has anyone ever heard of scabies turning into malaria?[2]

XVII.10

The *Book of Documents* says, "Just like shadow and echo." The *Rites of Zhou* says, "The sundial measures the shadow, in the morning and in the evening." *Mencius* says, "In a painting of shadow, one may miss the form." *Zhuangzi* says, "Wangliang asks Shadow." In these remarks the character should be always written as *jing*, as in the phrase *guang jing* (light). Since shadow is born of light (*guang*), it is called *jing*. *Huainanzi* mentions *jing zhu* ("shadow pole"), and the *Expanded Ya* says, "The gnomon (lit. sundial's pillar) casts a shadow (*jing*)." These cases are the same. In the Jin dynasty Ge Hong in his *Garden of Characters* for the first time added the "shan" radical to the character, and gives its pronunciation as a combination of [the initial of] *yu* [MC ʼjo] and [the final of] *jing* [MC kjaengX] (i.e., *ying*, MC ʼjaengX).[3] Henceforth people have made changes in the *Book of Documents*, the *Rites of Zhou*, *Zhuangzi* and *Mencius* in accordance with Ge Hong's version. That is quite mistaken.

---

2 Yan Zhitui's reasoning here is disputed (see Wang Liqi 428–30).

3 For Ge Hong, see note to IX.7. *Garden of Characters* (*Zi yuan*), also known as *Garden of Essential Characters* (*Yaoyong ziyuan*, see XVIII.13) is no longer extant.

XVII.11

太公六韜，有天陳、地陳、人陳、雲鳥之
陳。論語曰：“衛靈公問陳於孔子。”左
傳：“為魚麗之陳。”俗本多作阜傍車乘
之車。案諸陳隊，並作陳鄭之陳。夫行陳
之義，取於陳列耳，此六書為假借也，
蒼、雅及近世字書皆無別字，唯王羲之小
學章獨阜傍作車。縱復俗行，不宜追改六
韜、論語、左傳也。

XVII.11

Taigong's *Six Tactics* mentions the battle formations of "heaven, earth, humans, and clouds and birds."[1] The *Analects* says, "Duke Ling of Wei asked Confucius about battle formations." The *Zuo Tradition* mentions the drawing up of the Yuli [lit. fish-scale] formation. The common versions of these works usually write the character for "formation" as one with the *fu* radical plus *che* as in the phrase *checheng* ("chariot").[2] I note here that in all of the cases, the character should be written as *chen*, just like in "the domains of Chen and Zheng." The meaning of battle formation (*hang chen*) derives from the display of the arrayed troops (*chen lie*); this is based on the principle of "loaning and borrowing [of graphs]" in the "Six Scripts."[3] The *Cang*, the *Ya*, and all the philological works in recent times give no variant. Only Wang Xizhi's *Elementary Learning* writes the character as "*fu* radical plus *che*."[4] Even if this graphic form is popular nowadays, it does not seem right to make changes in the *Six Tactics*, the *Analects*, and the *Zuo Tradition*.

---

1 For Taigong, see note to V.15. *Liu tao* (*Six Tactics*) is a military work attributed to him, now lost.
2 That is, as *zhen* 陣.
3 Six Scripts refer to the six principles of making characters. One of them is *jiajie*, loaning and borrowing graphs, which means borrowing existing characters to represent new words.
4 Wang Xizhi (ca. 303–ca. 361) was best known for being a great calligrapher. *Elementary Learning* (*Xiaoxue zhang*) is no longer extant.

XVII.12

詩云：“黃鳥于飛，集于灌木。”傳云：
“灌木，叢木也。”此乃爾雅之文，故李
巡注曰：“木叢生曰灌。”爾雅末章又
云：“木族生為灌。”族亦叢聚也。所以
江南詩古本皆為叢聚之叢，而古叢字似冣
字，近世儒生，因改為冣，解云：“木之
冣高長者。”案：眾家爾雅及解詩無言此
者，唯周續之毛詩注，音為徂會反，又音
祖會反，劉昌宗詩注，音為在公反，又狙
會反，皆為穿鑿，失爾雅訓也。

XVII.12

A couplet from the *Poems* says, "The yellow birds fly around, / and roost on the clustering trees." The "Mao Commentary" says, "*Guan mu* means trees growing in a cluster." This is cited from the *Erya*. Therefore Li Xun's glossary says, "Trees growing together in a cluster are called *guan*."[1] The last section of the *Erya* again says, "Trees growing densely together (*zu*) are called *guan*." *Zu* also means clustering. Thus all the old versions of the *Poems* in the south give the character [in the "Mao Commentary"] as *cong*, just like in the phrase *congju* ("gather together"). The old graph for the character *cong*, however, resembles the character *zui* ("most X of all"). Henceforth Ru scholars in recent times emended the character *cong* [in the Mao commentary] to *zui* and offer the following interpretation: "The tallest and most towering of trees." I would like to note here that none of the *Erya* or *Poems* scholars has ever endorsed such a reading. Only Zhou Xuzhi's *Annotations of the Mao Poems* [adopts it and] gives the pronunciation of *zui* as a combination of *cu* [MC dzu] and *hui* [MC hwajH], or a combination of *zu* [MC tsuX] and *hui* [MC hwajH];[2] Liu Changzong's *Annotations of the Poems* does the same, but gives the pronunciation as a combination of *zai* [MC dzojX] and *gong* [MC kuwng], or of *ju* [MC tshjo] and *hui* [MC hwajH].[3] Both scholars followed a contrived interpretation and missed the glosses in the *Erya*.

---

1 Li Xun (fl. 175) was an Eastern Han scholar and the author of a commentary on the *Erya*.
2 Zhou Xuzhi (377–423) was a late Eastern Jin scholar of the classics and a recluse.
3 Liu Changzong was a fourth-century scholar of phonetics who authored phonological glossaries of several classics including the *Classic of Poetry* and the *Record of Rites*.

XVII.13

也是語已及助句之辭，文籍備有之矣。河
北經傳，悉略此字，其間字有不可得無
者，至如"伯也執殳，""於旅也語，"
"回也屢空，""風，風也，教也，"及
詩傳云："不戢，戢也；不儺，儺也。"
"不多，多也。"如斯之類，儻削此文，
頗成廢闕。詩言："青青子衿。"傳曰：
"青衿，青領也，學子之服。"按：
古者，斜領下連於衿，故謂領為衿。孫
炎、郭璞注爾雅，曹大家注列女傳，並
云："衿，交領也。"鄴下詩本，既無也
字，輩儒因謬說云："青衿、青領，是衣
兩處之名，皆以青為飾。"用釋"青青"
二字，其失大矣。又有俗學，聞經傳中時
須也字，輒以意加之，每不得所，益誠可
笑。

XVII.13

"Ye," a final particle [marking the end of a clause or sentence] and an auxiliary particle, is seen everywhere in texts. The versions of classics and commentaries to the north of the Yellow River all drop it. Nevertheless, there are sentences in which the particle cannot be omitted [without affecting the meaning of the sentences]. For instance, "My husband – he carries the lance"; "At the gathering after the sacrificial ceremony is over, one may speak"; "Ah Hui – he frequently goes hungry"; or "The word *feng* [*Airs*], it means *feng*, to influence, and to teach."[1] Also these examples in the commentary on the *Poems*: "'If he does not restrain himself': it means he should restrain himself; 'if he does not consider it difficult': it means he should consider it difficult." And then, "Not much: it means there is much."[2] In these cases, if one omits the particle *ye*, the sentences no longer make sense. A line from the *Poems* says, "Blue, blue is your lapel." The [Mao] commentary says, "Blue lapel: blue neckband, which indicates the garment worn by a student." I note that in ancient times the slanting neckband was connected to the lapel; therefore one may refer to collar (*ling*) as "lapel" (*jin*). Sun Yan's and Guo Pu's commentaries on the *Erya* as well as Cao Dagu's commentary on *The Biographies of Notable Women* all state, "Lapel: a crossing neckband."[3] The versions of the *Poems* found in Ye are devoid of the particle *ye*, which led various scholars to come up with this absurd interpretation: "Blue *jin* (lapel) and blue *ling* (neckband) refer to two different parts of the garment; both are decorated in blue." They thus explain the duplicative "blue, blue" (*qing qing*). What a howler! And then there are your run-of-the-mill students who have heard that commentaries on the classics need to have the particle *ye* from time to time, so they proceed to add it based on their subjective judgment; but they often do so in the wrong place, and that truly makes it even more ridiculous.

---

1 The four citations are respectively from the *Classic of Poetry*, the *Ceremonial Ritual* (*Yi li*), the *Analects*, and the "Mao Commentary."

2 All quotations are from the "Mao Commentary" to a poem in the "Lesser Hymns" of the *Classic of Poetry*.

3 Sun Yan (fl. early third century) was a disciple of Zheng Xuan and a great classicist scholar. Guo Pu: see note to XVII.2. Cao Dagu is Ban Zhao 班昭 (ca. 40s–110s), writer, scholar, historian, and the younger sister of Ban Gu. She married into the Cao family and was hence known as Madame Cao.

XVII.14

易有蜀才注，江南學士，遂不知是何人。
王儉四部目錄不言姓名，題云王弼後人。
謝炅、夏侯該，並讀數千卷書，皆疑是譙
周；而李蜀書，一名漢之書，云姓范名長
生，自稱蜀才。南方以晉家渡江後，北間
傳記，皆名為偽書，不貴省讀，故不見
也。

XVII.15

禮王制云："臝股肱。"鄭注云："謂攘
衣出其臂脛。"今書皆作擐甲之擐。國子
博士蕭該云："擐當作攘，音宣，擐是穿
著之名，非出臂之義。"案字林，蕭讀
是，徐爰音患，非也。

---

1 Wang Jian (452–489) was a prime minister, writer, scholar, and bibliographer
  who compiled in 473 the *Catalogue of Books in the Four Categories* (*Sibu shumu*
  四部書目) in the imperial library. For Wang Bi, see note to VIII.21a.

2 Xie Jiong is otherwise unknown. Xiahou Gai might have been Xiahou Yong
  夏侯詠 (see Additional Notes), a sixth-century scholar and author of a phonological glossary of the *Han History*. Qiao Zhou (199–270) was a famous writer and
  scholar of the Shu Han regime during the Three Kingdoms period.

3 Li Xiong 李雄 (274–334) established a kingdom in Shu (modern Sichuan), and
  later changed the name of it from Cheng 成 to Han 漢. This regime, fallen to
  the Eastern Jin in 347, was known as Cheng Han 成漢 or Li Shu 李蜀. The
  Book of Li Shu, now lost, is presumably a history of the regime, compiled by
  Chang Qu 常璩 (fl. 300s–350s) who had been a court official of the Cheng Han
  regime. Fan Changsheng (218–318) was a Daoist leader and played an important
  role in Li Xiong's founding of the kingdom.

XVII.14

The *Classic of Changes* has a commentary written by a "talent of Shu." Scholars in the south had no idea who he was. Wang Jian's *Catalogue of Books in the Four Categories* does not give his name, merely noting that he was a "descendant of Wang Bi."[1] Xie Jiong and Xiahou Gai, men who had read several scrolls of books, both suspected that it referred to Qiao Zhou.[2] Yet, the *Book of Li Shu*, also known as the *Book of Han*, says that a man with the surname of Fan and the given name of Changsheng had styled himself as "the talent of Shu."[3] After the Jin crossed the Yangzi River, people in the south regarded the accounts and records from the north as "forgeries," and did not care for reading them.[4] Hence they missed this information.

XVII.15

The "Kingly Institutions" chapter in the *Record of Rites* says, "To expose thighs and arms." Zheng Xuan's commentary states, "This means to take off one's clothes and reveal arms and legs." Nowadays the character for "taking off clothes" is written as *huan*, as in the phrase *huanjia* ("put on armor"). Xiao Gai, the Erudite of the National University, said, "*Huan* 擐 should be written as 揎 instead, which is pronounced as *xuan* [MC sjwen]. *Huan* means to put on clothes, and does not mean revealing the arms."[5] I note that according to the *Forest of Graphs*, Xiao Gai's reading is correct.[6] Xu Yuan gives the pronunciation of the character as *huan* [MC hwaenH], which is wrong.[7]

---

4 Chang Qu, the compiler of the *Book of Li Shu* (aka the *Book of Han*), went to live in Jiankang, the Eastern Jin capital, after the conquest of the Cheng Han regime. So his works were not exactly "accounts and records from the north" 北間傳記 as claimed by Yan Zhitui here.

5 Xiao Gai (fl. 550s–580s) was a grandson of Liang Emperor Wu's half-brother Xiao Hui 蕭恢 (476–526), the Prince of Boyang. He was taken to the north as a captive after Jiangling fell in 554, and was made an Erudite of the National University by the Sui emperor in the early 580s. He authored a linguistic commentary on the *Han History* and also on the *Wen xuan*.

6 The *Forest of Graphs* (*Zi lin*) was authored by Lü Chen (see note to VIII.38).

7 Xu Yuan was a fifth-century scholar (see note to IX.25).

XVII.16

漢書："田肎賀上。"江南本皆作宵字。
沛國劉顯，博覽經籍，偏精班漢，梁代謂
之漢聖。顯子臻，不墜家業。讀班史，呼
為田肎。梁元帝嘗問之，答曰："此無義
可求，但臣家舊本，以雌黃改宵為肎。"
元帝無以難之。吾至江北，見本為肎。

XVII.17

漢書王莽贊云："紫色鼃聲，餘分閏
位。"蓋謂非玄黃之色，不中律呂之音
也。近有學士，名問甚高，遂云："王莽
非直鳶髆虎視，而復紫色鼃聲。"亦為誤
矣。

XVII.16

The *Han History* says, "Tian Ken offered congratulations to the emperor." The versions in the south write the character [*ken*] as *xiao*. Liu Xian of Peiguo was widely read and in particular had great expertise in Ban Gu's *Han History*. In fact he was known as the "sage of *Han* [*History*]" in the Liang.[1] His son, Zhen, inherited the family legacy.[2] When reading the *Han History*, he would pronounce the name as Tian Ken [instead of Tian Xiao]. Liang Emperor Yuan once asked him about it. He replied, "There is no rhyme or reason. It is just that in the old version [of the *Han History*] in my family collection, the character was changed from *xiao* to *ken* with orpiment." Emperor Yuan was unable to counter him. After I came to the north, I saw versions that read *ken*.

XVII.17

In the *Han History* the appraisal of Wang Mang states: "He is like the color purple, the sound of a frog, or the surplus in a calendar occupying the intercalary position."[3] This means that the color is not the correct colors of black and yellow, and the sound does not accord with the measuring pipes. Recently, a scholar with a fine reputation said, "Wang Mang not only had shoulders like a hawk and eyes like a tiger; he was also purplish in his complexion and spoke with the croaky voice of a frog!" He was quite mistaken there.

---

1 Liu Xian (481–543) was a native of Peiguo (in modern Anhui) who authored a phonological glossary of the *Han History*.
2 Liu Zhen (527–598), son of Liu Xian, was an expert in the *Han History* and the *History of the Later Han*. After Jiangling fell, he was taken to Chang'an and later served in the Northern Zhou court.
3 Wang Mang: usurper of the Han throne. The incident is related, in slightly different phrasing, in an earlier chapter (see VIII.35).

XVII.18

簡策字，竹下施朿，末代隸書，似杞、宋
之宋，亦有竹下遂為夾者；猶如刺字之傍
應為朿，今亦作夾。徐仙民春秋、禮音，
遂以笑為正字，以策為音，殊為顛倒。史
記又作悉字，誤而為述，作妞字，誤而為
妞，裴、徐、鄒皆以悉字音述，以妞字音
妞。既爾，則亦可以亥為豕字音，以帝為
虎字音乎？

XVII.18

The character *ce* in the phrase *jiance* (bamboo or wooden slips) should be written as *ci* under the "bamboo" radical. In the clerical script of later times, *ci* resembles the character *song* as in "the domains of Qi and Song." Some even write a *jia* under the bamboo radical. Likewise, the character *ci* 刺 should have *ci* 朿 as a component, but nowadays people write *jia* instead. Xu Xianmin's phonological glosses for the *Spring and Autumn Annals* and for the *Rites* thus take *jia* 筴 as the correct graphic form, but give its pronunciation as *ce*. This has really turned it upside down. In the *Historian's Record*, the character *xi* is mistakenly written as *shu*; the character *du* is mistakenly written as *gou*.[1] Pei [Yin], Xu [Guang], and Zou [Dansheng] henceforth give the pronunciation of *xi* as *shu* and that of *gou* as *du*.[2] If so, can we likewise pronounce the character *shi* as *hai* and the character *hu* as *di* as well?[3]

1 The *Historian's Record*: see note to VIII.34.
2 Pei Yin 裴駰 (fl. early fifth century) was a scholar specializing in the *Historian's Record* who compiled a commentary on the work. Xu refers to Xu Guang (courtesy name Yemin 野民), brother of Xu Miao (Xu Xianmin): see note to VIII.38. Zou Dansheng: see note to VIII.34.
3 This refers to the *Lüshi Chunqiu* story that the character *hai* was confused with *shi* ("pig")" and also to a fourth-century common saying that after repeated copying the character *di* ("emperor") is erroneously transcribed as *hu* ("tiger").

XVII.19

張揖云："虙，今伏羲氏也。"孟康漢書古文注亦云："虙，今伏。"而皇甫謐云："伏羲或謂之宓羲。"按諸經史緯候，遂無宓羲之號。虙字從虍，宓字從宀，下俱為必，末世傳寫，遂誤以虙為宓，而帝王世紀因更立名耳。何以驗之？孔子弟子虙子賤為單父宰，即虙羲之後，俗字亦為宓，或復加山。今兗州永昌郡城，舊單父地也，東門有子賤碑，漢世所立，乃曰："濟南伏生，即子賤之後。"是知虙之與伏，古來通字，誤以為宓，較可知矣。

XVII.20

太史公記曰："寧為雞口，無為牛後。"此是刪戰國策耳。案：延篤戰國策音義曰："尸，雞中之主。從，牛子。"然則口當為尸，後當為從，俗寫誤也。

---

1 Zhang Yi was a third-century scholar (see note to VIII.38).
2 Meng Kang (fl. 220s–250s) was an official in the Wei court during the Three Kingdoms period. He authored a phonological glossary of the *Han History*.
3 Huangfu Mi was a third-century scholar and writer (see note to VIII.15a).
4 For Fu Zijian as magistrate of Shanfu (in modern Shandong), see note to X.4.
5 The character with "mountain" added underneath becomes *mi* 嵡.
6 Master Fu of Ji'nan (in modern Shandong) had been an Erudite in the Qin. Han Emperor Wen (r. 179–157 BCE) sought him out as an expert on the *Book of Documents*, who was in his nineties at the time.

XVII.19

Zhang Yi said, "Fu is the clan of Fu Xi today."[1] Meng Kang's glossary of the archaic characters in the *Han History* also says, "Fu is [written as] Fu today."[2] Huangfu Mi says, "Fu Xi is sometimes written as Mi Xi."[3] I note that in classics and histories as well as apocryphal texts, there is no such a name as Mi Xi. The character *fu* is written with the *hu* radical while the character *fu*, the *xian* radical; but since both characters have *bi* in the lower part, copyists in later times mistakenly wrote *fu* as *mi*, and the *Lineages of Emperors and Kings* [by Huangfu Mi] adopted it and came up with a new name. How do we know this to be true? Confucius had a disciple Fu Zijian who had served as magistrate of Shanfu.[4] He was a descendant of Fu Xi. The character *fu* was commonly written as *mi*, sometimes with the character *shan* (mountain) added underneath.[5] Today the county seat of Yongchang in Yanzhou is the old territory of Shanfu; by the east gate of the county seat there is a "Zijian's stele," which was erected in the Han. It says, "Master Fu of Ji'nan was a descendant of Zijian."[6] Thus it becomes quite clear that [the two different characters] *fu* and *fu* have been used interchangeably since ancient times, but are mistakenly written as *mi*.

XVII.20

The *Grand Scribe's Record* says, "Better be the beak of a chicken than the behind of an ox."[7] This is taken in a revised form from the *Intrigues of the Warring States*.[8] I note that Yan Du's phonological glossary of the *Intrigues of the Warring States* says, "*Shi* is the leader among chickens and *cong* is a calf."[9] Thus *kou* (mouth, beak) should have been written as *shi* (leader) and *hou* (behind) should have been written as *cong* (calf). This is a transcription error in common editions.

---

7 The *Grand Scribe's Record* (*Taishigong ji*) is another name for the *Historian's Record* (*Shi ji*), which is the more common version. Yan Zhitui occasionally refers to *Shi ji* as *Taishigong ji*, and my translation here reflects the difference.

8 The *Intrigues of the Warring States* (*Zhanguo ce*) is a collection of stories and speeches from the Warring States period of the fifth to third centuries BCE, compiled by the Western Han scholar Liu Xiang (see note to VII.2).

9 Yan Du (d. 167) was an Eastern Han scholar.

XVII.21

應劭風俗通云："太史公記：高漸離變名
易姓，為人庸保，匿作於宋子，久之作
苦，聞其家堂客有擊筑，伎癢，不能無出
言。"案：伎癢者，懷其伎而腹癢也。是
以潘岳射雉賦亦云："徒心煩而伎癢。"
今史記並作徘徊，或作徬徨不能無出言，
是為俗傳寫誤耳。

XVII.21

Ying Shao's *Comprehensive Meaning of Customs and Mores* says, "According to the *Grand Scribe's Record* [i.e., *Historian's Record*], Gao Jianli changed his name and worked for hire, hiding himself at Songzi. After a long time of toiling, he heard a guest playing the harp on the hall in the household that employed him. His skills itched, and he could not remain silent."[1] I note here that the phrase *jiyang* ("itching skills") means one has skills that one's belly is itching to show off. Therefore Pan Yue's "Rhapsody on Shooting Pheasants" says, "My heart is filled with nothing but agitation, itching to try my skill."[2] Nowadays the versions of the *Historian's Record* all give *paihuai* ("pacing to and fro") for *jiyang*. Some versions read: "He paced back and forth, unable to remain silent." This is an error made in transcription by common hands.

---

1 The *Comprehensive Meaning of Customs and Mores* (*Fengsu tong* or *Fengsu tongyi* 風俗通義), an encyclopedic work on rituals, social practices, and local cults of the Han, was authored by the famous scholar Ying Shao (see note to VIII.38) in the late second century. The incident related in the citation is about the musician Gao Jianli, a good friend of the swordsman Jing Ke 荊軻 (d. 227), who was forced into hiding after Jing Ke's failed assassination attempt on the King of Qin. Songzi is in modern Hebei.

2 Pan Yue was a Western Jin writer (see note to VIII.35). His rhapsody on pheasant shooting is mentioned in an earlier chapter (see IX.25).

XVII.22

太史公論英布曰:"禍之興自愛姬,生於
妒媚,以至滅國。"又漢書外戚傳亦云:
"成結寵妾妒媚之誅。"此二媚並當作
娼,娼亦妒也,義見禮記、三蒼。且五宗
世家亦云:"常山憲王后妒娼。"王充論
衡云:"妒夫娼婦生,則忿怒鬭訟。"益知
娼是妒之別名。原英布之誅為意賁赫耳,
不得言媚。

XVII.22

The Grand Scribe [Sima Qian] made this comment on Ying Bu: "His disaster, starting with his beloved concubine and born of jealousy (*du mei*), led to the destruction of his kingdom."[1] The "Biographies of the Imperial In-laws" in the *Han History* says, "[It] led to the execution of a favorite consort who was jealous (*du mei*)." In both cases the character *mei* ("to charm or to please") should be written as *mao*. *Mao* also means jealous; its definition can be found in the *Record of Rites* and the Three Cang Texts. The "Hereditary House of the Five Princes" also says, "Prince Xian of Changshan's queen consort was jealous."[2] Wang Chong's *Balanced Discourses* says, "A suspicious husband and jealous wife living together give rise to angry fights and litigations."[3] So we know even more clearly that *mao* and *du* are synonymous. Ying Bu's execution was due to his jealous suspicion of Fei He, which cannot be described as *mei*.

---

1 The Grand Scribe refers to Sima Qian, author of the *Historian's Record*. Ying Bu, also known as Qing Bu, was a general who had assisted the founding Han emperor, Liu Bang, in unifying the empire. He suspected that his favorite concubine was having an affair with a man named Fei He and tried to arrest him; Fei He escaped and accused Ying Bu of plotting a rebellion. Ying Bu was eventually executed by the Han court.

2 The "Hereditary House of the Five Princes" is from the *Historian's Record*. Prince Xian of Changshan was Liu Shun 劉舜 (r. 145–114 BCE), a son of Han Emperor Jing 景帝 (r. 156–141 BCE). He had many favorite concubines and his queen consort was alienated from him.

3 Wang Chong was an Eastern Han thinker; his work is cited in an earlier chapter (VI.30).

XVII.23

史記始皇本紀：“二十八年，丞相隗林、
丞相王綰等，議於海上。”諸本皆作山林
之林。開皇二年五月，長安民掘得秦時鐵
稱權，旁有銅塗鐫銘二所。其一所曰：
“廿六年，皇帝盡并兼天下諸侯，黔首大
安，立號為皇帝，乃詔丞相狀、綰，灋度
量，則不壹，歉疑者皆明壹之。”凡四十
字。其一所曰：“元年，制詔丞相斯、去
疾，灋度量，盡始皇帝為之，皆[]刻辭
焉。今襲號而刻辭不稱始皇帝，其於久遠
也，如後嗣為之者，不稱成功盛德，刻此
詔左，使毋疑。”凡五十八字，一字磨
滅，見有五十七字，了了分明。其書兼為
古隸。余被敕寫讀之，與內史令李德林
對，見此稱權，今在官庫；其“丞相狀”
字，乃為狀貌之狀，爿旁作犬；則知俗作
隗林，非也，當為隗狀耳。

---

1 Kaihuang was the first reign title of Sui Emperor Wen (r. 581–604); the Kaihuang
  era lasted from 581 to 600.

XVII.23

The "Basic Annals of the First Emperor [of Qin]" in the *Historian's Record* says, "In the twenty-eighth year of the emperor's reign [219 BCE], the prime ministers Wei Lin, Wang Wan, as well as others had a discussion by the sea." In all the versions the name [Wei Lin] is given as *lin*, as in the phrase *shanlin* (mountains and groves). In the fifth month of the second year of the Kaihuang era [June 582], a man in Chang'an dug out the iron weight of a scale dated to the Qin time.[1] On the side of the weight, there were two bronze-gilded inscriptions. One inscription read: "In the twenty-sixth year of his reign [221 BCE], the emperor annexed all the feudal domains under heaven, and the common people enjoyed great peace. He established the title 'emperor' (*huangdi*), and ordered the prime ministers, [Wei] Zhuang and [Wang] Wan, to regulate and equalize the units of measurement of length and volume, to clarify any uncertainties and unify all inconsistencies." There are forty characters in total. The other inscription read: "In the first year of his reign, the emperor issues this edict to the prime ministers, [Li] Si and [Feng] Quji:[2] the regulation and unification of the units of measurement of length and volume were all undertaken by the First Emperor, and statements have been [...] inscribed. The current ruler has inherited the emperor's title, but if the inscriptions do not specify the First Emperor, then in the distant future it will perchance be thought that his heir had done it, and the great achievements of the First Emperor might not be extolled. Henceforth this edict is inscribed on the left [of the first inscription?], so as to settle any doubt that may rise." There are fifty-eight characters in total. One character is illegible; but the remaining fifty-seven characters are perfectly clear. The inscriptions were written in the ancient clerical script. The emperor commanded me to transcribe and read them, and to collate with Li Delin, Director of the Imperial Secretariat.[3] The weights are now put away in the government storage. In the inscriptions, the words "prime minister Zhuang" all give *zhuang* as in the phrase *zhuangmao* (appearance), written as a *quan* beside the *qiang* radical. Thus I know "Wei Lin" in the popular editions is wrong; it should be Wei Zhuang instead.

---

2 The emperor here refers to Qin's Second Emperor 秦二世 (r. 209–207 BCE).

3 Li Delin (532–592) was a Northern Qi courtier, writer, and historian who served in the Sui court after the conquest of Qi.

XVII.24

漢書云：“中外禔福。”字當從示。禔，安也，音匙匕之匙，義見蒼、雅、方言。河北學士皆云如此。而江南書本，多誤從手，屬文者對耦，並為提挈之意，恐為誤也。

XVII.25

或問：“漢書注：為元后父名禁，故禁中為省中。何故以省代禁？”答曰：“案周禮宮正：‘掌王宮之戒令糾禁。’鄭注云：‘糾，猶割也，察也。’李登云：‘省，察也。’張揖云：‘省，今省詧也。’然則小井、所領二反，並得訓察。其處既常有禁衛省察，故以省代禁。”詧，古察字也。

---

1 This character 禔 is pronounced as *zhi*1 in modern Mandarin.
2 *Regional Expressions* (*Fangyan*) was an important lexicographical work authored by the Western Han scholar Yang Xiong (see note to VIII.48).
3 Empress Yuan, named Wang Zhengjun 王政君 (71 BCE–13 CE), was the consort of Han Emperor Yuan 元帝 (r. 48–33 BCE).

XVII.24

The *Han History* says, "Inside and outside of the court, all are peaceful and happy." The third character should be written with a *shi* radical; it means peaceful and is pronounced as *chi* [MC dzye] like in the phrase *chibi* ("spoon and ladle").[1] Its definition can be found in the Three Cang Texts, *Erya*, and *Regional Expressions*.[2] Northern scholars all say the same. However, many copies in the south misrepresent the character as having a *shou* ("hand") radical [i.e., *ti* 提]. When creating parallelism in literary compositions, writers would use the character [as a verb] in the sense of "carrying." I am afraid it is a mistake.

XVII.25

Someone asked, "The commentary to the *Han History* says, 'Because Empress Yuan's father was named Jin, the expression *jin zhong* ("in the forbidden palace") was changed to *sheng zhong*.' But why use *sheng* to replace *jin*?"[3] I replied, "According to the 'Palace Supervisor' chapter in the *Rites of Zhou*, [the Palace Supervisor is] 'in charge of the rules and regulations of the imperial palace, as well as investigating violations and enforcing the prohibitions.' Zheng Xuan's commentary says, '*Jiu* means to incise and to investigate.' Li Deng says, '*Sheng* means to investigate.'[4] Zhang Yi says, '*Sheng* now means to watch and investigate.' Thus, no matter whether the character 省 is pronounced as *xing* [MC sjengX] or *sheng* [MC srjengX], it can be interpreted as 'watching or investigating' in either case.[5] Since the imperial palace is always watched over by the guards, *sheng* was chosen to replace *jin*. *Cha* 詧 is the archaic graphic form of *cha* 察.

---

4 Li Deng was a third-century linguist who authored *Sound by Categories* (*Sheng lei*) (see note to VI.43).

5 Literally, "no matter whether the pronunciation is given as a combination of *xiao* [MC sjewX] and *jing* [MC tsjengX] or a combination of *suo* [MC srjoX] and *ling* [MC ljengX]." The first corresponds to the character's Middle Chinese pronunciation sjengX, and the second to srjengX.

XVII.26

漢明帝紀：“為四姓小侯立學。”按：桓
帝加元服，又賜四姓及梁、鄧小侯帛，是
知皆外戚也。明帝時，外戚有樊氏、郭
氏、陰氏、馬氏為四姓。謂之小侯者，或
以年小獲封，故須立學耳。或以侍祠猥
朝，侯非列侯，故曰小侯，禮云：“庶方
小侯。”則其義也。

XVII.26

"The Annals of Han Emperor Ming" says, "A school was established
for the junior lords of the four surnames."[1] Also, Emperor Huan at his
capping ceremony had bestowed silk on the families of the four surnames as well as on the junior lords of the Liang and Deng families.[2]
Thus we know that the four surnames referred to the families of the
imperial in-laws. During Emperor Ming's time, the imperial in-laws
were the families of Fan, Guo, Yin, and Ma. To call them "junior lords"
is either because the lords were still very young when enfeoffed and
so a school was established for them, or because they were the "lords
participating in the imperial sacrifices" or the "humble lords" but had
not been made the highest of the noble lords.[3] The *Record of Rites* says,
"The junior lords of various tracts." That is the same idea.

1 This citation is from the *History of the Later Han*. Han Emperor Ming (r. 58–
  75) was the second emperor of the Eastern Han.
2 Emperor Huan (r. 147–167) ruled toward the end of the Eastern Han. The "four
  surnames" refers to the clans of Fan 樊, Guo 郭, Yin 陰, and Ma 馬, all being
  imperial in-laws; so were the clans of Liang and Deng. The capping ceremony,
  usually performed when one turns twenty *sui*, marks a man's reaching adulthood.
3 That is, they were not the sons of the imperial princes who had the imperial
  surname, nor did they occupy the highest status among the nobility, which was
  known in the Han as Liehou 列侯, also called Chehou 徹侯 or, after Emperor
  Wu was enthroned in 141 BCE, Tonghou 通侯 (to avoid Emperor Wu's personal
  name Che),

XVII.27

後漢書云：“鸛雀銜三鱓魚。”多假借為
鱣鮪之鱣。俗之學士，因謂之為鱣魚。案
魏武四時食制：“鱣魚大如五斗奩，長一
丈。”郭璞注爾雅：“鱣長二三丈。”安
有鸛雀能勝一者，況三乎？鱣又純灰色，
無文章也。鱓魚長者不過三尺，大者不過
三指，黃地黑文；故都講云：“蛇鱓，卿
大夫服之象也。”續漢書及搜神記亦說此
事，皆作鱓字。孫卿云：“魚鱉鰍鱣。”
及韓非、說苑皆曰：“鱣似蛇，蠶似
蜀。”並作鱣字。假鱣為鱓，其來久矣。

XVII.27

The *History of the Later Han* says, "A stork held in its beak three eels [lit. *shan* fish]."[1] In many copies of the text *shan* 鱓 is written as 鱣, a loan character borrowed from *zhan wei* (sturgeon and tuna). Subsequently, your run-of-the-mill scholars took it to refer to the sturgeon [lit. *zhan* fish]. According to Wei Emperor Wu's *Foods Prescribed for the Four Seasons*, "A sturgeon is as big as a five-peck dresser, and as long as one ten-foot."[2] Guo Pu's *Erya* commentary says, "A sturgeon is as long as two or three ten-feet." Now, what sort of stork can hold even one sturgeon in its beak, let alone three? Also, a sturgeon is of a purely ashen color and has no pattern. An eel at its longest measures no more than three feet, and is no thicker than one's middle finger. It is of a yellow color and has a black pattern, and that is why the Assistant Tutor said [in the *History of the Later Han*], "Snakes and eels are in the image of the official robe of a high minister."[3] Both the *Sequel to the 'Han History'* and the *Comprehensive Record of Spirits* note this incident, and in both cases they give the character as *shan* 鱓.[4] The *Xunzi* says, "Fishes, turtles, pond loaches, and eels." *Han Feizi* and *Shuoyuan* both say, "An eel looks like a snake; a silkworm looks like a caterpillar." These texts all adopt the graphic form of *shan* 鱓. Judged from this, the use of *shan* 鱣 as a loan character for *shan* 鱓 must have a long history.

---

1 This is cited from the biography of Yang Zhen 楊震 (d. 124).

2 Wei Emperor Wu is Cao Cao's posthumous title (see note to VI.12). Only fragments from his *Foods Prescribed for the Four Seasons* (*Sishi shizhi*) are extant.

3 When a stork held three eels in its beak and flew to the front of the lecture hall where Yang Zhen was teaching classics, his Assistant Tutor said that this was an omen signifying Yang Zhen would become a high official, which turned out to be true.

4 The *Sequel to the 'Han History'* (*Xu Han shu*) was compiled by Sima Biao 司馬彪 (d. 306). *A Comprehensive Record of the Supernatural* (*Soushen ji*) was a collection of stories of the supernatural compiled by the Eastern Jin historian Gan Bao 干寶 (286–336). The current version of *Soushen ji* does not contain this story.

XVII.28

後漢書：“酷吏樊曄為天水郡守，涼州為之
歌曰：‘寧見乳虎穴，不入曄城寺。’”而
江南書本“穴”皆誤作“六”。學士因循，
迷而不寤。夫虎豹穴居，事之較者；所以班
超云：“不探虎穴，安得虎子？”寧當論其
六七耶？

XVII.28

The *History of the Later Han* says, "When Fan Ye, a cruel official, was magistrate of Tianshui, the people of Liangzhou made a ballad about him saying, 'I'd rather see the den of a suckling tigress, / than step into Ye's official quarters."[1] The copies in the south all mistakenly read *xue* ("den") for *liu* ("six") [so the line reads, "I would rather see six suckling tigresses"]. Scholars have all blindly followed conventions without understanding [the issue]. Tigers and leopards live in a den: this is quite obvious. Hence Ban Chao said, "If you don't visit a tiger's den, how can you capture tiger cubs?"[2] Why should it matter to make a distinction between six or seven tigers [since the dangerous nature of the situation is the issue here]?

---

1 This is from the biography of Fan Ye (fl. 20s–40s). Tianshui is in modern Gansu.
2 Ban Chao (32–102) was a famous Eastern Han general and diplomat, the younger brother of the historian Ban Gu and the older brother of the woman scholar and writer Bao Zhao.

XVII.29

後漢書楊由傳云："風吹削肺。"此是削
札牘之柿耳。古者書誤則削之,故左傳云
"削而投之"是也。或即謂札為削,王褒
童約曰："書削代牘。"蘇竟書云："昔
以摩研編削之才。"皆其證也。詩云:
"伐木滸滸。"毛傳云："滸滸,柿貌
也。"史家假借為肝肺字,俗本因是悉作
脯腊之脯,或為反哺之哺字。學士因解
云："削哺,是屏障之名。"既無證據,
亦為妄矣。此是風角占候耳。風角書曰:
"庶人風者,拂地揚塵轉削。"若是屏
障,何由可轉也?

XVII.29

The "Biography of Yang You" in the *History of the Later Han* says, "The wind blows on the scraped wood chips [*xue fei*]." This *fei* here refers to the shavings (*fei*) that came from scraping off (*xue* or *xiao*) wooden slips. In the old days, when making an error in writing [on a wooden slip], one would scrape it off. Hence the *Zuo Tradition* says, "Scrape off and cast away." Some people even refer to the wooden slip itself as a "scrape." For instance, Wang Bao's "Covenant for My Servant" states, "To write on a 'scrape' in place of a wooden tablet."[1] Su Jing's letter says, "In the past, with the talent of 'polishing the inkstone and ordering the scrapes'...."[2] These are all good pieces of evidence [to support the reading of *fei* as wood chips]. A line from the *Poems* says, "They cut down the trees, profuse are [the wood chips]." The "Mao Commentary" says, "*Xuxu* describes the look of the wood chips." The historian [of the *History of the Later Han*] used the loan character *fei* as in the phrase *ganfei* ("liver and lungs"). Subsequently common editions all write the character as *fu*, as in the phrase *fu xi* ("dried meat"), or as *bu* like in the phrase *fan bu* ("return the feeding").[3] Scholars, based on the latter reading, explain *xue bu* as "the name of a screen." Since there is no evidence for the explanation, it is a groundless speculation. The sentence [in Yang You's biography in the *History of the Later Han*] is talking about divination by observing the wind. Wind-divination books contain this saying, "The 'wind of the commoners' blows on the ground, stirs up dust, and turns over the wooden slips [*xue*]." Now, if *xue* were a screen, how could it turn over?

---

1 Wang Bao was a famous Western Han writer whose "Covenant for My Servant" ("Tong yue") is mentioned in an earlier chapter (see IX.2).

2 Su Jing (fl. 9 BCE–30s CE) was a scholar official whose life and career spanned the last years of the Western Han and the early years of the Eastern Han. This citation is from his biography in the *History of the Later Han*.

3 To return the feeding refers to the belief that a grown crow feeds its parents as repayment. Yan Zhitui implies here that the mistake of writing *fu* for the loan character *fei* has resulted from the shared radical of the two characters, and that *fu* is further miswritten as *bu*, which shares a graphic component with *fu*.

XVII.30

三輔決錄云："前隊大夫范仲公，鹽豉蒜果共一筩。"果當作魏顆之顆。北土通呼物一丛，改為一顆，蒜顆是俗間常語耳。故陳思王鷂雀賦曰："頭如果蒜，目似擘椒。"又道經云："合口誦經聲璨璨，眼中淚出珠子䃜。"其字雖異，其音與義頗同。江南但呼為"蒜符"，不知謂為顆。學士相承，讀為裹結之裹，言鹽與蒜共一苞裹，內筩中耳。正史削繁音義又音蒜顆為苦戈反，皆失也。

XVII.30

The *Conclusive Account of the Three Administrative Regions of Chang'an* says, "The Grandee of Qiansui, Fan Zhonggong, / puts his bean paste and garlic (*suan guo*) into one jar."[1] *Guo* here should be *ke* [MC khwaX], like in the name Wei Ke.[2] The northerners commonly refer to one piece or chunk (*kuai*) of something as one *ke*; *suan ke* is a popular expression [indicating a garlic bulb]. Hence Prince Si of Chen's "Rhapsody on the Sparrowhawk and the Sparrow" says, "Its head is like a garlic bulb…. Its eyes are like halved peppercorn."[3] A Daoist text says, "Chanting scriptures with pursed lips in a tiny voice; / tears flow from eyes like beads."[4] Although the character of *ke* 磔 here [as measure-word for beads] has a different graphic form, its sound and meaning are the same [as those of *ke* 顆]. In the south people simply call a garlic bulb *suan fu*, and do not know to say *suan ke*. Southern scholars have traditionally pronounced the character 果 [in the *Sanfu juelu* saying, cited above] as *guo* [MC kwaX], like in the phrase *guo jie* ("wrap up"), believing that the saying meant wrapping up salt and garlic together and putting them in a jar. The glossary of *The Abridged Dynastic Histories* gives its pronunciation as a combination of *ku* [MC khuX] and *ge* [MC kwa]; that is also mistaken.[5]

---

1 This work is cited in an earlier chapter (see VIII.32). The Grandee of Qiansui refers to the magistrate of the Nanyang commandery (in modern He'nan); this is a title created by Wang Mang (see note to VIII.35) during the Xin dynasty (9–23 CE).

2 Wei Ke (fl. 594 BCE) was a grandee in the domain of Jin during the Spring and Autumn Period.

3 Prince Si of Chen is the famous writer Cao Zhi (see note to VI.12). The rhapsody ("Yao que fu") is partially extant, relating a lively personified dialogue between the sparrowhawk and its prey, a sparrow.

4 This text is identified as the *Classic of Laozi's Conversion of the Hu People* (*Laozi hua Hu jing*) that probably dates to the fourth or fifth century.

5 *The Abridged Dynastic Histories* (*Zhengshi xuefan*) was authored by Ruan Xiaoxu 阮孝緒 (479–536), a scholar and bibliographer of the Liang. The mistake Yan Zhitui criticizes here is that the pronunciation offered in the glossary of *The Abridged Dynastic Histories* is MC khwa, with a level tone, and the correct pronunciation should be MC khwaX, with a rising tone.

XVII.31

有人訪吾曰：“魏志蔣濟上書云弊攰之
民，是何字也？”余應之曰：“意為攰即
是𩊚倦之𩊚耳。張揖、呂忱並云：‘支傍
作刀劍之刀，亦是剞字。’不知蔣氏自造
支傍作筋力之力，或借剞字，終當音九偽
反。”

XVII.31

Someone asked me, "In the *Record of Wei*, Jiang Ji sent a memorial to the throne, in which he uses the phrase 弊劂之民 ("exhausted people"). What is the second character here?"[1] I replied, "I believe it is the same as the character *gui*, as in the phrase *gui juan* ("extreme exhaustion"). Zhang Yi and Lü Chen both said that this character consists of the *zhi* radical and the component of *dao*, as in the phrase *dao jian* ("knife and sword"), and that it is interchangeable with the character *ji*. Now, I am not sure whether Jiang Ji had coined the character himself by adding *li*, as in the phrase *jin li* ("physical strength") to the *zhi* radical, perhaps as a borrowed character for *ji*. But in any case, it should be pronounced as a combination of *jiu* [MC kjuwX] and *wei* [MC ngjweH]."[2]

---

1 The *Record of Wei* is from the *Record of the Three Kingdoms* (*Sanguo zhi*) compiled by Chen Shou 陳壽 (233–297). Jiang Ji (d. 249) was a Wei official.
2 That is, MC kjweH, or *gui* in modern Mandarin pronunciation.

XVII.32

晉中興書：“太山羊曼，常頹縱宏任，飲
酒誕節，兗州號為䫉伯。”此字皆無音
訓。梁孝元帝常謂吾曰：“由來不識。唯
張簡憲見教，呼為㘍羹之㘍。自爾便遵承
之，亦不知所出。”簡憲是湘州刺史張纘
謚也，江南號為碩學。案法盛世代殊近，
當是耆老相傳；俗間又有䫉䫉語，蓋無所
不見，無所不容之意也。顧野王玉篇誤為
黑傍沓。顧雖博物，猶出簡憲、孝元之
下，而二人皆云重邊。吾所見數本，並無
作黑者。重沓是多饒積厚之意，從黑更無
義旨。

XVII.32

The *Book of the Jin Restoration* says: "Yang Man of Taishan was a free spirit who drank alcohol and was unrestrained in behavior. The people of Yanzhou all called him the Laidback Lord (Ta bo)."[1] The character *ta* has never received any glossing. Liang Emperor Xiaoyuan once said to me, "For the longest time I had had no idea what this character was. Only Zhang Jianxian was able to enlighten me. He told me it should be pronounced as *ta*, as in *tageng* ('gulp down food'). I have followed it ever since, although I still do not know the origin of this character." Jianxian was the posthumous title of Zhang Zuan, the Governor of Xiangzhou, who was widely considered as an erudite man in the south.[2] I note here that He Fasheng lived at a time very close to Yang Man; he must have heard this expression passed down from the elders. There is also a popular expression *tata*, which means seeing everything and tolerating everything. Gu Yewang's *Yu pian* mistakenly writes the character with the *hei* 黑 ("black") radical beside the graph *ta* 沓.[3] Gu Yewang was quite learned, but not as much as Jianxian and Emperor Xiaoyuan, who both said that the character should be written as *chong* 重 ("layers") plus *ta* 沓. None of the copies I have seen ever adopts the *hei* radical. *Ta* consisting of *chong* and *ta* means great abundance and accumulation; it makes no sense to give it the *hei* ("black") radical.

---

1 *The Book of the Jin Restoration* (*Jin zhongxing shu*) was authored by He Fasheng (fl. mid-fifth century); it records the history of the Eastern Jin. Yang Man was a member of the prominent Yang clan of Taishan (in modern Shandong); see VI.19.

2 Zhang Zuan (499–549) was a son-in-law of Liang Emperor Wu and thus Emperor Yuan's brother-in-law.

3 Gu Yewang (519–581) was a prominent scholar and writer whose career spanned the Liang and Chen dynasties. *Yu pian* was a dictionary that he compiled and presented to the court in 543.

XVII.33

古樂府歌詞，先述三子，次及三婦，婦是對舅姑之稱。其末章云：「丈人且安坐，調絃未遽央。」古者，子婦供事舅姑，旦夕在側，與兒女無異，故有此言。丈人亦長老之目，今世俗猶呼其祖考為先亡丈人。又疑丈當作大，北間風俗，婦呼舅為大人公。「丈」之與「大」，易為誤耳。近代文士，頗作三婦詩，乃為匹嫡並耦己之群妻之意，又加鄭、衛之辭，大雅君子，何其謬乎。

XVII.34

古樂府歌百里奚詞曰：「百里奚，五羊皮。憶別時，烹伏雌，吹扊扅。今日富貴忘我為。」吹當作炊煮之炊。案蔡邕月令章句曰：「鍵，關牡也，牡所以止扉也，或謂之剟移。」然則當時貧困，并以門牡木作薪炊耳。聲類作扊扅，又或作戾。

---

1 The music or words of Zheng and Wei refers to the romantic songs from the domains of Zheng and Wei in the Spring and Autumn Period that were considered "mutations" of the orthodox elegant music. Many "Three Wives" poems from the Southern Dynasties are still extant, and the authors include Wang Rong 王融 (467–493), Shen Yue 沈約 (441–513), Wu Jun 吳均 (469–520), Liu Xiaochuo 劉孝綽 (481–539), Xiao Tong 蕭統 (501–531), and others.

XVII.33

The lyric of an old ballad begins by describing three sons and then three wives. Here *fu* ("wife") is used in the sense of "daughter-in-law" in relation to the parents-in-law. The final stanza states, "May the elders sit and relax for a moment, / for the strings are not done being tuned just yet." In the olden days, a daughter-in-law waited upon her parents-in-law from morning to evening, no different from their own sons and daughters; henceforth the words of the song. "Elder" (*zhangren*) refers to one's senior; people nowadays still refer to their deceased forefathers as their "late elders." I also suspect that *zhang* [in the term *zhangren*] should probably have been *da* ("great"). In the north it is customary for a daughter-in-law to call her father-in-law *daren gong* ("great sir"). It is easy to confuse the graphs *zhang* 丈 and *da* 大. In recent times, literary men have written many poems on the topic of "Three Wives," always taking them as referring to one's own consorts and adding the words of Zheng and Wei.[1] Alas, how wrong are these cultured gentlemen!

XVII.34

There is an old ballad song about Baili Xi that goes, "Baili Xi, five sheepskins! / I remember when we parted, / I cooked our hen, / and burned the bolt for firewood. / Today you are rich and noble, and you forgot me."[2] *Chui* 吹 should be written as *chui* 炊, as in the phrase *chui zhu* ("to boil food on a fire"). According to Cai Yong's commentary on the "The Monthly Ordinances" chapter, "*Jian* 鍵 is a sliding bar used to secure a door. Some call it *yanyi* 剡移." It is clear that in the ballad at the time of [the couple's] parting, they were so poor that Baili Xi's wife had to take down the wooden sliding bar and used it as firewood to cook with. *Sound by Categories* reads *yan* [*yi*], which also has a variant form, *dian* 扂.

---

2 Baili Xi (fl. seventh century BCE) was a minister of the domain of Yu; after Yu fell, he was reduced to slavery and escaped to Chu. He was redeemed with five sheepskins by Duke Mu of Qin (683–621 BCE) and made prime minister of Qin. His wife, who had become separated from him, went to his residence to work as a maidservant and sang this song at a banquet, after which she was reunited with Baili Xi.

XVII.35

通俗文，世間題云河南服虔字子慎造。虔既是漢人，其敘乃引蘇林、張揖；蘇、張皆是魏人。且鄭玄以前，全不解反語，通俗反音，甚會近俗。阮孝緒又云李虔所造。河北此書，家藏一本，遂無作李虔者。晉中經簿及七志並無其目，竟不得知誰制。然其文義允愜，實是高才。殷仲堪常用字訓，亦引服虔俗說，今復無此書，未知即是通俗文，為當有異？或更有服虔乎？不能明也。

XVII.35

The *Common Writing* is commonly attributed to Fu Qian, courtesy name Zishen, of He'nan. Fu Qian lived in the Han dynasty, but his preface cites Su Lin and Zhang Yi, who both lived in the Wei dynasty.[1] Besides, prior to Zheng Xuan's time, the practice of marking the pronunciation of a character by giving a combination of two characters was completely unknown. Yet, the *Common Writing* uses this method that matches the recent custom very well. Ruan Xiaoxu, on the other hand, attributes this work to Li Qian.[2] In the north every household has a copy of this work, but none of the copies ever mentions Li Qian. Neither the Jin *Register of the Central Canon* nor the *Seven Accounts* includes this title.[3] In the end we have no idea who wrote it. Nevertheless, its content is accurate and apt, clearly and truly by the hand of a genius. Yin Zhongkan's *Glossary of Commonly Used Words* cites a *Popular Sayings* by Fu Qian.[4] Yin's work is no longer extant, and I wonder if the work he cited was one and the same as the *Common Writing* or a different work altogether. Or could there be another man named Fu Qian? There is no way to find out.

---

1 Fu Qian's *Common Writing* (*Tongsu wen*), Su Lin, and Zhang Yi are mentioned in an earlier chapter: see VIII.38.

2 Ruan Xiaoxu was a Liang scholar and bibliographer (see note to XVII.30), who compiled the *Seven Records* 七錄, a comprehensive book catalogue. A work known as the *Sequel to the 'Common Writing'* 續通俗文 is attributed to Li Qian in Tang bibliographies. Some scholars believe that he might be the same as Li Mi 李密 (224–287, aka Li Qian), a Shu official, scholar, and writer who later served in the Western Jin court.

3 Both were book catalogues, the former compiled by Xun Xu 荀勖 (d. 289) and the latter by Wang Jian. The *Seven Accounts* is to be differentiated from Wang Jian's other book catalogue presented to the throne in 473 (see XVII.14).

4 Yin Zhongkan (d. 399), the author of *Changyong zi xun*, was an Eastern Jin official.

XVII.36a

或問："山海經，夏禹及益所記，而有長沙、零陵、桂陽、諸暨，如此郡縣不少，以為何也？"答曰："史之闕文，為日久矣；加復秦人滅學，董卓焚書，典籍錯亂，非止於此。譬猶本草神農所述，而有豫章、朱崖、趙國、常山、奉高、真定、臨淄、馮翊等郡縣名，出諸藥物。爾雅周公所作，而云'張仲孝友'。仲尼修春秋，而經書孔丘卒；世本左丘明所書，而有燕王喜、漢高祖。

XVII.36a

Someone asked, "The *Classic of Mountains and Seas* is a record compiled by Yu and Yi of the Xia dynasty, yet it mentions Changsha, Lingling, Guiyang, Zhuji, and many such commanderies. Why is that?"[1] I replied, "Many texts have remained incomplete for a long time. In addition, the Qin tried to destroy learning;[2] Dong Zhuo burned books.[3] Hence the canon became muddled and disarrayed far beyond this one case. For instance, the *Materia Medica* was put together by Shennong, but contains the names of Yuzhang, Zhuyai, Zhaoguo, Changshan, Fenggao, Zhending, Linzi, Pingyu, and other commanderies and counties where various medicinal herbs grow.[4] *Erya* was written by the Duke of Zhou, but it says 'Zhang Zhong [a man from a later era of Zhou] was filial and brotherly.' Confucius produced the *Spring and Autumn Annals*, but the classic records the death of Confucius. The *Origins of the Lineages* was composed by Zuo Qiuming,[5] yet the work mentions Xi the Yan king as well as Han Emperor Gaozu.[6]

---

1 The *Classic of Mountains and Seas* (*Shanhai jing*) is an early work of geography, still extant, that mixes real and mythological places. Yu, like Yao and Shun, was a sage emperor in antiquity and was the legendary founder of the Xia dynasty; Yi, aka Boyi, was his minister. The commanderies listed here were established during the Qin and Han dynasties, long after the time of the reputed *Shanhai jing* authors.

2 This refers to the supposed First Qin Emperor's burning of books and killing of Ru scholars in 213–212 BCE.

3 Dong Zhuo (d. 192) was a general in the late Eastern Han. He seized control of the court in political turmoil and, when a coalition force of regional officials and warlords launched a campaign against him, forced the Han court to move to Chang'an and sacked the capital Luoyang, burning down its palaces.

4 *Materia Medica* (*Bencao*) is a book on medicinal plants, attributed to Shennong, a mythical sage ruler in antiquity who taught people the ways of agriculture and the use of herbal drugs.

5 A note in the "Song edition" states that this theory comes from Huangfu Mi's *Lineages of Emperors and Kings* (see XVII.19). Zuo Qiuming (fl. sixth century BCE), a historian of the domain of Lu in the Spring and Autumn Period, was the putative author of the *Zuo Tradition*.

6 Xi was the last king of the state of Yan (r. 255–222 BCE) at the end of the Warring States Period. Han Emperor Gaozu was the founder of the Han dynasty, Liu Bang.

XVII.36b

汲冢瑣語乃載秦望碑；蒼頡篇李斯所造，
而云漢兼天下，海內并廁，豨黥韓覆，畔
討滅殘；列仙傳劉向所造，而贊云七十四
人出佛經；列女傳亦向所造，其子歆又作
頌，終于趙悼后，而傳有更始韓夫人、明
德馬后及梁夫人嫕：皆由後人所羼，非本
文也。"

XVII.36b

"The *Miscellaneous Discourses* from the Ji tomb records the stele of Mount Qinwang.[1] The *Cang Jie pian* was created by [the Qin minister] Li Si, but it states that the Han unified all under heaven and people within the four seas joined the empire, and that Chen Xi's soldiers had their faces tattooed as criminals and Han Xin met his ruin, and all the rebels were suppressed and their remnants extinguished.[2] *The Biographies of Immortals* was written by Liu Xiang, but the eulogy states that seventy-four immortals are named in the Buddhist scriptures.[3] *The Biographies of Notable Women* was also written by Liu Xiang, whose son Liu Xin wrote the eulogies, and the book concludes with Queen Dao of Zhao;[4] yet its current version contains the biographies of Lady Han of Emperor Gengshi, Empress Ma of Bright Virtue, and Lady Liang Yi.[5] These examples have all been inserted by later hands, not included in the original versions."

---

1 The *Miscellaneous Discourses* (*Suoyu*) was found in a Warring States Period tomb in Ji county in 281. The stele on Mount Qinwang was erected by the First Qin Emperor, much later than the date of the tomb.

2 For *Cang Jie pian* and Li Si, see note to VI.43. Chen Xi (d. 196) and Han Xin (d. 196) were both generals who aided Liu Bang in the founding of the Han dynasty; they both rebelled after the Han was established and were suppressed and killed. For an alternative interpretation of this passage, see Additional Notes.

3 Liu Xiang (see note to VII.2) lived before Buddhism came to China.

4 Liu Xin, scholar and writer, died in 23 CE. Queen Dao of Zhao was the queen consort of King Daoxiang of Zhao (d. 236 BCE).

5 Lady Han was a consort of the Gengshi Emperor (d. 25); Empress Ma (d. 79) was the consort of Han Emperor Ming (r. 58–75); Lady Liang Yi (fl. 97) was an aunt of Han Emperor He (r. 89–105).

XVII.37

或問曰："東宮舊事何以呼鷗尾為祠
尾？"答曰:"張敞者吳人，不甚稽古，隨
宜記注，逐鄉俗訛謬，造作書字耳。吳人
呼祠祀為鷗祀，故以祠代鷗字；呼紺為
禁，故以糸傍作禁代紺字；呼盞為竹簡
反，故以木傍作展代盞字；呼鑊字為霍
字，故以金傍作霍代鑊字；又金傍作患為
鐶字，木傍作鬼為魁字，火傍作庶為炙
字，既下作毛為氅字；金花則金傍作華，
窗扇則木傍作扇：諸如此類，專輒不
少。"

XVII.37

Someone asked, "In *The Matters of the Eastern Palace in Recent Times*, why is the 'owl-tail' (*chi wei*) called *si wei*?"[1] I replied, "[The author] Zhang Chang was a man of Wu; he did not quite study the past.[2] He merely made notes in a casual manner, following the local customs and perpetuating their mistakes by coining new words. Wu people call temple sacrifices (*si si*) 'owl sacrifices' (*chi si*), so he replaced *chi* with *si* in the term *chi wei*. Wu people refer to [the color] *gan* (MC komH) as *jin* (MC kimH), so he created a graph consisting of the silk radical (*mi* 糸) and *jin* 禁, to replace the character *gan*. Wu people pronounce the character *zhan* [MC tsreanX] as a combination of *zhu* [MC trjuwk] and *jian* [MC keanX], so he replaced it with a graph consisting of the wood radical (*mu* 木) and *zhan* 展 [MC trjenX]. Wu people pronounce *huo* (MC hwak, "cauldron") as *huo* [MC xwak], so he made up a new graph consisting of the metal (*jin* 金) radical and *huo* 霍 to replace the original character. He also made a graph consisting of the metal radical next to *huan* 患, to replace the character *huan* ("circle or ring"); added the wood radical to *gui* 鬼 to replace *kui* 魁 ("ladle"); added the fire radical to *shu* 庶 to replace *zhi* ("roasted meat"); and added *mao* 毛 ("hair") under *ji* 既 to replace *ji* ("chignon"). He added the metal radical to *hua* 華 ("flower") to make a graph representing a metal flower, and added the wood radical to *shan* 扇 ("door leaf") to make a graph representing a window. There are many other examples of his arbitrary inventions."

---

1 The Eastern Palace was a name of the residence of the Crown Prince. *The Matters of the Eastern Palace in Recent Times* (*Donggong jiushi*) is also entitled *Jin donggong jiushi* 晉東宮舊事, written in the late fourth century or early fifth century. *Chi wei* is an ornamental roof-ridge tile.

2 Zhang Chang (fl. 370s) was an Eastern Jin official who was a native of Wu commandery (in modern Jiangsu); he was the father of the more famous minister Zhang Maodu 張茂度 (376–442). Wu was understood in contrast with north China from which Yan Zhitui's ancestors had immigrated.

XVII.38

又問：“東宮舊事‘六色罽緤’，是何等
物？當作何音？”答曰：“案說文云：‘
著，牛藻也，讀若威。’音隱：‘塢瑰
反。’即陸璣所謂聚藻葉如蓬者也。又郭
璞注三蒼亦云：‘蘊藻之類也，細葉蓬茸
生。’然今水中有此物，一節長數寸，細
茸如絲，圓繞可愛，長者二三十節，猶呼
為著。又寸斷五色絲，橫著線股間繩之，
以象著草，用以飾物，即名為著；於時當
絀六色罽，作此著以飾緄帶，張敞因造糸
旁畏耳，宜作隈。”

XVII.38

The person asked again, "*The Matters of the Eastern Palace in Recent Times* mentions a six-colored *ji* 緌. What is it? How should the [last] character 緌 be pronounced?" I replied, "According to *Shuowen*, '蒤 (*Potamogeton crispus*) is cow's-pondweed. It is pronounced as *wei*.' The *Subtleties of Sounds* gives the pronunciation of the character as a combination of *wu* [MC 'uX] and *gui* [MC kwoj].[1] This is the plant that Lu Ji has described as 'a water plant growing in clusters whose leaves are like those of mugwort.'[2] Guo Pu's commentary on the Three Cang Texts also says, 'It belongs to the same species of clustered pondweed, whose slender leaves grow profusely.' Nowadays there is indeed such an aquatic plant; each section of it is several inches long, slender like silk and quite lovely in its coiling and twining manner. The tall ones have twenty or thirty sections. People still call it *wei*. They also cut five-colored silk into inch-long sections, and string them horizontally with thread on a rope in imitation of the *wei* plant for decoration, which they subsequently name *wei*. I suppose that people at the time must have bound the six-colored woolen blankets (*liuse ji*) in a bundle with a colored sash that was made with the *wei* decoration.[3] Zhang Chang thereupon coined the character *wei* 緌 consisting of the silk radical (*mi* 糸) and the graph *wei* 畏. It should be written as *wei* 隈."

---

1 The full title of this work is *The Subtleties of Sounds of the 'Shuowen' (Shuowen Yin yin)*. Its authorship is unknown.

2 Lu Ji (fl. third century) was the author of a commentary on the names of plants, animals, insects, and fish that appear in the *Classic of Poetry*. He was not the same person as the poet Lu Ji (see VI.24).

3 I have followed the *Taiping yulan* version here in emending *gan* 紺 to *xie* 絏 (see Additional Notes).

XVII.39

柏人城東北有一孤山，古書無載者。唯闞
駰十三州志以為舜納於大麓，即謂此山，
其上今猶有堯祠焉；世俗或呼為宣務山，
或呼為虛無山，莫知所出。趙郡士族有李
穆叔、季節兄弟、李普濟，亦為學問，並
不能定鄉邑此山。余嘗為趙州佐，共太原
王邵讀柏人城西門內碑。碑是漢桓帝時柏
人縣民為縣令徐整所立，銘曰："土有
巏嶵，王喬所仙。"方知此巏嶵山也。巏
字遂無所出，嶵字依諸字書，即旄丘之旄
也，旄字，字林一音亡付反。今依附俗
名，當音權務耳。入鄴，為魏收說之，收
大嘉歎。值其為趙州莊嚴寺碑銘，因云：
"權務之精。"即用此也。

1　Boren is in modern Hebei.

2　Kan Yin (fl. early fifth century) was a scholar from Dunhuang (in modern Gansu); the *Records of the Thirteen Prefectures* (*Shisanzhou zhi*) is no longer extant in entirety.

3　Mushu was the courtesy name of Li Gongxu 李公緒 (fl. 540–550s); Jijie was the courtesy name of Li Gongxu's younger brother, Li Gai 李概, who was also known as a scholar and writer. Li Puji (fl. 540s) was from a prominent clan of Zhao commandery (in modern Hebei) and was known for his learning.

XVII.39

There is a solitary hill to the northeast of the city of Boren, which has never been recorded in ancient texts.[1] Only Kan Yin's *Records of the Thirteen Prefectures* holds that Shun had once gone into a vast mountain forest, and that it was on this hill.[2] Nowadays, atop the hill there is still a shrine dedicated to Yao. The locals call it Xuanwu Hill or Xuwu Hill, but no one knows where the name came from. Among the gentry of Zhao commandery, the brothers Li Mushu and Li Jijie, as well as Li Puji, were erudite men, but none of them could offer anything definitive about this hill in their native region.[3] When I served as administrative aide to the Governor of Zhaozhou, I once went together with Wang Shao of Taiyuan to read a stele inside the west city gate of Boren.[4] The stele had been erected by the people of Boren county for the county magistrate, Xu Zheng, during the reign of Han Emperor Huan.[5] The inscription says, "This land has the Quanwu Hill, where Prince Qiao became an immortal."[6] Only then did I realize that the hill was the Quanwu Hill. The etymology of *quan* is unknown; *wu*, according to various dictionaries, is the same as *mao* like in the phrase "Maoqiu."[7] The *Forest of Graphs* gives one of the pronunciations of the character *mao* as a combination of *wang* (MC mjang) and *fu* (MC pjuH). If we follow the popular local name, we should say Quanwu. When I came to Ye, I told Wei Shou about it, who exclaimed with great admiration.[8] He happened to be composing a stele inscription for the Zhuangyan Temple of Zhaozhou at the time, so he wrote the line, "The essence of Quanwu," based on this very discovery.

---

4 For Wang Shao, see VIII.40.

5 Han Emperor Huan ruled from 147 to 167.

6 Prince Qiao was Prince Jin (see XII.9). He was said to have become an immortal and ascended to heaven.

7 "Maoqiu" is the title of a poem from the *Classic of Poetry*; *mao* means a sloping hill high in front and low behind.

8 Wei Shou was a famous scholar and historian: see VII.20.

XVII.40

或問：“一夜何故五更？更何所訓？”答曰：“漢、魏以來，謂為甲夜、乙夜、丙夜、丁夜、戊夜，又云鼓，一鼓、二鼓、三鼓、四鼓、五鼓，亦云一更、二更、三更、四更、五更，皆以五為節。西都賦亦云：‘衛以嚴更之署。’所以爾者，假令正月建寅，斗柄夕則指寅，曉則指午矣；自寅至午，凡歷五辰。冬夏之月，雖復長短參差，然辰間遼闊，盈不至六，縮不至四，進退常在五者之間。更，歷也，經也，故曰五更爾。”

XVII.41

爾雅云：“朮，山薊也。”郭璞注云：“今朮似薊而生山中。”案朮葉其體似薊。近世文士，遂讀薊為筋肉之筋，以耦地骨用之，恐失其義。

---

1 The "Rhapsody on the Western Capital" ("Xidu fu") was composed by Ban Gu.
2 Day and night were divided into twelve two-hour periods named after the twelve Earthly Branches. *Yin* is roughly equivalent to 3:00 to 5:00 and *wu* is 11:00 to 13:00. From the beginning of *yin* to the end of *wu*, there are ten hours (five two-hour periods).

XVII.40

Someone asked, "Why are there five watches (*geng*) in one night? What does *geng* mean?" I replied, "Since the Han and Wei dynasties, a night has been divided into A, B, C, D, and E nights; also into 'drums' (*gu*): first drum, second, third, fourth, and fifth; and 'watches' (*geng*): first *geng*, second, third, fourth, and fifth. But they all use five as measurement. The 'Rhapsody on the Western Capital' says, 'Guarded by an office that sounds a drum for each of the watches (*yan geng*).'[1] The reason for this is that, in the first month of a year, the handle of the Dipper points to *yin* in the evening, but to *wu* in the morning; from [the beginning of] *yin* to [the end of] *wu*, five two-hour periods elapse.[2] From winter to summer, even though the length of a night may vary, the total number of the two-hour periods does not go beyond six [i.e., twelve hours] at the longest or under four [i.e., eight hours] at the shortest; it is always around five, give or take. *Geng* means to move or pass through something; therefore we say there are five *geng* each night."

XVII.41

The *Erya* says, "*Atractylodes* (*zhu*) is mountain thistle." Guo Pu's commentary explains, "*Atractylodes* looks like thistle but grows in the mountains." I note that the leaves of *Atractylodes* look like thistle leaves. But literary men in modern times pronounce *ji* (thistle) as *jin*, as in the phrase *jinrou* ("sinew and flesh; muscle"), and even pair the term with "earth's bones" (*di gu*, wolfberry) for the sake of parallelism in their writings.[3] I am afraid they have missed its real meaning.

---

3 That is, the "mountain thistle / mountain's sinews" and "earth's bones" are used as matching terms in a parallel couplet or sentence. Liang Emperor Yuan uses the phrase *shanjin digu* 山筋地骨 ("mountain's sinews and earth's bones") in his "Xuanlan fu" 玄覽賦.

XVII.42

或問："俗名傀儡子為郭禿，有故實乎？"答曰："風俗通云：諸郭皆諱禿。當是前世有姓郭而病禿者，滑稽調戲，故後人為其象，呼為郭禿，猶文康象庾亮耳。"

XVII.43

或問曰："何故名治獄參軍為長流乎？"答曰："帝王世紀云：'帝少昊崩，其神降于長流之山，於祀主秋。'案：周禮秋官，司寇主刑罰。長流之職，漢、魏捕賊掾耳。晉、宋以來，始為參軍，上屬司寇，故取秋帝所居為嘉名焉。"

XVII.42

Someone asked, "The puppet in puppet shows is commonly called 'Bald Guo.' Is there an old story behind this?" I replied, "The *Comprehensive Meaning of Customs and Mores* says, 'Men surnamed Guo all treat 'bald' as a taboo word.'[1] Presumably, in the old days someone surnamed Guo who suffered from baldness was a funny fellow and loved jesting, and so people in later times made puppets in his image and called them 'Bald Guo.' This is just like the Wenkang show that used Yu Liang's image."[2]

XVII.43

Someone asked, "For what reason is the Adjutant of Justice called Changliu?" I replied, "The *Lineages of Emperors and Kings* says, 'After Emperor Shaohao died, his spirit descended to Changliu Mountain. With regard to the annual cycle, he is in charge of autumn.'[3] I note that according to the 'Autumn Offices' chapter in the *Rites of Zhou*, a Minister of Justice is in charge of crime and punishment.[4] In Han and Wei times, the office of Changliu was responsible for capturing thieves and bandits. Since Jin and Song dynasties, the position was turned into an Adjutant, and placed under the supervision of the Minister of Justice. Hence people took the term designating the dwelling place of the autumn emperor to be a complimentary name for it."

---

1 This work is mentioned in an earlier chapter (see XVII.21).

2 Wenkang was the posthumous title of Yu Liang 庾亮 (289–340), the powerful Eastern Jin minister. After his death, his family entertainers missed him and made a mask in his image in a song-and-dance show. Some commentators believe Wenkang refers to a different musical show, popular in the sixth century, in which the protagonist is an "old Tatar" named Wenkang and has nothing to do with Yu Liang (Teng 181, note 4; Wang Liqi 506–7).

3 The *Lineages of Emperors and Kings* was a work by Huangfu Mi (see note to VIII.15a). Shaohao was a mythical emperor whose spirit became the god of the west, the direction associated with autumn.

4 Autumn is the season associated with law and order.

XVII.44a

客有難主人曰：“今之經典，子皆謂非，說文所明，于皆云是，然則許慎勝孔子乎？”主人拊掌大笑，應之曰：“今之經典，皆孔子手跡耶？”客曰：“今之說文，皆許慎手跡乎？”

XVII.44b

答曰：“許慎檢以六文，貫以部分，使不得誤，誤則覺之。孔子存其義而不論其文也。先儒尚得改文從意，何況書寫流傳耶？必如左傳止戈為武，反正為乏，皿蟲為蠱，亥有二首六身之類，後人自不得輒改也，安敢以說文校其是非哉？

XVII.44a

A guest challenged his host, saying, "What we regard as classics today you always say are wrong; but whatever the *Shuowen* sheds light on, you always accede to. Could Xu Shen [the *Shuowen* author] have possibly been superior to Confucius?" The host clapped his hands and laughed out loud, saying, "Are the copies of the classics we read today written out by the hand of Confucius?" The guest retorted, "Well, is the copy of the *Shuowen* we read today written out by the hand of Xu Shen?"

XVII.44b

The host responded, "Xu Shen checked the characters with the Six Methods and divided them by radicals, so that there would be no mistake.[1] If there is any mistake, it can be detected immediately. Confucius, however, was intent on preserving the meaning of a text but did not discuss the graphs themselves. Even previous Ru scholars were free to revise the graphs in order to follow the true meaning of a text, not to mention that the texts have gone through so much in transmission and circulation [and are thus riddled with errors]. If it is a case as in the *Zuo Tradition*, when the graphs *zhi* and *ge* were said to make up the character *wu*, *fan* and *zheng* to make up *fa*, *min* and *chong* to make up *gu*, or the character *hai* was said to have 'two as its head [upper part] and six as its body [lower part],' then the later-born naturally should not alter these characters arbitrarily, and in such cases how can we use the *Shuowen* to assess what is right or wrong?

---

1 The Six Methods refer to the six principles of making characters: *zhishi* 指事 ("indicating the concept"), *xiangxing* 象形 ("depicting the form"), *xingsheng* 形聲 ("formulating the sound"), *huiyi* 會意 ("joining the sense"), *zhuanzhu* 轉注 ("rotating characters"), and *jiajie* 假借 ("loaning and borrowing [characters]."

XVII.44c

"且余亦不專以說文為是也,其有援引經傳,與今乖者,未之敢從。又相如封禪書曰:'導一莖六穗於庖,犧雙觡共抵之獸。'此導訓擇,光武詔云'非徒有豫養導擇之勞'是也。而說文云:'導是禾名。'引封禪書為證,無妨自當有禾名導,非相如所用也。禾一莖六穗於庖,豈成文乎?縱使相如天才鄙拙,強為此語,則下句當云'麟雙觡共抵之獸',不得云犧也。吾嘗笑許純儒,不達文章之體,如此之流,不足憑信。大抵服其為書,隱括有條例,剖析窮根源,鄭玄注書,往往引其為證;若不信其說,則冥冥不知一點一畫,有何意焉。"

---

1 Sima Xiangru was a great writer of the Western Han (see note to VI.6). Hearing that he was gravely ill, Han Emperor Wu sent someone to his home for his writings. When the messenger arrived, Sima Xiangru had already died, but the messenger brought back a memorial he had written to the throne, in which he urged the emperor to perform the Feng and Shan ceremonies.

XVII.44c

"Besides, I do not believe that the *Shuowen* is always correct. If its citations from the classics and commentaries disagree with the versions we have today, I do not presume to follow them. For instance, Sima Xiangru's 'Memorial to the Throne about the Feng and Shan Ceremonies' says, 'Select (*dao*) a stalk with six ears of grain in the kitchen, / sacrifice the animal with two horns growing from one root.'[1] Here the word *dao* is glossed as 'selecting or choosing.' It is the same as in the edict of Han Emperor Guangwu, which says, '....not merely causing the trouble of cultivating in advance and selecting.'[2] The *Shuowen*, however, says, '*Dao* is the name of a grain,' and cites the Feng Shan memorial as its basis. Of course there might have been a kind of grain named *dao*, but that is not the sense in which Sima Xiangru used the word in his memorial. To say 'Grain, one stalk six ears, in the kitchen' – is that even grammatical? Even if Sima Xiangru had been clumsy and stupid, and had indeed come up with such a clause, then in the matching clause [for the sake of parallelism] he should have written, 'Unicorn, two-horns-sharing-one-root animal,' and should not have used 'to sacrifice,' a verb.[3] Once I laughed at Xu Shen for purely being a Ru scholar who did not understand the style of literary composition, and surely things in the *Shuowen* like the preceding are not worth following. In general, however, I admire his book for having sound principles in establishing a standard of judgment and being thorough and exhaustive in its etymological analysis. Zheng Xuan often cited the *Shuowen* for evidence when he wrote his commentaries. If we do not believe Xu Shen, then we would be completely ignorant of the reason for a dot or a stroke in a character – what good would that do?"

---

2 Han Emperor Guangwu (r. 25–57 CE) was the founder of the Eastern Han. This is from an edict issued in 37 CE forbidding regional officials to present rare delicacies to the throne.

3 That is, since the two clauses are parallel to each other, the characters in corresponding positions in the two lines should be in the same word-class. If in the first position of the first clause the author had used a noun ("grain"), in the same position of the second clause he should have also used a noun ("unicorn"), not a verb ("to sacrifice"). Again, many scholars dispute Yan Zhitui's argument here (see Wang Liqi 513–14).

XVII.45

世間小學者，不通古今，必依小篆，是正
書記；凡爾雅、三蒼、說文，豈能悉得蒼
頡本指哉？亦是隨代損益，互有同異。西
晉已往字書，何可全非？但令體例成就，
不為專輒耳。考校是非，特須消息。至如
"仲尼居"，三字之中，兩字非體，三蒼
"尼"旁益"丘"，說文"尸"下施
"几"：如此之類，何由可從？古無二
字，又多假借，以中為仲，以說為悅，以
召為邵，以閒為閑：如此之徒，亦不勞
改。

XVII.45

Many people who engage in philological study do not have the knowledge that encompasses both past and present; they invariably rely on the "small seal script" as the standard to make corrections in books and records.[1] But are the *Erya*, the Three Cang, and the *Shuowen* all able to completely preserve the original ideas of Cang Jie, the creator of characters? They, too, made changes to suit the times, and thus show differences in graphic forms. So how can we reject all the philological works produced since the Western Jin? They are acceptable as long as they have established a comprehensive set of principles and do not make arbitrary choices. When we assess the right and wrong of the graphic form of a character, we must particularly give careful consideration. For instance, of the three characters, "Zhongni ju" 仲尼居 ("Confucius's dwelling), two are not written in the correct form.[2] Yet, when the Three Cang Texts added a *qiu* to *ni*, and the *Shuowen* put a *ji* under *shi*, how can we just go ahead and follow their practices?[3] Furthermore, in ancient times a character often did not have any variant form [to express a different idea], and so people would use loan characters; thus *zhong* 中 is used as a loan character for *zhong* 仲, *shuo* 說 for *yue* 悅, *zhao* 召 for *shao* 邵, and *xian* 閒 for *xian* 閑. In such cases there is no need to bother correcting them.

---

1 The "small seal script" was the new script promulgated after the First Qin Emperor unified the empire in 221 BCE.

2 These three characters are the opening of the *Classic of Filial Piety* (see VII.18).

3 The character *ni* is written as 㞬, and the character *ju* written as 凥.

XVII.46

自有訛謬，過成鄙俗。亂旁為舌，揖下無
耳，鼋、鼉從龜，奮、奪從雚，席中加
帶，惡上安西，鼓外設皮，鑿頭生毀，離
則配禹，壑乃施豁，巫混經旁，皋分澤
片，獵化為獦，寵變成竉，業左益片，靈
底著器，率字自有律音，強改為別；單字
自有善音，輒析成異：如此之類，不可不
治。

XVII.47

吾昔初看說文，蚩薄世字，從正則懼人不
識，隨俗則意嫌其非，略是不得下筆也。
所見漸廣，更知通變，救前之執，將欲半
焉。若文章著述，猶擇微相影響者行之，
官曹文書，世間尺牘，幸不違俗也。

XVII.46

There are also errors that are turned into vulgar conventions. For instance, *luan* is written with *she* as a component; *yi* has no *er* on the right; *yuan* and *tuo* are written with the *gui* radical, and *fen* and *duo* with the *guan* radical; to write *xi* one adds a *dai* inside, and for *e* one puts *xi* on the top; *gu* is written with a *pi* on the side while the upper part of *zuo* becomes *hui*; *li* is matched with a *yu* while *he* acquires a *huo*; *wu* becomes confused with a part of *jing*, and *gao* takes one part from *ze*; *lie* is changed to *ge*, and *chong* is turned into *long*; on the left side of *ye* one adds a *pian*; at the bottom of *ling* one inserts a *qi*; the character *shuai* originally also has the pronunciation of *lü*, but people insist on changing it to fit its alternative pronunciation; likewise, *dan* is also pronounced *shan*, but they arbitrarily adopt another character to indicate the alternative pronunciation. In cases like these, one simply must correct them.

XVII.47

Earlier, when I first read the *Shuowen*, I became scornful of the characters commonly used in the world. I wanted to follow the correct forms, but feared that people might not recognize them; should I follow the common practice, I felt reluctant because I knew it was wrong. As a result, I almost became paralyzed and could no longer write anything! Later on, as I read more widely, and better understood the importance of flexibility and change, it has helped me correct my stubborn bias in nearly half of the cases. In one's own writings, one should still select characters that are more or less similar to their correct forms; but when it comes to government documents and correspondence with people in society, I hope you will not go against popular conventions.

XVII.48

案彌亙字從二閒舟，詩云"亙之秬秠"是
也。今之隸書，轉舟為日；而何法盛中興
書乃以舟在二閒為舟航字，謬也。

XVII.49

春秋說以人十四心為德，詩說以二在天下
為酉，漢書以貨泉為白水真人，新論以金
昆為銀，國志以天上有口為吳，晉書以黃
頭小人為恭，宋書以召刀為劭，參同契以
人負告為造：如此之例，蓋數術謬語，假
借依附，雜以戲笑耳。如猶轉貢字為項，
以叱為匕，安可用此定文字音讀乎？潘、
陸諸子離合詩、賦，拭卜、破字經，及鮑
昭謎字，皆取會流俗，不足以形聲論之
也。

---

1 The clerical script (*lishu*) was used in the Qin empire to facilitate writing in the
newly created bureaucracy.

2 He Fasheng's work is mentioned in an earlier chapter (see XVII.32).

3 The *Interpretation of the Spring and Autumn Annals* and the *Interpretation of the
Poems* are both apocryphal texts that are no longer extant.

4 The *New Treatises* (*Xin lun*) was written by Huan Tan 桓譚 (23 BCE–56 CE).

5 The *Unity of the Three* is a work on alchemy attributed to a Wei Boyang 魏伯陽
(fl. second century).

6 "Separation and combination" verses and rhapsodies are poetic writings based on
separating and combining components of a graph. For instance, one line can
indicate one component of a character and the next line another; when the two

XVII.48

I would like to further note that the character *gen*, as in the phrase *migen* ("extend"), follows the form of *zhou* 舟 ("boat") between the two strokes of the graph *er* 二 ("two"). This is the word used in the line from the *Poems*, "Extensive are the black millet and the double-kernelled millet." Nowadays the clerical script changes *zhou* to *ri* ("sun") [so that the graph appears as 亘].[1] He Fasheng's *Book of the Jin Restoration* takes it to be the character *hang* as in the phrase *zhouhang* ("boat"); that is a mistake. [2]

XVII.49

The *Interpretation of the Spring and Autumn Annals* says that a person (*ren*) with four and ten hearts (*shi si xin*) makes up the character *de*, and the *Interpretation of the Poems* says that two (*er*) under heaven (*tian*) makes *you*;[3] in the [*Later*] *Han History*, money (*huoquan*) becomes "the Genuine Being of the White River" (*baishui zhenren*); the *New Treatises* takes silver (*yin*) to be "the brother of gold" (*jin kun*);[4] in the *Records of the [Three] Kingdoms*, a mouth (*kou*) in heaven (*tian*) is Wu; the *Jin History* takes "respectful" (*gong*) to be "a lowly man with a yellow head" (*huangtou xiaoren*); in the *History of the Song*, the character *shao* is said to consist of *zhao* ("summon") and *dao* ("knife"); in the *Unity of the Three*, the character *zao* ("go to") is taken to be a person (*ren*) carrying a report (*gao*).[5] Examples like these are code words of diviners who put words together through borrowing and loaning in a joking manner. This is like twisting the graph *gong* into *xiang* or taking the graph *chi* as *bi*; how can you use that as a measure of a character's pronunciation? The "separation and combination" verses and rhapsodies composed by writers such as Pan [Yue] and Lu [Ji], the *Star Compass Divination*, the *Scripture of Splitting Characters*, and Bao Zhao's "Character Riddles" are all works designed to please the crowd.[6] They are not worth any consideration in terms of the principle of "formulating the sound."[7]

---

lines are combined, the character will emerge. One such poem by Pan Yue is extant. For Pan Yue and Lu Ji: see notes to VIII.35 and to VI.24. Bao Zhao 鮑照 (414?–466) was a famous Song writer. The graph for his given name would be changed to 昭 in the Tang to avoid the taboo name of Empress Wu Zhao 武曌 (r. 684–704). Three of his "Character Riddles ("Zi mi") are extant. The *Star Compass Divination* and the *Scripture of Splitting Characters* are lost.

7 *Xingsheng* ("formulating the sound") is one of the "Six Methods" of character-making discussed by Xu Shen (see note to XVII.44b).

XVII.50

河間邢芳語吾云："賈誼傳云日中必蔇。
注：'蔇，暴也。'曾見人解云：'此是
暴疾之意，正言日中不須臾，卒然便咻
耳。'此釋為當乎？"吾謂邢曰："此語
本出太公六韜，案字書，古者暴曬字與暴
疾字相似，唯下少異，後人專輒加傍日
耳。言日中時，必須暴曬，不爾者，失其
時也。晉灼已有詳釋。"芳笑服而退。

XVII.50

Xing Fang of Hejian once asked me, "The 'Biography of Jia Yi' says, 'The sun in mid-heaven must *wei*.'[1] The commentary glosses this character as *bao*. I once saw someone interpret it like this, 'The character means 'fierce and fast.' The phrase is saying that the sun is in mid-heaven only for one instant before it suddenly begins setting.' Is this a correct interpretation?" I said to Xing, "This phrase is originally from Taigong's *Six Tactics*.[2] According to lexical works, in ancient times the character *pu* in *pushai* ('expose to sun') was very similar to *bao* in *baoji* ('fierce and fast'), only with a slightly different bottom part; in later times people arbitrarily added the 'sun' radical (*ri*) to it. So the phrase is saying that when the sun is in mid-heaven, one must sun whatever needs to be sunned; otherwise one would miss the opportune time. Jin Zhuo has already given a detailed explanation of this."[3] Satisfied with the answer, Fang went away with a smile.

---

1 Jia Yi was a Western Han writer (see note to IX.2c). His biography is in both the *Historian's Record* and the *Han History*. Here the citation is from Jia Yi's memorial to the throne cited in his *Han History* biography. Nothing else is known about Xing Fang.
2 Taigong's *Six Tactics* is mentioned earlier (see XVII.11).
3 Jin Zhuo (fl. late third century–early fourth century) served at the Western Jin court and authored a linguistic commentary on the *Han History*.

音辭第十八

XVIII. 1

夫九州之人，言語不同，生民已來，固常
然矣。自春秋摽齊言之傳，離騷目楚詞之
經，此蓋其較明之初也。後有揚雄著方
言，其言大備。然皆考名物之同異，不顯
聲讀之是非也。逮鄭玄注六經，高誘解呂
覽、淮南，許慎造說文，劉熹製釋名，始
有譬況假借以證音字耳。

XVIII. Phonology

XVIII. 1

People of the Nine Regions all speak different tongues: this has always been the case since the birth of the folk. The [Gongyang] commentary on the *Spring and Autumn Annals* is marked in the Qi dialect; the *Li sao* is viewed as a classic in the Chu idiom.[1] This shows a clear linguistic distinction from the beginning. Later on, Yang Xiong authored the *Regional Expressions* (*Fangyan*), which is greatly comprehensive.[2] However, it only examines the differences in names of things, and does not reveal the right and wrong of their pronunciations. The commentators' practice of using homophones and loan characters to indicate pronunciation only began at the time when Zheng Xuan annotated the Six Classics, Gao You interpreted *Lü's View* and *Huainanzi*, Xu Shen created the *Shuowen*, and Liu Xi produced *A Glossary of Names*.[3]

---

1 The Gongyang commentary, known as the *Gongyang Tradition*, is one of the three major commentaries on the *Spring and Autumn Annals*; its author, Gongyang Gao 公羊高 (fl. fourth century BCE), was a native of Qi (in modern Shandong) in the Warring States Period. See note to VIII.2.

2 For *Regional Expressions*, see note to XVII.24.

3 The Six Classics annotated by Zheng Xuan include the *Classic of Changes*, the *Book of Documents*, the *Classic of Poetry* (the *Poems*), and the three ritual classics (*Yi li*, *Li ji*, and *Zhou li*). Gao You: see note to XVII.2. Liu Xi (fl. second century) is also written as 劉熙.

XVIII.2

而古語與今殊別，其間輕重清濁，猶未可
曉；加以內言外言、急言徐言、讀若之
類，益使人疑。孫叔言創爾雅音義，是漢
末人獨知反語。至於魏世，此事大行。高
貴鄉公不解反語，以為怪異。自茲厥後，
音韻鋒出，各有土風，遞相非笑，指馬之
諭，未知孰是。共以帝王都邑，參校方
俗，考覈古今，為之折衷。摧而量之，獨
金陵與洛下耳。

XVIII.2

However, the ancient speech was quite different from modern speech, and the distinction between stressed and unstressed, voiced and voiceless was not yet entirely clear. In addition, there are also confusing issues such as the internal and external sounds, the fast and slow utterances, and the practice of "reading X as Y."[1] Sun Shuyan wrote *Sounds and Meanings of Erya*, thus proving himself the only one toward the end of the Han dynasty who knew about the *fanqie* system.[2] By the Wei dynasty, this system had become so popular that people thought it strange that the Duke of Gaogui District did not understand it.[3] From this point onward, works about sounds and rhymes emerged like a swarm of wasps.[4] Scholars each followed their own regional customs, criticizing and mocking one another; as in the discussions of "fingers and horses," it is hard to know which was right and which was wrong.[5] If we focus on the imperial capitals, using regional customs as points of reference and investigating the past and present in order to find the middle way, then in the final analysis there are only Jinling and Luoyang [that can serve as standards].[6]

---

1 The internal and external sounds are explained by the modern linguist Zhou Zumo 周祖謨 (1914–1995) as "back and open vowels" and "front and closed vowels."

2 Sun Shuyan was Sun Yan (mentioned earlier, in XVII.13), also known as Sun Shuran 孫叔然. The *fanqie* system is to mark pronunciation by using a combination of the initial sound of one character and the final sound of another.

3 The Duke of Gaogui District was Cao Mao 曹髦 (r. 254–260), who was the fourth ruler of Wei in the Three Kingdoms Period.

4 For the phrase *fengqi* ("emerge like a swarm of wasps"), see Additional Notes.

5 The discussions of "fingers and horses" are those of the "Terminologists" (*mingjia*) of the late Warring States Period and are used to refer to debates about right and wrong.

6 Jinling is an old name of Jiankang, the capital of the Eastern Jin and Southern Dynasties; Luoyang was the former capital of the Eastern Han, the Western Jin, and from 494 to 534, the Northern Wei.

XVIII.3

南方水土和柔，其音清舉而切詣，失在浮
淺，其辭多鄙俗。北方山川深厚，其音沈
濁而鈋鈍，得其質直，其辭多古語。然冠
冕君子，南方為優；閭里小人，北方為
愈。易服而與之談，南方士庶，數言可
辯；隔垣而聽其語，北方朝野，終日難
分。

XVIII.4

而南染吳越，北雜夷虜，皆有深弊，不可
具論。其謬失輕微者，則南人以錢為涎，
以石為射，以賤為羨，以是為舐；北人以
庶為戍，以如為儒，以紫為姊，以洽為
狎。如此之例，兩失甚多。

XVIII.3

The water and soil in the south are soft and gentle; the human sounds are clear, elevated, and fast, but their weakness is shallowness and superficiality, and many of their expressions are low and unrefined. The mountains and rivers in the north are impenetrable and deep; the human sounds are sonorous, heavy, and blunt, but their strength is solidity and directness, and many of their expressions are from ancient times. If it is a gentleman speaking, the south is superior to the north; if it is a low-born rustic, then the north is better than the south. For in the south, even if they exchange their clothes, one can tell a gentry member and a commoner apart after hearing them say a few words; but in the north, if you listen to people talking on the other side of a wall, you will have a hard time distinguishing a patrician from a plebeian even after all day.

XVIII.4

Nevertheless, the southerners' speech is contaminated by Wu and Yue, while the northerners' speech is mixed with barbarian tongues. Each side has its great shortcomings, which cannot be discussed in detail here. I will only cite some minor errors: southerners mispronounce *qian* ("coin"; MC *dzjen*) as *xian* ("saliva"; MC *zjen*), *shi* ("stone"; MC *dzyek*) as *she* ("shoot an arrow"; MC *zyaeH*), *jian* ("lowly"; MC *dzjenH*) as *xian* ("envy"; MC *zjenH*), and *shi* ("this"; *dzyeX*) as *shi* ("lick"; MC *zyeX*); northerners mispronounce *shu* ("commoner"; MC *syoH*) as *shu* ("guard the fronter"; MC *syuH*), *ru* ("if"; MC *nyo*) as *ru* ("Ruist or Confucian"; MC *nyu*), *zi* ("purple"; MC *tsjeX*) as *zi* ("elder sister"; MC *tsijX*), and *qia* ("moisten": MC *heap*) as *xia* ("overly familiar"; MC *haep*). There are many such examples on both sides.

XVIII.5

至鄴已來，唯見崔子約、崔瞻叔姪，李祖
仁、李蔚兄弟，頗事言詞，少為切正。李
季節著音韻決疑，時有錯失；陽休之造切
韻，殊為疏野。

XVIII.6.

吾家子女，雖在孩稚，便漸督正之；一言
訛替，以為己罪矣。云為品物，未考書記
者，不敢輒名，汝曹所知也。

XVIII.5

Since coming to Ye, I have only seen Cui Ziyue and his nephew Cui Shan as well as the brothers Li Zuren and Li Wei who are devoted to phonological matters and have done some corrective work.[1] Li Jijie wrote *Resolving Doubts in Sounds and Rhymes*, but it makes mistakes from time to time;[2] Yang Xiuzhi produced a work on rhymes (*Qie yun*), which is quite careless.[3]

XVIII.6

The sons and daughters of my family, even during their early childhood, are drilled and corrected little by little. If they ever pronounce one thing wrong, I consider it my fault. As for objects and vessels made in our household, I will not presume to name them arbitrarily without consulting books and records first, as you boys know well.

1 Cui Ziyue (fl. 540s–560s) was a member of the prominent Cui clan of Qinghe (in modern Hebei). Cui Shan (interchangeable with Shan 贍, fl. 530s–560s) and Cui Ziyue were both known for their learning and elegance, regarded by contemporaries as "two heavenly beings." Li Zuren was the courtesy name of Li Yue 李岳, a brother of Li Shu (see VIII.4). The Li brothers were all known for their cultural refinement in the Northern Qi court.

2 Li Jijie was Li Gai (see note to XVII.39).

3 Yang Xiuzhi (509–582) was a high official as well as prominent scholar and writer of the north. His work on rhymes, known as the *Summaries of Rhymes* (*Yun lue* 韻略), has only survived in fragments. Referred to as *Qie yun* here, it should be differentiated from the *Qie yun* 切韻 compiled in 601 by Lu Fayan 陸法言 (fl. late sixth century to early seventh century) with Yan Zhitui's participation (see Introduction).

XVIII.7

古今言語，時俗不同；著述之人，楚夏各
異。蒼頡訓詁，反稗為逋賣，反娃為於
乖。戰國策音列為免。穆天子傳音諫為
閒。說文音戞為棘，讀皿為猛。字林音看
為口甘反，音伸為辛。韻集以成、仍、
宏、登合成兩韻，為、奇、益、石分作四
章。李登聲類以系音羿。劉昌宗周官音讀
乘若承。此例甚廣，必須考校。

1　The *Glossary of Cang Jie* (*Cangjie xungu*) was a work of linguistic commentary on the *Cang Jie pian* by Du Lin 杜林 (d. 47), an Eastern Han philologist.

2　Zhou Zumo explains that *mian* in the dialect of the Qing and Qi regions was pronounced as *wen* in the departing tone; hence the *Intrigues of the Warring States* gloss.

3　King Mu refers to King Mu of Zhou (see note to XIII.2). The *Biography of King Mu* is a fantastical account of his travels, discovered in the Warring States tomb in Ji County in the third century (see note to XVII.36b).

XVIII.7

Ancient and modern pronunciations vary according to the changing times and customs. Some authors speak with a Chu drawl while others with the Central Plains inflection. The *Glossary of Cang Jie* gives the pronunciation of *bai* (MC beaH) as a combination of *bu* (MC pu) and *mai* (MC meaH), and *wa* (MC 'wea), as *yu* (MC 'jo) and *guai* (MC kweajH).[1] The *Intrigues of the Warring States* gives the sound of *wen* (MC mjunX) as *mian* (MC mjenX).[2] The *Biography of King Mu* gives the sound of *jian* ("remonstrate"; MC kaenH) as *jian* ("interpose"; MC keanH).[3] The *Shuowen* reads *jia* (MC keat) as *ji* (MC kik), and *min* (MC mjaengX) as *meng* (MC maengX).[4] The *Forest of Graphs* gives the pronunciation of *kan* (MC khan) as a combination of *kou* (MC khuwX) and *gan* (MC kam), and reads *shen* (MC syin) as *xin* (MC sin). The *Collection of Rhymes* treats *cheng* (MC dzyeng), *reng* (MC nying), *hong* (MC hweang), and *deng* (MC tong) as belonging to two rhyme categories, and separates *wei* (MC hjwe), *qi* (MC gje), *yi* (MC 'jiek), and *shi* (MC dzyek) into four different groups.[5] Li Deng's *Sound by Categories* uses *xi* (MC hejH) to mark the pronunciation of *yi* (MC ngejH). Liu Changzong's phonological glossary of the *Zhou Offices* reads *cheng* ("ride"; MC zying) as *cheng* ("receive"; MC dzying).[6] There are numerous such examples, and one must carefully examine them.

---

4 Zhou Zumo points out that although *min* (MC mjaengX) and *meng* (MC maengX) belong to the same rhyme category in Middle Chinese, they are distinguished by being a closed sound ("of the third class") and an open sound ("of the second class") respectively.

5 Duan Yucai 段玉裁 (1735–1815) points out that according to the eleventh-century *Guang yun* (廣韻), which originates from the *Qie yun* compiled by Lu Fayan with Yan Zhitui's participation, *cheng, reng, hong,* and *deng* belong to four different rhyme groups. Again, according to *Guang yun, wei, qi, yi,* and *shi* belong to two different categories, with *wei* and *qi* grouped together and *yi* and *shi* grouped together, rather than falling under four different rhyme groups.

6 The *Zhou Offices* (*Zhou guan*) is another name for the *Rites of Zhou* (*Zhou li*).

XVIII.8

前世反語，又多不切，徐仙民毛詩音反驟
為在遘，左傳音切椽為徒緣，不可依信，
亦為眾矣。今之學士，語亦不正；古獨何
人，必應隨其訛僻乎？通俗文曰："入室
求曰搜。"反為兄侯。然則兄當音所榮
反。今北俗通行此音，亦古語之不可用
者。

XVIII.9

璵璠，魯人寶玉，當音餘煩，江南皆音藩
屏之藩。岐山當音為奇，江南皆呼為神祇
之祇。江陵陷沒，此音被於關中，不知二
者何所承案。以吾淺學，未之前聞也。

XVIII.8

Moreover, the *fanqie* system of earlier times is often inaccurate. Xu Xianmin's phonological glossary of the *Mao Poems* gives the pronunciation of *zhou* (MC dzrjuwH) as a combination of *zai* (MC dzojX) and *gou* (MC kuwH); his phonological glossary of the *Zuo Tradition* gives the pronunciation of *chuan* (MC drjwen) as a combination of *tu* (MC du) and *yuan* (MC ywen). Neither is reliable, and there are many such instances. If modern scholars do not always have correct pronunciations, why should we assume that ancient scholars were any better and that we must follow their idiosyncrasies? The *Common Writing* says, "*Sou* [MC srjuw] means searching everywhere within a room," and gives its pronunciation as a combination of *xiong* (MC xjwaeng) and *hou* (MC huw). Had this been right, then *xiong* should have been pronounced as a combination of *suo* (MC srjoX) and *rong* (MC hjwaeng) [rather than xjwaeng, the correct pronunciation]. Nowadays this erroneous pronunciation is widespread in the north. This is a case in which the ancient reading should not be used.

XVIII.9

"Yufan," the name of a precious jade of the State of Lu, should be pronounced as *yu2fan2* [MC yo bjon]. But in the south people all pronounce the second character as *fan1* [MC pjon], as in the phrase *fanping* ("screen, guard of border"). *Qi* in Mount Qi should be pronounced as *qi* ("strange"; MC gje), but in the south people pronounce it as *qi* [MC gjie] as in the phrase *shenqi* ("heaven and earth deities"). After the fall of Jiangling, these two pronunciations have spread all over the northwest.[1] I do not know their origin and basis. With my shallow learning, I simply have never heard of such pronunciations before.

---

1 After the Northern Wei army captured Jiangling, many southerners were taken captive to Chang'an, and thus spread the pronunciations.

XVIII.10

北人之音，多以舉、莒為矩。唯李季節云：“齊桓公與管仲於臺上謀伐莒，東郭牙望見桓公口開而不閉，故知所言者莒也。然則莒、矩必不同呼。”此為知音矣。

XVIII.11

夫物體自有精麤，精麤謂之好惡；人心有所去取，去取謂之好惡。此音見於葛洪、徐邈。而河北學士讀尚書云好生惡殺，是為一論物體，一就人情，殊不通矣。

XVIII.10

Most northerners pronounce *ju* 舉 ("raise up"; MC kjoX) and *ju* 莒 (place name; MC kjoX) as *ju* 矩 ("carpenter's square"; MC kjuX). Only Li Jijie had this to say, "When Duke Huan of Qi and Guan Zhong discussed attacking the state of Ju 莒 on the terrace, Dongguo Ya saw from a distance that Duke Huan said a word with parted lips, from which he guessed that the duke was speaking of [the domain of] Ju. Judging from this, I am sure that *ju* 莒 [place name] does not share the same sound as *ju* 矩 [carpenter's square]."[1] Now there you have a man who really "understands the tones."

XVIII.11

The substance of an object can be refined or coarse, and the different qualities are respectively referred to as *hao*3 ("good") and *e*4 ("bad"); the human mind has likes and dislikes, and the different sensibilities are respectively referred to as *hao*4 ("love or adore") and *wu*4 ("detest").[2] These pronunciations are found in the works of Ge Hong and Xu Miao. However, scholars to the north of the Yellow River would read "love life and detest killing" 好生惡殺 in the *Book of Documents* as *hao*4*sheng e*4*sha*.[3] That is, they pronounce the word 惡 as *e*4 in the sense of the quality of objects and the word 好 as *hao*4 in the sense of human sensibilities. That is not right.[4]

---

1 Li Jijie was the courtesy name of Li Gai (see XVII.39). Guan Zhong was a famous statesman of Qi from the seventh century BCE who helped Duke Huan of Qi achieve hegemony among the feudal lords. In modern Mandarin *ju* [place name] is pronounced in the third tone while *ju* [carpenter's square] is pronounced in the fourth tone.

2 At the end of this sentence, an original note in the "Song edition" indicates the pronunciation of the second 好惡: "The former character is pronounced as a combination of *hu* [MC xu] and *hao* [MC hawH]; the latter, a combination of *wu* [MC 'u] and *gu* [MC kuH]" 上呼號下烏故反. In modern Mandarin the pronunciation is *hao*4*wu*4, both in the fourth tone.

3 In the Song edition there is an original note that gives the pronunciation of 好 as a combination of *hu* 呼 [MC xu] and *hao* 號 [MC hawH], thus *hao*4 in modern Mandarin, and that of 惡 as a combination of *yu* 於 [MC 'jo] and *ge* 各 [MC kak], thus *e*4 in modern Mandarin.

4 That is, the correct pronunciation should be *hao*4*sheng wu*4*sha*.

XVIII.12

甫者，男子之美稱，古書多假借為父字；
北人遂無一人呼為甫者，亦所未喻。唯管
仲、范增之號，須依字讀耳。

XVIII.13

案諸字書，焉者鳥名，或云語詞，皆音於
愆反。自葛洪要用字苑分焉字音訓：若訓
何訓安，當音於愆反，"於焉逍遙，"
"於焉嘉客，" "焉用佞，" "焉得仁"
之類是也；若送句及助詞，當音矣愆反，
"故稱龍焉，" "故稱血焉，" "有民
人焉，" "有社稷焉，" "託始焉爾，"
"晉、鄭焉依"之類是也。江南至今行此
分別，昭然易曉；而河北混同一音，雖依
古讀，不可行於今也。

---

1 A note in the "Song edition" gives the appellation of Guan Zhong as Zhongfu
仲父 and that of Fan Zeng as *yafu* 亞父, both having the meaning of "uncle."
Duke Huan of Qi had respectfully addressed Guan Zhong (see XVIII.10) as
Zhongfu. Fan Zeng (278–204 BCE) was the councilor of Xiang Yu 項羽 (232–
202 BCE), a Chu general who, with the fall of the Qin dynasty, became the
main contender for the throne with Liu Bang, the eventual founder of the Han.

XVIII.12

The word *fu* 甫 [MC pjuX] is an honorific applied to a man. Ancient texts often replace it with the loan character *fu* 父 ["father"; MC bjuX]. In the north, no man is ever called *fu* 甫, which is something I do not understand. But of course, in Guan Zhong's appellation and Fan Zeng's appellation *fu* should be pronounced as the original character [i.e., as bjuX instead of pjuX].[1]

XVIII.13

According to various lexical works, *yan* is the name of a bird; but some say it is a modal word. In either case, it is pronounced as a combination of *yu* (MC 'jo) and *qian* (MC khjen). Ge Hong's *Garden of Essential Characters* was the first to make a distinction between its various meanings and ensuing pronunciations. If it is glossed as "what," "how," or "where," then it is pronounced as a combination of *yu* (MC 'jo) and *qian* (MC khjen); the examples include, among others, "Where is he taking his leisure?" "Where is he being a fine guest?" "How is eloquence necessary?" "How can he be called benevolent?"[2] If it is glossed as a final particle or an auxiliary word, then it should be pronounced as a combination of *yi* (MC hiX) and *qian* (MC khjen). The examples include, among others, "Therefore it says 'dragon.'" "Therefore it says 'blood.'" "Here are the common folk." "There are the altars of the God of Earth and the God of Grain." "This is the beginning." "Jin and Zheng were depended upon for help."[3] To the south of the Yangzi River people observe this distinction even today. It is very clear and makes it easy to recognize the difference. To the north of the Yellow River, however, people combine them into one pronunciation; though an ancient reading, it should not be practiced in modern times.

---

2 The first two examples are from the *Classic of Poetry*, the second two from the *Analects*.

3 The first two examples are from the *Classic of Changes*; the second two from the *Analects*; the last two are respectively from the Gongyang commentary on the *Spring and Autumn Annals* and the *Zuo Tradition*.

XVIII.14

邪者,未定之詞。左傳曰:"不知天之棄
魯邪?抑魯君有罪於鬼神邪?"莊子云:
"天邪地邪?"漢書云:"是邪非邪?"
之類是也。而北人即呼為也字,亦為誤
矣。難者曰:"繫辭云:'乾坤,易之門
戶邪。'此又為未定辭乎?"答曰:"何
為不爾。上先標問,下方列德以折之
耳。"

XVIII.15

江南學士讀左傳,口相傳述,自為凡例,
軍自敗曰敗,打破人軍曰敗。諸記傳未見
補敗反,徐仙民讀左傳,唯一處有此音,
又不言自敗、敗人之別,此為穿鑿耳。

XVIII.14

The character *ye* 邪 expresses uncertainty. The *Zuo Tradition* says, "I don't know if this is heaven forsaking Lu, or the lord of Lu having offended spirits and gods." *Zhuangzi* says, "Is it heaven, or is it earth?" In the *Han History* we find: "'Is it her, or is it not her?'" But the northerners pronounce *ye* 邪 [MC yae] as *ye3* 也 [MC yaeX]; that is a mistake.[1] Someone questioned me about this, saying, "The 'Appended Statements' [of the *Classic of Changes*] states, '*Qian* and *kun* – aren't they the gateway of change!' How can *ye* in this sentence be construed as a word of uncertainty here?" I replied, "But why not? In the context, the author has first marked it as a question, and then he proceeds to demonstrate the principle and offer his judgment."

XVIII.15

The scholars of the south read the *Zuo Tradition* based on oral teaching and transmission. They made their own rules. For instance, for an army to be defeated is called baejH [MC], but the same character, when used to indicate defeating the enemy, is pronounced paejH [MC].[2] I have not seen *bai* being pronounced as a combination of *bu* [MC puX] and *bai* [MC baejH] in any of the commentaries. Xu Xianmin's glossary [of the *Zuo Tradition*] only marks the sound in one place, but he does not distinguish between one's own defeat and defeating others. The distinction in pronunciation seems contrived.

---

1 The mistake lies in the misuse of tones, as indicated by the Middle Chinese pronunciations. In modern Mandarin the first *ye* is pronounced in the second tone while the second is in the third tone.

2 A note in the "Song edition" states that the second is pronounced as a combination of *bu* [MC puX] and *bai* [MC baejH] 補敗反.

XVIII.16

古人云："膏粱難整。"以其為驕奢自足，不能刻勵也。吾見王侯外戚，語多不正，亦由內染賤保傅，外無良師友故耳。梁世有一侯，嘗對元帝飲謔，自陳瘀鈍，乃成颸段，元帝答之云："颸異涼風，段非干木。"謂郢州為永州，元帝啟報簡文，簡文云："庚辰吳入，遂成司隸。"如此之類，舉口皆然。元帝手教諸子侍讀，以此為誡。

XVIII.17

河北切攻字為古琮，與工、公、功三字不同，殊為僻也。比世有人名暹，自稱為纖；名琨，自稱為袞；名洸，自稱為汪；名𩫖音藥，自稱為獡音爍。非唯音韻舛錯，亦使其兒孫避諱紛紜矣。

1　Emperor Yuan is mocking the marquis by punning. *Si* 颸 means a cool breeze; Duan is the surname of Duan Ganmu 段干木 (fl. fifth century BCE), who was well-known for his ability and ingerity but remained a recluse all his life.

2　The first line refers to the Wu army's capture of the city of Ying in 506 BCE; the second line refers to Bao Yong 鮑永 (d. 42 CE), a famously upright official who was the Director of Convict Laborers in the Eastern Han. Emperor Jianwen was being ironic about the marquis' mispronunciation of *ying* as *yong*.

XVIII.16

The ancients said, "The children of the rich and powerful are hard to rectify," since they tend to be arrogant, extravagant, self-satisfied, and unable to discipline and exert themselves. I have seen many noblemen and imperial in-laws who could not pronounce words correctly, largely due to the fact that they were influenced by their low-born sitters and tutors inside their home and lacked good teachers and friends outside. During the Liang dynasty, when a certain marquis was drinking and chatting with Emperor Yuan, he described himself as *chi dun* ("stupid and slow"), but he said *si duan* instead. In response Emperor Yuan said, "I suppose your *si* is not a cool breeze, and your *duan* is not Mr. Ganmu."[1] The same marquis also pronounced Ying prefecture as Yong prefecture. Emperor Yuan mentioned it in a letter to Emperor Jianwen, who replied, "Well, on the *gengchen* day the Wu army entered a city that turned out to be a Director of Convict Labor instead."[2] Examples such as these were numerous whenever he opened his mouth. Emperor Yuan personally wrote a note to his sons' tutors and cited this anecdote as a warning to them.

XVIII.17

In the north people pronounce the character *gong* ("attack"; MC kuwng) as a combination of *gu* (MC kuX) and *cong* (MC dzowng), different from the three characters, *gong* ("work"; MC kuwng), *gong* ("impartial"; MC kuwng), and *gong* ("achievement"; MC kuwng).[3] This is rather idiosyncratic. In recent times, someone is named Xian [MC siem], but he pronounces it as *jian* [MC tsjem];[4] someone is named Kun [MC kwon], but he pronounces it as *gun* [MC kwonX]; someone named Guang [MC kwang] pronounces it as *wang* [MC 'wang]; someone named Yao [MC yak] calls himself Shuo [MC syak]. Not only are the pronunciations wrong, but they will cause their sons and grandsons a great deal of trouble in avoiding taboo characters.

3 *Qie yun*, the lexical work completed in 601 that had credited Yan Zhitui for his contribution, gives both pronunciations for the character *gong* (attack), although here Yan Zhitui clearly thinks that one of the two, adopted in the north, is incorrect.

4 The pronunciation of *xian* 纖 is identical with that of *xian* 遅 (sjem), and Zhou Zumo suspects that *xian* 纖 is an error for *jian* 殲 or 瀸 (see Zhou Fagao 125b). However, *xian* 纖 has two pronunciations, *xian* (MC sjem) and *jian* (MC tshjem), so there is no need to emend the graph.

雜藝第十九

XIX.1

真草書跡，微須留意。江南諺云："尺牘
書疏，千里面目也。"承晉、宋餘俗，相
與事之，故無頓狼狽者。吾幼承門業，加
性愛重，所見法書亦多，而翫習功夫頗
至，遂不能佳者，良由無分故也。然而此
藝不須過精。夫巧者勞而智者憂，常為人
所役使，更覺為累；韋仲將遺戒，深有以
也。

XIX. Miscellaneous Arts

XIX.1

You should pay some attention to the formal script and the draft script. In the south there is a saying, "A letter or a note shows one's face across a thousand miles." People in the south inherited the customs from the Jin and Song dynasties and worked at it, so nobody's handwriting was entirely terrible. Since my early childhood I have followed our family tradition;[1] in addition, I am fond of the art and value it. Thus I have seen many model calligraphies and also spent considerable time on appreciation and practice. Even though in the end I am unable to achieve excellence, it is simply because I have no talent for it. Nevertheless, you do not need to excel in this art. "The clever person toils, and the wise worries." Excellence in calligraphy leads to many demands from others and can become a burden.[2] There is indeed a very good reason for Wei Zhongjiang's final instruction to his children.[3]

---

1 Yan Zhitui's father Yan Xie was a well-known calligrapher who was particularly good at the draft script, the clerical script, and the so-called "flying white" style. See his biography in the *Liang History* (*Liang shu* 50.727) and *Southern History* (*Nan shi* 72.1785).

2 Yan Xie's biography in the *Southern History* claims that his calligraphy graced "all the steles in the Jing Chu region." *Nan shi* 72.1785. Yan Zhitui's warning to his sons may well have been a lesson learned from his own father's example.

3 Wei Zhongjiang was Wei Dan 韋誕 (179–253), a famous calligrapher in the Wei during the Three Kingdoms Period. He was ordered by Emperor Ming to write the name of a newly-built tower at its top and was raised high up to do it. He was so frightened that his hair reportedly turned gray from the experience. He warned his children not to excel at calligraphy.

XIX.2

王逸少風流才士，蕭散名人，舉世惟知其
書，翻以能自蔽也。蕭子雲每歎曰："吾
著齊書，勒成一典，文章弘義，自謂可
觀；唯以筆跡得名，亦異事也。"王褒地
冑清華，才學優敏，後雖入關，亦被禮
遇。猶以書工，崎嶇碑碣之間，辛苦筆硯
之役，嘗悔恨曰："假使吾不知書，可不
至今日邪？"以此觀之，慎勿以書自命。
雖然，廝猥之人，以能書拔擢者多矣。故
道不同不相為謀也。

XIX.2

Wang Yishao was a talented man with panache, a free spirit.[1] The entire world only knows him for his calligraphy, so he has actually managed to obscure himself with his skill. Xiao Ziyun often said with a sigh, "I compiled the *Qi History* and made it into a complete standard work.[2] I consider the style and content of my writing as rather presentable. However, I have acquired a reputation only for my handwriting – this is a strange thing indeed!" Wang Bao, the scion of a great noble family, possessed deep learning and a quick mind.[3] Even though later in his life he was brought inside the Pass, he was treated with much respect. But because he was a master of calligraphy, he trudged amidst stele inscriptions and toiled with brush and inkstone. He once expressed his regret, saying, "Suppose I had not known anything about writing, isn't it true that I would not have been reduced to this state today?" Seeing these examples, you should be very careful not to pride yourself on your calligraphy. Still, low-born men are often promoted because of their calligraphic skill. Thus it is quite true that "those who do not share the same convictions cannot make plans together."[4]

---

1 Yishao was the courtesy name of Wang Xizhi, the best-known calligrapher in Chinese history (see note to VI.13).
2 For Xiao Xiyun as calligrapher, also see VII.5b. Xiao Ziyun compiled the *Jin History* (*Jin shu* 晉書), which is to be differentiated from the currently extant *Jin History* compiled in the early seventh century. It was his brother Xiao Zixian 蕭子顯 (487–537) who compiled the *Southern Qi History* (*Nan Qi shu* 南齊書).
3 This refers to the Liang nobleman Wang Bao (see note to VII.5a), not the Western Han writer. Wang Bao was taken to Chang'an as a captive after the fall of Jiangling and later served in the Northern Zhou court.
4 This is a quotation from the *Analects*.

XIX.3

梁武祕閣散逸以來，吾見二王真草多矣，
家中嘗得十卷。方知陶隱居、阮交州、蕭
祭酒諸書，莫不得羲之之一體，故是書之
淵源。蕭晚節所變，乃右軍年少時法也。

XIX.4

晉、宋以來，多能書者。故其時俗，遞相
染尚，所有部帙，楷正可觀，不無俗字，
非為大損。至梁天監之間，斯風未變；大
同之末，訛替滋生。蕭子雲改易字體，邵
陵王頗行偽字；朝野翕然，以為楷式，畫
虎不成，多所傷敗。至為一字，唯見數
點，或妄斟酌，逐便轉移。爾後墳籍，略
不可看。

XIX.3

Since the scattering of the Liang imperial library collection, I have seen many formal script and draft script pieces of the two Wangs.[1] Our family once obtained ten scrolls of them. Looking them over, I began to realize that Recluse Tao, Governor Ruan of Jiaozhou, and Libationer Xiao had each learned [one aspect of] Wang Xizhi's style, which is truly the source of great calligraphy.[2] The stylistic change in Xiao's calligraphy in his later years was actually the style adopted by General Wang of the Right Army [Wang Xizhi] in his youth.

XIX.4

Since the Jin and Song dynasties there were many able calligraphers who exerted influence on the world at large, so that all the books in circulation were tidy and presentable. Even though there were some vulgar characters, they did not do great harm. This tendency had not changed until the Tianjian era of the Liang [502–519]. But toward the end of the Datong era [535–546], errors and corrosions began to appear. Xiao Ziyun changed the graphic form of characters; the Prince of Shaoling loved to coin characters.[3] The court and country unanimously took them as models, but the attempt to paint a tiger failed miserably and led to many deteriorations.[4] It got to the point where they would use a few dots to represent a character or randomly rearrange and change parts for the sake of convenience. The books that were copied after the Datong era became completely unreadable.

---

1 The two Wangs are Wang Xizhi and his son Wang Xianzhi 王獻之 (344–386), famed calligrapher in his own right.

2 Recluse Tao refers to the famous Daoist master and alchemist Tao Hongjing (see note to XV.2). Governor Ruan of Jiaozhou was Ruan Yan 阮研 (courtesy name Wenji 文幾), acclaimed calligrapher of the time. Libationer Xiao was Xiao Ziyun, mentioned earlier (VII.5). He was made Libationer in 536. For the text and translation of the sentence, 莫不得義之之一體, see Additional Notes.

3 The Prince of Shaoling was Xiao Lun 蕭綸 (507–551), the sixth son of Liang Emperor Wu. Yan Zhitui is speaking of graphic forms rather than calligraphic styles here (see Additional Notes).

4 "The attempt to paint a tiger failed miserably" is an abbreviation of the saying, "One tries to paint a tiger, but ends up drawing a creature that resembles a dog" 畫虎不成反類狗.

XIX.5

北朝喪亂之餘，書跡鄙陋，加以專輒造字，猥拙甚於江南。乃以百念為憂，言反為變，不用為罷，追來為歸，更生為蘇，先人為老，如此非一，徧滿經傳。唯有姚元摽工於草隸，留心小學，後生師之者眾。泊於齊末，祕書繕寫，賢於往日多矣。

XIX.6

江南閭里間有畫書賦，此乃陶隱居弟子杜道士所為。其人未甚識字，輕為軌則，託名貴師，世俗傳信，後生頗為所誤也。

XIX.5

After the time of trouble in the north, calligraphy was unsightly.[1] Moreover, people coined characters at will, and it is even more clumsy and awful than in the south. For instance, they put together *bai* (hundred) and *nian* (concerns) to make *you* (worry), *yan* (speech) and *fan* (rebellion) to make *bian* (change), *bu* (not) and *yong* (use) to make *ba* (dismiss), *zhui* (chase) and *lai* (come) to make *gui* (return), *geng* (once more) and *sheng* (live) to make *su* (revive), *xian* (former) and *ren* (person) to make *lao* (old), and such examples fill the classics and commentaries. Only Yao Yuanpiao was good at draft script and formal script, and paid much attention to philological learning; many young people emulated him. As a consequence, near the end of the Qi, the copying done in the Imperial Library was much improved.

XIX.6

A "*Fu* on Painting and Calligraphy" had circulated among the commoners in the south. It was written by Daoist Du, a disciple of the Recluse Tao. That fellow had a very limited knowledge of characters, but nonchalantly made up many rules and standards, and availed himself of the name of his prestigious teacher. Ordinary people had faith in him, and many young men were misled by him.

---

1 Here Yan Zhitui refers to the time after the Northern Wei fell in 534 and was split into the Western Wei and Eastern Wei, and the latter was eventually replaced by the Northern Qi in 550.

XIX.7

畫繪之工，亦為妙矣；自古名士，多或能
之。吾家嘗有梁元帝手畫蟬雀白團扇及馬
圖，亦難及也。武烈太子偏能寫真，坐上
賓客，隨宜點染，即成數人，以問童孺，
皆知姓名矣。蕭賁、劉孝先、劉靈，並文
學已外，復佳此法。翫古知今，特可寶
愛。若官未通顯，每被公私使令，亦為猥
役。

XIX.7

The art of painting is, for its part, marvelous. Many famous gentlemen since ancient times were good at it. Our family once had a round white fan with a cicada and a sparrow and also a painting of a horse, both painted by Liang Emperor Yuan himself. They are truly peerless. The Crown Prince Wulie was particularly dexterous at portraiture.[1] He would casually dash off a sketch of several guests in his residence with a few dots and strokes, but even if you showed it to a child, the child would be able to name the people in the drawing. Xiao Bi, Liu Xiao-xian, and Liu Ling were all exceptional in this art in addition to [being known for] their cultural learning.[2] Appreciating the paintings of the past and learning those of the present, one finds them truly lovely and valuable. However, if a good painter does not attain to a prominent official position, he may end up getting so many requests from public and private spheres that it will become a tiresome chore.

---

1 The Crown Prince Wulie was Emperor Yuan's eldest son, Xiao Fangdeng (mentioned in IX.30).

2 Xiao Bi (courtesy name Wenhuan 文奐, d. 549) was a descendant of the Southern Qi royal family and served on Xiao Yi's staff. He offended the prince and eventually starved to death in prison. Liu Xiaoxian (fl. 520s–550s) was the younger brother of Liu Xiaochuo (mentioned in VI.45, IX.33–35). Liu Ling was Yan Zhitui's brother-in-law (see VIII.47).

XIX.8

吳縣顧士端出身湘東王國侍郎，後為鎮南
府刑獄參軍，有子曰庭，西朝中書舍人，
父子並有琴書之藝，尤妙丹青，常被元帝
所使，每懷羞恨。彭城劉岳，橐之子也，
仕為驃騎府管記、平氏縣令，才學快士，
而畫絕倫。後隨武陵王入蜀，下牢之敗，
遂為陸護軍畫支江寺壁，與諸工巧雜處。
向使三賢都不曉畫，直運素業，豈見此恥
乎？

XIX.8

Gu Shiduan of Wu county began his official career as Attendant Gentleman in the Prince of Xiangdong's establishment, and later was appointed as Penal Adjutant in the military headquarters of the Defender-general of the South.[1] He had a son, Ting, who was appointed Secretariat Drafter in the western court.[2] Both father and son possessed fine skills in zither-playing and calligraphy, and were especially good at painting. They were often employed in the capacity of painter by Emperor Yuan, and always felt shame and resentment. Liu Yue of Pengcheng was Liu Tuo's son. He served as Secretary in the headquarters of the Cavalry General and also magistrate of Pingshi county.[3] He was a bold and forthright gentleman of talent and learning and was also a peerless painter. He later went to Shu to serve the Prince of Wuling.[4] After the defeat at Xialao, he was ordered by Protector General Lu to paint a wall mural for the Zhijiang Temple, and was placed amongst all sorts of workers and craftsmen.[5] Had all three worthies had no knowledge of painting and merely kept to the pure profession, how would they have been humiliated like this?[6]

---

1 Xiao Yi, Liang Emperor Yuan, was enfeoffed as the Prince of Xiangdong in 514, and made Defender-general of the South and governer of Jiangzhou in 540.

2 The western court refers to Liang Emperor Yuan's court in Jiangling, to the west of Jiankang, the old Liang capital.

3 Liu Yue likely had served on the staff of Prince of Luling, Xiao Xu 蕭續 (504–547), Liang Emperor Wu's fifth son, who was made Cavalry General and governor of Jingzhou in 539 until his death in 547. Pingshi county was in Jingzhou or Jing prefecture (in modern Hubei).

4 The Prince of Wuling was Xiao Ji 蕭紀 (508–553), Liang Emperor Wu's eighth son, who was governor of Yizhou (in modern Sichuan) in 537 and stayed in Shu for many years. He proclaimed himself emperor in 552 and fought over the throne with Xiao Yi.

5 Xialao is in modern Hubei. Protector General Lu was Xiao Yi's general Lu Fahe 陸法和 (d. late 550s), who defeated Xiao Ji (see the preceding note). Zhijiang is in modern Hubei. A devout Buddhist, Lu Fahe had the walls of the Buddhist temple in Zhijiang painted with murals.

6 In this period the pure profession or enterprise (*suye*) often referred specifically to an engagement in cultural learning and classical scholarship.

XIX.9

弧矢之利，以威天下，先王所以觀德擇
賢，亦濟身之急務也。江南謂世之常射，
以為兵射，冠冕儒生，多不習此。別有博
射，弱弓長箭，施於準的，揖讓昇降，以
行禮焉。防禦寇難，了無所益。亂離之
後，此術遂亡。河北文士，率曉兵射，非
直葛洪一箭，已解追兵，三九讌集，常麇
榮賜。雖然，要輕禽，截狡獸，不願汝輩
為之。

XIX.10

卜筮者，聖人之業也；但近世無復佳師，
多不能中。古者，卜以決疑，今人生疑於
卜；何者？守道信謀，欲行一事，卜得惡
卦，反令怵怵，此之謂乎。且十中六七，
以為上手，粗知大意，又不委曲。凡射奇
偶，自然半收，何足賴也。

XIX.9

The bow and arrow are utilized to subdue and overpower. The former kings observed a man's virtue and selected worthies by means of archery; it is also an urgent matter in terms of self-protection. People to the south of the Yangzi River refer to regular archery as "military archery," and most gentry members and Ru scholars are not trained in it. There is also a "sporty archery," which uses a weak bow and long arrows to deploy toward a target, with courteous obeisance and ceremonious steps in performing the ritual. But it is completely useless as self-defense against invaders in a crisis. After disorder and dislocation, this technique was lost. Men of letters to the north of the Yellow River all know military archery very well. Not only are they like Ge Hong who could shoot one arrow to hold back the soldiers chasing him,[1] but they often receive imperial rewards at banquets held for nobles and ministers. In spite of that, if archery is to be used for hunting wild birds and fierce beasts, I do not want you boys to do it.

XIX.10

Divination was the undertaking of the sages. There are no more good divination masters these days; their predictions are mostly inaccurate. In ancient times divination was to resolve doubts; but in modern times it gives rise to doubts. How is that? Suppose you plan to do something, and you are observing all the right principles and placing your confidence in strategizing; but then your divination gives an inauspicious reading, which fills you with apprehension and anxiety – that is what I mean by divination giving rise to doubts. Besides, those who make correct predictions in six or seven cases out of ten are considered superior diviners; yet they only know the rough outline of an event with no details. When guessing at an odd or even number, one naturally gets it right in half of the cases; how can we rely on this?

---

1 According to the "Self-account" in his *Master of Embracing Simplicity* (*Baopuzi*), Ge Hong once shot dead two soldiers who were in pursuit of him.

XIX.11

世傳云：解陰陽者，為鬼所嫉，坎壈貧窮，多不稱泰。吾觀近古以來，尤精妙者，唯京房、管輅、郭璞耳，皆無官位，多或罹災，此言令人益信。儻值世網嚴密，強負此名，便有註誤，亦禍源也。

XIX.12

及星文風氣，率不勞為之。吾嘗學六壬式，亦值世閒好匠，聚得龍首、金匱、玉軨變、玉歷十許種書，討求無驗，尋亦悔罷。

XIX.11

People all say that those who understand the workings of *yin* and *yang* are disliked by spirits, so they suffer hardship and poverty, rarely enjoying a good and easy life. According to my observation, in recent times only Jing Fang, Guan Lu, and Guo Pu may be considered outstanding diviners.[1] None of them obtained any office, and two had a bad end. Thus I am even more convinced that the saying is right. If one lives in an age when the meshes of law are tight, then possessing such a reputation may get him in trouble and become a source of woe.

XIX.12

As for astrology and wind-divination, do not bother to do any of it. I once studied the Six Ren method, and was also lucky enough to meet some good diviners and get hold of a dozen works of divination, such as the *Dragon Head*, the *Golden Case*, *Yuling bian*, *Jade Calendar*, and so forth.[2] I studied them but to no effect, and soon gave it up with regret.

---

1 Jing Fang (77–37 BCE) was a Western Han scholar of the *Classic of Changes*, music theorist, and astrologer. Guan Lu (209–256) was known as one of the best diviners of his time. For Guo Pu, see note to XVII.2. Both Jing Fang and Guo Pu died by execution.
2 The Six Ren was a divination method. The texts mentioned here are all divination texts. "Dragon Head" and "Golden Case" are still extant in the Daoist Canon, but the last two titles cannot be traced.

XIX.13

凡陰陽之術，與天地俱生，亦吉凶德刑，
不可不信。但去聖既遠，世傳術書，皆出
流俗，言辭鄙淺，驗少妄多。至如反支不
行，竟以遇害；歸忌寄宿，不免凶終。拘
而多忌，亦無益也。

XIX.14

算術亦是六藝要事；自古儒士論天道，定
律歷者，皆學通之。然可以兼明，不可以
專業。江南此學殊少，唯范陽祖暅精之，
位至南康太守。河北多曉此術。

---

1 This alludes to Zhang Song 張竦 (d. 23 CE), who was killed by bandits because
he refused to travel on a "reversed branch" day, even though he knew there were
bandits in the region and ought to leave. The twelve Earthly Branches (*zi, chou,
yin, mao, chen, si, wu, wei, shen, you, xu, hai*) are used in combination with the
ten Heavenly Stems (*jia, yi, bing, ding, wu, ji, geng, xin, ren, gui*) to mark the
days of a month. The twelve branches end with *xu* and *hai*, and then the cycle
begins anew with *zi* and *chou*. However, if the very first day of a month is marked
with a *xu* or a *hai*, and the second day is marked with a *shen* or a *you*, and so
on, then this is regarded as "reversed" and unlucky. The Han court would not
accept any memorials to the throne on such a "reversed branch" day until Han
Emperor Ming (r. 58–75 CE) abolished the custom.

XIX.13

The art of *yin* and *yang* was born with heaven and earth; we cannot but believe that it foretells auspiciousness and misfortune as well as rewards and punishments. It is just that we are far away from the sages, and the books on such subjects circulating in the world all come from mediocre people: their words are vulgar and shallow; their predictions are often wrong. Even if a man observed the "reversed branch" days by not going out, he could still get killed.[1] Or a man might very well respect the "homecoming taboo" by spending a night elsewhere, but was unable to escape from a violent end.[2] It does a person no good to be restricted by many prohibitions.

XIX.14

Mathematics is an important skill among the six arts. Since times of old, a Ru scholar who discusses the way of heaven and determines astronomical and calendrical matters must be well-versed in it. You may learn it among other subjects, but should not specialize in it. To the south of the Yangzi River there were not many men who studied it. Only Zu Geng of Fanyang was an expert, who was last appointed to the position of Magistrate of Nankang.[3] To the north of the Yellow River many know it well.

2 On "homecoming taboo" days, one is not supposed to travel, whether leaving or coming home, or to move house. Here Yan Zhitui refers to a man named Chen Bojing 陳伯敬 (fl. 147–167) who was cautious all his life. If he was on the road on a "homecoming taboo" day, he would take up lodging in a hostel rather than come home. He was implicated in his son-in-law's misconduct and executed.

3 Zu Geng (fl. early sixth century), aka Zu Gengzhi 祖暅之, was a mathematician and the son of the famous mathematician and astronomer Zu Chongzhi 祖沖之 (429–500).

XIX.15

醫方之事，取妙極難，不勸汝曹以自命
也。微解藥性，小小和合，居家得以救
急，亦為勝事，皇甫謐、殷仲堪則其人
也。

XIX.16

禮曰："君子無故不徹琴瑟。"古來名
士，多所愛好。洎於梁初，衣冠子孫，不
知琴者，號有所闕；大同以末，斯風頓
盡。然而此樂愔愔雅致，有深味哉。今世
曲解，雖變於古，猶足以暢神情也。唯不
可令有稱譽，見役勳貴，處之下坐，以取
殘盃冷炙之辱。戴安道猶遭之，況爾曹
乎。

XIX.15

Medicine is extremely difficult to excel in. I do not encourage you boys to pride yourselves on it. If you want to acquire some basic knowledge about the nature of medicinal herbs and dabble in their mixing and combining in order to find first-aid remedies for family members, it may not be such a bad thing. In this Huangfu Mi and Yin Zhongkan are your models.[1]

XIX.16

The *Record of Rites* says, "A gentleman does not put away his zither and harp for no good reason." Many famous gentlemen since ancient times have been fond of the art of zither-playing. At the beginning of the Liang dynasty, if the son of a gentry family did not know how to play the zither, it was considered a defect [in his education]. Toward the last years of the Datong era [535–546], this trend completely disappeared. Nevertheless, zither music is graceful and harmonious, and truly has a profound flavor. Even though modern music has changed from the past, it is still adequate to elevate and delight one's spirit. Just do not become famous for it; otherwise you would be made to wait upon a nobleman and assigned to a lowly seat in his house, humiliated by being served dregs in a cup and cold leftovers. Even a great man like Dai Andao suffered such a fate, let alone you boys![2]

---

1 Huangfu Mi was a prolific third-century author (see VIII.15 and XVII.19) who, due to his own bad health, studied medicine and authored an acupuncture manual. Yin Zhongkan (see note to XVII.35) studied medicine because of his father's illness and became very good at it; he authored a medical text that is now lost.

2 Dai Andao was Dai Kui 戴逵 (d. 396), a distinguished Eastern Jin writer, painter, and sculptor also known for his zither playing. Upon being summoned to play the zither for a prince, he broke his zither, saying that he would not be an entertainer for a noble lord.

XIX.17

家語曰：“君子不博，為其兼行惡道故也。”論語云：“不有博弈者乎？為之，猶賢乎已。”然則聖人不用博弈為教；但以學者不可常精，有時疲倦，則儻為之，猶勝飽食昏睡，兀然端坐耳。至如吳太子以為無益，命韋昭論之；王肅、葛洪、陶侃之徒，不許目觀手執，此並勤篤之志也。能爾為佳。

XIX.18

古為大博則六箸，小博則二煢，今無曉者。比世所行，一煢十二棊，數術淺短，不足可翫。

XIX.19

圍棊有手談、坐隱之目，頗為雅戲；但令人耽憒，廢喪實多，不可常也。

---

1 This refers to the *School Sayings of Confucius* (*Kongzi jiayu*): see note to VII.3.
2 Wei Zhao (204–273, aka Wei Yao 韋曜) was a famous scholar and writer of the Wu court in the Three Kingdoms Period. The Crown Prince of Wu was Sun He 孫和 (224–253), who was made heir after his eldest brother died in 242 but was deposed in 250. Wei Zhao's treatise is preserved in the sixth-century anthology *Wen xuan*.

XIX.17

The *School Sayings* states, "A gentleman does not play the *bo* game, because it brings with it other bad habits."[1] The *Analects* says, "Are there not the *bo* game and the encirclement chess? If you engage in them, it is still better than doing nothing." Clearly, the sage did not consider these board-games as part of his educational curriculum; yet, a student cannot focus on study at all times, and he may occasionally play the games when he is tired, which should still be better than falling asleep after eating a full meal or sitting there doing nothing. The Crown Prince of Wu regarded chess as a useless game and commanded Wei Zhao to write a treatise on it.[2] Wang Su, Ge Hong and Tao Kan did not endorse looking at the games or touching them.[3] These instances demonstrate their aspiration to assiduousness. If you can do that, it will be excellent.

XIX.18

In ancient times a "greater *bo* game" used six sticks and a "lesser *bo* game" used two dice called *qiong*; nowadays no one knows anything about it. The game people play today has one die and twelve game pieces; the technique is so crude and simple that it is not worth one's while.

XIX.19

Encirclement chess is also known as "dialogue of hands" or "sedantary hermitage."[4] It is a rather elegant game. But one can easily become obsessed by it and neglect many others things in life. You should not play it often.

---

3 Wang Su (195–256) was a great scholar of the Wei from the Three Kingdoms Period who authored commentaries on the Confucian classics. Tao Kan (259–334) was an Eastern Jin general who played a crucial role in stabilizing the dynasty; he was well-known for his frugality and hard-working ethic. He was the great-grandfather of the famous poet Tao Yuanming (see note to IX.35).

4 *Wei qi*, encirclement chess or surrounding chess, is popularly known in English as Go, based on its Japanese name. "Dialogue of hands" (*shoutan*) and "sedentary reclusion" (*zuoyin*) are terms invented respectively by Wang Tanzhi 王坦之 (330–375) and Zhi Dun 支遁 (314–366).

XIX.20

投壺之禮，近世愈精。古者，實以小豆，為其矢之躍也。今則唯欲其驍，益多益喜，乃有倚竿、帶劍、狼壺、豹尾、龍首之名。其尤妙者有蓮花驍。汝南周璝，弘正之子，會稽賀徽，賀革之子，並能一箭四十餘驍。賀又嘗為小障，置壺其外，隔障投之，無所失也。至鄴以來，亦見廣寧、蘭陵諸王，有此校具，舉國遂無投得一驍者。

XIX.21

彈棊亦近世雅戲，消愁釋憒，時可為之。

XIX.20

The game of pitch-pot has become increasingly sophisticated in recent times. In ancient times one filled the target pot with small beans that prevented the arrow from jumping out. But today players only want the arrows to rebound (*xiao*), the more so the better. They have also devised names for different kinds of rebounding, such as leaning-on-the-pole, carrying-a-sword, wolf's pot, leopard tail, and dragon head. The most exquisite of the moves is called Lotus Flower Xiao. Zhou Gui of Ru'nan, the son of Zhou Hongzheng, and He Hui of Kuaiji, He Ge's son, could both make more than forty *xiao* with just one arrow.[1] He Ge once constructed a small screen and placed the target pot on the other side of the screen; he would throw the arrow into the pot across the screen and never miss. After I came to Ye, I saw that the Prince of Guangning and the Prince of Lanling had the game set.[2] However, there was no one in the whole country who could make a single *xiao*.

XIX.21

"Pellet chess" is also an elegant game of modern times. It dispels worries and relieves mental fogginess. You may do it now and then.

---

1 Zhou Hongzheng and He Ge are both mentioned earlier (see XI.5). He Hui (d. 540) was loved deeply by his father; he died before He Ge, who was so grieved that he became ill and died shortly after. He Hui might have been the same man who had a dalliance with Xiao Yi's wife, Xu Zhaopei 徐昭佩 (d. 549), who was known for her indiscretions.

2 The Prince of Guangning was Gao Xiaoheng 高孝珩 (d. 577), son of Gao Cheng 高澄 (521–549, posthumously Emperor Wenxiang 文襄). The Prince of Lanling was his younger brother, Gao Xiaoguan 高孝瓘 (541–573), better known as Changgong 長恭. Gao Xiaoguan was a fierce warrior but had such a good-looking face that he would wear a fearsome mask on the battlefield to intimidate his enemies; a great victory he won inspired a song-and-dance show that continued to be performed in the Tang.

終制第二十

XX.1

死者，人之常分，不可免也。吾年十九，
值梁家喪亂，其間與白刃為伍者，亦常數
輩；幸承餘福，得至於今。古人云："五
十不為夭。"吾已六十餘，故心坦然，不
以殘年為念。先有風氣之疾，常疑奄然，
聊書素懷，以為汝誡。

XX.2

先君先夫人皆未還建鄴舊山，旅葬江陵東
郭。承聖末，已啟求揚都，欲營遷厝。蒙
詔賜銀百兩，已於揚州小郊北地燒塼，便
值本朝淪沒，流離如此，數十年間，絕於
還望。今雖混一，家道罄窮，何由辦此奉
營資費？且揚都污毀，無復孑遺，還被下
溼，未為得計。自咎自責，貫心刻髓。

XX. Last Will

XX.1

Death is the common lot of all men; nobody can escape from it. When I was nineteen *sui*, I encountered the disorder and destruction that happened to the Liang dynasty, and several times I had to face a sharp blade. Fortunately, by the blessings inherited from my ancestors, I have managed to survive until now. The ancients said, "If one dies at fifty, it is not a life cut short." I am already in my sixties, so my heart is at peace, and I do not worry about the remaining years. Earlier I have suffered from the wind disease,[1] and I suspect I do not have much time left in this world. So I will write out here my long-cherished wishes as my final instructions for you.

XX.2

My late father and mother had never been returned to the family cemetery at Jianye; they were buried in the eastern suburbs of Jiangling instead. Toward the end of the Chengsheng era [554], I asked for [and received] the emperor's permission to move their coffins back to Yangdu [Jiankang], for which I received the imperial gift of one hundred taels of silver.[2] I already had bricks baked in the northern suburbs of Yangzhou. But right at that time, the dynasty fell, and I was displaced from my home region till today. Wandering for the past several decades, I have lost any hope of returning to the south. Now, although the world is unified, our family resources are exhausted. How can we raise the funds for the reburial? Besides, Yangdu has been devastated, and there is nothing left; it is also in a low and damp place, and so will not work out well for the coffins. I blame myself for this and my heart is pierced by guilt.

---

1 It is unclear what "wind disease" was. It may have been a form of diabetes.
2 Chengsheng was Liang Emperor Yuan's reign title.

XX.3

計吾兄弟，不當仕進；但以門衰，骨肉單弱，五服之內，傍無一人，播越他鄉，無復資廕；使汝等沈淪廝役，以為先世之恥；故靦冒人間，不敢墜失。兼以北方政教嚴切，全無隱退者故也。

XX.3

As I see it, we brothers should not have entered public service. However, the fortune of our clan is in decline, and our blood and flesh do not enjoy much power and status in society. Indeed there is nobody among close and distant relatives on whom we can rely. Moreover, we have been displaced from our native land and migrated to another region, so there is no inherited title to be passed on to our offspring. Should you boys be debased to the status of servants, it would be a disgrace to our ancestors. For this reason we have brazenly taken official posts, not daring to let the family tradition fall away. Besides, governmental regulations in the north are so austere that no one is permitted to seek reclusion and retirement.

XX.4

今年老疾侵，儻然奄忽，豈求備禮乎？一日放臂，沐浴而已，不勞復魄，殮以常衣。先夫人棄背之時，屬世荒饉，家塗空迫，兄弟幼弱，棺器率薄，藏內無塼。吾當松棺二寸，衣帽已外，一不得自隨，床上唯施七星板；至如蠟弩牙、玉豚、錫人之屬，並須停省，糧甖明器，故不得營，碑誌旒旐，彌在言外。載以鱉甲車，襯土而下，平地無墳；若懼拜掃不知兆域，當築一堵低牆於左右前後，隨為私記耳。靈筵勿設枕几，朔望祥禫，唯下白粥清水乾棗，不得有酒肉餅果之祭。親友來餽酹者，一皆拒之。汝曹若違吾心，有加先妣，則陷父不孝，在汝安乎？

XX.4

Now, as I get on in years and am afflicted by illness, once I am gone, how can I demand comprehensive funeral rites? As soon as I die, simply bathe my body and dress it in my ordinary clothes. It will not be necessary to perform the "soul-summoning" ritual.[1] At the time when my late mother passed away, there was a famine; our family was destitute, and we brothers were very young. Thus her coffin was simple and frugal, and no bricks were used inside the tomb vault. For me, you should use a pine coffin, two inches thick, and nothing to be put inside the coffin except for the cap and clothes I wear. Inside the coffin only place a seven-star board at the bottom; as for wax crossbow, jade pig, tin figurines, and so on, leave all of them out.[2] Do not use pottery jars of provisions and other spirit vessels, not to mention a stele inscription and soul streamer.[3] Take the coffin to the burial ground with a turtle-shell cart,[4] and lower it directly underground. Flatten the earth afterward; do not raise a mound above. If you worry about not being able to find the grave for future visits, then build a low wall all around it as a personal reminder for yourselves. Do not set up pillow and armrest at my spirit shrine. When making sacrificial offerings on the first and fifteenth days of the month, only prepare plain congee, clear water, and dried dates; there must not be any ale, meat, cakes, or fruit. Prevent relatives and friends from coming to make offerings. If you boys disobey my wishes and give me a better burial than what we gave our late mother, you will have made your father an unfilial son – how can you live with that?

---

1 The ritual was performed after a person died, in the hope to revive the deceased.

2 The seven-star board is a wooden board with seven holes, placed underneath the body at the bottom of the coffin. Wax crossbow, jade pig, and tin figurines were objects interred with the dead in this period, as evidenced by many excavated tombs in recent years.

3 Pottery jars, spirit vessels, and a stele inscription (with biographical information about the deceased and commemorative writing) were all to be placed inside a tomb. A spirit streamer, with the name and official position of the deceased written on it, was used in front of the coffin in the funerary procession and placed on the coffin during interment.

4 A turtle-shell cart was a low cart transporting a coffin, covered with curtains on all four sides, which were thought to resemble the hanging edges of a turtle's shell.

XX.5

其內典功德，隨力所至，勿刳竭生資，使
凍餒也。四時祭祀，周、孔所教，欲人勿
死其親，不忘孝道也。求諸內典，則無益
焉。殺生為之，翻增罪累。若報罔極之
德，霜露之悲，有時齋供，及七月半盂蘭
盆，望於汝也。

XX.6

孔子之葬親也，云："古者墓而不墳，丘
東西南北之人也，不可以弗識也。"於是
封之崇四尺。然則君子應世行道，亦有不
守墳墓之時，況為事際所逼也。吾今羈
旅，身若浮雲，竟未知何鄉是吾葬地；唯
當氣絕便埋之耳。汝曹宜以傳業揚名為
務，不可顧戀朽壤，以取堙沒也。

---

1 This refers to Buddhist funerary practices that are believed to help toward a better
   rebirth for the deceased. The Inner Scriptures are Buddhist scriptures.
2 Literally, "the sorrow of frost and dew." It is a phrase from the *Record of Rituals*,
   in which a son is moved by cold weather and seasonal change and longs for his
   deceased parents.

XX.5

As for the merit-earning ceremonies mentioned in the Inner Scriptures, you should perform them according to your financial capabilities.[1] Do not exhaust your funds and cause hunger and cold in your family. The four seasonal sacrifices are taught by the Duke of Zhou and Confucius with the hope that one shall not forget one's parents as soon as they die, but if you look into the Inner Scriptures, you will see that these sacrifices are completely useless. To kill animals for offerings will only increase our sins. If you want to repay the endless love of your parents and console your sadness and longing,[2] then offer my spirit a vegetarian meal from time to time, and do something at the Ullambana Festival on the fifteenth of the seventh month:[3] that is all I expect from you.

XX.6

When Confucius buried his parents, he said, "In ancient times people would build a grave only but raised no mound over it. Nevertheless, I, Qiu, am a man of east, west, south, and north; I cannot go without marking the grave."[4] Thereupon he raised a mound that was four-feet tall. This shows that a gentleman should act in accordance with the changing conditions of the world, and there are indeed times when he cannot stay close to his parents' tombs, especially when being pressed by circumstances. A displaced immigrant, I am like a floating cloud; I know not where my own grave will be. I should just be put in the ground as soon as I take my last breath. You boys should take it as your most important duty to pass on our family legacy and establish a reputation far and wide. Do not become so fondly attached to the dirt that you bring obscurity upon yourselves.

---

3 The Yulanpen Festival is also known as the Ghost Festival or Hungry Ghost Festival, on which rituals are performed to absolve the sins and relieve the sufferings of the dead. It derives from the *Ullambana Sutra* in which Maudgalyāyana redeems his deceased mother from hell.

4 This is from the *Record of Rituals*.

Other Works

神仙詩

紅顏恃容色
青春矜盛年
自言曉書劍
4 不得學神仙
風雲落時後
歲月度人前
鏡中不相識
8 捫心徒自憐
願得金樓要
思逢玉鈐篇
九龍遊弱水
12 八鳳出飛煙
朝遊采瓊實
夕宴酌膏泉
崢嶸下無地
16 列缺上陵天
舉世聊一息
中州安足旋

Poem on Immortals

With ruddy cheeks he has exulted in his looks;
in the years of green spring, he has taken pride in his youth.
He thought he was well-read and skilled in swordsmanship,
4 and did not bother to study the way of immortals.
Wind and clouds rising, he has fallen behind his times;
months and years have passed right before his eyes.
He can no longer recognize his face in the mirror;
8 stroking his chest, he pities himself in vain.
He wishes to acquire the essentials of the golden tower,
and to come into possession of the *Book of the Jade Lock*.[1]
Nine dragons roam in the Weak Waters,[2]
12 eight phoenixes emerge from the drifting mist.
In the morning, picking the alabaster fruit;
in the evening, drinking from the sweet springs.[3]
Vast and deep, he sees no ground when looking down;[4]
16 lightning tears holes in the sky above.
An entire lifetime is but taking one breath,
how can the Central Region be enough space for turning around?

---

1 The Master of the Golden Tower was a Daoist of Mount Song (in modern He'nan) who discovered the secret for finding treasures and used it to find minerals for making the elixir of immortality. Liang Emperor Yuan used Golden Tower as his own appellation and authored a work entitled *The Master of the Golden Tower*, in which he mentions the Mount Song Daoist.

2 Daoist deities are said to roam in a carriage hitched with nine dragons. The Weak Waters is so called because no boat can sail on it; it is said to surround a paradisial land in the Western Ocean and make it unreachable.

3 Alabaster fruit and sweet springs are both found in the immortals' land.

4 Lines 11–14 echo "Far Roaming" 遠遊 in the *Lyrics of Chu* as well as the Western Han writer Sima Xiangru's "*Fu* on the Great Man" 大人賦.

古意詩二首

I

十五好詩書
二十彈冠仕
楚王賜顏色
4　出入章華裏
作賦凌屈原
讀書誇左史
數從明月讌
8　或侍朝雲祀
登山摘紫芝
泛江採綠芷
歌舞未終曲
12　風塵暗天起
吳師破九龍
秦兵割千里
狐兔穴宗廟
16　霜露沾朝市
璧入邯鄲宮

1　King of Chu refers to Xiao Yi, Liang Emperor Yuan. As governor of Jingzhou, in
the Chu region, for many years before he ascended the throne, he is often figured
as a "King of Chu" in contemporary writings. The Zhanghua Terrace was built
by King Ling of Chu 楚靈王 (d. 529 BCE).

Ancient Theme: Two Poems

I

I loved the *Poems* and *Documents* at the age of fifteen;
at twenty, I dusted my cap, and entered service.
The King of Chu received me with kind countenance,
4 and I went in and out of the Zhanghua Palace.[1]
Composing rhapsodies, I surpassed Qu Yuan;
in reading I boasted being on a par with the Left Historian.[2]
Frequently I participated in banquets at the Bright Moon Tower,
8 at times I attended the sacrifices to the Morning Cloud.[3]
Climbing hills, I picked purple mushrooms;
sailing on the Yangzi River, I gathered green angelica.
Before the performance of song and dance was completed,
12 wind and dust darkened the sky.
Wu's army smashed the bells of nine dragons,
the Qin troops cut away a thousand square leagues of our territory.[4]
Foxes and rabbits made their home in the ancestral temple,
16 frost and dew soaked the court.
The jade disk entered the palace of Handan,

---

2 For Qu Yuan, see note to IX.2a. The Left Historian refers to Yixiang 倚相 (fl. 510 BCE), an official in the Chu court who was well-read in the ancient canons.

3 Xiao Yi built a large park at Jiangling, the provincial capital of Jiangzhou, when he was governor; in the park there were a Bright Moon Tower and also a Sunny Cloud Tower. The Morning Cloud is an allusion to the story that a King of Chu dreamed of the goddess of the Wu Mountain and had a romantic dalliance with her; upon departure she said that she would always be around as the morning cloud and evening rain. A shrine was dedicated to the goddess at the Wu Mountain. This may also be an allusion to a well-known love affair between Xiao Yi and a local Jingzhou girl who was compared to the goddess and connected to Sunny Cloud Tower in contemporary poems (see Additional Notes).

4 King Helü of Wu (see note to IX.23) invaded Chu in 506 BCE and captured the Chu capital, desecrating the former Chu king's tomb and smashing the bells (or, according to another source, a cauldron, symbol of the royal power) decorated with nine dragons. Qin, the powerful regime of the Warring States Period, is often used to indicate the Western Wei/Northern Zhou in writings of Yan's contemporaries. The first line of this couplet might refer to either Hou Jing's capture of Jiankang or the Western Wei army's taking of Jiangling.

劍去襄城水
不獲殉陵墓
20 獨生良足恥
憫憫思舊都
惻惻懷君子
白髮闚明鏡
24 憂傷沒余齒

II

寶珠出東國
美玉產南荊
隋侯曜我色
4 卞氏飛吾聲
已加明稱物
復飾夜光名
驪龍旦夕駭
8 白虹朝暮生
華彩燭兼乘

---

1 The priceless jade discovered by Bian He 卞和 (fl. 700s–670s BCE; see the second poem below) had been a treasure in the possession of Chu kings, but later it was owned by the state of Zhao, whose capital was Handan (in modern Hebei). Zhang Hua 張華 (232–300) had a precious sword named Longyuan 龍淵 (aka Longquan 龍泉); after he died, the sword flew into the river at Xiangcheng (in modern He'nan) and turned into a dragon. These two lines describe how Yan Zhitui left the south for the north.

the sword departed from the waters of Xiangcheng.[1]
Not able to follow my lord to the grave,
20 I survived, truly a cause for shame.
With sorrow I long for my former capital,
mournfully I think on my prince.
A white-haired man peeking into the bright mirror,
24 I will live out the remaining days of my life in grief.

II

A precious pearl emerges from the eastern region;
a beautiful jade is produced in the southern Jing.[2]
The Marquis of Sui brings forth my luster;
4 Master Bian enhances my reputation.[3]
Already "luminosity" is added to its name;
further adorned with the appellation of "nocturnal radiance."
Dawn and dusk, the dark dragon is startled;
8 a white nimbus appears around it morning and evening.[4]
One illuminates multiple carriages with its brilliance;

---

2 Chu was also called Jing or Jing Chu. The precious pearl was from Sui (see the note below) to the east of the Han River.

3 The Marquis of Sui (in modern Hubei) once saved a snake and was repaid by it with a precious pearl. Master Bian is Bian He, the man who recognized the invaluable jade inside an uncut stone and presented it to the Chu king.

4 In a *Zhuangzi* parable, a precious pearl is said to be guarded by a dark dragon in a deep ravine. The aura of a jade is likened to a white nimbus by Confucius in the *Record of Rites.*

價值詎連城
常悲黃雀起
12　每畏靈蛟迎
千刃安可捨
一毀難復營
昔為時所重
16　今為時所輕
願與濁泥會
思將垢石并
歸真川岳下
20　抱潤潛其榮

1 King Hui of Wei 魏惠王 (r. 370–319 BCE) once boasted that he had ten inch-long pearls, each of which could illuminate a number of carriages. King Zhao-xiang of Qin 秦昭襄王 (r. 306–251) once proposed to the King of Zhao to exchange fifteen cities for Bian He's jade.

2 The first line combines two allusions. The first is to an observation in *Zhuangzi* that, if someone uses a slingshot to shoot at a wren a thousand yards away, with the Marquis of Sui's pearl as pellet, he would be considered insane. The second is to a well-known story in early sources in which a praying mantis is about to catch a cicada without being aware that it is itself the target of a wren, nor does the wren know that it is itself about to be shot down by a human.

the other is worth more than many cities.[1]
Yet one often feels sad that the wren should fly up;[2]

12 and the other always fears being greeted by numinous *jiao*-dragons.[3]
How can one be given up for the wren of a thousand yards?
Once damaged, the other will be hard to acquire again.
In the past they were valued by the world;

16 today they receive only scorn.
I wish that they would sink into the mud,
or find a place amidst gravel.
Returning to their genuine essence
    by the river or at the foot of a hill,

20 they should hold onto their gentle and lustrous texture
    and conceal their light.

---

3 According to a story in Zhang Hua's 張華 (232–300) *Bowu zhi* 博物志, Tantai
Ziyu 澹臺子羽 once carried a precious jade to cross the Yellow River; the River
God wanted the jade, so he sent two *jiao*-dragons, fearsome mythological aquatic
creatures, to attack the boat. Tantai Ziyu killed the *jiao*-dragons, but once he
crossed, he threw the jade into the river to show that he was not greedy about
the jade – he just refused to be robbed. The River God, however, returned the
jade to him, perhaps out of embarrassment. After this happened three times, Ziyu
destroyed the jade and left.

和陽納言聽鳴蟬篇

聽秋蟬
秋蟬非一處
細柳高飛夕
4 長楊明月曙
曆亂起秋聲
參差攬人慮
單吟如轉簫
8 群噪學調笙
乍飄流曼響
多含斷絕聲
垂陰自有樂
12 飲露獨爲清
短綏何足貴
薄羽不羞輕
螗蜋翳下偏難見
16 翡翠竿頭絕易驚
容止由來桂林苑
無事淹留南斗城
城中帝皇里

A Companion Piece to Adviser Yang's "Listening to the Singing Cicadas"[1]

Listening to the autumn cicadas –
the autumn cicadas are found more than one place.
From the Slender Willow in twilight, it soars high;
4 the moon shines bright over the Tall Poplar at dawn.[2]
Then and there, autumn sounds arise in disarray,
tumultuously, disrupting and churning one's thoughts.
A solitary chanting resembles a melodious flute;
8 vocalizing as a group emulates the tuning of panpipes.
Drifting for a while, its long echo flows on,
always containing the sound of a broken heart.
Hiding in the shade has its pleasure;
12 drinking dew, it alone remains pure.
How could its short mandible be worth prizing?
Yet it does not feel ashamed of the lightness of its delicate wings.
Shadowed by the praying mantis,
    it is particularly hard to spot;
16 on top of the pole decorated with kingfisher feathers,
    it is startled most easily.[3]
It has always been lingering in the Cassia Park;
now for no reason it tarries in the City of the Southern Dipper.[4]
The city is the dwelling place of emperor and kings,

---

1 Yang was the Northern Qi writer Yang Xiuzhi (see note to XVIII.5). Yang's poem is no longer extant. See Additional Notes for the circumstances of this poem's composition.

2 While "slender willow" and "tall poplar" are trees, they are also place names in Han-dynasty Chang'an: Slender Willow was where the Western Han general Zhou Yafu 周亞夫 (d. 143 BCE) had his military camp, and Tall Poplar was the name of one of the Han palaces.

3 The praying mantis is here figured as a prey trying to catch the unsuspecting cicada (see note to "Ancient Theme: Two Poems" II). In a *Zhuangzi* parable an old man uses a pole to catch cicadas.

4 The Cassia Park was a park in Wu during the Three Kingdoms Period, here representing the south. The city of the Southern Dipper refers to Chang'an, because the northern wall of the city was supposed to be modeled on the shape of that constellation.

20 金張謚許史
　　權勢熱如湯
　　意氣謚城市
　　劍影奔星落
24 馬色浮雲起
　　鼎俎陳龍鳳
　　金石諧宮徵
　　關中滿季心
28 關西饒孔子
　　詎用虞公立國臣
　　誰愛韓王游說士
　　紅顏宿昔同春花
32 素鬢俄頃變秋華
　　中腸自有極
　　那堪教作轉輪車

---

1 Jin Midi 金日磾 (d. 134–86 BCE) and Zhang Anshi 張安世 (d. 62 BCE) were Western Han officials whose descendants continued to occupy prominent positions for several generations. The Xu and Shi families were imperial in-laws: Xu Pingjun 許平君 (88–71 BCE), the consort of Han Emperor Xuan 宣帝 (r. 73–49 BCE) was from the Xu family; Emperor Xuan's grandmother was a Shi. The phrase "Jin, Zhang, Xu, and Shi" is used to refer to the rich and powerful families in the capital.

20 and of the families of Jin, Zhang, Xu, and Shi.[1]
    Their power and influence are as hot as boiling water;
    their aims and airs stir up clamor in the marketplace.
    The gleam of their swords speeds past like a shooting star;
24 from the colors of their horses, floating clouds arise.
    In cauldrons and on platters display
        the meat of dragons and phoenixes;
    metal bells and stone chimes
        perform a harmony of the *gong* and *zhi* tones.
    The land within the Pass is filled with the likes of Ji Xin;
28 to the west of the Pass, a rich store of Confuciuses.[2]
    Why bother using the Lord of Yu's state-defending minister?
    Who'd be fond of the persuader in the court of the King of Han?[3]
    Ruddy cheeks were once like spring flowers;
32 but in an instant pale temple-hair turns into autumnal flecks of
        white.
    The intestines have their limit:
    how could they be made into turning wheels?[4]

---

2 "Within the Pass" generally refers to the region to the west of the Hangu Pass
   (in modern He'nan) that was the former territory of the state of Qin; "to the
   west of the Pass" is the region to the west of the Hangu Pass or the Tong Pass
   潼關 (in modern Shaanxi). Ji Xin (see note to XII.9), was a chivalrous figure widely admired by people "within the Pass." Yang
   Zhen (see XVII.27), the learned Eastern Han scholar, was called by his contempo-
   raries "the Confucius to the west of the Pass" 關西孔子. This couplet says that
   the regime of the Northern Zhou has many talented ministers.
3 The state-defending minister of the Lord of Yu refers to Gong Zhiqi (see note to
   VII.3). The persuader in the court of the King of Han refers to the famous
   Warring States strategist Su Qin (see note to VIII.25), who talked King Xuan of
   Han 韓宣王 (d. 312 BCE) into forming an alliance with the other states against
   Qin. Here Gong Zhiqi and Su Qin are figures for the Northern Qi courtiers.
   Yan Zhitui is saying that the Northern Zhou has its own talented ministers and
   will not use the services of the courtiers from Qi.
4 "Intestines like turned wheels" is a figurative phrase indicating an intensely dis-
   tressed state.

從周入齊夜度砥柱

俠客重艱辛
夜出小平津
馬色迷關吏
4 雞鳴起戍人
露鮮華劍彩
月照寶刀新
問我將何去
8 北海就孫賓

Passing by Dizhu at Night on the Way from Zhou to Qi[1]

The man-at-arms does not treat hardship lightly,
under the night's cover he leaves Xiaopingjin.[2]
The color of my horse bewilders the officer at the pass;
4 at roosters' crow, the solders on the frontier rise.[3]
Dew refreshes the radiance of my patterned sword,
moonlight gleams on the precious blade.
If you ask me where I am going –
8 I will go to Beihai and seek Sun Bin.[4]

---

1 Dizhu or the Whetstone Pillar was the name of a large pillar-like rock formation
  in the current of the Yellow River (in modern He'nan); it no longer exists. This
  poem was supposedly written in 556 when Yan Zhitui fled from the Northern
  Zhou to the Northern Qi, hoping to eventually return to the south via Qi (see
  the Introduction as well as his rhapsody, ll.239–240).
2 Xiaopingjin was an Eastern Han pass fording over the Yellow River (in modern
  He'nan).
3 Gongsun Long 公孫龍, the third-century BCE "terminologist" (see note to
  XVIII.2) who famously posited that "a white horse is not a horse," was blocked
  by the officer at the pass for not having his papers with him. Tian Wen 田文 (d.
  279 BCE) or the Lord of Mengchang 孟嘗君, aristocrat and statesman of the
  state of Qi, escaped from Qin in 299 BCE, but when he got to the Hangu Pass,
  he found that the gates would not open until cockcrow. One of his retainers
  simulated cockcrow and the gates were opened, and Tian Wen successfully fled.
4 Sun Bin of Beihai (in modern Shandong) is Sun Binshi 孫賓石 (fl. second century), shortened for the sake of line length and rhyming. Also known as Sun
  Song, he saved the scholar Zhao Qi who was fleeing arrest (see note to XII.9).

觀我生賦

仰浮清之藐藐
俯沉奧之茫茫
已生民而立教
4　乃司牧以分疆
內諸夏而外夷狄
驟五帝而馳三王
大道寢而日隱
8　小雅摧以云亡
哀趙武之作孽
怪漢靈之不祥
旍頭翫其金鼎
12　典午失其珠囊
瀍澗鞠成沙漠
神華泯為龍荒
吾王所以東運
16　我祖於是南翔

---

1 The title, "viewing my life," is from the "Viewing" (*guan* 觀) hexagram in the *Classic of Changes*: "Here the viewing is of my own life: a noble man will be without misfortune" 觀我生, 君子無咎.

2 The floating clarity refers to heaven and the sunken depths, the earth.

3 The "various Xia states" refers to the states in the Central Plains enfeoffed by the Zhou. Yi and Di respectively refer to the eastern and northern tribal people, a term indicating "barbarians." The Five Emperors are mythical rulers in high antiquity and there are various groupings. The Three Kings are the founders of the Xia, Shang, and Zhou dynasties.

Rhapsody on Viewing My Life[1]

I look up at the vastness of the floating clarity,
then look down at the massiveness of the sunken depths.[2]
After the birth of the folk, teachings were established,
4 and territories were divided, presided over by shepherding officers.
Within were the various Xia states; without, Yi and Di barbarians;
time rushed for the Five Emperors, and raced for the Three Kings.[3]
The great Way lies concealed day by day;
8 the tradition of the Lesser Odes is damaged and lost.[4]
One laments the wayward behavior of King Wu of Zhao,
and is amazed by the inauspicious actions of Han Emperor Ling.[5]
The yak-tail banner toyed with the Golden Tripods;
12 the house of Sima lost its bag of pearls.[6]
The region between the Chan and Jian Rivers had turned into desert;
the divine Hua realm was reduced to the wasteland of the Dragon
    City.[7]
Thereupon my Lord and King moved east;
16 thereupon my ancestor soared to the south.[8]

---

4 The *Lesser Odes* from the *Classic of Poetry* represents the elegant music of the
   Zhou; the damage and neglect of its tradition signify the loss of moral orthodoxy.

5 King Wu of Zhao is also known as King Wuling of Zhao 趙武靈王 (r. 325–299
   BCE). He had advocated wearing Hu/Tatar-style clothes that were convenient for
   practicing horsemanship and archery. Han Emperor Ling (r. 168–189) loved Hu/
   Tatar fashion, furniture, and music. These were considered omens for Hu invasion of Chinese land.

6 The yak-tail banner constellation is the Pleiades, which is supposed to govern the
   region of the nomadic Xiongnu (see XVI.7). It represents the Hu barbarians. The
   Golden Tripods are the nine tripods symbolizing dynastic rule and power, created
   in the Xia dynasty and passed down. Dianwu is a word puzzle whose answer is
   Sima, the surname of the Jin royal house. The pearls are the Five Planets (Venus,
   Jupiter, Mercury, Mars, and Saturn); losing the pearls refers to the loss of control
   over the regular movement of the stars and hence the loss of political legitimacy
   and domination.

7 The region between the Chan and Jian Rivers was Luoyang, the capital of the
   Western Jin. The Dragon City was where the Xiongnu made sacrifices to heaven.

8 My Lord and King refers to Sima Rui 司馬睿, Jin Emperor Yuan 元帝 (r. 317–
   323), aka Zhongzong (see Yan Zhitui's original note below), who founded the
   Eastern Jin. Yan Zhitui's ninth-generation progenitor, Yan Han, had moved south
   with Sima Rui in 307 (see Introduction).

晉中宗以琅邪王南渡，之推琅邪人，故稱吾王。

去琅邪之遷越

宅金陵之舊章

作羽儀於新邑

20 樹杞梓於水鄉

傳清白而勿替

守法度而不忘

逮微躬之九葉

24 頹世濟之聲芳

問我辰之安在

鍾厭惡於有梁

養傅翼之飛獸

梁武帝納亡人侯景，授其命，遂為反叛之基。

28 子貪心之野狼

武帝初養臨川王子正德為嗣，生昭明後，正德
還本，特封臨賀王，猶懷怨恨。經叛入北而
還，積財養士，每有異志也。

---

1 Langye (in modern Shandong) was the fief of Sima Rui before he ascended the throne. It was Yan Zhitui's ancestral home.

2 Jinling was the old name of Jianye, changed to Jiankang in the Eastern Jin.

3 Medlar and catalpa are trees of fine timber, a metaphor for talented men.

4 Yang Zhen (see XVII.27) once said he wanted to pass on "purity and integrity" to his descendants as his legacy.

Jin Zhongzong crossed the Yangzi River to the south as the Prince of
Langye. I, Zhitui, am originally from Langye; therefore I address him as
"my Lord and King."[1]

After leaving behind the relocation from Langye,
we settled at Jinling, still observing our old family practices.[2]
Fine plumed trappings were set up at the new metropolis,
20   medlar and catalpa were planted in the river land.[3]
The legacy of purity and integrity was transmitted without cease,
the family never became forgetful in preserving laws and measures.[4]
My insignificant self is of the ninth generation,
24   by now our family's fragrant reputation, passed on through the ages,
      has declined.
If you ask me wherein my misfortune lies –
it dates from the time when heaven grew weary of the Liang.
The emperor nurtured the winged tiger,[5]

Liang Emperor Wu took in the refugee Hou Jing, who offered his
service.[6] This became the foundation for rebellion and insurrection.[7]

28   and adopted as his own son the savage wolf with a greedy heart.

Emperor Wu had adopted Zhengde, son of the Prince of Linchuan, as his
heir. After Prince Zhaoming was born, Zhengde was returned to his own
family. He was enfeoffed as the Prince of Linhe as a special honor, but he
still harbored resentment. He had once capitulated to the north, and after
returning to the south, he stored wealth and kept retainers with
traitorous intentions.[8]

---

5 The text reads "winged beast" *fei shou*, presumably changed by a Tang editor or
   copyist from "winged tiger" (*fei hu* 飛虎), an established phrase, to avoid the
   taboo name of the father of the Tang founding emperor.
6 For my translation of the phrase *shou qi ming* 授其命, see Additional Notes.
7 Hou Jing's capitulation was accepted in 547; he rebelled in 548.
8 Xiao Zhengde (d. 549) was a son of Emperor Wu's brother Xiao Hong 蕭宏
   (Prince of Linchuan, 473–526). Emperor Wu, sonless for a long time, had adopted Zhengde as heir. After the birth of his eldest son, Prince Zhaoming (Xiao
   Tong 蕭統, 501–531), he disowned Zhengde. Zhengde fled to the Northern Wei
   in 525 but returned to Liang in 526; he was pardoned and his title restored. He
   was made the Commandery Prince 郡王 of Linhe in 532.

初召禍於絕域
重發釁於蕭牆

> 正德求征侯景,至新林,叛投景,景立為主,
> 以攻臺城。

雖萬里而作限
32 聊一葦而可航
指金闕以長鍛
向王路而蹴張
勤王踰於十萬
36 曾不解其搤吭
嗟將相之骨鯁
皆屈體於犬羊

> 臺城陷,援軍並問訊二宮,致敬於侯景也。

武皇忽以厭世
40 白日黯而無光
既饗國而五十
何克終之弗康

---

1 The Solemn Screens are walls within the palace complex, so named because a minister is supposed to act solemnly when getting close to the ruler. Trouble within the Solemn Screens refers to internal trouble.

2 Xinlin was to the southwest of Jiankang. The Palace City or Taicheng was the imperial palace complex within the capital. Xiao Zhengde conspired with Hou Jing and enabled Hou Jing's army to cross the Qinhuai River and besiege the Palace City for nearly five months. Hou Jing declared Zhengde the emperor, but once the Palace City fell, Hou Jing deposed him and finally executed him.

First calamity was invited from afar;
then trouble ensued within the Solemn Screens.[1]

> Zhengde asked to wage battle with Hou Jing. When he advanced to
> Xinlin, he rebelled and surrendered to Hou Jing. Jing established him as
> the lord and proceeded to attack the Palace City.[2]

Though the border was drawn ten thousand leagues away,
32 now with a little skiff one could cross over.[3]
Long halberds were pointed to the golden towers;
on the King's Highway cross-bows were drawn with feet.
More than one hundred thousand troops came to the emperor's rescue,
36 but none could loosen the hold over the throat.
Alas, the upright generals and ministers
all bowed to those curs and goats.

> After the fall of the Palace City, all rescue armies inquired after the Two
> Palaces and paid respects to Hou Jing.[4]

Soon after, the Martial Emperor had had enough of the world,[5]
40 the white sun was eclipsed and lost its brilliance.
He had enjoyed the throne for fifty years;
why must the end be in such disgrace?[6]

---

3 A little skiff is literally "a bundle of reeds." The lines, "Who said the Yellow River
is wide? / On a bundle of reeds one can cross it," are from the *Classic of Poetry*.
It was used by Cao Pi, Wei Emperor Wen (see note to X), to refer to the Yangzi
River once. Yan Zhitui may be using this allusion to also refer to the Qinhuai
River, which Hou Jing crossed with Xiao Zhengde's help (see above).

4 That is, the rescue armies accepted their defeat. The Two Palaces refer to Emperor
Wu and the Crown Prince, Xiao Gang.

5 Emperor Wu's posthumous title, *wu*, means martial.

6 Emperor Wu ruled from 502 to 549, nearly fifty years. He died soon after Hou
Jing captured the Palace City.

嗣君聽於巨猾

44 每凜然而負芒

自東晉之違難

寓禮樂於江湘

迄此幾於三百

48 左衽淪於四方

詠苦胡而永歎

吟微管而增傷

世祖赫其斯怒

52 奮大義於沮漳

　　孝元帝時為荊州刺史。

授犀函與鶴膝

建飛雲及艅艎

北徵兵於漢曲

56 南發餫於衡陽

　　湘州刺史河東王譽、雍州刺史岳陽王詧並隸荊
　　州都督府。

---

1 Xiao Gang the Crown Prince succeeded to Emperor Wu but was completely under Hou Jing's control.

2 The Yangzi River and the Xiang River (in Hu'nan) represent the south.

3 "Those wearing lapels on the left" refers to the non-Han peoples.

4 In the *Analects* Confucius had said of Guan Zhong, the famous Qi statesman of the Spring and Autumn Period, "Were it not for Guan Zhong, I would have had unbound hair and worn my lapels on the left."

5 This quotation is from a poem in the "Greater Odes" section of the *Classic of Poetry*.

The successor monarch yielded to the great evildoer,
44 ever anxious and fearful, as if having thorns in his back.[1]
The Eastern Jin had sought a shelter from catastrophe,
    and lodged the rites and music at the Yangzi and Xiang rivers.[2]
Since then, it had been nearly three hundred years,
48 and those wearing lapels on the left had spread to all sides.[3]
Chanting about suffering from the barbarians,
    I heaved long sighs;
I recited "Were it not for Guan [Zhong],"
    which only increased my sadness.[4]
Emperor Shizu "rose majestic in his wrath,"[5]
52 upholding the great principle by the Ju and Zhang Rivers.[6]

> At the time Emperor Xiaoyuan was the Governor of Jingzhou.

He issued forth rhinoceros chain-mail and crane's-knee lances,
    and established the fleet of Flying Cloud and Yuhuang warships.
To the north he summoned troops from the bends of the Han River;
56 to the south he asked for provisions from Hengyang.[7]

> The [Commandery] Prince of Hedong, Yu, who was then Governor of
> Xiangzhou, and the [Commandery] Prince of Yueyang, Cha, who was
> then Governor of Yongzhou, were both under the military command of
> Jingzhou.[8]

---

6 Shizu was the temple name of Xiao Yi, Emperor Yuan/Xianyuan. "Ju and Zhang
   Rivers" refers to the region of Chu.
7 The Han River flows through Xiangyang 襄陽 (in modern Hubei), the seat of
   Yongzhou or Yong prefecture. Hengyang commandery was part of Xiangzhou or
   Xiang prefecture and is in modern Hu'nan. The former was the territory of Xiao
   Cha and the latter, that of Xiao Yu (see below).
8 Xiao Yu (519–550), Commandery Prince of Hedong, was the second son of Xiao
   Tong, the Crown Prince Zhaoming. Xiao Cha (519–562), Commandery Prince
   of Yueyang, was the third son of Xiao Tong, and later with the support of the
   Western Wei, became the ruler of the Later Liang (Emperor Xuan 宣帝, r. 555–
   562). Xiao Yi had requested troops from Xiao Yu and provisions from Xiao Cha
   to help suppress Hou Jing's rebellion.

昔承華之賓帝

實兄亡而弟及

> 昭明太子薨，乃立晉安王為太子。

逮皇孫之失寵

60 歎扶車之不立

> 嫡皇孫驩出封豫章王而薨。

間王道之多難

各私求於京邑

襄陽阻其銅符

64 長沙閉其玉粒

> 河東、岳陽皆昭明子。

遽自戰於其地

豈大勛之暇集

子既殯而姪攻

68 昆亦圍而叔襲

褚乘城而宵下

杜倒戈而夜入

---

1 This couplet and the original note narrate how after Xiao Tong's death in 531 Emperor Wu had decided to designate Xiao Gang, the Prince of Jin'an, as heir, rather than Xiao Tong's eldest son, Xiao Huan (510–541). Xiao Huan was enfeoffed as Commandery Prince of Yuzhang instead (see ll. 59–60 and the original note).

In the past, when the resident of the Chenghua Palace
    became a guest of the heavenly god,
in truth it was his younger brother who succeeded him.

> After Crown Prince Zhaoming died, the Prince of Jin'an was made heir
> apparent.[1]

The imperial grandson had lost the emperor's favor,
60 and sadly was not chosen for the throne.

> Emperor Wu's eldest grandson, Huan, was sent to the provinces as
> [Commandery] Prince of Yuzhang and subsequently passed away.

Taking advantage of the hardships on the King's Way,
they each sought for private profit at the capital city:
Xiangyang refused to match the bronze tally,
64 and Changsha begrudged the precious grain.[2]

> [The Commendary Princes of] Hedong [Xiao Yu] and Yueyang [Xiao
> Cha] were both sons of Prince Zhaoming.

They all rushed to fight among themselves in their territories,
how could they have time to accomplish the great deed?[3]
A son was destroyed, and a nephew was assaulted;
68 the elder brother was besieged, and the uncle was attacked.[4]
Chu climbed over the city wall in the evening;
Du turned halberd around, and surrendered at night.

---

2 Xiao Yu (of Changsha) and Xiao Cha (of Xiangyang) defied Xiao Yi's orders and
   refused to send him troops and provisions (see the above note to ll. 55–56).

3 The great deed refers to the annihilation of Hou Jing. Only after Xiao Yi defeated
   and killed Xiao Yu in early 550 (see below) did he launch a formal campaign
   against Hou Jing.

4 This and the following three couplets lament the infighting among the members
   of the Liang royal family. The author's original note explains the references to
   son (Xiao Fangdeng), nephew (Xiao Yu), elder brother (Xiao Yu), and uncle (Xiao
   Yi).

孝元以河東不供船艎，乃遣世子方等為刺史。
大軍掩至，河東不暇遣拒。世子信用羣小，貪
其子女玉帛，遂欲攻之，故河東急而逆戰，世
子為亂兵所害。孝元發怒，又使鮑泉圍河東。
而岳陽宣言大獵，即擁眾襲荊州，求解湘州之
圍。時襄陽杜岸兄弟怨其見劫，不以實告，又
不義此行，率兵八千夜降，岳陽於是遁走。河
東府褚顯族據投岳陽，所以湘州見陷也。

行路彎弓而含笑
72 骨肉相誅而涕泣
周旦其猶病諸
孝武悔而焉及

方幕府之事殷
76 謬見擇於人羣
未成冠而登仕
財解履以從軍

時年十九，釋褐湘東國右常侍，以軍功加鎮西
墨曹參軍。

---

1 Xiao Fangdeng is mentioned several times in Yan Zhutui's *Family Instructions* (see VI.47, IX.30, XIX.7).

2 Bao Quan (d. 552) was unable to defeat Xiao Yu. Later Wang Sengbian (see II.5) was sent to take over the command of the army.

3 This happened in the autumn of 549. Du An (d. 549) was a general under Xiao Cha's command. Later that year, however, Du An was captured by Xiao Cha who had him executed.

Because [the Commandery Prince of] Hedong did not provide warships, Emperor Xiaoyuan sent his son and heir, Fangdeng, to replace him as governor of Xiangzhou.[1] When the heir's army arrived, Hedong did not have time to mount a defense. Trusting the council of his crooked advisors and coveting Hedong's women and wealth, the heir planned to launch an attack. Hedong became desperate and fought back, and the heir was killed. Emperor Xiaoyuan was so enraged that he sent Bao Quan to besiege Hedong.[2] Subsequently [the Commandery Prince of] Yueyang declared he would go on a great hunting trip, leading his army to attack Jingzhou in hope of lifting the siege of Xiangzhou. At the time, Du An of Xiangyang and his brothers resented that they were being coerced and had not been told the truth, nor did they approve of this campaign, so they surrendered to Xiaoyuan with eight thousand soldiers in the middle of the night.[3] Thereupon Yueyang fled. Chu Xianzu on the staff of Hedong went to join Yueyang, and Xiangzhou fell.[4]

When a stranger on the road draws his bow, one can face it with a
    smile;
72 but when assailed by one's own flesh and blood, one weeps.
This had once deeply troubled the Duke of Zhou;
this had given rise to Emperor Xiaowu's remorse, but too late.[5]

At the time the affairs at the military headquarters were numerous,
76 I was, by error, selected from the crowd.
Before reaching the age of capping, I already entered service;
having just "taken off the shoes," I joined the army.[6]

    At the time I was nineteen *sui*. My first appointment was the Right
    Attendant of the princedom of Xiangdong. Later, I was additionally
    appointed Adjutant of the Defender-general of the West in the Section of
    Justice due to military merit.[7]

---

4 Xiangzhou fell to Wang Sengbian in early 550 and Xiao Yu was killed. Nothing else is known about Chu Xianzu. His betrayal of Xiao Yu, described as climbing over the city wall at night (to flee), is clearly believed by Yan Zhitui to have led to the fall of Xiangzhou.
5 King Wu of Zhou's brothers, Guanshu 管叔 and Caishu 蔡叔, plotted a rebellion; another brother, the Duke of Zhou, campaigned against them, had Guanshu killed and Caishu exiled. Xiaowu refers to Han Emperor Wu, whose heir was slandered and forced to commit suicide; later the emperor realized the son's innocence and regretted.
6 A courtier must take off his shoes when entering the palace to see the ruler.
7 Xiao Yi was Prince of Xiangdong. He was made Defender-of-the-West General in 547.

非社稷之能衞

80 □□□□□□

　　童汪錡。

僅書記於階闥

罕羽翼於風雲

及荊王之定霸

84 始儺恥而圖雪

舟師次乎武昌

撫軍鎮於夏汭

　　時遣徐州刺史徐文盛領二萬人屯武昌蘆州拒侯
　　景將任約，又第二子綏寧度方諸爲世子，拜中
　　撫軍將軍、郢州刺史以盛聲勢。

濫充選於多士

88 在參戎之盛列

慚四白之調護

厠六友之談說

1　Line 80 is missing and the text of the original note is corrupt. According to the
　Zuo Tradition, Wang Qi was a young boy loved by a nobleman of Lu. They both
　died in battle. Confucius approved of Wang Qi being given the burial of a grown
　man because he was able to defend the state.

2　This with more than a hint of criticism refers to the fact that Xiao Yi did not
　launch the campaign against Hou Jing until he first defeated his nephew Xiao
　Yu. Xiao Cha was driven to seek aid from the Western Wei to attack Xiao Yi.

It was not that I was able to defend the state,

80 ....

> the young boy Wang Qi.[1]

I was merely keeping records in the court;
rarely could I function as a worthy aide in wind and clouds.

Only after the King of Jing secured his hegemony
84 did he begin to eradicate shame and take vengeance.[2]
His naval fleet camped at Wuchang,
and the Protector General was stationed at the ford of the Xia River.[3]

> At the time Xu Wensheng, Governor of Xuzhou, was put in charge of
> an army of 20,000 solders at Wuchang's Luzhou to repel Ren Yue, Hou
> Jing's general.[4] The Marquis of Suining, Fangzhu, who was the second
> son, was made heir apparent, and was also appointed Capital Protector
> General and governor of Yingzhou in order to enhance the repute and
> status of the resistance forces.[5]

Filling a position among the many worthy gentlemen,
88 I found myself in the overflowing ranks of military advisers.
In assisting and sheltering, I was put to shame by the Four White-
    heads,
I did no more than partake in the conversations of the Six Friends.[6]

---

3 Wuchang is in modern Hubei. The Xia River joins the Yangzi River near Wuchang.
4 Xu Wensheng (d. 551) was governor of Qinzhou 秦州. Xuzhou is either an
   original mistake or a copyist error.
5 Xiao Fangzhu (537–552) was Xiao Yi's second son, half-brother of Xiao Fangdeng.
6 The Four White-heads were the four elders who served as guardians of Liu Bang's
   eldest son, Liu Ying 劉盈, later Han Emperor Hui 漢惠帝 (r. 194–188 BCE).
   The "Six Friends" were the six tutors selected for the Crown Prince in the last
   years of the Western Jin.

時遷中撫軍外兵參軍，掌管記，與文珪、劉民
英等與世子遊處。

雖形就而心和
92 匪余懷之所說

緊深宮之生貴
矧垂堂與倚衡
欲推心以屬物
96 樹幼齒以先聲
中撫軍時年十五。

懍敷求之不器
乃畫地而取名
仗禦武於文吏
以虞預為郢州司馬，領城防事。

100 委軍政於儒生
以鮑泉為郢州行事，總攝州府也。

值白波之猝駭
逢赤舌之燒城
王凝坐而對寇

---

1 This is the advice given to someone who was going to be a tutor to the heir
apparent of the domain of Wei in *Zhuangzi*.

2 This couplet says that Xiao Fangzhu had led a privileged and sheltered life, never
having been exposed to any danger growing up. Line 94 derives from a saying,
"The son of a family with a thousand gold pieces does not sit under the eaves

> At the time I was promoted to Adjutant of the Protector General in the Section for Outer Troops, and placed in charge of secretarial matters. Together with Wen Gui, Liu Minying, and others, I attended the heir apparent.

Though "affable in appearance and agreeable in heart,"
92 I did not take delight in it.[1]

The heir apparent was born precious in the deep palace,
not to mention "sitting under the eaves" or "leaning against the railing."[2]
He desired to be sincere and earnest to inspire his people,
96 seeking to establish a noble reputation at a tender age.

> At the time, the Protector General was fifteen *sui*.

Alas, in widely seeking out counselors, he did not consider their capacities;
instead he employed men whose fame was as empty as a drawing on the ground.
He delegated military defense to a civil officer,

> He made Yu Yu the Constable of Yingzhou in charge of city defense.

00 and entrusted army affairs to a Ru scholar.[3]

> He appointed Bao Quan as the Executive Director of Yingzhou in charge of the prefectural headquarters.

They suffered the sudden strike of the "White Water" bandits,
and were caught up in the burning of the city by "fiery tongues."[4]
Yet, they behaved like a Wang Ningzhi, who faced the rebels and did nothing,

---

and the son of a family of a hundred gold pieces does not lean against the railing." Sitting under the eaves and leaning against a railing refer to risky situations (tiles might fall and railings might collapse). Another interpretation of 倚衡 is to ride on the shaft of a chariot (and to be in danger of falling off).

3 Yu Yu was the author of a work entitled *Essentials of Food* 食要 commissioned by Xiao Yi. Bao Quan was a scholar of the classics and a poet. Yu Yu, Bao Quan, and Xiao Fangzhu were all captured by Hou Jing's general Song Zixian 宋子仙 (d. 551). Yu and Bao were killed and their bodies dumped into the Yangzi River; Xiao Fangzhu was killed by Hou Jing in 552.

4 The "White Water bandits" refers to the rebels in Baibo (in modern Shanxi) at the end of the Eastern Han. Fiery tongues' burning of a city is a figure for slandering, from the Western Han writer Yang Xiong's *Taixuan jing* 太玄經.

104 向詡拱以臨兵

> 任約為文盛所困，侯景自上救之，舟艦弊漏，軍饑卒疲，數戰失利。乃令宋子仙、任約步道偷郢州城，預無備，故陷賊。

莫不變蝯而化鵠
皆自取首以破腦
將睥睨於渚宮
108 先憑陵於地道

> 景欲攻荊州，路由巴陵。

懿永寧之龍蟠

> 永寧公王僧辯據巴陵城，善於守禦，景不能進。

奇護軍之電掃

> 護軍將軍陸法和破任約於赤亭湖，景退走，大潰。

犇虜快其餘毒
112 縲囚膏乎野草
幸先主之無勸
賴滕公之我保

---

1 Wang Ning is Wang Ningzhi 王凝之 (d. 399), son of the famous calligrapher Wang Xizhi and administrator of Kuaiji (in modern Zhejiang). When Sun En's 孫恩 (d. 402) rebel army attacked the city, he did nothing but pray to the Daoist gods and was killed when the city fell. Xiang Xu (d. 184) was an eccentric scholar. During the Yellow Turban Uprising, he suggested reciting the *Classic of Filial Piety* to the rebel troops and believed that they would then disband on their own.

04 or like a Xiang Xu, who confronted the enemy by folding his hands,[1]

> Ren Yue was trapped by Xu Wensheng, and Hou Jing himself went upriver to his rescue. His warships were dilapidated and leaky, his soldiers hungry and tired, and they lost several battles. Thereupon Hou Jing ordered Song Zixian and Ren Yue to take their troops to Yingzhou by land and launch a sneak attack. Yu Yu had made no preparations and lost the city to the rebels.

There was none who was not transformed into a gibbon or a crane;
all, as a result of their own doing, had their heads cut off, and their
  brains dashed out.[2]
Before the rebel forces cast their sideways glance at Zhugong,
08 they first wreaked havoc through the Underwater Tunnel.[3]

> Hou Jing was going to attack Jingzhou by way of Baling.[4]

I admire the Duke of Yongning who coiled like a dragon,

> Wang Sengbian, the Duke of Yongning, was in command at the city of Baling. He was good at defending the city and Jing could not advance.

I marvel at the Protector General who swept the rebels like lightning.[5]

> Lu Fahe, Protector General, defeated Ren Yue at Chiting Lake. Jing retreated and fled, and his army fell apart.

The fleeing rebels indulged in spreading their leftover poison,
12 their prisoners' bodies were turned into fertilizer of wild plants.
Fortunately there was no Former Ruler to urge my execution,
instead I had a Lord of Teng who preserved my life.[6]

---

2 This couplet alludes to the violent end of Xiao Fangzhu, Yu Yu, and Bao Quan. By order of one of Hou Jing's generals, Yu Yu and Bao Quan had their heads smashed by a huge rock. "Transformation into gibbon or crane" is an allusion to the story that after King Mu of Zhou's failed campaign, the officers turned into gibbons or cranes and the soldiers into sand or insects.

3 Zhugong was the name of an old Chu palace in Jingzhou. Here it indicates Xiao Yi's Jingzhou headquarters, Jiangling. An Underwater Tunnel was said to exist at Baling beneath the Dongting Lake.

4 Baling is in modern Hu'nan.

5 Wang Sengbian: see II.5. Lu Fahe: see XIX.8.

6 The Former Ruler refers to Liu Bei 劉備 (161–223), who had urged Cao Cao to kill the captured general Lü Bu 呂布 (d. 199). The Lord of Teng was Xiahou Ying 夏侯嬰 (d. 172 BCE); he saved Han Xin 韓信 (d. 196 BCE) from execution, who was to play a crucial role in the founding of the Western Han.

之推執在景軍，例當見殺。景行臺郎中王則初
無舊識，再三救護，獲免，囚以還都。

剟鬼錄於岱宗

116　招歸魂於蒼昊

時解衣訖而獲全。

荷性命之重賜

銜若人以終老

賊棄甲而來復

120　肆觜距之鵰鳶

積假履而弒帝

憑衣霧以上天

用速災於四月

124　奚聞道之十年

臺城陷後，梁武曾獨坐歎曰：「侯景於文為小
人百日天子。」及景以大寶二年十一月十九日
僭位，至明年三月十九日棄城逃竄，是一百二
十日，蓋天道紀大數，故文為百日。言與公孫
述俱棄十二，而旬歲不同。

---

1 It was believed that the souls of the dead would go to the underworld at Mount
  Tai.
2 Taking off one's clothing to be executed was a phrase that also appears in other
  sources (see Additional Notes). This practice was perhaps designed to make it
  easier for the executioner.
3 Abandoning or casting away one's armor means being defeated. Having suffered
  defeat at Baling, Hou Jing returned to Jiankang in the autumn of 551.

I was a captive in Hou Jing's army and was supposed to be executed.
Wang Ze, the Director of Hou Jing's Branch Department of State Affairs,
with whom I had had no prior acquaintance, intervened on my behalf
more than once. Thus I was able to escape death, and was taken back to
the capital as a prisoner.

From the register of ghosts at Mount Tai my name was taken off,
116   my soul was summoned back from the gray heavens.[1]

At the time I had already taken off my robe [i.e., getting ready to die],
but was saved at the last minute.[2]

I owed to that man my second life,
I am grateful to him till the end of my days.

The rebel [Hou Jing] abandoned his armor and returned,
120   the vultures and kites wantonly used their beaks and claws.[3]
Augmenting his borrowed power, he committed regicide,
and ascended heaven by treading on fog.[4]
This only sped up their collapse in a matter of four months,
124   How could he have achieved "hearing the Way" for ten years?

After the fall of the Palace City, Liang Emperor Wu once said with a sigh
while sitting alone: "The graphs of Hou Jing's name can be split into 'a
small man being emperor for one hundred days." Hou Jing usurped the
throne on the nineteenth day of the eleventh month in the second year
of Dabao [January 1, 552], and fled from the capital city on the nineteenth day of the third month in the following year [April 28, 552].[5] It
came to 120 days. The way of heaven records only the general numbers;
therefore the graphs read "a hundred days." This couplet states that Hou
Jing and Gongsun Shu both received the number of twelve, but one in
terms of a group of ten days and the other, in terms of years.[6]

---

4   After Hou Jing returned to Jiankang, he deposed Xiao Gang, Liang Emperor
Jianwen, and murdered him shortly after. Hou Jing first set another Liang prince
on the throne, but soon deposed him and proclaimed himself emperor ("ascended
heaven").

5   Dabao was the reign title of Emperor Jianwen.

6   Gongsun Shu (d. 36 CE) was a warlord who established a regime in Shu (in
modern Sichuan). He had a dream in which someone said his rule would last
twelve years. He told his wife upon waking, who replied, "'If one hears the Way
in the morning, one may die in the evening,' let alone twelve years!" His wife
cited Confucius' remark from the *Analects*.

観我生賦

就狄俘於舊壤

陷戎俗於來旋

慨黍離於清廟

128 愴麥秀於空廛

籥鼓臥而不考

景鐘毀而莫懸

野蕭條以橫骨

132 邑闃寂而無煙

疇百家之或在

> 中原冠帶隨晉渡江者百家，故江東有百譜，至
> 是在都者覆滅略盡。

覆五宗而翦焉

獨昭君之哀奏

136 唯翁主之悲絃

> 公主子女見辱見儷。

經長干以掩抑

> 長干，舊顏家巷。

展白下以流連

> 靖侯以下七世墳塋皆在白下。

---

1 Di and Rong were names of non-Han tribes, here representing "barbarians."

2 "Millet Ripe" ("Shuli") is a poem from the *Classic of Poetry* that laments the decline of Zhou. "Sprouting Wheat" ("Maixiu") was composed by a Shang descendant to lament the ruins of Shang.

3 See Additional Notes for my translation of this line.

As a captive of the Di tribe on my home soil,
I was brought back, trapped in the ways of the Rong.[1]
I lamented the millet ripening in the ancestral temple,
28 pained to see sprouting wheat in vacant neighborhoods.[2]
The great drums lay silent and unstruck,
the majestic bells, destroyed, were suspended no more.
The suburbs were deserted, strewn with bones;
32 townships empty and quiet, no cooking smoke anywhere.
Which of the one hundred clans was still there?[3]

> Of the "caps and sashes" of the Central Plain, those who had crossed the
> River with the Jin house amounted to a hundred clans.[4] Hence there
> were a hundred clan genealogies to the east of the Yangzi River. By now,
> however, those in the capital were almost completely destroyed.

All of the imperial princes were terminated.[5]
There was only Zhaojun's sorrowful music,
36 and the sad melody of the Commandery Princess.[6]

> Princesses and imperial daughters were dishonored and matched in
> marriage [with the rebels].

My heart was heavy when I passed by Changgan;

> The old Yan Family Lane was in Changgan.

gazing at Baixia, I was unable to tear myself away.[7]

> From Marquis Jing on down, the graves of all seven generations of my
> family were at Baixia.

---

4 "Caps and sashes" refers to the gentry.
5 *Wuzong* ("imperial princes") is literally "five clans," referring to the descendants
   from the sons by the same father and five different mothers, a term used to
   designate the descendants of the sons of Han Emperor Jing by five mothers. Hou
   Jing had killed most of Xiao Gang's sons.
6 Wang Zhaojun 王昭君 (fl. 33–20 BCE) was a Western Han palace lady married
   off to the Xiongnu khan. Wengzhu, translated as Commandery Princess, was a
   title given to the daughters of imperial princes in the Han. Here it refers to Liu
   Xijun 劉細君 (d. 101 BCE), daughter of a Western Han prince, who was married
   off to the king of Wusun 烏孫. The daughters of the Liang royal house were
   taken by the rebels. Hou Jing himself married Princess Liyang 溧陽公主, Xiao
   Gang's daughter.
7 Changgan was to the south of Jiankang and Baixia, to the northwest.

深燕雀之餘思
140 感桑梓之遺虔
得此心於尼甫
信茲言乎仲宣

邊西土之有眾
144 資方叔以薄伐

    永寧公以司徒為大都督。

撫鳴劍而雷咤
振雄旗而雲窣
千里追其飛走
148 三載窮於巢窟
屠蚩尤於東郡
挂郅支於北闕

    既斬侯景，烹屍於建業市，百姓食之，至于肉
    盡齕骨，傳首荊州，懸於都街。

弔幽魂之冤枉
152 掃園陵之蕪沒
殷道是以再興
夏祀於焉不忽

---

1 Mulberry and catalpa are planted about the homestead and remind one of one's
parents who have planted them.

Cherishing an intense homesickness that was shared even by swallows
    and sparrows,
40 I was moved by lasting longing for my parents that was stirred by the
    sight of mulberry and catalpa trees.[1]
I now understood the feelings of Confucius,
and I found Zhongxuan's words to be so true.[2]

The people of the distant land to the west
44 relied on Fangshu to undertake the campaign.[3]

> The Duke of Yongning in his capacity of the Minister of Education was
> appointed the Commander-in-chief.

He grasped his singing sword, which roared like thunder;
his virile banners were raised, fluttering like clouds.
For a thousand leagues he pursued the flying birds and running
    beasts,
48 after three years they were finally chased down to their nests and lairs.
He slayed Chiyou in the eastern commandery;
and hung Zhizhi's head on the northern palace tower.[4]

> After Hou Jing was executed, his body was boiled in the marketplace of
> Jiankang. People ate up his flesh and even chewed his bones. His head
> was sent to Jingzhou, where it was hung in the streets of the capital
> Jiangling.[5]

He offered condolences to the souls of those who died by injustice,
52 and swept clean the weeds overgrowing the imperial mausoleums.
The way of Yin was henceforth resurrected,
and the sacrifice of Xia was no longer neglected.[6]

---

2 When Confucius was traveling in the domain of Chen, he expressed homesickness
   for his home state of Lu. Zhongxuan is Wang Can (see VIII.19), who described
   his longing for home in his famous "Rhapsody on Climbing the Tower" 登樓賦
   during his exile in Jingzhou.
3 Fangshu was a worthy minister of King Xuan of Zhou (r. 827–782 BCE) who
   undertook campaigns against the barbarian tribes.
4 Chiyou was the mythical tribal leader who fought against the Yellow Emperor,
   and later the name became synonymous with an evildoer. Zhizhi was a Xiongnu
   khan who attacked the Han and was killed in 36 BCE.
5 Hou Jing's head was sent to Jiangling on June 18, 552. It had been about three
   years since he first rebelled.
6 By Yin (Shang) and Xia dynasties Yan Zhitui refers to the Liang.

但遺恨於炎崑

156　火延宮而累月

　　　　侯景既走，義師採稆失火，燒宮殿蕩盡也。

指余櫂於兩東

侍昇壇之五讓

欽漢官之復睹

160　赴楚民之有望

攝絳衣以奏言

忝黃散於官謗

　　　　時為散騎侍郎，奏舍人事也。

或校石渠之文

The only regret was that Kunlun had been set ablaze:[1]
156   the fire extended to the palaces and burned for months.

> After Hou Jing fled, the imperial troops, while gleaning wild grain,
> accidentally set a fire that burned the palace complex to the ground.

Pointing my oars at the twin Eastern Gates,
I attended upon the five deferrals on the altar.[2]
I appreciated how we once again were seeing the Han officials,
160   I hastened to join the ruler in whom the Chu people placed their
        hope.[3]
Gathering up my crimson robe,
    I presented my speech to the throne;
braving criticism for inadequacy,
    I filled in as a Gentleman Attendant at the Palace Gate.[4]

> At the time I was made Gentleman Cavalier Attendant, performing the
> duty of Secretary.

Sometimes I collated the texts of the Stone Dyke Tower,[5]

---

1 This refers to the saying in the *Book of Documents* that when the Kunlun is ablaze,
   both jade and stone are burned indiscriminately.
2 The Twin Eastern Gates refers to the two eastern gates of the capital Ying of the
   state of Chu, here designating Jiangling. Han Emperor Wen (r. 179–157 BCE)
   was said to have deferred five times before he agreed to take the throne. When
   asked by his ministers to become emperor, Xiao Yi deferred a number of times
   before he finally accepted.
3 When Emperor Guangwu (r. 25–57 CE) resurrected the Han rule, the people
   of Chang'an were pleased to "once again see the majestic bearings of the Han
   officials."
4 Crimson robe indicates a military office (Wang Liqi 680). Yan Zhitui had served
   as adjutant in the Section for Outer Troops in Xiao Fangzhu's military headquarters; but after he made his way back to Jiangling, he was appointed Gentleman
   Cavalier Attendant.
5 The Stone Dyke Tower was the name of an imperial library in the Western Han,
   here referring to Emperor Yuan's book collection.

王司徒表送祕閣舊事八萬卷，乃詔比校部分，
為正御、副御、重雜三本。左民尚書周弘正、
黃門郎彭僧朗、直省學士王珪、戴陵校經部，
左僕射王褒、吏部尚書宗懷正、員外郎顏之
推、直學士劉仁英校史部，廷尉卿殷不害、御
史中丞王孝紀、中書郎鄧藎、金部郎中徐報校
子部，右衞將軍庾信、中書郎王固、晉安王文
學宗善業、直省學士周確校集部也。

164　時參柏梁之唱
　　　顧甌甌之不算
　　　濯波濤而無量
　　　屬瀟湘之負罪
　　　　　陸納。

168　兼岷峨之自王
　　　　　武陵王。

1　Zhou Hongzheng: see VIII.17 and VIII.22. Nothing is known about the other
　　three, although one wonders if Wang Gui and the earlier Wen Gui (see original
　　note to ll. 88–89) may have been the same person.

2　Wang Bao was the famous writer (see XIX.2). One wonders if Liu Renying could
　　have been Liu Minying (see original note to ll. 88–89).

3　Yin Buhai (505–589) was a well-known administrator in the Liang court; he was
　　taken to Chang'an after the fall of Jiangling but was released and sent back south.
　　After the Sui conquered Chen in 589, his son came from the north to fetch him,
　　and he died on his way north. Xu Bao (d. 588), also known as Xu Jian 徐儉,
　　was Xu Ling's eldest son and Zhou Hongzheng's son-in-law.

The Minister of Education Wang [Sengbian] sent to Jiangling eighty
thousand scrolls from the imperial library. Emperor Yuan ordered to have
them collated and classified, and for each book to have three copies
made: the primary-imperial copy, the secondary-imperial copy, and the
miscellaneous-duplicate copy. Zhou Hongzheng, the director of the
Census Section, Peng Senglang, Gentleman of the Palace Gate, Wang Gui
and Dai Ling, Academicians on Duty in the Secretariat, collated the
Classics.[1] Wang Bao, Left Chief Administrator, Zong Huaizheng,
Minister of Personnel, Yan Zhitui, Supernumerary Gentleman Cavalier
Attendant, and Liu Renying, Academician on Duty in the Secretariat,
collated the Histories.[2] Yin Buhai, Chief Minister for Law Enforcement,
Wang Xiaoji, Palace Aide to the Censor-in-chief, Deng Jin, Attendant
Gentleman in the Secretariat, and Xu Bao, Gentleman of the Interior in
the Treasury Bureau, collated the Masters.[3] Yu Xin, Right General of the
Guards, Wang Gu, Attendant Gentleman in the Secretariat, Zong
Shanye, Instructor of the Prince of Jin'an, and Zhou Que, Academician
on Duty in the Secretariat, collated the Literary Collections.[4]

64   and often participated in versification on the Boliang Terrace.[5]
      I looked upon myself: this crude small vessel that did not amount to
          much
      now was bathed in endless billowing waves.
      At this juncture there was one
          who committed a crime by the Xiao and Xiang Rivers,
              That is, Lu Na.[6]
68   and there was also one
          who proclaimed himself king at the Min and Emei Mountains.
              That is, the Prince of Wuling.[7]

---

4 Yu Xin (513–581) was one of the most famous pre-Tang writers. Wang Gu (513–
   575) was the maternal nephew of Liang Emperor Wu. Zhou Que (529–587) was
   son of Zhou Hongzhi (500–575) and nephew of Zhou Hongrang (see VI.24).
   The Prince of Jin'an was Xiao Fangzhi 蕭方智 (543–558), Emperor Yuan's ninth
   son, but nothing is known about Zong Shanye, who was presumably a member
   of the prominent Zong clan of Jiangling.
5 Han Emperor Wu had reputedly composed "linked verse" with his officials on
   the Boliang (Cypress Beam) Terrace.
6 Lu Na, the governor of Xiangzhou, rebelled against Emperor Yuan in 552 but
   eventually surrendered. The Xiao and Xiang Rivers were in Xiangzhou (in modern Hu'nan).
7 The Prince of Wuling, Xiao Ji (see note to XIX.8), fought with Xiao Yi for the
   throne. Min and E are the Min Mountain and the Emei Mountain, both in
   Sichuan (Xiao Ji's fief).

竛既定以鳴鸞
修東都之大壯

> 詔司農卿黃文超營殿。

驚北風之復起
172 慘南歌之不暢

> 秦兵繼來。

守金城之湯池
轉絳宮之玉帳

> 孝元自曉陰陽兵法，初聞賊來，頗為厭勝，被
> 圍之後，每歎息，知必敗。

徒有道而師直
176 翻無名之不抗

> 孝元與宇文丞相斷金結和，無何見滅，是師出
> 無名。

民百萬而囚虜
書千兩而煙煬
溥天之下

---

1 Literally, repair the Great Grandeur of the eastern capital. The Great Grandeur is the name of a hexagram in the *Classic of Changes*, and the image of the hexagram evokes the shape of houses and palaces. In 553, Emperor Yuan had expressed the intention to move the capital back to Jiankang.
2 In 555 BCE, the state of Jin heard Chu was going to attack Jin. The Jin musician Shi Kuang 師曠 said he had sung a northern air and a southern air; the southern air was weak and had the sound of death, and so he knew the Chu army would not prevail.

Once order was restored, we awaited chariot bells to ring like simurghs,
setting out to repair the palaces of the eastern capital.[1]

> The emperor [Emperor Yuan] commanded Huang Wenchao, Chamber-
> lain for the National Treasury, to work on the palaces [at Jiankanag].

We were startled by the second rising of the north air,
72 and grieved by the weakness of the southern song.[2]

> The Qin army subsequently arrived.[3]

Keeping to the deep moat of a city as strong as metal,
the commander vacillated in the jade enclosure of the crimson
      palace.[4]

> Emperor Xiaoyuan was well-versed in *yin-yang* techniques and military
> strategies. When he first heard of the coming of the enemy troops, he
> was engaged in the method of suppression.[5] After the city was besieged,
> however, he would sigh frequently, certain of his defeat.

In vain we had the true way and our troops were honorable;
76 ultimately we failed to withstand the unrighteous army.

> Emperor Xiaoyuan made a metal-breaking pact with Prime
> Minister Yuwen, who nevertheless destroyed him.[6] This was a case of
> undertaking an unrighteous campaign.[7]

A million people were made captives;
several thousand cartloads of books were burned to ashes.[8]
In all the world under Heaven,

---

3 The Western Wei invaded and attacked Jiangling in 554.

4 The jade enclosure refers to the headquarters of an army commander.

5 The method of suppression here refers to a sort of black magic that was supposed
  to overpower the target of the spell.

6 The metal-breaking pact alludes to the saying, "If two people share the same
  heart, the sharpness [brought about by their alliance] will enable them to even
  break metal" 二人同心其利斷金. Prime Minister Yuwen refers to Yuwen Tai
  宇文泰 (507–556), the real power behind the Western Wei throne.

7 *Shichu wuming* 師出無名 is literally undertaking a military campaign with no
  (right) reason.

8 Emperor Yuan ordered to have his book collection burned on the eve of the fall
  of Jiangling. The Western Wei army took numerous people from Jiangling as
  captives to Chang'an, and many were made slaves.

180 斯文盡喪

> 北於墳籍少於江東三分之一，梁氏剝亂，散逸
> 湮亡。唯孝元鳩合，通重十餘萬，史籍以來，
> 未之有也。兵敗悉焚之，海內無復書府。

憐嬰孺之何辜
矜老疾之無狀
奪諸懷而棄草
184 踣於塗而受掠
冤乘輿之殘酷
軫人神之無狀
載下車以黜喪
188 拚桐棺之薨葬
雲無心以容與
風懷憤而慅悢
井伯飲牛於秦中
192 子卿牧羊於海上
留釧之妻，人銜其斷絕

---

1 In his *Account of Wronged Souls* 冤魂志, Yan Zhitui records a heart-breaking story
of a gentry member surnamed Liu who was forced to abandon his young son to
die in snow during the march to Chang'an. The man had already lost his entire
family during the Hou Jing Rebellion, and he begged the Wei commander for
his son's life in vain. He was so devastated that he fell sick and died shortly after
(*Yuanhun zhi* 88–89).

80 this culture of ours was completely lost.

> The books of the north were less than one third of those of the south.
> After the Liang fell into chaos, the imperial book collection [at Jiankang]
> was dispersed and destroyed. Emperor Xiaoyuan gathered the scattered
> books, and rebuilt a collection that amounted to over a hundred
> thousand scrolls. There had never been a book collection like this in the
> historical record. After his defeat, he had the entire collection burned.
> Afterward there was no great library left within the four seas.

I pitied the young children – what crime had they?
I commiserated with the elderly and the sick,
    who suffered for no reason.
Babies were snatched from their parents' arms,
    abandoned amidst the grass;[1]
84 adults stumbled and fell on the road, and received scourging.
I was cut to the quick by the cruel fate
    unjustly suffered by him who mounted the imperial chariot,[2]
I was pained by how men and gods
    could have committed such appalling deeds.
His body was transported by a crude cart,
    with no proper funerary rites;
88 it was placed in a coffin made of plain paulownia wood,
    buried hastily among the weeds.[3]
Even the heartless clouds lingered and hovered;
the wind, harboring bitterness, blew sad and strong.
Jingbo was made to water his oxen in the land of Qin;
92 Ziqing was to tend the flock of sheep by the North Sea.[4]
For the wife who left behind her bracelet,
    her man was distraught by their severance;

---

2 That is, Emperor Yuan.
3 After Emperor Yuan died, he was not given a proper burial.
4 Jingbo was a grandee of the domain of Yu that was conquered by Jin in 655 BCE.
   His story was confused with that of Baili Xi (see XVII.34), another grandee of
   Yu, who after Yu's conquest became a shepherd in Qin. Ziqing is Su Wu (d. 60 BCE),
   the faithful Han emissary to Xiongnu, who was detained for nineteen years and
   made a shepherd at the North Sea (Lake Baikal).

擊磬之子，家纏其悲愴

小臣恥其獨死
196　實有愧於胡顏
　　　牽痾疢而就路
　　　　　時患腳氣。
　　　策駑蹇以入關
　　　　　官給疲驢瘦馬。
　　　下無景而屬蹈
200　上有尋而亟騫
　　　嗟飛蓬之日永
　　　恨流梗之無還

　　　若乃五牛之旌
204　九龍之路
　　　土圭測影
　　　璿璣審度
　　　或先聖之規模
208　乍前王之典故
　　　與神鼎而偕沒
　　　切仙弓之永慕

---

1 The wife leaving her bracelet was Madam Wei 衛, wife of a Wang Da 王達, who was taken captive by Xianbei invaders in 302/303. She left a letter and her hairpin

for the son who struck the chime-stone,
  his family was entangled in grief.[1]

I, this humble subject, ashamed by my survival,
96 had no face left for not having died.
Debilitated by illness, I embarked on the journey,
    At the time I was suffering from beriberi.
whipping on the lame nag, I entered the pass.
    The officials were given feeble donkeys and emaciated horses.

No light [in the ravine] below, as we took one step after another;
00 seeking [clouds] above, as we frequently gathered up our robes.[2]
I lamented the eternal wandering of the blown tumbleweed;
I regretted that the floating peach-wood puppet would never go home.[3]

As for the banners carried by the five oxen,
04 the imperial carriage drawn by the nine dragons,[4]
the gnomon template used for measuring the sun's shadow,
the astrolabe for calculating the stars –
they were either fashioned and designed by previous sages,
08 or created as standards and precedents by former kings,
but now have all but vanished with the divine cauldrons,
evoking our lasting longing for the immortal bow.[5]

---

and bracelet for her family when passing through Zhangwutai (in modern Liaoning). The son striking a chime-stone was a slave whose father had died by execution and who was separated from his mother for three years without having seen her; the story is recorded in *Mr. Lü's Annals* (*Lüshi chunqiu*).

2 This couplet describes the captives' journey to Chang'an through mountainous landscape.

3 The peach-wood puppet floating on the river is a figure of utter helplessness (despite its being shaped in human form) from the *Intrigues of the Warring States*.

4 The five oxen drawing the imperial carriage carried banners on their backs. The nine dragons refer to the legendary steeds acquired by Han Emperor Wen.

5 The "divine cauldrons," the symbol of imperial power, were said to disappear in chaotic times and reappear in an age of peace and prosperity. The "immortal bow" had belonged to the Yellow Emperor; it dropped to the ground when he ascended to heaven, and courtiers who were unable to follow him clasped the bow and wept over his departure. These lines speak to the looting and the destruction of the precious objects and paraphernalia of the Liang, symbolic of the power of the state, and the death of the Liang emperor.

爾其十六國之風教
212　七十代之州壤
接耳目而不通
詠圖書而可想
何黎氓之匪昔
216　徒山川之猶曩
每結思於江湖
將取弊於羅網
聆代竹之哀怨
220　聽出塞之嘹朗
對皓月以增愁
臨芳樽而無賞

日太清之內釁
224　彼天齊而外侵
始蹙國於淮澔
遂壓境於江潯

侯景之亂，齊氏深斥梁家土宇，江北淮北唯餘
廬江、晉熙、高唐、新蔡、西陽、齊昌
數郡。至孝元之敗，於是盡矣，以江為界也。

The customs and teachings of the sixteen states,
212 the land passed down by the seventy generations,[1]
though separated from my ears and eyes in the past,
were well visualized in the course of my readings.
Yet how different were their people now!
216 Only mountains and waters still retained their old look.
I often thought of withdrawing to the rivers and lakes,
but I feared being caught in traps and nets.[2]
I listened to the melancholy bamboo flute of the Dai,
220 or to the shrill sound of "Going out the Frontier."[3]
Facing the bright moon only increased my sorrow;
even the goblet of sweet ale failed to bring relief.

In the old days, as internal trouble began during the Taiqing era,[4]
224 Heaven's Navel had made raids from outside.[5]
At first they reduced the state to the Huai riverbanks,
then they pressed on the territory to the Yangzi shores.

> During the Hou Jing Rebellion, the [Northern] Qi had taken a large part
> of Liang's territory. To the north of the Yangzi and Huai rivers, only
> Lujiang, Jinxi, Gaotang, Xincai, Xiyang, and Qichang commanderies
> were left. When Emperor Xiaoyuan was defeated, even those
> commanderies were all taken, with the Yangzi River now as the boundary
> line between the two states.

---

1 The "sixteen states" were those enfeoffed to the sons of King Wen of Zhou. The
    phrase "seventy generations" alludes to the descendants of the legendary emperor
    Shennong. The sixteen states and seventy generations indicate the ancient Han
    civilization of the Chinese heartland.
2 That is, he longed to withdraw from public service but was afraid being punished
    by law.
3 The music of Dai refers to northern music. "Going out the Frontier" is the title
    of a Han music piece inspired by Hu/Tatar music.
4 Taiqing is the name of Liang Emperor Wu's last reign (547–549).
5 The region of Qi (modern Shandong) is referred to as "tian Qi," a phrase from
    the *Historian's Record*, which states that Qi is the land corresponding to the navel
    (qi) of heaven. Here it is used to refer to the Northern Qi.

獲仁厚之麟角

228　剋儁秀之南金

爰眾旅而納主

車五百以夏臨

　　　齊遣上黨王渙率兵數萬納梁貞陽侯明為主。

返季子之觀樂

232　釋鍾儀之鼓琴

　　　梁武聘使謝挺、徐陵始得還南，凡厥梁臣，皆
　　　以禮遣。

竊聞風而清耳

傾見日之歸心

試拂蓍以貞筮

236　遇交泰之吉林

　　　之推聞梁人返國，故有犇齊之心。以丙子歲旦
　　　筮東行吉不，遇泰之坎，乃喜曰："天地交泰
　　　而更習坎重險，行而不失其信，此吉卦也，但
　　　恨小往大來耳。後遂吉也。"

譬欲秦而更楚

假南路於東尋

1　Unicorn's horns are a figure for rare talented people, also members of the nobility.
The "southern gold" is a figure for talented men of the south. This refers to Qi's
acquisition of many Liang royal family members and courtiers.

2　Ming refers to Xiao Yuanming 蕭淵明 (d. 556), son of Liang Emperor Wu's elder
brother, Xiao Yi 蕭懿 (d. 500). He was captured during a failed military campaign
against Qi in 547. After Emperor Yuan's death, Qi ordered Gao Huan (533–558)
to escort Xiao Yuanming back to be the new Liang emperor in early 555.

They captured the kind and generous "unicorn's horns,"

228   they overpowered the outstanding "southern gold."[1]

They sent a multitude of troops to escort a ruler,

and five hundred chariots arrived from afar.

> Qi sent Gao Huan, the Prince of Shangdang, to lead an army of tens of
> thousands to escort Liang's Marquis of Zhenyang, Ming, back to be the
> Liang ruler.[2]

They returned the music-observing Jizi,

232   and released the zither-strumming Zhong Yi.[3]

> Liang Emperor Wu's emissaries, Xie Ting and Xu Ling, were able to
> return to the south.[4] All Liang courtiers were sent back with proper rites.

As I got wind of the news, I secretly perked my ears;

my heart was bent on going home to see the sun again.

I shook the milfoil to divine the portent,

236   and encountered the auspicious "interaction in peace."

> When I heard that the Liang people were allowed to return south,
> I planned to flee to Qi. On the new year's day of the *bingzi* year
> [January 28, 556], I made a divination about the outcome of the
> eastward journey. I came across the "Tai" ("Peace") and "Kan" ("Pit")
> hexagrams. I was delighted, saying to myself, "'Heaven and earth interact
> in peace,' and then there is the 'double pits with twofold perils.' But
> 'despite treading [in danger], one does not lose faith.' This is auspicious.
> I only dislike the 'small going and great coming.' But the outcome
> should be auspicious."

Like the man who wanted to go to Qin by way of Chu,

so did I seek a path to the south by traveling east.[5]

---

3 Jizi or Ji Zha (see note to X.10a), the Wu prince, traveled to Lu; he was treated
   with a performance of the music of various states and made insightful comments
   about each piece. Zhong Yi was a musician of Chu who became a captive in Jin.
   When the lord of Jin asked him to play music, he played his native tunes, and
   was permitted to return to his homeland.

4 Xu Ling (507–583) was a famous writer and poet of the Liang. Xie Ting, mayor
   of Jiankang, and Xu Ling were sent on a diplomatic mission to the Eastern Wei
   in 548. After the Hou Jing Rebellion broke out, they were detained in Qi until
   555. Xu Ling later served in the Chen court.

5 Tian Jiu 田鳩 had wanted to see King Huiwen of Qin 秦惠文王 (r. 337–311
   BCE) but could not, so he went south to Chu and managed then to become an
   emissary to Qin.

乘龍門之一曲
240 歷砥柱之雙岑
　　冰夷風薄而雷响
　　陽侯山載而谷沉
　　侔挈龜以憑濬
244 類斬蛟而赴深
　　昏揚舲於分陝
　　曙結纜於河陰

　　　　水路七百里一夜而至。

　　追風飆之逸氣
248 從忠信以行吟

　　遭厄命而事旋
　　舊國從於採芑
　　先廢君而誅相
252 訖變朝而易市

　　　　至鄴，便值陳興而梁滅，故不得還南。

　　遂留滯於漳濱
　　私自憐其何已

---

1 The Dragon Gate is a gorge of the Yellow River, with steep cliffs facing each
  other like a gateway. Dizhu or the Whetstone Pillar: see note to the poem "Passing
  by Dizhu at Night on the Way from Zhou to Qi."
2 Pingyi is the river god and Yanghou, the god of billows.
3 The Duke of Zhou and the Duke of Shao had divided their fiefs respectively to
  the east and west of Shan county (in modern Shaanxi). The "dividing line at
  Shan" refers to the Western Wei territory. Heyin, literally the south shore of the

Taking advantage of the river's bend at the Dragon Gate,
40 I passed through the twin peaks of Dizhu.[1]
Pingyi's wind struck, his thunder roared,
Yanghou's surf overbore the mountains and sank the valley.[2]
Like grabbing the turtle's severed head over the depths,
44 or reaching the river's bottom and slaying the *jiao*-dragon,[3]
in twilight we raised sail from the dividing line at Shan,
at dawn we tied the hawser at Heyin.[4]

> We traveled seven hundred leagues by river and arrived in one night.

Pursuing the lofty air of the whirlwind,
48 I chanted on the journey, relying on faithfulness and constancy.

I encountered bad luck, as the situation changed:
my old state had gone with the "gathered white millet."[5]
The ruler was first deposed, then the prime minister put to death;
52 the court was ultimately changed, and the marketplace, transformed.[6]

> After I arrived at Ye, the Chen dynasty was established and the Liang was terminated, and so I was unable to return to the south.

Thus I was trapped, tarrying by the Zhang River,
feeling endless pity for my life.

Yellow River, is the name of a county in modern He'nan and represents the Northern Qi territory.

4 The warrior Gu Yezhi 古冶子 had reputedly killed a gigantic turtle that attacked Duke Jing of Qi's (r. 548–490 BCE) horse when they were crossing the Yellow River. Zhou Chu 周處 (236–297) was said to have killed a man-eating tiger and a fierce *jiao*-dragon (perhaps a species of crocodile) in his youth.

5 The people of the state of Qi had sung a song of "gathering the white millet" and predicting the Tian clan would replace the Jiang house to rule Qi. This refers to the Liang's replacement by Chen. Since Qi's Tian clan was believed to have descended from the noble house surnamed Chen, the allusion here is particularly appropriate.

6 Defeated by Qi's army, Wang Sengbian deposed Emperor Yuan's son and successor, Xiao Fangzhi, and established Xiao Yuanming as emperor in the summer of 555. Soon afterward, Chen Baxian 陳霸先 (503–559), another Liang general, attacked and killed Wang Sengbian, deposed Xiao Yuanming, and put Xiao Fangzhi back on the throne. He forced Xiao Fangzhi to abdicate in 557 and established the Chen.

謝黃鵠之迴集

256 恧翠鳳之高峙

曾微令思之對

空竊彥先之仕

纂書盛化之旁

260 待詔崇文之裏

> 齊武平中，署文林館，待詔者僕射陽休之、祖
> 孝徵以下三十餘人，之推專掌，其撰修文殿御
> 覽、續文章流別等皆詣進賢門奏之。

珥貂蟬而就列

執麾蓋以入齒

> 時以通直散騎常侍遷黃門郎也。

款一相之故人

> 故人祖僕射掌機密，吐納帝令也。

264 賀萬乘之知己

祗夜語之見忌

---

1 In a song sung by Liu Xijun, a Han princess married off to the Wusun, she
   wishes to fly home like a yellow swan. The phoenix is selective about its dwelling
   place and only perches on the paulownia tree.

2 Lingsi was the courtesy name of Hua Tan 華譚 (d. 322), a native of Wu. After
   Jin's conquest of Wu, he presented a series of good answers to the civil service
   examination questions devised by Jin Emperor Wu 晉武帝 (r. 265–290). Yanxian
   was the courtesy name of Gu Rong 顧榮 (d. 312), another native of Wu who
   had served the Western Jin.

3 Shenghua (Flourishing Civilization) was the name of a palace gate in the Eastern
   Han; it is mentioned in a memorial presented to the throne in 177 by the scholar

I was humbled by the roosting yellow swan,
256 and put to shame by the cyan-plumed phoenix's lofty perch.[1]
I had not presented the replies of a Lingsi,
yet I usurped the office of a Yanxian.[2]
We compiled books by the Shenghua Gate,
260 and awaited imperial edicts in the Chongwen Institute.[3]

> During the Wuping era of the Qi, more than thirty men were appointed
> Attendees at the Grove of Letters Institute, including Chief Administrator
> Yang Xiuzhi, Zu Xiaozheng, and so forth, and I was put in charge.[4] After
> we compiled the *Imperial View at the Xiuwen Hall*, the *Sequel to the
> 'Collection of Literature Arranged by Genre,'* and other works, we would go
> to the Jinxian Gate and present them to the throne.[5]

My hat decorated with sable and cicada, I went into the ranks;
with banners and canopy I took my place among my peers.

> At the time, I was promoted to be Gentleman of the Palace Gate, from
> Senior Recorder for Comprehensive Duty.

On close terms with the prime minister, an old friend,

> My old friend, Chief Administrator Zu, handled the secrets of the state
> and relayed the imperial orders.[6]

264 I felt fortunate that the ruler appreciated me.[7]
Only because of those nocturnal conversations
    I had become the target of envy,

> Cai Yong (133–192) (see VI.9) advising the emperor to uphold a higher standard
> in appointing scholars. Chongwen (Promoting Culture) is the name of an insti-
> tute for scholars established by Wei Emperor Ming (r. 227–239).

4 Wuping was the name of the second reign-period (570–577) of the Northern
   Qi's Last Ruler 後主, Gao Wei 高緯 (556–577, r. 565–577). The Grove of
   Letters Institute (Wenlin guan) was established in the spring of 573. Yang Xiuzhi:
   see XVIII.5. Zu Xiaozheng is featured in several sections in the *Family Instructions*; see, for instance, VI.19.

5 *The Imperial View at the Xiuwen Hall* was a large encyclopedia. The *Collection of
   Literature Arranged by Genre* (*Wenzhang liubie*) was an influential early anthology
   compiled by Zhi Yu 摯虞 (d. 311); it had a sequel compiled by Kong Ning 孔寗
   (Kong Ningzi 孔寗子, d. 425), which was different from the one mentioned
   here.

6 This was Zu Xiaozheng.

7 *Wansheng*, the ruler, is literally "[the one with] the ten thousand chariots."

寧懷刷之足恃
諫譖言之矛戟
268　惕險情之山水
由重裘以寒勝
用去薪而沸止

　　時武職疾文人，之推蒙禮遇，每搆創痏。故侍
　　中崔季舒等六人以諫誅，之推爾日隣禍，而儕
　　流或有毀之推於祖僕射者，僕射察之無實，所
　　知如舊不忘。

予武成之燕翼
272　遵春坊而原始
唯驕奢之是修
亦佞臣之云使

---

1 The warlord Cao Cao often spoke with Du Xi 杜襲 (fl. 196–231) till late at night, which incited jealousy in Wang Can (see VIII.19). This might also be a reference to Han Emperor Wen's late-night conversation with Jia Yi (200–168 BCE). In the latter case, the emperor only spoke with Jia Yi about supernatural matters, not about state affairs. The Lord of Jingguo 靖郭君 (fl. 341–301 BCE), prime minister of the state of Qi, gave a hairbrush to his attendant, who was subsequently considered an important person by others because of his perceived closeness to the prime minister.

how could one rely on the gift of a hairbrush?[1]
I was pierced by slanderous words,
   which were like spears and halberds;
268 I became apprehensive about human feelings,
   which were more perilous than mountains and waters.[2]
Thanks to the heavy fur, I was able to overcome cold;
because the firewood was removed, water stopped boiling.

> At the time, the military officers detested men of letters. I received
> favorable treatment from the emperor, and so was often hurt by slander.
> Therefore, when Cui Jishu, the Palace Attendant, and five others were
> executed for remonstrating,[3] I was almost caught up in tragedy myself on
> that day. Some colleagues slandered me to Chief Administrator Zu, who
> looked into it and found it to be without basis, and continued to treat
> me just as before.

I had provided a swallow's wing [support] to Emperor Wucheng,
272 and we must trace the Spring Ward to its roots.[4]
Only arrogance and extravagance were ever cultivated,
and sycophants were employed in service.

---

2 The remark that the human heart is more perilous than mountains and rivers is
  attributed to Confucius in *Zhuangzi*.
3 Cui Jishu (d. 573), Zhang Diaohu 張雕虎 (519–573), Liu Ti 劉逖 (525–573),
  Feng Xiaoyan 封孝琰 (523–573), Pei Ze 裴澤, and Guo Zun 郭遵 remonstrated
  with the Last Ruler about his decision to go to Jinyang and were all executed on
  the same day in the winter of 573.
4 Emperor Wucheng refers to Gao Zhan 高湛 (537–569, r. 561–565). He decided
  to abdicate to his son, Gao Wei (the Last Ruler), in the summer of 565. The
  Spring Ward, also known as the Spring Palace, is the name of the residence of
  the Crown Prince. This couplet and the original note following it offer criticism
  not only of the Last Ruler but also of his father, Emperor Wucheng, who did not
  set a good example for his son and heir.

武成奢侈，後宮御者數百人，食於水陸貢獻珍
異，至乃厭飽，棄於廁中。褌衣悉羅纈錦繡珍
玉，織成五百一段。爾後宮披遂為舊事。後主
之在宮，乃使駱提婆母陸氏為之，又胡人何洪
珍等為左右，後皆預政亂國焉。

惜染絲之良質
276　惰琢玉之遺祉
用夷吾而治臻
昵狄牙而亂起

祖孝徵用事，則朝野翕然，政刑有綱紀矣。駱
提婆等苦孝徵以法繩己，譖而出之。於是教令
昏僻，至于滅亡。

誠怠荒於度政
280　惋驅除之神速
肇平陽之爛魚
次太原之破竹

晉州小失利，便棄軍還并，又不守并州，犇走
向鄴。

寔未改於弦望

1 *Zhicheng* is the name of an expensive brocade fabric.
2 Madame Lu was Lu Lingxuan 陸令萱 (d. 576), who had been a wet nurse to
  Gao Wei, the Last Ruler. She and her son Luo Tipo (aka Mu Tipo 穆提婆,
  d. 577) became extremely powerful in the last years of Gao Wei's reign.

Emperor Wucheng was extravagant. The ladies in his harem, numbering several hundreds, ate rare delicacies from land and water offered as tribute; when sated, they would throw the rest of the food into the latrine. They were all dressed in silk, gauze, brocade, and fine embroideries decorated with precious jewels; the *zhicheng* brocade they used cost 500 cash per section.[1] This henceforth became an established custom in the inner palace. When the Last Ruler was in the Spring Ward, he put Luo Tipo's mother, Madame Lu, in charge [of the household]; he also used He Hongzhen, a Tatar, and others like him as his attendants.[2] Later they all intervened in governance and brought chaos to the state.

How regrettable that fine nature was influenced like dyed silk,
76 and that inherited blessings were spoiled by the unpolished jade.
When Yiwu was used, good government ensued;
but intimacy with Diya led to chaos.[3]

When Zu Xiaozheng was in power, court and commons were at peace, and there was order in state administration and legal matters. Luo Tipo and his like resented how Zu Xiaozheng controlled them with law, so they slandered him and sent him into exile. Thereafter imperial instructions became muddled and deviant, and the state eventually came to ruin.

Truly the court was indolent and profligate in governance,
80 yet I regret how swiftly it was swept away.
It began at Pingyang, like a fish rotting from within;
then Taiyuan fell, as easily as splitting bamboo.[4]

After a minor defeat at Jinzhou, the [Last Ruler] abandoned the army and went to Bingzhou; instead of defending Bingzhou, he further fled to Ye.[5]

Indeed the moon had not yet become full again,

---

3 Yiwu was Guan Zhong (see XVIII.10), the statesman of Qi who helped Duke Huan of Qi achieve hegemony. In his late years Duke Huan trusted several malevolent courtiers including Diya (better known as Yiya 易牙), the palace chef; they conspired together and caused the decline of Qi.

4 Pingyang and Taiyuan (known as Jinyang) were both part of Jinzhou or Jin prefecture (in modern Shanxi).

5 Gao Wei left Bingzhou in the charge of Gao Yanzong (see below) and fled to Ye on January 17, 577. For the dating of the events in the last months of the Northern Qi rule, I follow Sima Guang's (1019–1086) *Comprehensive Mirror in Aid of Governance* 資治通鑑.

284 遂□□□□□
及都口而昇降
懷墳墓之淪覆
迷識主而狀人
288 競已棲而擇木
六馬紛其顛沛
千官散於犇逐
無寒瓜以療饑
292 靡秋螢而照宿
　　　　時在季冬，故無此物。

讎敵起於舟中
胡越生於輦轂
壯安德之一戰
296 邀文武之餘福
屍狼藉其如莽
血玄黃以成谷

84   and then....[1]
      When [the capital?]....rose and fell,
      I was grieved by the destruction of the ancestral tombs.
      Befuddled in recognizing the [right] ruler and evaluating men,
88   the nesting birds vied with one another to select a new roost.[2]
      The Six Steeds stumbled and fell into disorder;
      as a thousand officials dispersed in flight.[3]
      There were no cold melons to cure hunger,
92   nor autumn fireflies to illuminate camping at night.[4]

            It was in the last month of winter, so we had none of those things.[5]

      Those sharing the boat turned into foes;
      Hu and Yue appeared at the hubs of the imperial chariot.[6]
      How stalwart was the Prince of Ande, fighting one last battle,
96   seeking whatever was left from the blessings of Wen and Wu.[7]
      Corpses were piled up and scattered like weeds;
      blood flowing black and yellow in streams.

---

1 The text is corrupt here and in the next line.
2 Many courtiers, including Mu Tipo, left Gao Wei and surrendered to the Northern Zhou at this juncture.
3 The Six Steeds refers to the emperor's carriage.
4 The first line alludes to the story that when the King of Wu fled from the King
   of Yue's army, he found a snake melon (also known as snake cucumber) in the
   wilds and ate it. In the chaos at the end of the Eastern Han, the "Young Emperor"
   Liu Bian 劉辯 (176–190, r. 189) and his brother were kidnapped by palace
   eunuchs and had to travel on foot at night by the light of fireflies.
5 It was the twelfth month of the *bingshen* year (January 5 to February 3, 577).
6 That is, they became adversaries. This comes from a memorial written by the
   Western Han writer Sima Xiangru, in which he urged Han Emperor Wu to stop
   hunting expeditions because of the inherent danger of hunting, comparing an
   animal attack to Hu and Yue barbarians emerging at the hubs of the imperial
   chariot.
7 The Prince of Ande refers to Gao Yanzong 高延宗 (544–577), the son of Gao
   Cheng 高澄 (posthumous title Emperor Wenxiang 文襄帝, 521–549), nephew
   of Emperor Wucheng (see above). Emperors Wen and Wu may refer to Gao
   Huan 高歡 (496–547, posthumous title Emperor Shenwu 神武), the father of
   Northern Qi's founding emperor Gao Yang 高洋 (Emperor Wenxuan 文宣帝,
   r. 550–559). This could also refer to Emperors Wenxuan and Wucheng.

後主犇後，安德王延宗收合餘燼，於并州夜
戰，殺數千人。周主欲退，齊將之降周者告以
虛實，故留至明而安德敗也。

天命縱不可再來
300　猶賢死廟而慟哭

乃詔余以典郡
據要路而問津

　　　除之推為平原郡，據河津，以為犇陳之計。

斯呼航而濟水
304　郊鄉導於善鄰

　　　約以鄴下一戰不剋，當與之推入陳。

不羞寄公之禮
願為式微之賓
忽成言而中悔
308　矯陰疏而陽親
信詔謀於公王
競受陷於姦臣

> After the Last Ruler fled, Gao Yanzong, the Prince of Ande, gathered the
> remaining forces and fought a nightlong battle at Bingzhou, slaying
> several thousand enemy soldiers. The Zhou ruler was about to retreat,
> but a Qi general who surrendered to Zhou told him the real situation, so
> the Zhou ruler stayed till dawn, and the Prince of Ande was defeated.[1]

Even if heaven's mandate could not be obtained again,
300 it was still more worthy than bursting into tears and committing
    suicide in the ancestral temple.[2]

Then an imperial edict ordered me to take charge of a commandery,
occupying an important route for the sake of the ford.

> I was appointed Magistrate of Pingyuan commandery to hold the Yellow
> River's ford, so as to execute the plan of seeking refuge in Chen.

It was to summon the boat and cross the water,
304 and I was to act as a guide and take my ruler to our good neighbor.

> The emperor agreed that, should the imperial army not prevail in
> the battle defending Ye, he would go to Chen with me.

The emperor was not embarrassed to become a dependent lord,
and was quite willing to be a guest in the time of decline.
But neglecting a pact already made, he changed his mind midway;
308 showing affection on the surface, he secretly became estranged.
He believed a flattering plot put forth by noble lords,
and eventually suffered downfall at the hands of wicked vassals.

---

1 This bloody battle took place on the night of January 20, 557.
2 This refers to the Prince of Beidi 北地王, Liu Chen 劉諶 (d. 263), who was the
  son of Liu Shan 劉禪 (r. 223–263), the Last Ruler of the Shu-Han regime in the
  Three Kingdoms Period. On the eve of Shu-Han's defeatt, Liu Chen refused to
  surrender to the Wei army; he wept, killed his wife and children, and committed
  suicide in the ancestral temple.

丞相高阿那肱等不願入南，又懼失齊主則得罪
於周朝，故疏間之推。所以齊主留之推守平原
城，而索船渡濟向青州。阿那肱求自鎮濟州，
乃啟報應齊主云：“無賊，勿怱怱。”遂道周
軍追齊主而及之。

攘九圍以制命

今八尺而由人

四七之期必盡

百六之數溢屯

趙郡李穆叔調妙占天文算術，齊初踐祚計止於
二十八年。至是如期而滅。

予一生而三化

備荼苦而蓼辛

在揚都值侯景殺簡文而篡位，於江陵逢孝元覆
滅，至此而三為亡國之人。

鳥焚林而鎩翮

魚奪水而暴鱗

嗟宇宙之遼曠

愧無所而容身

夫有過而自訟

Gao E'nagui, the prime minister, and some others did not want to go to the south. They also feared that, if they let the Qi ruler get away, they would be held responsible by the Zhou court. So they spoke ill of me to the Qi ruler and alienated him from me. Thereupon the Qi ruler left me in charge of Pingyuan but ordered a boat to go himself to Qingzhou instead. E'nagui requested to command Jizhou himself, and sent a report to the Qi ruler, saying, "The enemy is nowhere to be seen. Do not panic." He then showed the way to the Zhou army, which pursued the Qi ruler and captured him.[1]

In the past his wishes were carried out through the nine regions,
12 but now this body eight *chi* tall was at the mercy of others.
The period of "four sevens" was fated to come to an end;
the number of "one hundred and six" had suddenly been reached.[2]

Li Mushu of Zhao commandery was very good at divination through his command of astronomy and arithmetic.[3] When Qi was first founded, he had prophesied that it would only last twenty-eight years. Now it was indeed conquered at the predicted time.

This life of mine has undergone three transformations,
16 filled with the bitter flavor of sow-thistle and knotweed.

At Yangdu, Hou Jing assassinated Emperor Jianwen and usurped the throne. At Jiangling, Emperor Xiaoyuan met with destruction. By now I have three times become a man of a fallen state.

A bird has had its home grove burned, its wings clipped,
a fish is taken out of water, its scales exposed to the sun.
Alas, so vast is the universe,
20 I am mortified that there is no place to lodge this body of mine.
When making a mistake, one should reproach oneself,

---

1 Gao Wei went to Jizhou on February 24, 557, and then left for Qingzhou the next day. He planned to go to Chen from Qingzhou, but Gao E'nagui, his trusted minister, lulled him into believing that the Zhou army was still faraway. Gao E'nagui subsequently surrendered Jizhou, which allowed the Zhou army to chase and capture Gao Wei on February 28. For my rendering of *dao*, see Additional Notes.

2 "Four sevens" equals twenty-eight, explained in the original note that follows this couplet. There are a number of divination theories regarding the number 106; simply put, it indicates disaster and disorder.

3 For Li Mushu, see XVII.39. I render *suanshu* as arithmetic to distinguish from *shushu* 數術 or 術數, numerology. It is, however, possible that Li Mushu was skilled in numerology rather than arithmetic.

始發矇於天真
遠絕聖而棄智
324　妄鎖義以羈仁
舉世溺而欲拯
王道鬱以求申
既銜石以填海
328　終荷戟以入榛
亡壽陵之故步
臨大行以逡巡
向使潛於草茅之下
332　甘為畎畝之人
無讀書而學劍
莫抵掌以膏身
委明珠而樂賤
336　辭白璧以安貧
堯舜不能榮其素樸
桀紂無以汙其清塵
此窮何由而至
340　茲辱安所自臻
而今而後
不敢怨天而泣麟也

thus beginning to recover from blindness and return to one's true nature.
Far from "forsaking sagacity and abandoning wisdom,"
524   I have been vainly fettered by righteousness and trapped by benevolence.[1]
When the world was drowning, I wanted to save it;
when the kingly way was blocked, I sought its expansion.
But after having tried to use pebbles to fill the ocean,
528   eventually I entered a thorny thicket carrying a halberd.[2]
Having lost the former gait of Shouling,
I face Mount Taihang, unable to advance.[3]
Suppose that I had hidden myself in a thatched hut,
532   content to be a man plowing the fields,
having never read a book or studied swordsmanship,
or clapped my hands to make a sacrifice of my body,[4]
but rather declined the bright pearl and took pleasure in lowliness,
536   refused the white jade and remained complacent in poverty,
then even Yao and Shun could not extol my simplicity,
nor could Jie and Zhou tarnish my purity.[5]
Where can this adversity have come from?
540   How can I have suffered from such humiliation?
From today, and hereafter,
I will not dare complain of heaven or weep for the captured unicorn.[6]

---

1 The Daoist philosophy advocates "forsaking sagacity and abandoning wisdom,"
   and dismissing Confucian concepts of "righteousness and benevolence."
2 A legend had it that the young daughter of the Fiery Emperor drowned in the
   eastern sea and turned into a bird named Jingwei, which vowed to fill the ocean
   with branches and pebbles from the western hills. "Carrying a halberd and entering a thicket" is a figure for being trapped in a difficult situation.
3 A Zhuangzi parable tells of a man from Shouling who admired the way the
   people of Handan walked; he emulated them but was unable to do it, meanwhile
   forgetting how he used to walk, so he had to crawl back to Shouling. Mount
   Taihang is featured in several well-known earlier poems in which the speaker is
   daunted by the prospect of getting through the mountain range.
4 Clapping one's hands is a gesture indicative of getting excited and animated in
   talking, and usually describes a persuader or a counselor.
5 Yao and Shun were mythical sage rulers; Jie and Zhou were the last evil kings of
   Xia and Shang.
6 The appearance of a unicorn is a sign of a peaceful and prosperous time. In 481
   BCE, Confucius wept at the capture of a unicorn during the Duke of Lu's hunting trip, since the unicorn had appeared at the wrong time and died in captivity.

稽聖賦

1.

豪豕自為雌雄[1]
決鼻生無牝牡

2.

黿鱉伏乎其陰
麢鸙孕乎其口[2]

3.

魚不咽水

4.

雀奚夕瞽?
鷗奚晝盲?

5.

雎鳩奚別？
鴛鴦奚雙？

---

1 That is, the porcupine.
2 That is, the hare.

Rhapsody on Questioning the Sages [Fragments]

1.

A "prickly pig" can be both female and male;[1]
the "cracked nose" is genderless at birth.[2]

2.

The giant and lesser soft-shelled turtles hatch eggs through their
   genitals;
the cormorant gives birth through its mouth.

3.

Fish does not swallow water.

4.

Why is the sparrow visionless at night?
Why is the owl sightless during the day?

5.

Why do the fish-hawks stand apart?[3]
Why are the mandarin ducks paired?

---

3 Under the entry on fish-hawks 雎鳩 in *Pi Ya* (*Augmented Ya*) 7, Lu Dian 陸佃
(1042–1102) cites a common saying that fish-hawks would fly in pair when
mating but stand apart from each other when perching.

6.

蛇曉方藥
鴆善禁呪

7.

蠐螬行以其背
蟪蛄鳴非其口

8.

蛷旋於影
蜮射於光

9.

竹布實而根枯
蕉舒花而株槁

---

1 A fifth-century story collection records that a farmer once saw a snake taking an herb to heal an injured snake, and the farmer later used the same herb to cure human wounds and sores.

2 *Zhen* is a fabulous bird that supposedly has poisonous feathers. Some ornithologists speculate that it may be the crested serpent eagle, which lives in southern China and eats snakes. According to *Pi ya*, the *zhen* bird can cast a spell on a rock and use the rock to kill snakes for food.

6.

Snake understands the way of medicine;[1]
the serpent eagle is good at casting spells.[2]

7.

Grubs walk with their back;[3]
the kempfer cicada sings, but not with its mouth.[4]

8.

The earwig urinates at shadow;[5]
the sand-spitter spews toward light.[6]

9.

When bamboo forms fruit, its roots wither;
when plantain spreads flowers, its stalk wilts.

---

3 *Qicao*, grubs, are the larvae of scarab beetles and live underground.
4 Cicadas produce sounds by contracting the ribbed membranes at the base of their
   abdomen.
5 *Qiu* is also called *qusou* 蠼螋, earwig, which is a mostly nocturnal insect living
   in crevices. It is believed to urinate in a person's shadow and make the person
   develop a rash.
6 *Yu* is said to spew water or sand at a person and cause harm (some say it spews
   at a person's shadow). Some scholars believe *yu* is the bombardier beetle, but that
   does not fit the early medieval Chinese description of *yu* as a river-dwelling
   creature that resembles a turtle but has three legs. It is best to take it as a fabulous
   creature.

10.

瓜寒於曝
油冷於煎

11.

芩根為蟬

12.

魏嫗何多
一孕四十
中山何夥
有子百廿

13.

水母

---

1 The reasons for a melon to manage to remain cool in the sun are said to be manifold. One of them is that the melon is spherical and does not have much surface for the sun to shine on for its volume.

2 Oil's boiling point is much higher than that of water.

3 *Chan* should probably be emended to *shan* 鱓 (eel). See Additional Notes.

10.

Melon stays cool in the sun;[1]
oil remains cold when boiled.[2]

11.

The root of the runner-reed metamorphoses into cicadas.[3]

12.

Why was the Wei woman so fecund,
rearing forty at one pregnancy?[4]
Why was the Zhongshan prince so fertile,
siring one hundred and twenty children?[5]

13.

"Water-mother"[6]

---

4 As Wang Liqi points out, Wei should be Zheng 鄭. According to the *Bamboo Annals* 竹書紀年, a chronicle interred in the tomb of King Xiang of Wei in 296 BCE and discovered in the late third century, in 487 BCE "a woman in the state of Zheng gave birth to forty children, twenty of whom died."

5 The Prince of Zhongshan 中山, Liu Sheng 劉勝 (165–113 BCE), of the Western Han, was said to have sired more than one hundred and twenty children.

6 That is, jellyfish. See Additional Notes.

14.

爰有女人
感彼死馬
化為蠶蟲
衣被天下

14.

There was a woman,
who was moved by a dead horse;
she transformed into the silkworm,
and subsequently clothes the entire world.[1]

---

1 This refers to the legend about the origin of the silkworm. A girl's father was
  kidnapped and she made an oath to marry whoever could get her father back;
  her father's horse carried him back, but the father became angry upon learning
  of the daughter's oath and killed the horse, leaving the horse's hide to dry in the
  courtyard. The hide rose up, wrapped the girl in it, and flew away. Later, the
  hide was found on a mulberry tree, and the girl turned into a silkworm eating
  mulberry leaves and producing silk.

Abbreviations

Baopuzi neipian	Ge Hong 葛洪 (283–343), *Baopuzi neipian* 抱朴子內篇, comp. Wang Ming 王明. Taibei: Liren shuju, 1981.
Bao Tingbo	鮑廷博 (1728–1814), *Yanshi jiaxun* 顏氏家訓. Shugu tang ying Song ben chongdiao 述古堂影宋本重雕. Zhibuzu zhai congshu 知不足齋叢書 11.
Beihu lu	Duan Gonglu 段公路 (fl. 869–871), Beihu *lu* 北戶錄. In *Yingyin Wenyuange siku quanshu* 景印文淵閣四庫全書, Vol. 589. Taibei: Shangwu yinshuguan, 1983.
Bei Qi shu (BQS)	Li Baiyao 李百藥 (564–647), comp. *Bei Qi shu* 北齊書. Beijing: Zhonghua shuju, 1972.
Bei shi (BS)	Li Yanshou 李延壽 (fl. 620s–650s), comp. *Bei shi* 北史. Beijing: Zhonghua shuju, 1972.
Chen Yinke	Chen Yinke 陳寅恪, "Cong shishi lun *Qie yun*" 從史實論切韻. *Lingnan xuebao* 嶺南學報 9.2 (1949): 1–18.
Cheng Rong	Cheng Rong 程榮 (fl. late 16th c.) collated, *Yanshi jiaxun* 顏氏家訓. *Han Wei congshu* 漢魏叢書 edition. With Yan Rugui 顏如環 1518 preface and Yan Zhibang 顏志邦 1578 preface.
Chuxue ji	Xu Jian 徐堅 (659–729), comp. *Chuxie ji* 初學記. Beijing: Zhonghua shuju, 1962.
Dien	Albert E. Dien, trans. with introduction and notes. *Pei Chi shu 45: Biography of Yen Chih-t'ui*. Würzburger Sino-Japonica. Bern: Herbert Lang, 1976.
Fu Yue	傅鑰 (傅太平) (1482–1540), *Yanshi jiaxun* 顏氏家訓. *Sibu congkan* edition. Shanghai Hanfen lou photo-reprint of Fu Yue's printed edition with Zhang Bi's 張璧 1524 preface.
Gu shi ji	Feng Weine 馮惟訥 (1513–1572), comp. *Gu shi ji* 古詩紀. In *Yingyin Wenyuan ge siku quanshu* 景印文淵閣四庫全書, Vol. 1379. Taibei: Shangwu yinshuguan, 1983.

Jin shu   Fang Xuanling 房玄齡 (578–648) et al., comp.
                       Jin shu 晉書. Beijing: Zhonghua shuju, 1974.

Jiu Tang shu   Liu Xu 劉昫 (887–946), comp. *Jiu Tang shu* 舊唐
                       書. Beijing: Zhonghua shuju, 1975.

Liang shu   Yao Cha 姚察 (533–606) and Yao Silian 姚思廉
                       (557–637), comp. *Liang shu* 梁書. Beijing:
                       Zhonghua shuju, 1973.

Lidai minghua ji   Zhang Yanyuan 張彥遠 (815–907), *Lidai min-
                       ghua ji* 歷代名畫記. Beijing: Renmin meishu chu-
                       banshe, 1963.

Lu Qinli   Lu Qinli 逯欽立, comp. *Xian Qin Han Wei Jin
                       nanbeichao shi* 先秦漢魏晉南北朝詩. Beijing:
                       Zhonghua shuju, 1983.

Lu Wenchao   Lu Wenchao 盧文弨 (1717–1796). *Yanshi jiaxun*
                       顏氏家訓. Baojing tang jiaoding ben 抱經堂校定
                       本. *Sibu beiyao* 四部備要 edition. Shanghai:
                       Zhonghua shuju.

Mengzi zhushu   *Mengzi zhushu* 孟子注疏. In *Shisanjing zhushu* 十
                       三經注疏, compiled by Ruan Yuan 阮元 (1764–
                       1849). Taibei: Yiwen yinshuguan, 1955.

Nan Qi shu   Xiao Zixian 蕭子顯 (489–537), comp. *Nan Qi
                       shu* 南齊書. Beijing: Zhonghua shuju, 1972.

Nan shi   Li Yanshou 李延壽 (fl. 620s–650s), comp. *Nan
                       shi* 南史. Beijing: Zhonghua shuju, 1975.

Pei xi   Guo Zhongshu 郭忠恕 (d. 977), *Pei xi* 佩觽. In
                       Yingyin Wenyuan ge siku quanshu 景印文淵閣四
                       庫全書, Vol. 224. Taibei: Shangwu yinshuguan,
                       1983.

Pi Ya   Lu Dian 陸佃 (1042–1102), *Pi Ya* 埤雅. In *Ying-
                       yin Wenyuange siku quanshu* 景印文淵閣四庫全書,
                       Vol. 222. Taiwan: Shangwu yinshuguan, 1983.

Quan Tang wen   *Quan Tang wen* 全唐文. Beijing: Zhonghua shuju,
                       1996.

Ruan Ji   *The Poetry of Ruan Ji*, trans. Stephen Owen, in
                       The Poetry of Ruan Ji and Xi Kang. Boston/Berlin:
                       De Gruyter, 2017.

Shi ji   Sima Qian 司馬遷 (ca. 145 BCE–ca. 86 BCE).
                       Shi ji 史記. Beijing: Zhonghua shuju, 1975.

Shishuo xinyu	Liu Yiqing 劉義慶 (403–444), comp., with Liu Xiaobiao's 劉孝標 (462–521) commentary. *Shishuo xinyu jianshu* 世說新語箋疏, annot. Yu Jiaxi 余嘉錫. Shanghai: Shanghai guji chubanshe, 1993.
Shi tong	Liu Zhiji 劉知幾 (661–721), *Xin Shi tong jiaozhu* 新史通校注, annot. Zhao Lüfu 趙呂甫. Sichuan: Chongqing chubanshe, 1990.
Song shu	Shen Yue 沈約 (441–513), comp. *Song shu* 宋書. Beijing: Zhonghua shuju, 1974.
Sui shu	Wei Zheng 魏徵 (580–643) et al., comp. *Sui shu* 隋書. Beijing: Zhonghua shuju, 1973.
Taiping guangji	Li Fang 李昉 (925–996) et al., comp. *Taiping guangji* 太平廣記. Beijing: Zhonghua shuju, 1981.
Taiping yulan	Li Fang 李昉 (925–996) et al., comp. *Taiping yulan* 太平御覽. Taibei: Shangwu yinshuguan, 1975.
Teng Ssu-yü	Teng Ssu-yü, trans. with an introduction and notes, *Family Instructions for the Yen Clan*. Leiden: Brill, 1968.
Tian 2018	Tian, Xiaofei. "Yu Xin's 'Memory Palace': Writing Trauma and Violence in Early Medieval Chinese Aulic Poetry." In *Memory in Medieval Chinese Text, Ritual, and Community*, ed. Wendy Swartz and Robert Ford Campany. Leiden: Brill, 2018; 124–157.
Wang Liqi	Wang Liqi 王利器, annot. *Yanshi jiaxun jijie (zengbu ben)* 顏氏家訓集解增補本. Beijing: Zhonghua shuju, 1993.
Wenjing mifu lun	Henjō-Kongō 遍照金剛 [Kūkai 空海] (774–835). *Wenjing mifu lun huijiao huikao* 文鏡秘府論彙校彙考, annot. Wang Liqi 盧盛江. Beijing: Zhonghua shuju, 2006.
Wen xuan	Xiao Tong 蕭統 (501–531), comp. *Wen xuan* 文選. Shanghai: Shanghai guji chubanshe, 1986.
Wenyuan yinghua	Li Fang 李昉 (925–996) et al., comp. *Wenyuan yinghua* 文苑英華. Beijing: Zhonghua shuju, 1966.

Wulei xianggan zhi	*Dongpo xiansheng wulei xianggan zhi* 東坡先生物類相感志, attri. Su Shi 蘇軾 (1037–1101) / Zanning 贊寧 (919–1001). *Siku quanshu cunmu congshu zibu* 四庫全書存目叢書子部 116. Ji'nan: Qi Lu shushe, 1997.
Xin Tang shu	Ouyang Xiu 歐陽修 (1007–1072) and Song Qi 宋祁 (998–1061), comp. *Xin Tang shu* 新唐書. Beijing: Zhonghua shuju, 1975.
Xu Jiaxun	Dong Zhenggong 董正功 (fl. 11th c.?), *Xu Jiaxun* 續家訓. *Xuxiu siku quanshu* 續修四庫全書, Vol. 1122. Shanghai: Shanghai guji chubanshe; 1–40.
Yan Kejun	Yan Kejun 嚴可均 (1762–1843), comp. *Quan shanggu sandai Qin Han sanguo liuchao wen* 全上古三代秦漢三國六朝文. Beijing: Zhonghua shuju, 1987. Note: in all citations from Yan Kejun I give the volume title as divided by dynasty, such as *Quan sanguo wen* (*Complete Three Kingdoms Prose*), followed by *juan* number and page number.
Yan Shihui	Yan Shihui 嚴式誨 (1890–1976). *Yanshi jiaxun* 顏氏家訓 (annotated by Zhao Ximing 趙曦明 and Lu Wenchao 盧文弨) with 1930 colophon and collation notes by Yan Shihui. Chengdu: Yanshi xiaoyi jiashu 嚴氏孝義家塾, 1928 first printing. *Xuxiu siku quanshu* 續修四庫全書, Vol. 1121. Shanghai: Shanghai guji chubanshe; 597–707.
Yinchuang zalu	*Yinchuang zalu* 吟窗雜錄. Beijing: Zhonghua shuju, 1997.
Yiwen leiju	Ouyang Xun 歐陽詢 (557–641) et al, comp. *Yiwen leiju* 藝文類聚. Shanghai: Shanghai guji chubanshe, 1999.
Yongcheng jixian lu	Du Guangting 杜光庭 (850–933), *Yongcheng jixian lu* 墉城集仙錄. *Siku quanshu cunmu congshu zibu* 四庫全書存目叢書子部 258. Ji'nan: Qi Lu shushe, 1997.
Yuanhun zhi	Yan Zhitui 顏之推, *Yuanhun zhi jiaozhu* 冤魂志校注. Collated and annot. by Luo Guowei 羅國威. Chengdu: Ba Shu shushe, 2001.

Zhang Aitang   Zhang Aitang 張藹堂, trans. and annot. *Yan Zhi-
                        tui quanji yizhu* 顏之推全集譯注. Ji'nan: Qi Lu
                        shushe, 2004.

Zhou Fagao   Zhou Fagao 周法高, annot. *Yanshi jiaxun huizhu*
                        顏氏家訓彙注. 4 volumes. Taibei: Academia Sini-
                        ca, 1960.

Zhou shu   Linghu Defen 令狐德棻 (582–666) et al., comp.
                        Zhou shu 周書. Beijing: Zhonghua shuju, 1971.

Zizhi tongjian   Sima Guang 司馬光 (1019–1086), comp. *Zizhi
                        tongjian* 資治通鑑. 2 volumes. Beijing: Zhonghua
                        shuju, 1997 (revised from the 1956 edition).

Additional Notes

Family Instructions for the Yan Clan 顏氏家訓

I.
序致第一 reads 序致篇第一 in the Cheng Rong editions, and *pian* 篇 appears in all subsequent chapter titles. It reads 序致篇一 in the Fu Yue edition, and the subsequent chapter titles all follow the pattern.

I.1
耳 appears as the less common variant graph 尒 throughout the Bao Tingbo edition.
今所以復為此者: a note in the "Song edition" says that *jin* 今 is absent in a different edition.

I.2
凡人 reads 兄弟 in the Yan Sishen edition according to Wang Liqi (Wang 3).

I.3
誨誘 appears as 誘誨 in the 1789 print of the Lu Wenchao edition, but was corrected by Lu Wenchao in the errata in the 1792 reprint. Wang Liqi notes that except for the "Song edition" that he consulted, all editions read 誨誘 (4).

I.4
家塗 also reads 家徒 in the Cheng Rong edition.
不備邊幅 is emended to 不脩邊幅 in the Lu Wenchao edition.

I.5
三十 is a variant for 二十 given in a note in the "Song edition," which is adopted only in the Lu Wenchao edition. I follow the Lu Wenchao edition here.

I.6
經目過耳 also reads 經目過耳也 according to a note in the "Song edition," which is adopted by the Lu Wenchao edition.

以為汝曹後車耳: a note in the "Song edition" says that 車 also reads 範. This variant reading appears in the Fu Yue and Cheng Rong editions.

II.2
子生 reads 生子 only in the Lu Wenchao edition, which Wang Liqi follows.

咳嘔 also reads 孩提 according to a note in the "Song edition."

仁孝禮義 also reads 孝禮仁義 according to a note in the "Song edition." Lu Wenchao emends it to 孝仁禮義, citing a *Han shu* passage, which Wang Liqi follows on the basis that "filial piety" is the foremost of all moral values (Wang 10). The Cheng Rong edition reads 仁智禮義.

當及嬰稚 reads 當撫嬰稚 in the Cheng Rong edition.

II.3
宜誡翻獎 also reads 宜訓翻獎 according to a note in the "Song edition."

應訶反笑 also reads 應訶反笑 according to a note in the "Song edition."

驕慢 also reads 憍慢 according to a note in the "Song edition."

方復 also reads 方乃 according to a note in the "Song edition."

無威 also reads 無改悔 according to a note in the "Song edition."

增怨 also reads 增怨懟 according to a note in the "Song edition."

II.11
若由此業 also reads 若用此業 according to a note in the "Song edition."

III.1
有夫婦而後有父子 reads 有夫婦而後有父母 in the Bao Tingbo edition. I follow the Lu Wenchao edition here.

盡此三而已矣 reads 此三而已矣 in the Lu Wenchao edition (with a note of the "Song edition" variant) and others.

III.2
悖亂之行 reads 悖亂之人 in the Lu Wenchao edition (with a note of the "Song edition" variant) and others.

篤厚之行 reads 篤厚之人 in the Lu Wenchao edition (with a note of the "Song edition" variant) and others.

III.3
異於他人 reads 易於他人 according to a note in the "Song edition."

III.4
皆有歡笑 reads 皆有歡愛 in the Lu Wenchao edition (with a note of the "Song edition" variant) and others.

III.6
何怨愛弟不及愛子乎 reads 何為愛弟不及愛子乎 in the Lu Wenchao edition.

良久方應 reads 良久方答 in the Lu Wenchao edition (with a note of the "Song edition" variant) and others.

IV.1
以賢父御孝子: 以 is missing in the Cheng Rong and Fu Yue editions.

IV.2
江左 reads 江右 in the Cheng Rong edition.

或不 reads 或未 in the Lu Wenchao edition and others.

IV.7
取其老者 reads 引其老者 in the Lu Wenchao edition and others.

V.3
如有周公之才之美 reads 雖有周公之才之美 in the Fu Yue and Cheng Rong editions.

施則奢 reads 奢則施 in the "Song edition." Lu Wenchao has a note saying all old editions read 奢則施 but emends it to 施則奢 in the context. The emendation is correct.

V.7
竟無捶撻之意 also reads 竟無捶撻 according to a note in the "Song edition," which is adopted in the Lu Wenchao edition and others.

V.9
誓滿千人 reads 誓滿一千 in the Lu Wenchao edition and others.

朝夕肴膳 reads 朝夕每人肴膳 in the "Song edition" and is marked as a variant reading in a note, which is adopted in the Fu Yue and Cheng Rong editions. I follow the variant reading.

便無以兼 reads 更無以兼 in Cheng Rong edition and is marked as a variant reading in a note in the Lu Wenchao edition.

V.10
常貧 reads 嘗貧 in the "Song edition" and is marked as a variant reading in a note. I follow the variant reading, which is also adopted in the Lu Wenchao edition.

V.13
河北人事 also reads 河北人士 according to a note in the "Song edition."

V.15
先人遺體 reads 先人傳體 in the Lu Wenchao edition and others.

V.18
部秩 reads 部帙 in the Cheng Rong edition, adopted by Wang Liqi with a long note (Wang 56). The emendation is not necessary.
犬鼠 also reads 蟲鼠 according to a note in the "Song edition," and reads 大鼠 in the Cheng Rong edition.

V.19
勿妖妄之費 is emended to 勿為妖妄之費 in the Lu Wenchao edition, followed by Wang Liqi and Zhou Fagao.

VI.1
節文 reads 節度 in the Fu Yue and Cheng Rong editions.
聊記以傳示子孫 reads 聊記錄 in the Fu Yue and Cheng Rong edition.

VI.2
蓋知 is emended to 益知 in the Lu Wenchao edition, followed by Wang Liqi and Zhou Fagao.

VI.3
又臧逢世，臧嚴之子也 reads 又有臧逢世，臧嚴之子 in the Lu Wenchao edition.

VI.8
凡名子者 reads 名子者 in the Fu Yue and Cheng Rong edition.
譚裏、譚周 reads 譚裏、譚友、譚同 in the Fu Yue and Cheng Rong editions, adopted in the Lu Wenchao edition.

VI.9
亦鄙事也 reads 亦鄙才也 in Bao Tingbo's "Song edition" and is emended according to the other editions.

VI.10
況當之者乎 reads 況名之者乎 in the Fu Yue and Cheng Rong editions.

VI.12
陳思王稱其父曰家父，母曰家母: 曰 reads 為 in the Fu Yue and Cheng Rong editions. Lu Wenchao adopts 為 with a note that the "Song edition" reads 曰.

及南北風俗 is emended to 今南北風俗 by Wang Liqi following the "Song edition" he consulted (Wang 74).

蔡邕書集呼其姑姊為家姑家姊: 姑姊 reads 姑女 in all but the Wang Liqi and Zhou Fagao editions. Wang Liqi emends 姑女 to 姑姊 with a note saying he follows the Fu Yue (Fu Taiping) edition. Zhou Fagao also makes the same emendation but says that he follows a Qing reprint of the Yan Zhibang edition in Zheng Zhen's collection (Zhou 18a). Yan Shihui's 嚴式誨 (1890–1976) collation note says that the Fu Yue (Taiping) edition reads 姑姊 (Yan Shihui 679), but Zhou Fagao believes that in this case Fu Taiping is a mistake for Yan Zhibang.

VI.15
皆古之道也: 皆 is present in the "Song edition" but absent in the Fu Yue and Cheng Rong editions.

VI.18a
江南人事不獲已 reads 江南事不獲已 in the Fu Yue and Cheng Rong editions. A note in the "Song edition" states that after this line, a different edition has ten extra characters that read: 乃陳文墨，懂懂無自言者. The extra line reads 乃陳文墨，懂懂無言者 in the Fu Yue and Cheng Rong editions.

勿使煩重 also reads 勿取煩重 according to a note in the "Song edition," which is the reading in the Fu Yue and Cheng Rong editions.

VI.19
北土風俗 also reads simply 北土 according to a note in the "Song edition" and in the Fu Yue and Cheng Rong editions.

VI.20

從父兄弟姊妹巳孤 reads 從兄弟姊妹巳孤 in the Lu Wenchao, Fu Yue, and Cheng Rong editions.

北土人多呼為姪 reads 北土人多呼為姪 in the Lu Wenchao, Fu Yue, and Cheng Rong editions.

並是對姑立稱 reads 並是對姑之稱 in the Lu Wenchao, Fu Yue, and Cheng Rong editions.

VI.21

甚以惻愴 also reads 甚心惻愴 according to a note in the "Song edition," which is the reading in the Fu Yue and Cheng Rong editions.

VI.25

乃有對面以相戲者 also reads 乃有對面以為戲者 according to a note in the "Song edition."

VI.26

字固因呼為字: the Lu Wenchao edition eliminates 因 with a note saying that it seems to be an error. Wang Liqi and Zhou Fagao both follow the Lu Wenchao edition.

VI.30

天奪其算 reads 天奪之算 in the Fu Yue and Cheng Rong editions.

亦不諭: a note in the "Song edition" says these three characters are absent in a different edition. It reads 亦不論 in the Cheng Rong edition.

VI.34

北朝頓丘李構: 構 is replaced with a note "the imperial first name of the Retired Emperor" 太上御名 in the Bao Tingbao "Song edition" throughout the work. The Retired Emperor refers to Southern Song Emperor Gaozong 高宗 (r. 1127–1162) whose name was Zhao Gou 趙構. He retired in 1162 and passed the throne to Emperor Xiaozong 孝宗 (r. 1163–1189). The "Song edition" was put into print during Emperor Xiaozong's reign.

同集談讌 reads 同席談讌 in the Lu Wenchao edition.

VI.35

江陵 reads 江寧 in the Lu Wenchao edition.

亦當不可絕食也 also reads 亦不可絕食也 or 亦當不可絕食 according to a note in the "Song edition."

VI.37

精神傷沮 reads 精神傷怛 in the Cheng Rong edition.

VI.38

來歲有社 also reads 來歲一社 or 來歲社 according to a note in the "Song edition." Zhao Ximing emends it to 來歲社日, followed by Wang Liqi and Zhao Fagao.

忌之外 reads 忌之日 in the "Song edition." 忌之外 is the variant reading recorded in a note in the "Song edition." 日 is adopted by the Lu Wenchao edition, followed by Zhou Fagao; 外 is the reading in the Fu Yue and Cheng Rong editions and followed by Wang Liqi, who believes 忌之日 is wrong.

猶應感慕 reads 猶應思慕 according to a note in the "Song edition." It reads 尤應感慕 in the Lu Wenchao edition.

VI.42

梁孝元帝年少之時 also reads 梁孝元年少之時 according to a note in the "Song edition."

VI.43

于耒反 reads 于來反 in the Fu Yue and Cheng Rong editions.

VI.45

怨讎 reads 死讎 in the "Song edition" with a note saying that it also reads 怨讎 in a different edition.

VI.47

親拜中兵參軍李猷焉 also reads 親拜中兵參軍李猷 according to a note in the "Song edition."

VI.48

申父交之敬 also reads 申父友之敬 according to a note in the "Song edition."

VI.49
黃門侍郎裴之禮，好待賓客，或有此輩，對賓杖之，僮僕引接，折旋俯仰，莫不盡敬，與主無別 also reads 黃門侍郎裴之禮，號善為士大夫，有如此輩，對賓杖之，其門生僮僕，接於他人，折旋俯仰，辭色應對，莫不盡敬，與主無別也 according to a note in the "Song edition." The variant reading is adopted in all other editions.

VII.1
神醉魂迷 reads 心醉魂迷 in all other editions.

VII.2
言笑舉對 reads 言笑舉動 in all other editions.

VII.3
校其長短，覈其精麤，或能彼不能此矣 also reads 校長短，覈其精麤，或彼不能如此矣 according to a note in the "Song edition."

VII.5a
一皆使典之 also reads 一皆使之 according to a note in the "Song edition."
時云 is absent in another edition according to a note in the "Song edition."
王君一字 reads 王褒數字 in all other editions. It also reads 王君數字 according to a note in the "Song edition."

VII.8
關中至今譽之 reads 關中人至今譽之 in the Lu Wenchao edition.

VII.9
齊國之亡 also reads 齊亡之跡 according to a note in the "Song edition," which is adopted in all other editions.

VIII.3a
討論貨賄 reads 計論貨賄 in the Cheng Rong edition.
沈思 also reads 深思 in the Cheng Rong edition.
射則不能穿札 reads 射既不能穿札 in the Fu Yue and Cheng Rong editions.

VIII.3b

便自為足，全忘修學 also reads 便謂為足，安能自苦 according to a note in the "Song edition." The latter is the adopted reading in the Fu Yue and Cheng Rong editions.

VIII.4b

鹿獨戎馬之間 reads 孤獨戎馬之間 in the Cheng Rong edition.

VIII.5

汝可不自勉耶 reads 安可不自勉耶 in all other editions.

VIII.7

文義習吏 reads 文義習史 in the Fu Yue and Cheng Rong editions.

VIII.8b

如秋荼 reads 幾秋荼 in the Cheng Rong edition.

VIII.9b

執轡如組 also reads 執轡生組 according to a note in the "Song edition." 早刑時捨 also reads 早刑晚捨 according to a note in the "Song edition." The latter is the reading adopted in the Fu Yue and Cheng Rong editions.

VIII.10a

以致甘腝 reads 以致甘腝 in the "Song edition" with a note saying that it also reads 以致甘旨 in a different edition. It reads 腝 in all other editions.

VIII.12

今世人讀書者: *jin* is absent in a different edition according to a note in the "Song edition."
黍穭 reads 黍稗 in the "Song edition."

VIII.14

一月廢置 also reads 一日廢置 according to a note in the "Song edition." 便至荒蕪矣 also reads 便荒蕪矣 according to a note in the "Song edition."

VIII.15a

始授孝經 is emended to 始受孝經 in the Lu Wenchao edition. It is unnecessary.

VIII.16

不肯專於經業 also reads 不肯專儒 according to a note in the "Song edition." The latter is the reading adopted in the Lu Wenchao, Fu Yue, and Cheng Rong editions, followed by Wang Liqi and Zhou Fagao.

VIII.18

爭此得勝 reads 以此得勝 in all other editions.

VIII.20

與諸博士爭宗廟事 reads 與諸博士議宗廟事 in all other editions.

VIII.21b

傾動專勢 reads 傾動權勢 in the Cheng Rong edition.

VIII.21c

清談雅論，辭鋒理窟，剖玄析微，妙得入神，賓主往復，娛心悅耳，然而濟世成俗，終非急務 also reads 清談高論，剖玄析微，賓主往復，娛心悅耳，非濟世成俗之要也 according to a note in the "Song edition." The latter reading is adopted in all other editions.

VIII.22

故置學生 reads 召置學生 in all other editions.

VIII.24

閒齋 reads 閉齋 in the Fu Yue edition.
以自寬痛 also reads 以寬此痛 according to a note in the "Song edition."

VIII.25

亦云勤篤 also reads 亦為勤篤 according to a note in the "Song edition." 常無燈，折荻尺寸，然明讀書 also reads 燈燭難辦，常買荻，尺寸然明讀書 according to a note in the "Song edition." It reads 燈燭難辦，常買荻，尺寸折之，然明夜讀 in the Lu Wenchao, Fu Yue, and Cheng Rong editions, followed by Wang Liqi and Zhou Fagao.

VIII.26
卒成大學 also reads 卒成學士 according to a note in the "Song edition."

VIII.28
齊有主宦者 also reads 齊有宦者 according to a note in the "Song edition."

後主之奔青州 also reads 齊主之奔青州 according to a note in the "Song edition."

齊王 reads 齊主 in the Lu Wenchao edition, followed by Wang Liqi and Zhou Fagao.

以學著忠誠 also reads 以學成忠 according to a note in the "Song edition."

VIII.29
父當以教為事 also reads 父當以學為教 according to a note in the "Song edition." The latter reading is adopted in all other editions.

我自欲之 reads 吾自安之 in the Lu Wenchao edition.

VIII.30
謬誤羞慙者多矣 also reads 謬誤差失，慙者多矣 according to a note in the "Song edition." The Lu Wenchao edition reads 謬誤差失者多矣.

VIII.31
孟勞者 is absent in a different edition according to a note in the "Song edition." This is the case in the Fu Yue and Cheng Rong editions.

VIII.34
遂謂朝士言 also reads 遂一一謂言 according to a note in the "Song edition." This is the reading in the Fu Yue and Cheng Rong editions.

VIII.36
必稱陝西 reads 必稱峽西 in the Lu Wenchao edition.

海郡 reads 海邦 in the Lu Wenchao edition.

VIII.38
笑呂忱 reads 忽呂忱 in all other editions.

專皮、鄒 is emended to 專徐、鄒 in the Wang Liqi edition (221–22).

VIII.39

而有名峙者 reads 而有名峙者 in the Lu Wenchao and Cheng Rong editions, followed by Wang Liqi.

手邊 reads 手傍 in the Fu Yue edition (followed by Wang Liqi and Zhou Fagao) and 木傍 in the Lu Wenchao and Cheng Rong editions.

VIII.42

城南門 reads 城西門 in the Lu Wenchao, Fu Yue, and Cheng Rong editions, followed by Wang Liqi and Zhou Fagao.

VIII.43

忩遽者 reads 怱遽者 in the Cheng Rong edition and 忽遽者 in the Fu Yue edition, and 怱遽者 in the Lu Wenchao edition, followed by Wang Liqi and Zhou Fagao. 忩 and 怱 are variant forms of the same character.

VIII.44

初晴日晃 reads 初晴日明 in the Fu Yue and Cheng Rong editions.

命將取來 reads 命取將來 in all other editions.

VIII.45

舉俗 reads 舉族 in the Cheng Rong edition.

鳲 and 音分 are emended to 鳩 and 音介 in the Lu Wenchao edition, followed by Wang Liqi and Zhou Fagao.

VIII.46

梁世有蔡朗諱純 reads 梁世有蔡朗父諱純 in the Lu Wenchao edition; Wang Liqi reads 梁世有蔡朗者諱純. 蔡朗諱純 is correct and there is no need to emend it.

露葵菜 reads 露葵 in all other editions.

覈究 reads 覆究 in the Fu Yue and Cheng Rong editions.

IX.1

不可暫無 also reads 施用多途 according to a note in the "Song edition." The latter reading is adopted in all other editions.

IX.2b

詆忤鄉里 reads 詆訶鄉里 in the Fu Yue and Cheng Rong editions.

IX.4

至無才思 reads 至於無才思 in the Fu Yue and Cheng Rong editions.

IX.5

得其評裁 reads 得其評論者 in the Fu Yue and Cheng Rong editions.
知可施行: this is absent in the Fu Yue and Cheng Rong editions; the absence is marked as a variant reading in a different edition according to a note in the "Song edition."
便稱才士 reads 遂稱才士 in the Fu Yue and Cheng Rong editions.
要動俗蓋世 reads 要須動俗蓋世 in the Lu Wenchao, Fu Yue, and Cheng Rong editions.

IX.6

何事非君 reads 何事我為 in the Fu Yue edition.

IX.7

壯士 reads 壯夫 in the Lu Wenchao, Fu Yue, and Cheng Rong editions, followed by Wang Liqi and Zhou Fagao.
袁亮以勝老子 reads 桓譚以勝老子 in all other editions.

IX.8

席毗 reads 辛毗 in the Fu Yue and Cheng Rong editions.
譬若朝菌 reads 譬若榮華 in all other editions.
千丈松樹 reads 十丈松樹 in the Fu Yue and Cheng Rong editions.
可哉 reads 可矣 in the Fu Yue and Cheng Rong editions.

IX.9

猶乘騏驥 reads 猶人乘騏驥 in all other editions.

IX.12

撰西府新文紀無一篇見錄者 reads 撰西府新文史記無一篇見錄者 in the Cheng Rong edition and 撰西府新文史訖無一篇見錄者 in the Fu Yue edition. The Wang Liqi edition reads 撰西府新文, 訖無一篇見錄者 by following and emending the variant reading in the Fu Yue edition.

IX.14

各為朋黨 reads 各有朋黨 in all other editions.

IX.17
世人或有引詩 also reads 世人或有文章引詩 in all other editions.

IX.19
遂嘗以忤人 reads 遂嘗以此忤人 in all other editions.

IX.21
譬婦為考 reads 匹婦於考 in all other editions.
倪天之和 reads 倪天之妹 in the Yan Sishen edition (Wang Liqi 283).

IX.22
製作大意 reads 製作本意 in all other editions.

IX.23
疎失厥體 reads 殊失厥體 in the Fu Yue edition.
何不逝赧王、靈帝乎 reads 胡不逝赧王、靈帝乎 in the Lu Wenchao
edition, followed by Wang Liqi. It reads 祠不逝 in the Cheng Rong
edition, which seems to be a typographical error.

IX.24
略舉一兩端以為誡云: 云 is absent in all other editions.

IX.26
痛心拔惱 reads 痛心拔腦 in the Lu Wenchao edition, followed by Wang
Liqi and Zhou Fagao.
何故方言有如也 reads 何故言有如也 in all other editions except for
Wang Liqi.

IX.32
常云: 常 is absent in the Fu Yue and Cheng Rong editions.
蓮車 reads 蓮居 in all editions, but in this case should be emended to
蓮車 as in the Wang Liqi edition (see Wang 298, 301). 居 and 車 are
homophones, and a misunderstanding of Liu Xiaochuo's criticism (懵
懵不道車) may have led to the writing of 居 rather than 車. That is,
many have taken 不道車 as meaning "not mentioning 'carriage'." The
correct interpretation is "unorthodox (or unrighteous) carriage."

IX.34
亦為冠絕 reads 並為冠絕 in the Fu Yue and Cheng Rong editions.

X.3
拱把之梁 reads 拱抱之梁 in the Fu Yue and Cheng Rong editions.
仲由之言信 reads 仲由之證鼎 in the "Song edition," in which the former is given as a variant in a note.

X.4
慮 reads 宓 in the Fu Yue and Cheng Rong editions.

X.5
以孝著聲 reads 孝悌著聲 in the Fu Yue and Cheng Rong editions.
於苫塊之中 reads 以苫塊之中 in the Cheng Rong edition.

X.6
遞共吹噓 reads 遞相吹噓 in the Fu Yue and Cheng Rong editions.
亦常出境聘 reads 亦嘗出境聘 in all other editions.
面相討試 reads 面相討試爾 in the "Song edition."

X.7
大弊事也 reads 太弊事也 in the Cheng Rong edition.

X.8
功績遂損敗矣 reads 功績遂敗損矣 in the Fu Yue and Cheng Rong editions.

X.9
而聖人以為名教乎 reads 而聖人以為教乎 in the Fu Yue and Cheng Rong editions.

X.10b
獲其庇廕者亦眾矣 reads 獲其庇廕者眾矣 in the Fu Yue and Cheng Rong editions.
世之汲汲者 reads 世人汲汲者 in the Fu Yue and Cheng Rong editions.
松柏偕茂者 reads 松柏偕茂 in the Fu Yue and Cheng Rong editions.

XI.1
士君子之處世 reads 夫君子之處世 in the Fu Yue and Cheng Rong editions.

XI.2
開略有術 reads 開悟有術 in the "Song edition."

XI.3
處廊廟之下 reads 處廟堂之下 in all other editions.

XI.4
所以處於清高 reads 所以處於清名 in the Fu Yue and Cheng Rong editions.

蓋護其短也 reads 益護其短也 in the Cheng Rong edition.

XI.6
A note in the "Song edition" says that this section is absent in a different edition. This passage is missing in the Fu Yue and Cheng Rong editions.

XI.7
因晉中興，南渡江，卒為羈旅 reads 因晉中興而渡江，本為羈旅 in the Fu Yue edition.

At the end of this chapter, the "Song edition" has an additional section, with a note saying that this additional section appears at the end of Chapter XVI ("Keeping Faith") in a different edition. All other editions have this section at the end of Chapter XVI (as XVI.23 in this volume).

XII.2
不如熟一 reads 不如執一 in all other editions.

胡書 is absent in all other editions. The Wang Liqi edition follows the "Song edition."

XII.3
或無絲毫之益 reads 或無私毫之益 in the "Song edition."

XII.4

事途迴穴 is emended from 事途迴冗 in the Zhou Fagao and Wang Liqi edition. 穴 appears as the variant graph 冗 in the Fu Yue and Cheng Rong editions.

XII.7

便為"弗索何獲" reads 便謂"弗索何獲" in the Lu Wenchao edition, followed by Wang Liqi and Zhou Fagao.

不然亦至也 reads 不求亦至也 in the Lu Wenchao edition, followed by Wang Liqi and Zhou Fagao.

XII.8

必以利治 is emended to 必以利殆 in the Wang Liqi edition. It is not necessary.

XII.10

亦不足恤焉 reads 又不足恤焉 in all other editions.

XII.11a

大抵諸儒所爭 reads 大抵諸儒所執 in the Lu Wenchao edition.

恥為此讓 reads 恥為此議 in the Fu Yue and Cheng Rong editions.

此好名之辱也 also reads 此好名好事之為也 according to a note in the "Song edition."

XIII.1

唯在少欲知足 reads 唯在少欲知止 in the Fu Yue and Cheng Rong editions.

XIII.3

皆以義散之 reads 以義散之 in all other editions.

XIII.5

夜填坑谷 reads 夜殯坑谷 in the Lu Wenchao edition and (erroneously) 夜損坑谷 in the Cheng Rong edition.

慎之哉 is not repeated in the Lu Wenchao edition.

XIV.1a

春秋之世 reads 春秋世 in the Lu Wenchao edition, followed by Wang Liqi.

顏高、顏鳴、顏息、顏羽之徒 reads 顏高、顏鳴、顏羽之徒 in the Fu Yue and Cheng Rong editions.

XIV.1b

趙有顏㝡 also reads 趙有顏聚 according to a note in the "Song edition."

XIV.2

逞弄拳擊: 擊 appears in its more common graphic form 腕 in the Fu Yue and Cheng Rong editions.

XIV.3

不能爲主畫規 reads 不能爲主盡規 in the Lu Wenchao edition, followed by Wang Liqi.

若居承平之世 reads 若承平之世 in the Fu Yue and Cheng Rong editions.

XIV.4

便騎乘 reads 便乘騎 in all other editions.

正可稱武夫兒 reads 上可稱武夫兒 in the Cheng Rong edition.

即自稱武夫兒 reads 即稱武夫兒 in all other editions.

XV.1

或難鍾值 reads 或難種植 in the Lu Wenchao and Cheng Rong editions.

幼少之日 reads 幼小之日 in the Lu Wenchao edition.

公私驅役 reads 公私勞役 in the Lu Wenchao edition.

千萬不過一爾 reads 千萬不過一爾 in the Fu Yue and Cheng Rong editions.

學若牛毛 reads 學如牛毛 in all other editions.

暄寒 reads 寒暄 in all other editions.

XV.2

有單服杏仁、枸杞、黃精、朮煎者 reads 有單服杏仁、枸杞、黃精、朮、車前 in all other editions. It reads 有單服杏仁、枸杞、黃精、朮煎、車前者 in another edition according to a note in the "Song edition."

不能一一說爾 is absent in another edition according to a note in the "Song edition."

XV.3

早朝建齒三百下為良 reads 早朝叩齒三百下為良 in all other editions. 建齒 is the term used in *The Master of Embracing Simplicity*.

即便平愈 reads 即平愈 in the Fu Yue and Cheng Rong editions.

XV.4

諸欲餌藥 reads 凡欲餌藥 in all other editions.

不可輕脫 reads 不可輕服 in the Cheng Rong edition.

XV.5

夫養生者先須慮禍 reads 夫養生先須慮禍 in the Fu Yue and Cheng Rong editions.

石崇冀服餌之徵 also reads 石崇冀服餌之延年 according to a note in the "Song edition."

XVI.1

家世業此 reads 家世歸心 in all other editions.

其間妙旨 reads 其間妙音 in the Cheng Rong edition.

略重勸誘爾 reads 略動勸誘爾 in the "Song edition."

XVI.3

漸極為異 reads 漸積為異 in the Wang Liqi edition only, which appears to be an error.

不淫之禁也 reads 不酒之禁也 in the Wang Liqi edition, with a note saying that he emended it based on the citation of this passage in the *Guang Hongming ji* (Wang, 368, 371).

固民之性 reads 因民之性 in the Fu Yue and Wang Liqi editions. Wang states that he emended 固 to 因 based on the "Song edition" and other editions that he has consulted (Wang 371). The emendation is not necessary.

XVI.5

莫著天地 reads 莫若天地 in all other editions.

XVI.10

原憲、伯夷之凍餒 is emended to 伯夷、原憲之凍餒 in the Wang Liqi edition based on *Guang Hongming ji* citation. It is unnecessary.

便生怨尤 reads 便可怨尤 in the Fu Yue and Cheng Rong editions.

則亦堯、舜之云虛 reads 則堯、舜之云虛 in the Lu Wenchao edition.

XVI.12

失國賦算 reads 空國賦算 in all other editions.

XVI.13

頓欲棄之哉 reads 頓欲棄之乎 in the *Guang Hongming ji* citation (see Wang Liqi 396–97), in which it is followed by the sentence: 故兩疎得其一隅, 累代詠而彌光矣 ("The two Shu partially understood this issue, and even with their partial understanding they were eulogized and honored for generations"). The "two Shu" are the Western Han scholars Shu Guang 疏廣 and his nephew Shu Shou 疏受, who became tutors to the Crown Prince in 67 BCE. They retired after five years at the height of their fame, and were given a gift of twenty catties of gold by the emperor and fifty catties of gold by the Crown Prince. They spent all the gold entertaining their kinsfolk rather than pass it on to their children and were praised for their wisdom. The sentence in this context means that even if the two Shu only understood to a limited extent the importance of valuing one's own self, they were commended for generations.

XVI.14

汝曹若觀俗計 reads 汝曹若顧俗計 in the Fu Yue edition.

XVI.16

每沐輒二三十枚 reads 每沐輒二三十枚 in the Lu Wenchao edition, followed by Wang Liqi.

XVI.17

後生一兒頭俱是鰌 reads 後生一兒頭是鰌 in all other editions.

XVI.19

投醒而覺體痺 reads 稍醒而覺體痺 in all other editions. 投 has the meaning of "by the time when" and is correct here.

XVI.23

倚作舅姑之大 reads 倚作舅姑之尊 in all other editions.
惡口加誣 reads 毒口加誣 in all other editions.
卻成教婦不孝己身 reads 卻云教以婦道, 不孝己身 in the Fu Yue and Cheng Rong editions.

但憐己之子女 reads 但怜己之子女 in the Fu Yue and Cheng Rong editions.

不愛其婦 reads 不愛己之兒婦 in all other editions.

不得與為鄰 reads 慎不可與為鄰 in all other editions.

何況交結乎 reads 仍不可與為援 in the Fu Yue and Cheng Rong editions.

避之哉，避之哉 reads 宜遠之哉 in the Fu Yue and Cheng Rong editions, and reads 避之哉 in the Lu Wenchao edition, followed by Wang Liqi.

XVII.1

接余也 reads 菨余也 in the Fu Yue and Cheng Rong editions.

XVII.2

禮云苦菜秀爾雅毛詩傳並以荼苦菜也 reads 爾雅毛傳並以荼苦菜也又禮云苦菜秀 in the Fu Yue and Cheng Rong editions. Lu Wenchao emends the text accordingly, followed by Zhou Fagao and Wang Liqi.

XVII.4

案毛傳云 reads 案毛詩云 in the Fu Yue and Cheng Rong editions.

諸侯六閑四種 reads 諸侯六閑 in the Lu Wenchao edition.

XVII.5

月令云 reads 月令 in the Lu Wenchao edition.

但呼為旱蒲 reads 但呼為早蒲 in the Fu Yue and Cheng Rong editions.

馬莧堪食 reads 堪食 in the Lu Wenchao, Fu Yue, and Cheng Rong editions.

俊晤 reads 俊悟 in the Fu Yue and Cheng Rong editions.

其伯父縚 reads 其伯父劉縚 in the Fu Yue and Cheng Rong editions.

XVII.6

恐為少誤 reads 恐有少誤 in the Lu Wenchao and Cheng Rong editions, followed by Zhou Fagao.

XVII.8

先儒未有釋者 reads 先儒未有釋書 in the Cheng Rong edition.

五尺犬為猶 reads 六尺犬為猶 in the Lu Wenchao edition.

然後敢渡 reads 然後渡 in the Fu Yue and Cheng Rong editions.

XVII.9

左傳曰 is missing in the Lu Wenchao edition.

變而成痁 reads 變而成瘕 in all other editions.

XVII.10

景 in 惟景響, 土圭測景, 景朝景夕, 圖景失形, 罔兩問景 all read 影 in the Fu Yue and Cheng Rong editions, followed by Wang Liqi.

故即為景 reads 故即謂為景 in all other editions.

傍始加彡: a note in the "Song edition" gives the pronunciation for 彡: 音杉.

XVII.11

案諸陳隊 reads 案諸陳字 in the Fu Yue and Cheng Rong editions.

唯王羲之小學章 reads 唯王羲小學章 in the Lu Wenchao edition.

XVII.12

皆為叢聚之叢 reads 皆為蕞聚之蕞 in the Lu Wenchao, Fu Yue and Cheng Rong editions.

又音祖會反 is missing in all other editions. Wang Liqi notes that this appears in an "original note" in the "Song edition" he consults.

又狙會反 reads 又祖會反 in all other editions.

XVII.13

曹大家注列女傳 reads 曹大家注烈女傳 in the Fu Yue and Cheng Rong editions. 列 is correct.

益誠可笑 reads 益成可笑 in the Lu Wenchao edition, followed by Wang Liqi and Zhou Fagao.

XVII.14

夏侯該: according to a note in the "Song edition," in another edition there is a note about 該, stating that He Ning's 和凝 (898–955) version cannot decide whether this character should be Yan 諺 or Yong 詠.

南方以晉家渡江後 reads 南方以晉渡江後 in the Fu Yue and Cheng Rong editions.

XVII.17

而復紫色蠅聲 reads 復紫色蠅聲 in the Fu Yue and Cheng Rong editions.

XVII.18

則亦可以亥為豕字音 reads 亦可以亥為豕字音 in the Fu Yue and Cheng Rong editions.

XVII.19

是知慮之與伏 reads 是慮之與伏 in the Lu Wenchao edition.

XVII.21

聞其家堂客有擊筑 reads 聞其家堂上有客擊筑 in all other editions.

XVII.23

皆[ ]刻辭焉 does not have the empty space in the Fu Yue and Cheng Rong editions. The Lu Wenchao edition makes a note about the empty space.

刻此詔左 appears as 刻此詔□左 in the Lu Wenchao edition; □ appears as an empty space in the Cheng Rong edition. The Fu Yue edition reads 刻此詔于左.

XVII.24

而江南書本，多誤從手 reads 而江南書多誤，從手 in the Lu Wenchao edition, with a note saying that since the text says 恐為誤 below, the 誤 in 多誤 here may be an error.

恐為誤也 reads 恐為誤 in the Fu Yue and Cheng Rong editions.

XVII.25

猶割也 is absent in another edition according to a note in the "Song edition."

XVII.26

為四姓小侯立學。按： reads 為四姓小侯立學校 in the Fu Yue and Cheng Rong editions.

XVII.27

鱣長二三丈 reads 鱣長二丈 in the Fu Yue and Cheng Rong editions.

XVII.28

不入曄城寺 is emended to 不入冀府寺 in the Lu Wenchao edition based on Fan Ye's biography in the *History of the Later Han*. However, *chengsi* 城寺 has the meaning of official headquarters and needs no emendation. 寧當論其六七耶 reads 寧當論其六七乎 in the Fu Yue and Cheng Rong editions.

XVII.29

此是削札牘之柿耳 reads 此是削札牘之梯耳 in the Fu Yue and Cheng Rong editions.

俗本因是悉作脯腊之脯 reads 俗本悉作脯腊之脯 in the Fu Yue and Cheng Rong editions.

或為反哺之哺字 reads 或為反哺之哺 in the Fu Yue and Cheng Rong editions.

XVII.30

北土通呼物一凸 reads 北士通呼物一凸 in the Cheng Rong edition.

目似擘椒 reads 目似[ ]椒 in the Cheng Rong edition, with an empty space for 擘.

言鹽與蒜共一苞裏 reads 言鹽豉與蒜共苞一裹 in the Fu Yue and Cheng Rong editions.

XVII.32

常頹縱宏任 reads 常頹縱任俠 in all editions except Dong Zhenggong (Dong 17), which I follow. This sentence appears in Liu Xiaobiao's 劉孝標 (462–521) commentary on the fifth-century anecdotal collection *Shishuo xinyu* 世說新語, which reads 曼頹縱宏任, cited from "Yang Man's Unofficial Biography" 羊曼別傳 (*Shishuo xinyu* 6).

此字皆無音訓 reads 此字更無音訓 in the Fu Yue and Cheng Rong editions.

當是耆老相傳 reads 當時耆老相傳 in the Lu Wenchao edition.

蓋無所不見 reads 蓋無所不施 in all other editions.

而二人皆云重邊 reads 而二人皆曰重邊 in the Lu Wenchao edition.

XV.34

牡所以止扉也 reads 所以止扉 in all other editions.

聲類作戹廖 reads 聲類作戹 in all other editions.

XVII.35
甚會近俗 reads 甚為近俗 in the Fu Yue and Cheng Rong editions.

XVII.36b
黥鯨韓覆: several modern translators (Teng 177; Zhang Aitang 251) take "tattoo" here as a reference to Ying Bu, aka Qing Bu or the Tattooed Bu 黥布, another general who also rebelled and was executed (see XVII.22). But there is a mention in Chen Xi's biography in the *Historian's Record* that his soldiers were tattooed as criminals after being defeated by the imperial army. The clause reads much more naturally with *qing* here as a verb than having a list of three names followed by one verb.

畔討滅殘: according to a note in the "Song edition," another edition reads 畔討戚映.

XVII.37
逐鄉俗訛謬 reads 遂鄉俗訛謬 in the Cheng Rong edition.

木傍作鬼為魁字 reads 木傍作鬼為槐字 in the Fu Yue and Cheng Rong editions.

XVII.38
即陸璣所謂聚藻葉如蓬者也 reads 即陸機所謂聚藻葉如蓬者也 in all other editions.

又郭璞注三蒼 reads 郭璞注三蒼 in the Fu Yue and Cheng Rong editions.

於時當紲六色闟 reads 於時當紲六色闟. I follow the *Taiping yulan* variant 紲 here, which makes better sense.

張敞因造糸旁畏耳 reads 張敞因造絲旁畏耳 in the Cheng Rong edition.

XVII.39
土有嚾嘐 reads 山有嚾嘐 in the Lu Wenchao edition.

因云權務之精 reads 曰權務之精 in the Fu Yue and Cheng Rong editions.

XVII.40
盈不至六 reads 盈不過六 in the Lu Wenchao edition.

XVII.42
當是前世有姓郭而病禿者 reads 當是前代人有姓郭而病禿者 in all other editions.

滑稽調戲 reads 滑稽戲調 in all other editions.

XVII.43

其神降于長流之山: a note in the "Song edition" states that this is from the *Shanhai jing*, with 流 reading 留.

於祀主秋 reads 於祀為秋 in the Lu Wenchao edition.

XVII.44a

子皆謂非 reads 子皆為非 in the Lu Wenchao edition.

說文所明 reads 說文所言 in all other editions.

XVII.44c

導是禾名 reads 𥛏是禾名 in the Lu Wenchao edition. Lu Wenchao states that 導 is adopted in the *Han History*, followed by the sixth-century *Wen xuan*; but 𥛏 is adopted in the *Historian's Record*.

XVII.45

互有同異 reads 各有同異 in the Fu Yue and Cheng Rong editions.

說文 "尸" 下施 "几" reads 說文 "居" 下施 "几" in the Bao Tingbo "Song edition," as well as the Fu Yue and Cheng Rong editions. I follow the emendation in the Lu Wenchao edition here.

XVII.49

宋書以召刀為劭 reads 宋書以召刀為邵 in the Lu Wenchao edition with a long note explaining the emendation.

拭卜 is emended to 栻卜 in the Wang Liqi edition.

XVII.50

古者暴曬字與暴疾字相似 reads 古者暴曬字與暴疾字相似 in the Fu Yue and Cheng Rong editions.

XVIII.1

自春秋摽齊言之傳 reads 自春秋標齊言之傳 in the Lu Wenchao edition.

離騷目楚詞之經 reads 離騷目楚辭之經 in the Lu Wenchao edition.

XVIII.2

加以內言外言 reads 加以外言內言 in the Fu Yue and Cheng Rong editions.

鋒出 is glossed by Wang Liqi as "emerge like [a multitude of] blades" (539). But most likely it should be taken as the same as 蜂出 (variant form: 蠢出), "emerge profusely and chaotically like a swarm of wasps," as in *Shi ji* 15.685: "矯稱蠢出, 誓盟不信."

摧而量之 reads 權而量之 in the Cheng Rong edition.

XVIII.6

吾家子女 reads 吾家兒女 in all other editions.

XVIII.8

入室求曰搜 reads 入室求曰搜 in all editions and 入室求曰[句] 搜 in the Lu Wenchao edition. I emend it according to the *Xu Jiaxun* edition cited in Wang Liqi (Wang 545).

XVIII.10

東郭牙望見桓公 reads 東郭牙望桓公 in all other editions.

XVIII.13

焉者鳥名 reads 焉字鳥名 in all other editions
或云語詞 reads 或云語辭 in the Lu Wenchao edition.

XVIII.14

而北人即呼為也字 reads 而北人即呼為也 in the Lu Wenchao edition.
此又為未定辭乎 reads 此又為未定乎 in the Lu Wenchao edition.
下列德以折之耳 reads 下乃列德以折之耳 in the Lu Wenchao edition.
It reads 下方刌德以折之耳 in the Cheng Rong edition.

XVIII.16

外無良師友故耳 reads 外無賢師友故耳 in the Cheng Rong edition.

XVIII.17

比世有人名暹 reads 北世有人名暹 in the Cheng Rong edition.
名斠: a note in the "Song edition" gives the pronunciation: 音藥.
自稱為獢: a note in the "Song edition" gives the pronunciation: 音爍.

XIX.2

舉世惟知其書 reads 舉世但知其書 in the Lu Wenchao edition.

XIX.3

梁武祕閣散逸以來 reads 梁氏祕閣散逸以來 in all other editions.
方知陶隱居、阮交州、蕭祭酒諸書 reads 方知陶隱居、阮交州、蕭祭酒 in the Lu Wenchao edition.
莫不得義之之一體 reads 莫不得義之之逸體 in the Bao Tingbo "Song edition" and reads 莫不得義之之體 in all other editions. Yan Shihui suggests that 莫不得義之之逸體 should read 莫不得義之之一體 based on a citation in Zhang Yanyuan's 張彥遠 (ca. 815–ca. 877) *Fashu yaolu* 法書要錄 (Yan Shihui 693), which makes good sense.

XIX.4

邵陵王頗行偽字: according to a note in the "Song edition" here, another edition has a note here stating: "For example, writing *cao* ("grass") on top of *qian* ("front") or *chang* ("length; strength") besides *neng* ("ability"), and so on" (前上為草、能傍作長之類是也). This statement appears as part of the text proper in the Fu Yue and Cheng Rong editions, and demonstrates clearly that Yan Zhitui is speaking of graphic forms rather than calligraphic style here.
逐便轉移 reads 遂便轉移 in the Fu Yue and Cheng Rong editions.

XIX.5

姚元摽工於草隸 reads 姚元標工於楷隸 in the Fu Yue and Cheng Rong editions (followed by Wang Liqi), and reads 姚元標工於草隸 in the Lu Wenchao edition (followed by Zhou Fagao).

XIX.6

此乃陶隱居弟子杜道士所為 reads 乃陶隱居弟子杜道士所為 in the Lu Wenchao edition.

XIX.7

吾家嘗有梁元帝手畫蟬雀白團扇及馬圖 reads 吾家嘗有梁元帝手畫蟬雀白團扇及馬圖 in the Lu Wenchao edition, and reads 吾家常有梁元帝手畫蟬雀白團扇及馬圖 in the Fu Yue and Cheng Rong editions.
翫古知今 reads 翫閱古今 in all other editions.

XIX.9

江南謂世之常射 reads 江南為世之常射 in the Fu Yue and Cheng Rong editions.

XIX.10

今人生疑於卜 reads 今人疑生於卜 in the Lu Wenchao edition.

XIX.12

玉輅變、玉歷十許種書 reads 玉變、玉歷十許種書 in the Fu Yue and Cheng Rong editions. In the "Song edition" there is a note saying that a different edition reads 玉變、玉歷十許種書. It is possible, as Wang Liqi surmises, that *Yuling* 玉輅 is an error for *Yuqian* 玉鈐 (*Jade Lock*), a phrase that appears in several Daoist titles (see Yan Zhitui's "Poem on Immortals" in this volume).

XIX.13

至如反支不行 reads 如反支不行 in the Lu Wenchao edition.

XX.2

已啟求揚都 reads 啟求揚都 in the Fu Yue and Cheng Rong editions.

XX.4

隨為私記耳 reads 隨為私記 in the Fu Yue and Cheng Rong editions.

XX.5

及七月半盂蘭盆，望於汝也 reads 及盡忠信，不辱其親，所望於汝也 in the Fu Yue and Cheng Rong editions. The variant deletes the mention of the Buddhist festival and makes the statement strictly "Confucian."

"Poem on Immortals" 神仙詩

Lu Qinli 2283; *Wenyuan yinghua* 225; *Gu shi ji* 110; Wang Liqi 718; Zhang Aitang 425–26.

"Ancient Theme: Two Poems" 古意詩二首

I

Lu Qinli 2283; *Yiwen leiju* 26; *Gu shi ji* 110; l. 7 cited in *Taiping yulan* 196; Wang Li 709; Zhang Aitang 431–32.

7 數從明月讌 reads 屢陪明月宴 in *Taiping yulan*.

8 During his first tenure as governor of Jingzhou (526–539), Xiao Yi had an affair with a local girl named Li Tao'er 李桃兒. He took her with him when called back to the capital in 539, but it was a violation of regulations, and his brother and successor, Xiao Xu 蕭繹 (504–547), threatened to inform the emperor of his misconduct. Xiao Yi was forced to send Li Tao'er back to Jingzhou, and wrote a poem in which he referred to her as the goddess of Wu Mountain (Lu Qinli 2060). The love story was well-known to contemporaries and celebrated in poems, in which Xiao Yi's Sunny Cloud Tower, with its allusion to the goddess of Wu Mountain, is associated with Li Tao'er (Tian 2018: 146).

23 不獲殉陵墓 reads 未獲殉陵墓 in *Gu shi ji*.

II

Lu Qinli 2283; *Yiwen leiju* 26; *Gu shi ji* 110; Wang Liqi 712; Zhang Aitang 432–33.

10 價值詎連城 reads 價直距連城 in *Yiwen leiju*.

"A Companion Piece to Adviser Yang's 'Listening to the Singing Cicadas'" 和陽納言聽鳴蟬篇

Lu Qinli 2284; *Chuxue ji* 30; *Gu shi ji* 110; Wang Liqi 714–15; Zhang Aitang 428–29.

According to *Bei shi* 30, after the Northern Qi was conquered by the Northern Zhou in 577, several Qi courtiers who were brought to Chang'an, the Zhou capital, wrote poems on this topic together. Besides Yan Zhitui's piece, the one by Lu Sidao (see note to IX.33) is also extant. The acclaimed poet Yu Xin was said to have read all the poems and particularly admired Lu Sidao's piece.

2 *Chuxue ji* reads 秋蟬悲非一處.

31–34 *Gu shi ji* has a note saying that the lines beginning with 紅顏宿昔同春花 contain some lacunae. These four lines are set apart from the preceding lines in Wang Liqi. 秋華 reads 秋草 in *Gu shi ji*, followed by Lu Qinli, Wang Liqi, and Zhang Aitang; but 秋華 is correct because 華 (MC hwae) rhymes with 花 (MC xwae) and 車 (MC tsyhae).

"Passing by Dizhu at Night on the Way from Zhou to Qi" 從周入齊夜度砥柱

Lu Qinli 2283–84 and 2190 (under Daoist Master Huimu, see note below); *Wenjing mifu lun* "East"; *Wenyuan yinghua* 289; *Yinchuang zalu* 1, 14; *Gu shi ji* 110; Wang Liqi 720–21; Zhang Aitang 427.

Gu shi ji has a note saying, "The *Beautiful Couplets of Liang Lyricists* (*Liang ciren liju* 梁詞人麗句) attributes it to a Daoist master Huimu 惠慕道士 instead, and the title reads 'I Encountered the Northern Enemies and Was About to Flee, and Composed This Poem' ("Fanlu jiang tao zuo" 犯虜將逃作)." The editorship of the *Beautiful Couplets of Liang Lyricists* is attributed to the Tang poet Li Shangyin 李商隱 (ca. 813–ca. 858); the work consists of poems by fifteen sixth-century authors, including the Western Liang (or Later Liang) Emperor Ming 梁明帝 (Xiao Kui 蕭歸, r. 562–585) as well as ghosts' poems and children's rhymes. It is preserved through the twelfth-century work, *Yinchuang zalu* (14).

1 俠客重艱辛 reads 俠客倦艱辛 in *Wenjing mifu lun*; it reads 使客倦艱辛 in *Shige* (*Yinchuang zalu* 1) and 客子倦艱辛 in *Liang ciren liju* (*Yinchuang zalu* 14, and Lu Qinli 2190).

4 雞鳴起成人 reads 雞鳴越成人 in *Shige* (*Yinchuang zalu* 1).

5 露鮮華劍彩 reads 露鮮花斂影 in *Shige* (*Yinchuang zalu* 1) and Lu Qinli 2190; it reads 露鮮花劍影 in *Wenjing mufu lun* as well as *Liang ciren liju* (*Yinchuang zalu* 14).

8 北海就孫賓 reads 北海問孫賓 in *Shige* (*Yinchuang zalu* 1).

"Rhapsody on Viewing My Life" 觀我生賦

Bei Qi shu 45; Lu Wenchao *Zhuan* 2b–16a; Yan Kejun, *Quan Sui wen* 13.4088–90; Wang Liqi 657–703; Dien 42–71; Zhang Aitang 307–39.

25 問我辰之安在 is emended from 問我良之安在 in Lu Wenchao, followed by Wang Liqi and Zhang Aitang. I adopt the emendation here.

27 Original Note: *Shouming* 授命 means to offer one's life and service to one's lord or one's state. Rather than "giving him [Hou Jing] life," *shou qi ming* here refers to "offering his [Hou Jing's] service." The phrase is used in the same sense as in a forged letter of submission to the Wu ruler, written by the Wu courtier Hu Zong 胡綜 (183–243) in the name of the Wei courtier Wu Zhi 吳質 (177–230): "Now, with sincerity, I, your subject, offer my service from afar" 今臣款款, 遠授其命.

55–56 Original Note: 湘州刺史河東王譽 reads 相州刺史河東王譽 in several editions of *Bei Qi shu* (see collation notes). Xiang 湘, which is adopted in the text proper, is correct.

60 扶車 ("assisting the carriage") is unclear. Lu Wenchao suggests it is an error for 綠車, also known as 皇孫車 (Imperial Grandson's Carriage), a type of carriage for the imperial grandson to ride in. Qian Daxin 錢大昕 (1728–1804), on the other hand, proposes that it is a corruption of Fusu 扶蘇 (d. 210 BCE), the eldest son of the First Qin Emperor who failed to become his successor (see Wang Liqi 665). Lu Wenchao's suggestion makes more sense, since this couplet is about the imperial grandson, not about the son, Xiao Tong. Fusu died of suicide under order of a forged imperial decree after the passing of the First Emperor; the circumstances do not fit Xiao Tong's death.

60 Original Note: 嫡皇孫 reads 嬌皇孫 in Yan Kejun.

67 子既殞 reads 子既損 ("A son was lost") in Yan Kejun and Wang Liqi. Either variant does not change the meaning of this phrase.

69–70 Original Note: 府 in 河東府褚顯族據投岳陽 reads 符 in one of the *Bei Qi shu* editions. Dien believes that Yueyang here refers to the city of Yueyang in Xiangzhou, not the Prince of Yueyang (Dien 135). However, there is no evidence supporting this claim.

79–80 Original Note: 汪 reads 注 in the base editions of *Bei Qi shu* and is emended to 汪.

85–86 Original Note: "Suining du" 綏寧度 is unclear. Qian Daxin believes *du* 度 should be *hou* 侯 (marquis).

104 向詡 reads 白詡 in all older editions of *Bei Qi shu*, Lu Wenchao, and Yan Kejun. It is emended in Wang Liqi (see Wang 670–71), Dien (50), and Zhang Aitang (315). I adopt the emendation.

108 地道 reads 他道 in *Bei Qi shu*, Lu Wenchao, and Yan Kejun. It is emended in Wang Liqi (see Wang 670–71), Dien (50), and Zhang Aitang (315). I adopt the emendation.

113 先主 reads 先生 in *Bei Qi shu* and is emended to 先主 in Lu Wenchao.

115–16 Original Note: Shen Jiong 沈炯 (502–560) uses the term "taking off clothing" in speaking of his own impending execution (and his last-minute escape) at the hand of Hou Jing's general Song Zixian in his "Rhapsody on the Returned Soul" ("Guihun fu" 歸魂賦), and the account of his experience in Qiu Yue's 丘悅 (fl. 708) *Summary Documents of the Three Kingdoms* (*Sanguo dianlue* 三國典略) uses the term "taking off clothing to go to execution" 解衣就戮.

122 衣霧: I take 衣霧 as 依霧, "relied-on fog," which makes more sense in the context than "[those who are] clothed in fog." Dragons and snakes were thought to rely on cloud and fog to ascend to the sky (see Lu Wenchao 7b). It also forms a better parallel with 假履 (literally, "borrowed shoes") in the next line.

123–24 Original Note: 十一月十九日 (January 1, 552) reads 十二月十九日 (January 30, 552) in Lu Wenchao, Yan Kejun, and Wang Liqi. 蓋天道紀大數 reads 芧天道紀大數 in *Bei Qi shu* and 芧天道繼大數 in all other editions; I emend 芧 to 蓋 based on the collation note in *Bei Qi shu*. The original note is missing in Zhang Aitang. Dien states that *Zizhi tongjian* 資治通鑑 gives the *yichou* 乙丑 day of the eleventh month (December 22, 551). However, *Zizhi tongjian* gives the *jichou* 己丑 day of the eleventh month, which was exactly the nineteenth day (*Zizhi tongjian* 164).

133 *Chou* 疇 is used here in the sense of "who," as in: "Who dares not to respectfully follow the excellent command of my king" 疇敢不祇若王之休命 (from the *Book of Documents*), or "Who could defy and lose reason, and yet preserve his life" 疇逆失而能存 (from Sima Xiangru, "On *Feng* and *Shan* Ceremony").

155–56 Original Note: 侯景既走，義師採穭失火 reads 侯景既平，我師採穭失火 in Lu Wenchao, Yan Kejun, Wang Liqi, and Zhang Aitang. 穭 reads 檑 in various editions of *Bei Qi shu* and is emended to 穭.

163 Original Note: 吏部尚書宗懷正、員外郎顏之推: Dien believes the text is corrupt and this line should be emended to 吏部尚書宗懍、正員郎顏之推 (Dien 152). Zong Lin 宗懍 (500–563) was a native of Jiangling and was made Minister of Personnel by Emperor Yuan. 王孝紀 reads 王孝純 in Lu Wenchao, Yan Kejun, and Wang Liqi. 宗善業 reads 宗菩業 in Lu Wenchao, Yan Kejun, and Dien, and reads 宗菩善 in Wang Liqi and Zhang Aitang.

175–76 Original Note: Lu Wenchao, Wang Liqi, and Zhang Aitang all take Prime Minister Yuwen 宇文丞相 as Yuwen Jue 宇文覺 (542–557), the son of Yuwen Tai.

177–78 民百萬而囚虜，書千兩而煙煬 reads 人民百萬而囚虜，書史千兩 而煙煬 in *Lidai minghua ji* 1.

180 斯文盡喪 reads 斯民盡喪 in Yan Kejun.

180 Original Note: 墳籍 reads 墳典 in one *Bei Qi shu* edition.

186 輈人神之無狀: Lu Wenchao believes 無狀 is an error, perhaps because the phrase is already used in l.182 (矜老疾之無狀). He proposes emending to 無杖 ("not to be relied on").

195–96 小臣恥其獨死，實有愧於胡顏: 恥其獨死 is literally "ashamed about dying alone." It is taken by Dien to mean his being ashamed by Emperor Yuan's lonely death (Dien 59); but one would not refer to his ruler's death in such bald terms. *Huyan* 胡顏 is literally "what face [does one have for not hastening to die]." The couplet here can be compared with ll. 23–24 in "Ancient Theme" I: 不獲殉陵墓，獨生良足恥.

198 Original Note: 官給疲驢瘦馬 reads 官疲驢瘦馬 in *Bei Qi shu* and Yan Kejun.

203 五牛 reads 玄牛 in *Bei Qi shu* and Yan Kejun.

210 仙弓 reads 仙宮 in *Bei Qi shu* and Yan Kejun.

242 陽侯 reads 陽度 in *Bei Qi shu* and is emended to 侯 in Lu Wenchao.

267 諫 reads 諫 in *Bei Qi shu* and Yan Kejun.

269–70 Original Note: 之推爾日隣禍，而儔流或有毀之推於祖僕射者 reads 之推爾日隣禍而免，儔流或有毀之推於祖僕射者 in Lu Wenchao (13b), Wang Liqi (698), and Zhang Aitang (335).

271 予 reads 子 in one of the *Bei Qi shu* editions and Yan Kejun.

276 惰琢玉之遺祉: Lu Wenchao believes 惰 should be 墮, "to ruin."

277–78 Original Note: this note is missing in Zhang Aitang.

279 度政: Lu Wenchao suspects that it should be 庶政.

304 郊鄉導: *Bei Qi shu* collation note suspects that 郊 should read 效.

309 信詔謀於公王 reads 信詔謀於公主 in a number of editions of *Bei Qi shu*, Lu Wenchao, Yan Kejun, and Wang Liqi. I follow the emendation, though imperfect, in *Bei Qi shu* (see collation note).

309–310 Original Note: in the name 高阿那肱, 肱 should be pronounced *gong* but was pronounced as *gui* 瓌 by contemporaries (*Bei Qi shu* 50). *Dao* 道 here is pronounced as, and interchangeable with, *dao* 導, "to lead or show the way," as in "Our humble domain will show you the way" 敝邑為道 (*The Zuo Tradition*, Duke Yin 5), or "I shall go before and show you the way" 來吾道夫先路 (from "Li sao" in the *Lyrics of Chu*). To translate *dao* as "on the road" as Dien did (69) does not make grammatical sense in the context.

314 屯: I take *zhun* here as a verb, "reach the fullness of," not as the name of the hexagram.

313–14 Original Note: 趙郡李穆叔調妙占天文算術: commentators believe that 調 here is superfluous.

317 鳥棽林 reads 鳥棽株 in Yan Kejun.

328 入榛 reads 入秦 in B*ei Qi shu*, Lu Wenchao, and Yan Kejun.

334 膏身: Lu Wenchao takes it to mean "nourish one's person," and so do Dien's and Zhang Aitang's translations. However, in early and early medieval writings, when *shen* is used with *gao*, it is always for the body to become a source of nourishment, i.e., to die and sacrifice one's body. For instance, 身膏草野 (*Han History*); 爭膏身於夷狄以要功名 (*History of the Later Han*). I translate the phrase accordingly.

"Rhapsody on Questioning the Sages" 稽聖賦 [Fragments]

Wang Liqi, "*Yan Zhitui ji* jiyi" 顏之推集輯佚 (Wang 722–23), except for #8 and #14. Zhang Aitang, 442–44. Note: Zhang Aitang follows Wang Liqi, but mistakenly removes #11 to a list of "Erroneous Attributions to Yan Zhitui" (Zhang 449).

Note: The rhapsody had two commentaries, one by Yan Shigu and the other by Li Chunfeng 李淳風 (602–670).

1.
Cited in Cui Guitu's 崔龜圖 (ca. 9th century?) commentary on the *Record of the Northern Gateway* (*Beihu lu* 北戶錄) 1. The "Northern Gateway" was the name of a mythical kingdom in the farthest south, and this work is an account of the customs and products of Lingnan (in modern Guangxi and Guangdong) by Duan Gonglu 段公路 (fl. 869–871). *Xin Tang shu* claims that Duan was the grandson of the prime minister Duan Wenchang 段文昌 (773–835).

2.
Cited in *Augmented Ya* (*Pi Ya* 埤雅) 2, "Explaining Fishes," a work by Lu Dian 陸佃 (1042–1102). The citation attributes the rhapsody to Yan Zhou 顏籀 (Yan Shigu's given name), mixing the commentator with the author of the rhapsody.

3.

Cited in *Pi Ya* 7, introduced simply with "Yan Zhitui says." Wang Liqi decides that it is from his "Rhapsody on Questioning the Sages."

4.

Cited in *Pi Ya* 7, introduced with "Yan Zhitui says."

5.

Cited in *Pi Ya* 7.

6.

Cited in *Pi Ya* 10.

7.

Cited in *Pi Ya* 11.

8.

Cited in *Pi Ya* 11.

Note: this fragment is not included in Wang Liqi's "*Yan Zhitui ji* jiyi" 顏之推集輯佚.

9.

Cited in *Pi Ya* 15.

10.

Cited in *Pi Ya* 16.

11.

Cited in the *Account of Species Responding to One Another* (*Wulei xianggan zhi* 物類相感志) 16, an encyclopedic work in eighteen scrolls attributed to Su Shi 蘇軾 (1037–1101). However, according to Song bibliographies, there was a *Wulei xianggan zhi* in ten scrolls authored by the Buddhist monk Zanning 贊寧 (919–1001). In *Wulei xianggan zhi*, this fragment is cited in the entry on "Cicadas" 蟬. The citation is followed by a quotation from the commentary on the rhapsody:

注：抱朴子曰：﹁有自然之蟬，有荇菜莖、芩根、土龍之屬皆化蟬。﹂

According to its commentary, *Baopuzi* says, 'There are naturally formed cicadas; there are also cicadas transformed from the stems of water-fringe, the root of runner-reed, or earthworms and their like.'

The *Baopuzi* citation is followed by a comment presumably made by the compiler of *Wulei xianggan zhi*, which is (erroneously) taken by Wang Liqi as part of the *Baopuzi* citation (Wang 723):

今驗水澤巨樹處多水蟲登岸，冗有烈化出為蟬也。

Nowadays we can testify to this by observing that where are big trees near a body of water, there are often water bugs climbing onto the shore, some of which may turn into cicadas.

I take *rong* 冗 here as *rong* 容, "perhaps" (cf. Wang Liqi's transcription of the last line: 空有裂化出為蟬也). The *Baopuzi* citation above appears in *Taiping yulan* 937.4298, with minor differences (田地既有自然之鱓而有荇菹苓根土龍之屬化為鱓), and this has been included in Appendix I of *Baopuzi neipian*. However, one should note that *Taiping yulan* includes the *Baopuzi* citation under the entry on "Eel" (*shanyu* 鱓魚), not on "Cicada" (*chan* 蟬). There is another item from *Taiping yulan* (1000.4556) citing *Baopuzi*: "The root of the *qin* plant turns into eel" 蔜根化為鱓. *Qin* is identified as an aquatic plant and probably an alternative graph for *qin* 芩.

12.
Cited in *The Carried Bodkin* (*Pei xi* 佩觿) by Guo Zhongshu 郭忠恕 (d. 977).

13.
Wang Liqi gives the following passage, cited in *Beihu lu* 1 as being from Yan Zhitui's rhapsody:

水母，東海謂之蛇 (音蜡)，正白濛濛如沫。

"Water-mother" is called jellyfish [pronounced as *zha*] on the east coast. It is pure white, varied and numerous, like foam.

Wang Liqi believes that this passage, unrhymed, is not part of the rhapsody itself but rather of Yan Shigu's commentary. He is likely correct, although we cannot be certain whether it is from the commentary by Yan Shigu or by Li Chunfeng. It is reasonable to assume that the commentary is about *shuimu* ("water-mother") mentioned in Yan Zhitui's rhapsody.

The full citation from *Beihu lu* reads as follows and should be given in its entirety in Wang Liqi for the reason I will explain below:

稽聖賦云：水母，東海謂之蛇 (音蜡)，正白濛濛如沫，生物，皆別無眼耳，故不知避人，常有蝦依隨之，蝦見人驚，此物亦隨之而驚，以蝦為目自衛也。

According to "The Rhapsody on Questioning the Sages," water-mother is called jellyfish [pronounced as *zha*] on the east coast; it is pure white, varied and numerous, like foam. It is a living creature, but has no eyes or ears, so it does not know to avoid people. A shrimp is always attached to it. When it sees people, the shrimp is startled, and the creature to which the shrimp is attached also becomes startled. Thus it uses the shrimp as its eyes for self-defense.

This is in turn cited from the *Account of the Southern Yue* (*Nan Yue zhi* 南越志) by Shen Huaiyuan 沈懷遠 (fl. 454–465), which is preserved, with only minor differences, in Li Shan's 李善 (d. 689) commentary on Guo Pu's 郭璞 (276–324) "Rhapsody on the Yangzi River" ("Jiang fu" 江賦) in *Wen xuan* 12.563:

海岸間頗有水母，東海謂之蛇，正白，濛濛如沫，生物，有智識，無耳目，故不知避人。常有蝦依隨之，蝦見人則驚，此物亦隨之而沒。

By the seashores there are a great many "water-mothers." It is called jellyfish on the east coast. It is pure white, varied and numerous, like foam. It is a living creature with sentience, but has no eyes or ears, so it does not know to avoid people. But a shrimp is always attached to it. When it sees people, the shrimp is startled, and this creature to which the shrimp is attached also vanishes with the shrimp.

Thus the commentary on Yan Zhitui's rhapsody must have come from *Nanyue zhi* and should be quoted in its entirety.

14.

Cited in Du Guangting 杜光庭 (850–933), *A Record of the Immortals Gathering at Yongcheng* (*Yongcheng jixian lu* 墉城集仙錄) 6; also in *Taiping guangji* 479.3945 (cited from *Yuanhua zhuan shiyi* 原化傳拾遺, with *Yuanhua zhuan* perhaps being a variant version of *Yuanhua ji* 原化記, a late ninth century story collection).

Note: this fragment does not appear in Wang Liqi's "*Yan Zhitui ji* jiyi" 顏之推集輯佚.

爰有女人 reads 安有女 in *Taiping guangji*.

*

Note: Wang Liqi gives a fragment that he finds in the *Sound and Meaning of All Scriptures* (*Yiqie jing yinyi* 一切經音義) by the Buddhist monk Huilin 慧琳 (737–820) and believes it to be from Yan Zhitui's rhapsody: "The crow dwells in fire, but does not burn; the hare resides in water, but does not drown" 烏處火而不燋, 兔居水而不溺 (*Yiqie jing yinyi* 51). Upon close examination, there is no clear indication that this is the case. Rather, it seems to be Huilin's summary of a passage from Wang Chong's *Lun heng*. Huilin does cite Li Chunfeng's commentary on Yan Zhitui's rhapsody, but it seems to merely consist of a citation from Ge Hong's *Baopuzi*. There is no clear evidence that Li Chunfeng was refuting Yan Zhitui in his commentary as Wang Liqi speculates here (Wang 724).

Appendix

Yan Zhitui's Biography in Dynastic Histories

Yan Zhitui's biography appears in the "Biographies of Men of Letters" 文苑傳 in two dynastic histories: the *History of the Northern Qi* (*Bei Qi shu* 北齊書, subsequently *BQS*), compiled by Li Baiyao 李百藥 (564–647), son of prominent Northern Qi/Zhou/Sui courtier and writer Li Delin 李德林 (see *Family Instructions* XVII.23); and the *Northern History* (*Bei shi* 北史, subsequently *BS*) compiled by Li Yanshou 李延壽 (fl. 620s–650s), son of Li Dashi 李大師 (570–628).[1] *BQS* was completed in 636 while BS was completed in 659. Both works had been started by the father and finished by the son, a pattern that was first set by the Western Han historian Sima Qian 司馬遷 (ca. 145 BCE–ca. 86 BCE) and his father Sima Tan 司馬談 (d. 110 BCE).

The two versions of Yan Zhitui's biography are largely identical. There are two notable differences: first, the *BQS* version is considerably longer than the *BS* version primarily because it includes Yan Zhitui's "Rhapsody on Viewing My Life" in its entirety; the *BS* version neither includes the rhapsody nor even makes any mention of it; second, the *BS* version refers to Xiao Yi by his princely title, in contrast to the *BQS* version that refers to him by name, and is generally more respectful in its description of the southern dynasty. This attitude evokes Li Yanshou's statement in the "Self-Account" ("Zixu" 自序), at the end of the *Northern History*, in which he recalls his late father's intent in creating a more balanced history of the north and south:

> 大師少有著述之志，常以宋、齊、梁、陳、魏、齊、周、隋南北分隔，南書謂北為索虜，北書指南為島夷。又各以其本國周悉，書別國並不能備，亦往往失實。常欲改正，將擬吳越春秋，編年以備南北。

Dashi aspired since his youth to be an author who would write and transmit. In his mind, Song, Qi, Liang, Chen, Wei, Qi, Zhou, and Sui were divided into south and north, and the southern books would refer to northerners as "braided savages" and the northern

---

1 *Bei Qi shu* 45.617–26. *Bei shi* 83.2794–796.

books would refer to southerners as "island barbarians"; each side was comprehensive and inclusive in recording the history of their own state but was unable to be complete in recording the history of the other state, not to mention that they frequently got the facts wrong. Therefore, Dashi wanted to rectify the situation. He planned to emulate the *Spring and Autumn Annals of Wu and Yue* and compile a chronological history of the south and north.[2]

The Chinese text consists of the *BQS* version followed by the *BS* version. My translation is based on the *BQS* version. I only offer a translation of the *BS* version when there is substantial difference beyond minor variations in phrasing. I also underline the two versions' differences for the reader's easy comparison.

---

2 *Bei shi* 100.3343. The *Spring and Autumn Annals of Wu and Yue* was an account of the conflicts of two southern states, Wu and Yue, during the early part of the fifth century BCE. The work is equally divided into two halves, the first devoted to Wu, and the second to Yue; the compiler does not take sides with either state.

BQS 1

顏之推字介，琅邪臨沂人也。<u>九世祖含，從晉元東渡，官至侍</u>
<u>中、右光祿、西平侯</u>。父勰，<u>梁湘東王繹鎮西府諮議參軍</u>。世
善周官、左氏，<u>之推早傳家業</u>。

BS 1

顏之推字介，琅邪臨沂人也。<u>祖見遠、父協，並以義烈稱</u>。世
善周官、左氏<u>學</u>，<u>俱南史有傳</u>。

BQS 1

Yan Zhitui, whose courtesy name was Jie, hailed from Linyi of Langye.[1] His ninth-generation ancestor, Han, followed Jin Emperor Yuan and crossed to the east [of the Yangzi River].[2] He eventually reached the positions of Palace Attendant and Grand Master of Splendid Emolument of the Right, and he was enfeoffed as Marquis of Xiping. Yan Zhitui's father, Xie, was Administrative Advisor at the military headquarters of the Liang Prince of Xiangdong, Xiao Yi, Defender-general of the West.[3] The Yan family specialized in the *Zhou Offices* and the *Zuo Tradition*.[4] Zhitui inherited the family legacy from an early age.

BS 1

Yan Zhitui, whose courtesy name was Jie, hailed from Linyi of Langye. His grandfather Jianyuan and his father Xie were both known for their unyielding uprightness.[5] His family specialized in the study of *Zhou Offices* and the *Zuo Tradition* for generations. Yan Jianyuan and Yan Xie each has a biography in the *Southern History*.[6]

---

1 In modern Shandong. This was the Yan clan's ancestral home.

2 Yan Xie's biography in the *Liang History* states that Yan Han was Yan Xie's seventh-generation ancestor (*Liang shu* 50.727), which would make Yan Han the eighth-generation ancestor of Yan Zhitui. The *Liang History* begins the count with Yan Han's son, but the *BQS* begins with Yan Han himself, hence the difference.

3 The character for *xie* in *BQS* is different from the character for *xie* in *BS* (勰 vs. 協). *Liang shu* and *Nan shi* both read 協.

4 Both are Confucian classics. *Zhou Offices* is another name for the *Rites of Zhou* (*Zhou li*).

5 This refers to Yan Jianyuan's suicide upon Liang's replacement of Qi, and Yan Xie's refusal to serve in the Liang imperial court due to the circumstances of his father's death. See *Liang shu* 50.727 and *Nan shi* 72.1784–785.

6 See *Nan shi* 72.1784–785. Both are in "Biographies of Men of Letters" 文學傳.

BQS 2

年十二，值繹自講莊、老，便預門徒。虛談非其所好，還
習禮、傳，博覽羣書，無不該洽，詞情典麗，甚為西府所
稱。<u>繹</u>以為其國<u>左</u>常侍，加鎮西墨曹參軍。好飲酒，多任縱，
不修邊幅，時論以此少之。

BS 2

<u>之推</u>年十二，遇<u>梁湘東王</u>自講莊、老，<u>之推</u>便預門徒。虛談非
其所好，還習禮、傳。博覽書史，無不該洽，辭情典麗，甚為
西府所稱。<u>湘東王</u>以為其國<u>右</u>常侍，加鎮西墨曹參軍。好飲
酒，多任縱，不修邊幅，時論以此少之。

BQS 3

<u>繹</u>遣世子方諸出鎮郢州，以<u>之推</u>掌管記。值侯景陷郢州，[<u>之推</u>
被執，]⁶ 頻欲殺之，賴其行臺郎中王則以獲免。被囚送建業。
景平，還江陵。時<u>繹已自立</u>，以<u>之推</u>為散騎侍郎，奏舍人事。

BS 3

<u>湘東</u>遣世子方諸鎮郢州，以<u>之推為中撫軍府外兵參軍</u>，掌管
記。遇侯景陷郢州，頻欲殺之，賴其行臺郎中王則以免。景
平，還江陵。時<u>湘東即位</u>，以<u>之推</u>為散騎侍郎，奏舍人事。

---

1 Twelve *sui* is roughly eleven years old by Western reckoning.
2 See Yan Zhitui's account of his experience in *Family Instructions*, VIII.22.
3 Xiao Yi's headquarters at Jingzhou to the west of the Liang capital Jiankang.
4 This was Yan Zhitui's first official post. It is related in the author's note to ll. 77–
  78 of the "Rhapsody on Viewing My Life." However, instead of Left Attendant,
  the note reads "Right Attendant," as does the *BS* version.
5 Cf. Yan Zhitui's description of his youthful self in his *Family Instructions*, I.4. *Ren
  zong* indicates being reckless and unrestrained in behavior; but it does not necessarily imply being "lax in one's responsibilities" (Dien 37). Being careless about
  appearances forms an interesting contrast with the description of his father Yan
  Xie in the latter's biography: "Although Xie's family only had meager means, he
  cared about appearances, and would not go out unless in a horse-drawn carriage"
  協家雖貧素, 而修飾邊幅, 非車馬未嘗出游 (*Nan shi* 72.1785).

BQS 2

When Zhitui was at the age of twelve *sui*, [Xiao] Yi personally lectured on *Zhuangzi* and *Laozi*, and Zhitui became one of the students.[1] He did not, however, care for empty talk,[2] and applied himself to the ritual classic [the *Zhou Offices*] and the [*Zuo*] *Tradition* instead. He read widely, and was well-versed in all sorts of topics. His writing was beautiful and elegant, and received much praise in the Western Headquarters.[3] Yi made Zhitui Left Attendant of his princedom, and later also appointed him Adjutant of the Defender-general of the West in the Section of Justice.[4] Fond of drinking, Zhitui was unrestrained in behavior and careless about his personal appearance.[5] As a result, he was not highly regarded by contemporaries.

BQS 3

Yi sent his heir Fangzhu to be governor of Yingzhou, and put Zhitui in charge of secretarial matters [on Fangzhu's staff].[7] When Hou Jing seized control of Yingzhou, [Zhitui was captured] and several times was about to be executed, but each time he was saved by Wang Ze, the Director of Hou Jing's Branch Department of State Affairs.[8] He was subsequently taken to Jiankang as a prisoner. After Hou Jing was defeated, he returned to Jiangling. At the time, Yi had already set himself up on the throne,[9] and he made Zhitui Gentleman Cavalier Attendant performing the duty of Secretary.[10]

---

6 These four characters are added based on the citation in *Taiping yulan* 642.3004.

7 This is narrated in the "Rhapsody on Viewing My Life," ll. 85–92, and the author's original notes to these lines. The *BS* version notes that Yan Zhitui's official title at the time was Adjutant of the Protector General in the Section for Outer Troops, a piece of information that can be found in Yan Zhitui's rhapsody.

8 This is narrated in the "Rhapsody on Viewing My Lufe," ll. 111–18; the author's original note to these lines records the name and office of his savior, as a token of his gratitude.

9 The *BS* version reads, "At the time, *the Prince of Xiangdong had already taken the throne.*"

10 Again, this biographical detail can be gleaned in the original notes to ll. 161–62 of the "Rhapsody on Viewing My Life."

BQS 4

後為周軍所破。大將軍<u>李顯慶</u>重之，<u>薦</u>往弘農，令掌其兄陽平
公遠書翰。<u>值</u>河水暴長，具船將妻子<u>來奔</u>，經砥柱之險，時人
稱其勇決。

BS 4

後為周軍所破，大將軍<u>李穆</u>重之，<u>送</u>往弘農，令掌其兄陽平公
遠書翰。<u>遇</u>河水暴長，具船將妻子<u>奔齊</u>，經砥柱之險，時人稱
其勇決。

BQS 5

<u>顯祖</u>見而悦之，即除奉朝請，引於內館中，侍從左右，頗被顧
眄。<u>天保末，從至天池</u>，以為中書舍人，令中書郎段孝信將勅
書出示之推。之推營外飲酒，孝信還以狀言，顯祖乃曰：「且
停。」由是遂寢。<u>河清末，被舉為趙州功曹參軍</u>。<u>尋</u>待詔文林
館，除司徒錄事參軍。

BS 5

<u>文宣</u>見，悦之，即除奉朝請，引於內館中，侍從左右，頗被顧
眄。<u>後從至天泉池</u>，以為中書舍人，令中書郎段孝信將勅示之
推。之推營外飲酒，孝信還以狀言，文宣乃曰：「且停。」由
是遂寢。<u>後</u>待詔文林館，除司徒錄事參軍。

---

1 I accept the *BQS* collation note's emendation of Li Xian to Li Xianqing, which
  was the courtesy name of Li Mu 李穆 (510–586), as well as the emendation of
  the name Qingyuan to Yuan, as Li Mu's elder brother Li Yuan was indeed the
  Duke of Yangping. *BQS* 45.617. Li Mu took part in the Jiangling campaign.

2 The phrasing *lai ben* ("fled here"), as opposed to the phrase *ben Qi* ("fled to Qi")
  in the *BS* version, reveals the different points of view of the *BQS* historian and
  the *BS* historian. Yan Zhitui relates his decision to flee to Qi and the boat journey
  in the "Rhapsody on Viewing My Life" in ll. 223–48.

3 Xianzu was the temple name of the Northern Qi Emperor Wenxuan 文宣, Gao
  Yang 高洋 (r. 550–559). The *BS* version reads "[Emperor] Wenxuan" for "Xianzu." Audience Attendant was one of the numerous low-ranking members of the

BQS 4

Later, Jiangling was captured by the Zhou army. Li Xianqing, the Great General, valued him, and sent him to Hongnong [in modern He'nan] with a recommendation, where he was put in charge of correspondence for Li Xian's elder brother, Yuan, the Duke of Yangping.[1] It so happened that the Yellow River was flooding at the time. He fitted out a boat, took his family, and braving the danger of Dizhu fled here [to Qi].[2] Contemporaries commended him for his courage and decisiveness.

BQS 5

Emperor Xianzu met him and took a liking to him.[3] He appointed Zhitui Audience Attendant, introduced him into the inner halls, and kept him around, receiving him with much favor. Toward the end of the Tianbao era [550–559], Zhitui followed Xianzu to Tianchi.[4] Xianzu was going to appoint him Secretariat Drafter, and ordered Duan Xiaoxin, Gentleman Attendant in the Secretariat, to take the appointment edict to show Zhitui. Zhitui, however, was drinking somewhere outside the camp. Xiaoxin reported back to Xianzu, who then said, "Let the matter rest for the time being." Subsequently the appointment never took place. At the end of the Heqing era [562–564], he was recommended to be an Administrator in the Labor Section at Zhaozhou.[5] Subsequently, he became an Attendee at the Grove of Letters Institute, and was then appointed Administrative Supervisor under the Minister of Education.[6]

Department of Scholarly Counselors 集書省, whose functions included attending personally on the emperor, compiling court documents, examining all memorials to the throne, and offering feedback of various sorts to the emperor.

4 This Tianchi should be Qilian Chi 祁連池 in Shanxi. This happened in the sixth month of the last year of the Tianbao era (July 559). See *Bei Qi shu* 4.65. The *BS* version gives Tianquan Chi (in Luoyang), which is an error.

5 Heqing was the second reign title of the Northern Qi Emperor Wucheng 武成 (r. 561–565). Zhaozhou was a prefecture (in modern Hebei). Yan Zhitui related an anecdote about his Zhaozhou sojourn in *Family Instructions*, VIII.42.

6 In his rhapsody, Yan Zhitui relates the impossibility of returning to the south via the Northern Qi in ll. 249–58 and his appointment in 573 at the Grove of Letters Institute in ll. 259–60 and the original note to this couplet.

BQS 6

之推聰穎機悟，博識有才辯，工尺牘，應對閑明，大為祖珽所
重，令掌知館事，判署文書。<u>尋</u>遷通直散騎常侍，俄領中書舍
人。

帝時有取索，恒令中使傳旨，之推稟承宣告，館中皆受進止。
所進文章，皆是其封署，於進賢門奏之，待報方出。兼善於文
字，監校繕寫，處事勤敏，號為稱職。

帝甚加恩接，<u>顧遇逾厚</u>，為勳要者所嫉，常欲害之。崔季舒等
將諫也，之推取急還宅，故不連署。及召集諫人，之推亦被喚
入，勘無其名，<u>方得免禍</u>。尋除黃門侍郎。

BS 6

之推聰穎機悟，博識有才辯，工尺牘，應對閑明，大為祖珽所
重，令掌知館事，判署文書。遷通直散騎常侍，俄領中書舍
人。帝時有取索，恒令中使傳旨，之推稟承宣告，館中皆受進
止。所進文書，皆是其封署，於進賢門奏之，待報方出。兼善
於文字，監校繕寫，處事勤敏，號為稱職。帝甚加恩接。為勳
要者所嫉，常欲害之。崔季舒等將諫也，之推取急還宅，故不
連署。及召集諫人，之推亦被喚入，勘無名，得免。尋除黃門
侍郎。

---

1 Zu Ting was Zu Xiaozheng, a talented Qi courtier featured in a number of
sections in Yan Zhitui's *Family Instructions*. He wielded considerable power during
the reign of Gao Wei, the Last Ruler. He was ousted from the court in 573 and
thereafter died in the provinces.

BQS 6

Intelligent and quick-witted, Zhitui possessed broad learning, and was talented and eloquent. He was skillful at composing letters, and was knowledgeable and lucid in responding to inquiries. He was highly regarded by Zu Ting, who put him in charge of the affairs at the Grove of Letters Institute, and authorized him to sign off on the documents [prepared by the Institute].[1] Subsequently he was promoted to be Senior Recorder for Comprehensive Duty, and shortly afterward, he became Secretariat Drafter.

Whenever the emperor needed anything, he always sent a eunuch to convey the message.[2] Zhitui received it from the emperor and announced it to the other members of the Institute, who all took instructions from him. The literary writings presented to the emperor by the Institute were all sealed and signed by Zhitui, who would take them in [to the imperial palace] and await [for the emperor's acknowledgment] at the Jinxian Gate. He would only leave after he received a reply from the emperor. In addition, he was excellent with language and script, and supervised and collated copying and compiling. Diligent and quick in handling affairs, he was considered competent in his office.

The emperor treated him very well with increasing favor and generosity. This aroused jealousy in the powers that be, who constantly wanted to harm him. When Cui Jishu and others were about to remonstrate with the emperor, Zhitui happened to be taking a leave and was at home, so he did not sign his name on the petition.[3] When the emperor summoned all who had remonstrated, Zhitui, too, was called in. He only managed to escape execution when it was discovered upon investigation that his name was not on the petition. Shortly afterward, he was appointed Gentleman of the Palace Gate.[4].

---

2 The emperor here refers to Gao Wei, the Last Ruler.

3 Cui Jishu and the other courtiers petitioned the Last Ruler not to leave the capital Ye to go to Jinyang (modern Taiyuan, Shanxi). This incident happened in the winter of 573 (see the original note to ll. 267–70 of Yan Zhitui's "Rhapsody" and the footnote). Note that *quji* means taking time off from duty for personal reasons, with official permission. It does not mean that Yan Zhitui "became apprehensive" about what was going to transpire (Dien 40).

4 The events narrated in this section are related in ll. 261–70 of Yan Zhitui's rhapsody.

BQS 7

及周兵陷晉陽，帝輕騎還鄴，窘急計無所從，之推因宦者侍中鄧長顒進奔陳之策，仍勸募吳士千餘人以為左右，取青徐路共投陳國。帝甚納之，以告丞相高阿那肱等。阿那肱不願入陳，乃云吳士難信，<u>不須募之</u>。勸帝送珍寶累重向青州，且守三齊<u>之</u>地，若不可保，徐浮海南渡。雖不從之推<u>計</u>策，然猶以為平原太守，令守河津。

BS 7

及周兵陷晉陽，帝輕騎還鄴，窘急計無所從。之推因宦者侍中鄧長顒進奔陳策，仍勸募吳士千餘人以為左右，取青徐路共投陳國。帝納之，以告丞相高阿那肱等。阿那肱不願入陳，乃云吳士難信，勸帝送珍寶累重向青州，且守三齊地，若不可保，徐浮海南度。雖不從之推策，然猶以為平原太守，令守河津。

BQS 8

齊亡入周，大象末為御史上士。隋開皇中，太子召為學士，甚見禮重。尋以疾終。有文三十卷，撰家訓二十篇，並行於世。<u>曾撰觀我生賦，文致清遠，其詞曰：[…]</u>

BS 8

齊亡入周。大象末為御史上士。隋開皇中，太子召為文學，深見禮重。尋以疾終。有文<u>集</u>三十卷，撰家訓二十篇，並行於世。

---

1 This happened in January 577.
2 Deng Zhangyong was a eunuch who was favored by the Last Ruler and held great power in the last years of the Qi (*BQS* 50.693).
3 Qingzhou or Qing prefecture is in modern Shandong and Xuzhou or Xu prefecture is in modern Jiangsu.
4 The Three Qi refers to the coastal region to the east of modern Shandong.
5 Pingyuan (in modern Shandong) was on the Yellow River and not far from the coast.

BQS 7

When the Zhou army attacked and captured Jinyang, the emperor returned to Ye with a small retinue.[1] He was in desperate straits and did not know what to do. Through the eunuch Palace Attendant Deng Zhangyong, Zhitui suggested fleeing to Chen.[2] He further advised the emperor to muster over a thousand Wu gentry as followers and together seek refuge in the state of Chen by way of Qingzhou and Xuzhou.[3] The emperor was quite receptive to the plan, and told his prime minister Gao E'nagui and the others about it. E'nagui was unwilling to go to Chen, so he said to the emperor that men of Wu were difficult to trust and there was no need to rally them. Instead, he urged the emperor to send treasures, properties, and family to Qingzhou, and to try to hold the territories of the Three Qi;[4] and, should they be unable to defend the Three Qi, then they could take to the sea and cross to the south unhurriedly. Even though the emperor did not follow Zhitui's counsel, he nevertheless appointed him Magistrate of Pingyuan and ordered him to defend the river ford.[5]

BQS 8

After Qi fell, he joined the Zhou court. At the end of the Daxiang era [579–580], he was appointed Senior Serviceman of the Censorate.[6] In the middle of the Kaihuang era [581–600], the Crown Prince summoned him to be an Academician and treated him with great courtesy and respect.[7] Shortly after, he died of illness. He left [a collection of] literary writings in thirty scrolls, and the *Family Instructions* in twenty chapters, both of which are circulating in the world. He once composed a "Rhapsody on Viewing My life," which has a lucid and noble air. It reads as follows: [...].[8]

---

6 Daxiang was the reign title of the last Northern Zhou emperor (Emperor Jing 靜 帝, r. 579–581).

7 Kaihuang was the first reign title of Sui Emperor Wen. The Crown Prince here refers to Yang Yong 楊勇 (d. 604), the eldest son of Sui Emperor Wen, who was deposed in 600 by Emperor Wen in favor of Yang Yong's younger brother, Yang Guang 楊廣, later Emperor Yang (r. 605–618).

8 *BQS* cites the rhapsody in its entirety, which is omitted here. The sentence about the rhapsody and the rhapsody itself are absent in the *BS* biography.

BQS 9

之推在齊有二子，長曰思魯，次曰敏楚，[1] 不忘本也。之推集在，
思魯自為序錄。

BS 9

之推在齊有二子，長曰思魯，次曰敏楚，蓋不忘本也。之推
集，思魯自為序。

---

1 The collation note in *BQS* points out that *min* 敏 should be min 愍, which is interchangeable with *min* 愍.

BQS 9

Zhitui had two sons when he was in Qi. The elder one was named Silu, and the younger one, Minchu, meant to commemorate their origins.[2] Zhitui's collection is extant, and Silu himself composed prefatory matter for it.

---

2 See Introduction for the meanings of the names.